Escape from Bellevue

Escape from Bellevue

A Dive Bar Odyssey

Christopher John Campion

GOTHAM BOOKS

GOTHAM BOOKS
Published by Penguin Group (USA) Inc.
375 Hudson Street, New York, New York 10014, U.S.A.
Penguin Group (Canada), 90 Eglinton Avenue East, Suite 700, Toronto,
Ontario M4P 2Y3, Canada (a division of Pearson Penguin Canada Inc.);
Penguin Books Ltd, 80 Strand, London WC2R 0RL, England;
Penguin Ireland, 25 St Stephen's Green, Dublin 2, Ireland
(a division of Penguin Books Ltd);
Penguin Group (Australia), 250 Camberwell Road, Camberwell,
Victoria 3124, Australia (a division of Pearson Australia Group Pty Ltd);
Penguin Books India Pvt Ltd, 11 Community Centre,
Panchsheel Park, New Delhi - 110 017, India;
Penguin Group (NZ), 67 Apollo Drive, Rosedale, North Shore 0632,
New Zealand (a division of Pearson New Zealand Ltd);
Penguin Books (South Africa) (Pty) Ltd, 24 Sturdee Avenue,
Rosebank, Johannesburg 2196, South Africa

Penguin Books Ltd, Registered Offices:
80 Strand, London WC2R 0RL, England

Published by Gotham Books,
a member of Penguin Group (USA) Inc.

First printing, March 2009
1   3   5   7   9   10   8   6   4   2

Gotham Books and the skyscraper logo are trademarks of Penguin Group (USA) Inc.

LIBRARY OF CONGRESS CATALOGING-IN-PUBLICATION DATA

Campion, Christopher John.
Excape from Bellevue : a dive bar odyssey / by Christopher John Campion.
p. cm.
ISBN 978-1-592-40426-1 (hardcover)
1. Campion, Christopher John. 2. Singers—New York (State)—New York—Biography.
3. Alcoholics—New York (State)—New York—Biography. 4. Dramatists, American—Biography.
5. Nightlife—New York (State)—New York. 6. New York (N.Y.)—Biography. I. Title.
CT275.C274515A3 2009
974.7'1043092—dc22   2008042360

Printed in the United States of America
Set in Bembo
Designed by Elke Sigal

This book is dedicated to
Mom, Dad, Bobby, Kevin, Donna, Eileen, and Billy,
whose faith, love, humor, and music
have shaped my life.

We are the Campions,
my friends.

Contents

Though the events that take place in this book are real and lifted directly from my life, I've had to, in certain cases, change the names of people and places or create fictional or composite characters to supplant real ones in order to protect the anonymity of the innocent and not so innocent (namely my felonious friends). Also, I'm reporting on a very foggy time in my life so if I got anything wrong by way of time lines and facts, I apologize. What you need to know is that I was in Bellevue three times, the second of these incarcerations I escaped, and I have thankfully emerged from it all with enough of my marbles intact to tell you this story. Of this I'll swear on a stack of Stones records. In this current climate of "memoir witch hunts," I think it's important to say that. In other words, I'm asking you to read this book, have a good time, and don't bust my balls. . . .

Love,
Chris

"The only people for me are the mad ones. The ones who are mad to love, mad to talk, mad to be saved; the ones who never yawn or say a commonplace thing, but burn, burn, burn like fabulous yellow roman candles exploding like spiders across the stars."

—JACK KEROUAC

"Lord, I believe. Help my unbelief."

—MARK 9:24

S tanding in the wings, I could hear the crowd getting louder and
louder and some drunken leather lung yelling out, "C'mon,
Drops, get out here!" Then above the noise they began singing,
"You're a dropout . . ."—the chorus to one of our staple tunes, "The
Dropout Song."

The scene was the Paradise Rock Club in Boston and it was the
fall of 1992. The Knockout Drops were playing behind our very
first EP, *The Burning Bush Chronicles*, and on the bill with us was my
brother's band, The Bogmen, who were about to be signed by Arista
Records and were already huge in Boston.

They'd circulated our cassette to all of their fans and started a
brushfire of anticipation for this Paradise show, as well as a few others
we had scheduled in the area. There were no Web sites back then so if
you were an unsigned band (in our case from NYC), you never knew
if your stuff was catching on until you got to a place. Needless to say,
we were all excited to play the show—all but me, that is.

I had a scorching sore throat that had reduced my voice to a
whisper and my heroic intake of cocktails and cocaine wasn't helping matters. My brother Bill, lead singer of The Bogmen, came over
to me and, seeing my look of helpless desperation, offered a solution.
"Here," he said, "drink some of this Thai stick tea. It'll dilate your
larynx and you'll be singing like a birdie, trust me." There were potent stems of marijuana floating in this cup so I was a tad reluctant.
I generally didn't smoke weed before I went on because it made me

a little spacey, and I liked to chat up the crowd in between songs; a blow-and-booze combo was my preferred gasoline (the PB & J of all long-distance revelers) but this seemed harmless enough. It was tea, for chrissakes.

He put a little honey in it so it tasted pretty good, and I quickly downed a cup. I grabbed another and started warming up my voice a bit, and before long, I was singing "Fat Bottomed Girls" just like Freddie Mercury and leading everyone backstage through choruses of it, every so often going for refills of the tea. True to my brother's word the potion had worked. I don't think I had sounded this good . . . *ever*! I figured the more of it I drank, the better my voice, right? I also thought that because it was tea, it wouldn't really get me that high since it was diluted with water, which shows you that I'm no Bill Nye, the Science Guy. In fact, the stuff goes right into your bloodstream with about three times the THC level—so not only does it get you stoned faster, it's far more potent—information that would have been useful at the time.

As I was milling about, I felt an ominous transformation occurring. I was morphing in my head from a Jaggeresque cock-of-the-walk to a cowering little kindergartener. What the hell was happening? I had gotten paranoid from strong weed before so I knew that feeling, but *this*? *This* was something different. It was as if my brain had released panzer divisions of self-doubt and fear into my system and the tanks of inner hysteria relentlessly kept coming. I wanted my mommy. Goddamn it, I wanted my mommy RIGHT NOW!

Then the stage manager came running over to me, visibly upset. He was a red-faced, red-haired, pure Boston Irish heat-miser-looking guy named Patrick, and in his wicked New England accent he barked, "The band is on, where the hell have you been?" I couldn't talk at all at this point 'cause I was tripping hard. I thought any answer I gave would sound like I was speaking in tongues—and in my head, I was. After a few seconds he realized he wasn't gonna get a reply and had to cajole me into moving: "We got six hundred screaming kids out there; get your ass onstage!"

I gingerly walked out to an eruption of applause, as the band launched into "The Dropout Song." I could feel my rib cage being vibrated by its thunderous beat and swirling, distorted guitar line. I stood behind the center mic with a lone spotlight on me—lathered in beads of flop sweat, eyes darting back and forth—a statue of fear. They kept playing and I did nothing. I couldn't remember the words to my own song so I started spitting some low-volume gibberish into the mic.

The room was rattling with everyone jumping up and down in unison. Finally Phil, my bass player, came over and yelled above the music, "What the hell is wrong with you?" None of those guys were privy to my little backstage tea experiment. I squinted back at him and uttered a line that will forever go down in Knockout Drops history. "I dunno, man. . . . I feel like everyone is staring at me." I'll never forget the laugh that came out of him when he said, "They are! You're onstage or haven't you noticed that? Now start singing, asshole; we can discuss your nervous breakdown later."

Side stage, there was a guy named Smitty hanging out and dancing. He'd popped me up with some key hits earlier in the evening, so I ran over there and shook him down. You know Smitty. He's the guy with the brown hair, nervous smile, and shifty eyes with perpetual sweat gathering over his upper lip. He seems normal to you upon first glance but then you look again and realize that he's jacked out of his mind. There's a Smitty at every show.

He lovingly packed my beak full of blow, and I took a huge pull out of the bottle of Jameson's that was on top of one of the big speakers—ahhhhhhhhh, warm, fuzzy, and familiar . . . MOTHER'S MILK! Cocaine was always a maintenance drug for me, but booze was the great love of my life. *Everything's gonna be all right. There's nothing Jameson's can't get me through*, I thought.

I was right. It went on to be one of the greatest shows we ever did. There would be many more nights to come, on bigger stages and in front of more people, where Jameson's would derail me, but this time it had my back. I thought it always would. I was wrong. Well, it did for a bit and then it didn't. You'll be hearing about all that in just a little while.

Have you ever been to Bellevue? You really should go. It's lovely this time of year. Between 1998 and 2000, I was there three times—so I'll be taking you there three times. I call these "The Wonder Years" 'cause I'm still wondering, "What the fuck happened?"

Don't worry, I'm not here to hijack you for some "shock and awe" journey of what it's like to be a down-and-dirty drunk. We've all heard that twice-told yarn, and I'm as tired of it as you are. It just so happens that I was a down-and-dirty drunk, but don't be confused. This is not a cautionary tale of woe or eventual triumph, but rather it's a story about the tireless pursuit of a dream and a desperate quest for faith. In other words, it's about growing up.

Chapter One

Livers with Feet

I threw up at my first Holy Communion. This was the first in a life-time series of public pukings. I apologize if I get a bit misty-eyed, but who doesn't get sentimental about their first time, right? Unlike the installments that followed, this did not come about as a result of bludgeoning myself, repeatedly, with the happy stick. This episode was brought on by the wonder and fear of a loving, yet invading, God.

For some people this might be a traumatic and paralyzing memory, but not me. Don't get me wrong—it was an unfuckinbearable humiliation while it was happening, but I've found in this life that any dreary experience that makes for a funny story afterward is usually worth it. Laughter defangs trauma. Of course, that little chestnut is coming from a guy who found himself in the psych ward at Bellevue three times within a two-year span (two and a half if you count my escape), so you might not want to be getting your credos from me just yet. Another reason I wasn't indelibly scarred by this unfortunate event is that I'm pretty much unembarrassable. Believe it or not, that's a skill. It's also a good way to be if you're going to grow up and navigate the world in a seismic stupor. It's all in the training.

I remember waking up early that spring morning in 1975, and my stomach felt like it had an undertow in it. Something just wasn't right. There are six of us in my folks' Irish Catholic brood: my three brothers, two sisters, and myself. At nine years old I'd already experienced the twenty-four-hour flu bug blowing through the house a few times so I knew what that was. The last go-round we all got it at the same time, turning the house into one giant vomitorium, everybody in their pajamas for two days with pots next to their beds, groaning. I'm kind of diggin' the Dickensian image of that but don't be misled, I'm from Huntington, Long Island. We got through that epidemic like every other family on the block by eating dry cereal, drinking ginger ale, and doing Mad Libs. This was the pre–video game era of the seventies when your only shot at bedridden amusement came home from the stationery store.

Anyway, my stomach was churning, making these slushy, watery sounds, and I got an image in my head of watching the sudsy clothes through the washing machine window, which I found hypnotically soothing. I pictured the mashed potatoes in my stomach from last night's dinner doing the same thing, and this picture was yielding an entirely different feeling, but I wasn't sure if it was the flu thing just yet. I thought maybe I was just nervous because this was the day I was gonna receive Jesus for the first time.

After Mom and I had gotten through saying my prayers the previous evening (an Our Father, a Hail Mary, and a Glory Be, for you Catholics following at home), she'd leaned in, kissed my forehead, and said, "Try to get some sleep 'cause tomorrow's a big day. You'll be receiving Jesus for the first time and that means he'll be alive in you." Then she gently left the room, reaching her hand around the doorway to click off the light.

I lay there in the dark, staring at the ceiling, pondering her statement: "He'll be alive in you." What did that mean? Was I gonna transform into something different now? What if I didn't like it? Clearly I was having some control issues with my incoming tenant, God. My mind was off the rails, racing. I fixated on this one spot on the ceiling where the paint was chipped off and looked like a whale, just trying to wrap my head around the concept. Then my oldest brother Bobby's shadowy figure appeared on the roof outside my window, and signaling me with the "shhh" finger over his lips, he motioned for me to quietly open it.

A couple of months before this I had been having a recurring nightmare that a murderer was climbing through my window in the middle of the night trying to stab me to death. About three times a week I'd dream that a rabid psychopath resembling Chuck Connors (the guy who played the Rifleman) was easing my window open and putting a knife to my throat. On the show *The Rifleman*, he was a good guy, but he had this cockeyed sort of evil look to him that had me convinced he was a violent fuckin' weirdo in real life. My older brothers and I would watch those old reruns, but I never once voiced my opinion about it.

In the dream I'd see his spastic eyes rise to just above my mattress, and as he was about to swipe the hot blade under my chin, I'd come to in a full gallop, en route to my parents' bedroom. Mom would let me climb into bed with them, but Dad wasn't too keen on the idea, saying, "Listen, it was just a dream and you have to learn how to sleep through the night on your own after something like this. You don't wanna grow up and be some kind of pansy, do you?" "Bob, he's trembling; just let him lay down in here for a while," Mom would say. To which he'd reply, "C'mon, Pat, we're not raising Little Lord Fauntleroy here," and deposit me back in my bed.

The rest of the night would be spent eyes wide-open, staring at the whale above my head imagining I was riding him through deep ocean swells, or looking at all the teams' mascots on my NBA bedsheets, trying to memorize them and stave off the terror. The latter would usually work and I'd fall asleep somewhere in the middle when I got to around the Milwaukee Bucks. I didn't resent my dad for being a hardass about it. I didn't wanna be a pussy either, but I couldn't prevent that dream from coming back even after I stopped watching *Rifleman* reruns.

After one of these harrowing 'mares I was in their room and the dream had been so vivid it rendered me practically catatonic. To get me to return to my own bed, Dad tried using a little child psychology, appealing to my nine-year-old machismo. I was wearing these Buffalo Bills pajamas with the number 32 on them that Mom had gotten me because O. J. Simpson was my favorite NFL running back. I used to weave through the furniture in the living room at top speed, an orange nerf football tucked under my arm, in those pajamas pretending I was O. J., ripping off one of his patented long open-field runs.

My dad saw the Bills' insignia on my shirt and said, "You've got to sleep in your own bed, buddy. You know, I'll bet the Juice has nightmares sometimes." I looked up surprised and said, "He does?" "Sure, we all do at one time or another, but you gotta be brave and not give into them 'cause they can't hurt you if they're not real, right? I'll tell ya one thing, I'd be willing to bet that the Juice isn't running into his mother's bed every time he has a nightmare about a guy with a knife." No, I suppose he didn't.

The nightmares kept happening and they were contemplating sending me to a child shrink—which, of course, my dad was very much against—but then one night my mom busted Bobby coming through my window and the mystery was solved. He'd been sneaking in and out of my window a couple of times a week for months. The next day Dad cut down the tree next to the window, and lo and behold, the nightmares stopped. Every once in a while he'd still sneak in by shimmying up the drainpipe instead, tapping on the window for me to let him in.

So on my Communion eve, there he was again, crouched and off kilter in my window, desperately waving me over. Bobby was seventeen and had just come from some keg party down the street where his band, The Old #7, was playing. He was their shaggy singer. Earlier that evening I'd heard them do a cover of the Grateful Dead tune "Bertha" from my windowsill. I sat quietly with my chin resting on the tops of my hands, listening to my brother's voice rise above the overly distorted guitars and buoyant party chatter of a hundred drunken teenagers. I heard it faintly through the breeze and the rustle of the swaying evergreens, the smell of fresh-cut grass and the giggles of errant chicks cutting through our yard to get back to the party, igniting a romantic spring trance in me. I wanted to be under the moon at that kegger too! I was gonna try and sneak out for a peak but thought better of it knowing I had my Communion the next day.

I'd heard Bobby come up the stairs earlier as I was lying there, not sleeping, but I guess he'd slid in, said good night to the folks, and snuck back out.

His hair was light brown and longish—straggly, wavy, and a little in his eyes, which were deep blue. He himself kind of looked like Jesus. He reeked that night of the usual things. His jean jacket still had the outside emanating from it: cold air, pot smoke, and beer, with a little charcoal twinge to it too. It all whooshed off him, coming through the window, as he steadied himself using his hand on the top of my head to guide his feet through, then slid his other hand onto my shoulder to ensure himself a soft landing, almost taking us both down. "Shit, that was close. Thanks," he said, huffing and puffing. I scurried back into bed.

While I had him, knowing he'd been getting Communion for years, I asked, "Hey, Bobby, what does Mom mean that tomorrow Jesus will be alive in me?" "Didn't anyone explain this to you yet— like in CCD or something?" he asked. CCD was a weekly after-school religion class that Catholic kids going to public school attended in people's private homes. The teachers volunteered through the church and to this day I don't know what those letters meant—back then they meant juice and cookies in some smiley church lady's weird-smelling living room.

"I guess not, or maybe I just wasn't listening. Do you know?" I asked, sitting up attentively. "Well," he said, taking a moment to formulate his answer, "it means that tomorrow for the first time you'll be eating his flesh. Now go to sleep, you little dick, you'll wake Mom and Dad." And as quickly as he came in, he left.

That may have been when my stomach started to quake. Tender moment, I admit, but I still think he could've put it better. I mean, I wouldn't have expected him to go into a lecture on the difference between tran- and consubstantiation, but a little more explanation than "you'll be eating his flesh" might've helped.

I had a sleepless night wrestling with this new theology and a few of life's other imponderables. If Jesus is the son of God and Jesus *is* God, then why didn't God send him down here right away when he made the world to get it all off on the right foot instead of making dinosaurs? Aren't dinosaurs really just monsters? Why did God put monsters here first (still a good question)? Are there cavemen in heaven? There can't be 'cause they lived before Jesus, right? What happened to all the people that lived before Jesus? Did they get to go to heaven or were they just training dummies for God?

These were the things that were firing through my head, and one question led to another and another and another till I saw the sun put a shadow on my wall. That's the first time I ever witnessed a daybreak (another first of many). I fell asleep for about ten minutes and woke up nauseous as hell to the sound of Mom calling for me to wake up and get ready.

Dad did his usual drill sergeant routine, rousting everybody, getting them into the station wagon for church. "Hey, Eil, how long does it take for you to eat a bowl of cereal?" he said pointedly to my sister Eileen, who is three years older than me and had been the last Campion to make her Communion. She was sitting at the kitchen table staring intensely at the back of the cereal box, slowly spooning it into her mouth. "You shouldn't be eating that so close to Communion anyway. . . . Nothing for an hour before, remember?" "Oh yeah," she said. "Why not again?" He paused, obviously not having a ready-made answer. " 'Cause Jesus doesn't feel like sharing your stomach with your Cocoa Puffs." Then he grabbed the bowl and tossed it in the sink.

Whenever my dad encountered a kid question he couldn't answer or when he just plain didn't feel like giving an involved response, he'd make something up. One time we were all watching the movie *Jesus of Nazareth* around Easter and I asked him, "Dad, what's Jesus's last name?" and without diverting his eyes from the screen, he said, "O'Leary."

The drive down to the church felt like a runaway toboggan ride, which wasn't helping me any. We were late as usual, so to make up time Dad kept it pegged the whole way, crossing the double yellow line and weaving through the slow-moving cars of the suburban streets. Everyone we rocketed past had the same look of surprised horror on his face. "Bob, please," Mom said, urging him to slow down. "Pat, we're late . . . I know what I'm doing." Then to avoid the light on the corner he used his special shortcut through the A&P parking lot across from Saint Pat's Church.

We screeched past the supermarket with Dad accelerating over the speed bump, causing the tailgate to drag for about ten feet and make the mellifluous sound that only a metal bumper on concrete can make, paralyzing some little old lady behind her shopping cart directly in front of us. Dad veered to her right, singeing her housecoat, then smiled and waved to her as if nothing out of the ordinary had transpired. We all turned quickly to have a look through the back windshield and saw her, discombobulated and dumbfounded, readjusting her bonnet that the car had blown to the side of her head, her cart full of packages slowly rolling away. "Bob, what are you try-ing to do? Get us all killed in front of the church?" Mom screamed, draping both her arms around my four-year-old little brother, Billy, who was on her lap, under her seat belt. "What? I saw her," he said, looking sheepishly into the rearview to see if she was all right. She was. I wasn't.

Dad parked the car while we went inside, and Mom tried to find a pew where the family could all fit. This was never an easy task. She shuffled us back and forth a couple of times, up and down the center aisle, peering around till we were all thoroughly embarrassed from being on display in our un-cool good clothes. (I was a pretty unhappy camper in a pair of desert boots and a sport coat, lemme tell ya.) Then my sister Donna, who was fourteen, asked, "Mom, can't we just spread out this time? Look, there's three spots right here." "No, we're gonna sit altogether as a family," Mom snapped back. Donna tugged on Mom's arm and whispered urgently, "We can go three here and there's room for the rest over there." "I said no." "But everyone's looking at us," Donna said, mortified by the ninth-grade social rami-fications. "Good, let 'em look . . . I don't mind . . . I think we're all lookin' pretty good today," Mom said, picking a piece of lint off of Billy's mini maroon blazer, embarrassing Donna further with her total disregard for volume.

She found an open pew toward the back and everyone crammed in. I went to sit down with them and she said, "No, no, hon, you sit up there with the other Communion kids," which I did, but because I was late I had to sit in the last row of them where the kids ran into the rest of the congregation.

I sat down and focused all my attention on this big dome skylight above the altar to take my mind off my queasy stomach. When I was five, I used to look up at that thing and think that it was specifically designed for God to drop in—that it was his designated entrance. It was enormous and beautiful, round with stained glass, and threw down these magnificently colored beams of light. It looked like God's porthole or, better still, a porthole to God. I tried to keep my eyes on it to get my mind off the ugliness that was happening inside me. One of the other kids saw how peaked I looked and said, "Wow, are you all right? Should we tell your mom?" I couldn't manage words so I just shook my head no, exhaled, and continued fighting it off. I *had* to make my Communion.

Right as the priest called all the kids to form an orderly line up to the altar for their first Eucharist experience, I felt it coming on. I got about halfway down the row, turned, and barfed all over this cranky bald guy's plaid pants.

He was the nervous, overprotective father of the girl next to me. It's always been my theory that the pattern of his pink and kelly green Haggar menswear (straight outta the Johnny Miller collection) triggered my puking mechanism.

He let out this high-pitched scream, as the unwanted wave began sopping him. It was such a ladylike sound that I think everybody in the church thought it was his wife who had caught the splash, but when he started hopping around like Lee Trevino being electrocuted by lightning on the tenth fairway, with a lake-size stain of regurgitated milk and Cap'n Crunch shrapnel covering his crotch, everyone knew it was he who'd been hit.

If I could show you the guy right now, you'd love the fact that I vomited on him—he was so puke-on-able. He had horn-rim glasses, combative little eyes, and a tensed-up face—the kind of person that turns you down for a loan at the bank and you just know it's his favorite part of the job. I like to think God acted through me that day, using me as his infirmed instrument of justice.

Needless to say, mass hysteria ensued at Saint Patrick's Church in Huntington that day. Kids were frantically trampling one another, desperate to get out of the pew. Parents were instructing their children to run for safety and shield their Sunday best from the tsunami of sick boy! "Get out of his way, Paulie, we're going to a restaurant after this," Mrs. Aruliano urged her young son.

I remember hearing these kinds of things and thinking that they were acting just like the panicky little Japanese people I saw on the four-thirty movie when they encountered Godzilla, only this time *I was Godzilla!!!* I didn't wanna be Godzilla. I just wanted my Jesus wafer like everybody else, goddammit, but I couldn't stop heaving. As you well know, once that succession of awfulness starts, it ain't stoppin' till the tank is empty.

I didn't have any better ideas on where to turn so I just kept letting it fly in the same direction. Why wipe out a whole new area full of innocent people? That's when the guy with the womanly scream really started to freak out. "Turn the other way . . . turn the other way . . . Somebody get him to a toilet, he's ruining the whole ceremony," he shrieked so everyone in the overly packed church could hear him.

Then a cloud of Old Spice aftershave descended from behind me, and I felt two strong hands hook under my armpits. All of a sudden I was airborne, as if in the bucket of a payloader, my chin on my chest, still ralphing on myself. The lady-screamer yelled at my dad, "It's about time, get him out of here!" I dangled there from Dad's hands, my eyes crossed, throw-up coiling off my chin. He looked at the lady-screamer with complete contempt and said, "Easy, pal, or I'll have to hold him over you till he finishes."

He cleaned me up in the bathroom in back of the church, which was behind this gigantic, ornately carved wooden door that Dad had to pull hard to get open. I imagined that the door was meant to remind the priests that they were holy even as they were squattin' one out. In fact, I even recall thinking, *Maybe this is where the expression holy shit comes from.*

Dad had a far-off look in his eyes and started cracking up as he wiped me down with wet paper towels. In between chuckles he said, "You're bringing back some not-so-fond memories for me right now. You're not gonna believe this but I threw up at my first Communion too." I looked at him suspiciously. "Really?" "Yeah, all over a guy's suit just like you but mine was a very nice man. You picked a better target." He gestured with his head in the direction of the girly-screamer. "If they're not so fond, then why are you laughing?" I asked him. "Well, 'cause when you're older even your not-so-fond ones become fond ones. Time has a way of doing that." He smiled that smile parents give kids when they tell them something they know one day will come back and mean something to them. I guess that time for me is right now, eh?

Then he looked past my shoulder and said, "I can see from here that the line is nearing the end. We gotta get you out there. Can you make it?" he asked, his voice going up like a coach's, trying to inspire. "Yeah, but we better go quick," I replied, not feeling that confident.

"C'mon . . . let's go . . . twenty-three skidoo. It'll all be over in a flash and we'll have you in the car and on the way home in no time, you'll see," he said as he grabbed my hand and whisked me up the center aisle to the high altar.

All eyes were upon me as my dad pulled on my arm, hurrying me to the front of the church. Some of the kids had that "it's the return of the monster" expression going while the adults just looked on with pity. I didn't fuckin' like that at all. "Who the hell do you think you're pitying?" I wanted to say. "I'll puke you all the way back to your car, asshole." Even at nine I had a pretty big ego and a fairly foul mouth to go with it, but mostly in my head. We weren't allowed to curse at home.

There was no one left on line as I approached Father McGiever, who was standing there holding out the host with more than just a worried look on his face. My dad stopped short of him and gave me a little push. "Go get 'em."

Nowadays most Catholics receive the Communion host in their hands but back then there was only one way and that was to stick out your tongue and the priest would gently lay it on there. He looked down at me, his red, ruddy face full of fear, his ceremonial vestiges rustling, his hand trembling as he rose the Eucharist up high and in an ominous tone authoritatively addressed me with, "BODY OF CHRIST." I mumbled Amen, opened my mouth, and stuck out my tongue, petrified of the geyser within. Father McGiever lowered his hand to rest "the living God" down on my tongue, and as he drew nearer with it I felt it coming again. It was definitely on its way. "Oh no, it's coming up and I can't stop it," I said to myself, terrified for the worst. I decided to petition the big fellah right then and there. It was my only shot. "Oh no . . . no . . . God, make it stop, please? . . . C'mon, haven't I suffered enough? . . . Hasn't *everyone* suffered enough? . . . Oh no . . . no . . . oh no . . . please stop this, would ya? . . . GOD, DO YOU HATE MEEEEEEEEE???"

Father McGiever delicately placed the wafer on my tongue with surgical focus, knowing the slightest fumble on his part could trigger an eruption. Our eyes then locked, mine full of terror, his full of more terror, as I stood there motionless with my mouth still open and the little white disc perched at the end of my outstretched tongue.

Then with the surging force of a tidal wave, out it came, "AHH-HHHHHHHT." Father McGiever smiled and said, "Amen indeed, Christopher."

It was only a burp. God heard my prayer. I was a believer.

. . .

After my puke-a-thon at the church, it was back to our house for a big celebration. This was a family gathering, and for a Communion no less, but that didn't really matter because by three P.M. the place was so filled up with smoke and loud, slurring voices that walking in you'd probably think you were standing in the middle of an OTB. You can't swing a dead cat without hitting an alcoholic in my family, so pretty much all of our parties looked like that. I don't have a perverse sense of pride over that or anything but I don't say it with any shame either, that's for shit sure. It is what it is. Anatomically speaking, we're all livers with feet.

Growing up Campion, we were always busy doing one of three things: getting ready for, cleaning up from, or idling smack dab in the middle of a raging party. This time our house was being stampeded by my relatives from Woodside, Queens, where Mom and Dad and all my extended family are from. This bunch are true salt-of-the-earth types with natural conversation volumes that would blow out your eardrum if you mistakenly leaned in too close while one of 'em was telling you a story.

I always loved when they came to the house because they all had cadences like insult comics, none more than my cousin Georgie, their ringleader, whose speech fell somewhere between Rodney Danger-field and Jackie Gleason. Georgie is Dad's nephew and is about twenty years older than me, so he always seemed like more of an uncle.

He was this hilariously cocky fuck, the oldest of three brothers (my cousins Bobby and Tommy), a good-looking guy with dirty-blond hair—greasy, parted on the side—brown eyes, and a dark complexion. He'd been an all-city athlete who once played high school basketball against Lew Alcindor (now Kareem Abdul-Jabbar), a story I'd make him tell me every time I saw him. Georgie was kind of like a Wood-side version of John Wayne—just replace the six-gun with a broom handle for stickball.

Huntington is mostly a middle-class suburb (with some poorer and richer parts) but in terms of space and average income, it's a far cry from my parents' humble outer-borough beginnings. The Woodside crew had a playful contempt for this and would bust my dad's balls to no end about how he'd gone suburban soft. "Hey, Uncle Bob, do you take tea at three around here or what? I'm standin' here at ten after three wit my saucer ready and no tea . . . what gives? I guess I'll have to break with convention and just have a beer then, but I don't want any of yas givin' me a dirty look, cuz, hey, I tried," my cousin Tommy said, waving around one of Mom's good china teacups. Tommy was a short, stocky guy with a glorious beer gut who looked like De Niro playing the older Jake La Motta at the end of *Raging Bull.*

Dad was able to move the family out of Woodside and into Huntington when my older brothers and sisters were little after graduating from St. Johns on the GI Bill (following his naval service in Korea). He rose up IBM's corporate ladder as a top salesman in the sixties, and started his own company in the mid-seventies that bought, sold, and leased mainframe computers.

We lived in a big white Georgian Colonial on a hill with columns in front of it on a full acre of property, which may have given the Woodsiders the illusion that we had money. The truth of it was that Dad did well, but there were a lot of us. It was your average middle-class upbringing, but in a bigger house.

The party was in full swing now with my parents' Louis Prima records hissing and popping through the stereo, one of those old behemoth wooden jobbies where the equalizer-amplifier and speakers were built right into it, with a compartment on the far left for vinyl storage. It was a spectacular piece of furniture that took up half the living room wall. Georgie's wife, Patti, was tiring of the older generation's tunes so she snuck over and clicked the humungous metal knob from stereo to radio and on came "The Hustle." She started dancing to it and grabbed my hand. "C'mon, Communion boy, it's time for you to learn how to dance."

As she was guiding me through the steps it came around to the chorus and we both yelled out, "Do the hustle!" when Georgie burst in and grabbed my forearm. "What're you tryin' to do to this kid?" he said. "Didn't you see him wipe out half the Catholic population at Saint Pat's earlier? He's sick!" "He's okay now. That was just nerves, I checked him out. Whatta you know anyway? . . . I'm the nurse," she said, continuing to smile at the ceiling and dance, honoring the apex of her buzz. "Yeah, okay, have another highball, Florence Nightingale, and while you're at it, find another victim. I need him for a second."

Georgie pulled me into the middle of the party in front of everyone and handed me a gift. "What is it?" I asked him. "A good way to find out would be to open it, dummkopf. It's a gift from Patti and me for your Communion. Now I was explaining to your mom, here in the family room before, that we all know you're evil now. We've had our suspicions for some time but today confirmed it, what with that display of rejecting God so vehemently back at the church . . . doing a three-sixty with your head like the chick from *The Exorcist* and helicoptering puke all over the congregation . . . embarrassing us all . . . well, mostly yourself really . . . giving new meaning to the word *pew . . . pee . . . uuuu*," he said, closing his nostrils with his fingers. "But I decided that none of that matters and that you should get a present anyway." "Georgie!" Mom said, laughing with everyone but glaring at him. "Now, don't get me wrong. I was proud as hell watching the kid walk outta there with his head held high and throw-up on his shirt. It takes a real man to do something like that," he said to Mom, backing off his jokey assault. "Really?" I said. "No, not really. It was disgusting. Now, open the damn gift already," he said impatiently.

I ripped off the paper and there staring back at me was a shiny, new, AM/FM, Panasonic pocket transistor radio. "WHOA, COOL!" I said excitedly. "You got your AM and FM on there. AM for the Knicks and Rangers and FM for rock 'n' roll," he instructed. I hugged him and Patti. "Thanks a lot!"

He then pulled me into the pantry on the sly. "I also gotcha one of these," and he pulled out the little white earpiece attachment. "I know how your mom makes you go to bed before the games are over, so now if you hook this thing to your ear under the covers you can listen to the rest of it and she won't hear a thing. If she catches you with it, just say you found it in the box, not that you got it from me, okay?"

That little radio transported me to so many new places. I loved it so much, from its metallic smell to its flickering little red indicator light that I would look at on top of my dresser in the still of the night, as if it were suspended in midair. It acted as a lighthouse in my child-hood world, guiding me into the harbor of new things. To this day I re-create that phenomenon by finding a low-budget station, turning off the lights, and leaving the radio on when I want the world to go away. Fuck the Internet, gimme the radio.

I would hide under the covers in my room with that earpiece wedged between my head and the pillow, listening to Marv Albert call Knick games—"Earl the Pearl drives the lane . . . he shoots . . . HE SCORES!"—or Bill "the Big Whistle" Chadwick doing play-by-play for the Rangers—"Guy Lafleur brings it into the Rangers zone . . . shottttttttttt . . . SAVE!"

I remember staring out the windows of Huntington Elementary, sitting in Mrs. Bergheim's third-grade class, exhausted after staying up to listen to the Islanders-Flyers playoff game. "Chris Campion!" she yelled, startling me outta my sleepy daydream. I looked up at her, lost. "I asked you a question. Can you answer it, please?" "Um . . . I dunno . . . three?" I said, taking a stab. "I asked you if there was room for all of us up there on Mars with you." "I know," I said. "And I told you I can take three." "Go to the principal's office and tell Mr. Good not to send you back till you can prove that you can be in this class. And clean yourself up . . . run a comb through your hair or some-thing. Whaddya have—a night job?" she hollered, pointing toward the door. Mrs. Bergheim was a cranky old bat but a great teacher, with a funny sense of humor.

My adrenaline would be running so high from listening to these games (that and the fear of getting caught) that I would have to click it over to FM and listen to music to ramp myself down. Deejays like Dennis Elsas and Tony Pig would spin new releases from Led Zep-pelin, The Who, The Kinks, and talk about them with encyclopedic knowledge that I would lap up, committing all the little factoids about the artists to memory.

On Sunday nights I'd listen to the King Biscuit Flower Hour, which broadcasted live concerts of all the biggest bands, and if I could keep my eyes open, that segued right into Dr. Demento, who did wacky comedy routines and audio send-ups. I really loved that show because it was all adult content and it felt like I'd snuck into the back of an R-rated movie.

They were all great but my favorite of these radio guys was Scottso Muni from 102.7 WNEW-FM. He had this low, grumbling tobacco-ravaged voice that would come through the speakers and just put you in the booth with him. I'd picture the city lights shining through the window off his face, cigarette smoke billowing up into a groovy lamp, as he interviewed newfound heroes like John Lennon and Pete Townshend. Unlike other deejays he seemed to know all these rock stars (on a personal and friendly level) and really made you feel like you were hanging with them listening to their conversation. He was definitely the audio Yoda of my formative rock 'n' roll years—a beacon for any budding insomniac.

On the day that Georgie gave me that radio the Stones had just come out with a greatest hits compilation and were pushing "Angie" as a single. Every station played it over and over and I couldn't get enough of it. I knew every word by sundown, thusly beginning a lifelong love affair with the Rolling Stones. Scottso might've been my Yoda, but the Stones were my demigods.

I loved everything about them: their uncompromising attitude, the unkemptness of Mick's and Keith's appearance that suggested a total disregard for personal hygiene (what kid wouldn't respect that?), the fact that my dad hated them, everything. I completely freaked for their music. I responded to the unabashedly irreverent lyrics in songs like "Live with Me," "Stray Cat Blues," and "Midnight Rambler," without yet knowing their full meaning. There was something uniquely filthy and fiercely bold in their playing that brought it all home for me. Scottso spun these album tracks because, unlike today's deejays, he had the freedom to play whatever he wanted. The deejays weren't entirely controlled by the bottom-feeding, scumbag beast we know as the corporate rock machine today.

Every time I heard a Stones song I'd grab a hairbrush, put it up to my mouth, find the closest mirror, and start singing into it, like I was Mick fronting the band. Every once in a while my mom or someone else would walk in and catch me, but I didn't care. I felt it in my marrow.

Mick and the boys provided my earliest inspiration, but it was my oldest brother Bobby's band, The Old #7, that delivered the second-life sentencing, bite. Around this time my brother Kevin nicknamed

Bobby Throb, short for heartthrob, thanks to all the girls he was getting from singing in the band. Later on he and many others also took to calling him Hollywood Bob, but we'll just stick with Throb for now.

They'd rehearse in our garage, which sat about 150 feet away from the house, a perfect space to jam out and crank up. It also meant that they could have people down there partying and watching them practice without my parents knowing. Every day I'd come home from school and they'd be there, drinking beers with a gaggle of stoned teenage girls in Indian skirts twirling in front of them, as they rocked out an Allman Brothers or Lynyrd Skynyrd song.

This was during the whole Southern rock craze that swept Huntington in the mid- to late-seventies. These guys were from Long Island but dressed like they were from El Paso, Texas, in cowboy boots and hats, wearing bandanas around their necks and shit. I liked some of that stuff when they played it, but I was way more into The Who, The Dead, and of course, the Stones.

The scene was what I was really digging. I could see that live music really got people off. It got me going and I was only a little kid. These girls were going crazy during every tune and the band was only practicing! *What do they do at the real gigs?* I thought, while I bumped butts with these beautiful gals and sprouted an involuntary little boner in my green Toughskins.

The guys in the band became like my own personal rock stars. My brother was the lead singer. You had Dad Nud (the "ud" pronounced "ood" as in *wood*) on rhythm guitar and vocals, Paul Dykes banging on the drums, and rounding it out was Stumpy Restin shredding the world's loudest lead guitar.

They were kinda striking to look at too. Dad Nud stood at 6 feet 5 and was sort of a handsome-looking Frankenstein with a booming voice, Throb was 6 feet 2, and Stumpy was 5 feet 5, so they sloped downward from one side of the stage to the other. When looking at them you'd almost wish they had a midget to play accordion or something to complete the geometry of the thing, ceiling to floor. They all had long brown hair except Stumpy; his was long and blond but would 'fro up like one of the Brady kids.

Every Saturday night, Old #7 would play in the garage and have a little party down there, which made for an interesting juxtaposition to my parents' soirees that would be going on simultaneously in the house. Talk about your two different worlds.

My parents' parties looked like something out of an Elizabeth Taylor–Richard Burton movie—with martinis going, people on love seats chatting away, and light music wafting in the backround. There were lots of sideburns, plaids, and snazzy blazers with elbow patches; the men all smelling of Vitalis and Marlboro Reds; the women, my friends' mothers, unrecognizable in their caked-on blue eye shadow.

Billy was only four so he'd be fast asleep. Donna and Kevin were high school age so they'd be down at the garage partying with the band, and Eileen and I would be up in my parents' bedroom, stuck watching Carol Burnett. We loved *The Carol Burnett Show*, but being surrounded by party noises on all sides made it feel like jail.

We would wait for the precise moment when the voices got a little louder downstairs and the music got turned up to make our move. When the big band stuff, like the Dorsey Brothers, hit the turntable, that was our cue to go.

First, we'd shoot out to the landing on the stairs and spy through the spindles to get a good glimpse of where the party was at (in terms of people's drunkenness). Once the adults were good and tanked our neighbor, Mrs. Posillico, a talented natural musician who could play anything by ear, would get on the piano and they would all start singing standards. When they started bellowing *"Won't you come home, Bill Bailey"* (which my dad always took the lead on), that's when we knew we could nick down to the garage without fear of getting caught. Once they began singing, there was no stopping them. They were like crackheads for the sound of their own voices and the memories that these songs brought them. The sentimentality would be at such a high level in the room that, even if we did get snagged coming back in, there'd be no reprisal, just hugs and encouragement to sing along if we knew the words.

We would watch as our living room detached like an Apollo capsule into this other dimension. It was always fascinating to see the change in people. Shy people like Mrs. Markham, who was near mute and sidled next to her husband when the night began, would be up on the piano belting and hiking up her skirt. I'd think to myself, *God, music and booze really go together,* and of course they do. I defy you to find a better marriage. Why do you think karaoke bars clean up so much? Two beers deep and any idiot thinks he can sing. I guess like most marriages you take the good with the bad.

In the garage, the scene was in some ways comparable because everyone was too ruined to know their own name but that's where the similarities ended.

The pot smoke would hit our noses midway on the walk over, like a big-toe dip in the water. Then Eileen and I would follow it down through the large open doors of the garage. The big back-drop behind the drum kit was a shot of the front of a Jack Daniel's bottle (hence the name Old #7). There'd be floor lights shining up at the band as they plowed through some high-octane number like the Dead's "One More Saturday Night" with an enthusiastic, shoulder-to-shoulder crowd packed in.

It was like having a speakeasy on your own property, only no one spoke easy. It was louder than hell in there. There'd be fifty to a hundred people hanging out in and around the garage, passing bowls, and filling up beers at the keg hidden behind our lawnmower (like that was good enough camouflage for a parental raid).

There was a single-room apartment above the garage that was supposedly the maid's quarters around the time the house was built in 1907, but it had long since been out of use. My folks told Throb he and his friends could fix it up and use it as a sort of clubhouse. He took that ball and ran amok with it. Within a week it looked like an opium den–hippie fuck palace, equipped with multiple lava lamps and pink shag carpeting. It also served as a flophouse for all his wayward teen fuckup friends who'd been bounced from their houses, and he had no shortage of them.

When you walked in, the first thing you saw was a poster that read STONED AGAIN with a cartoon drawing of a guy going through the different stages of stoned-dom, starting in the first frame with his head in his hands and elbows on the table, then his face progressively melting till the last square where there was nothing but a pair of empty hands and a puddle between them. That kinda says it all in a nutshell, don'tcha think? My best friend, Monk, and I would stow away in a little crawl space and watch my brothers Bobby and Kevin and their various girlfriends get high and make out.

One day we were in there spying and Throb was diligently trying to unsnap this girl's bra. We had the little cabinet door cracked open as Throb played Beat the Clock, his chin on the girl's shoulder, facing us, the young lady turned the other way, as he desperately tried to crack the code on the brassiere before she changed her mind and said forget it. (Every guy knows he has about sixty seconds before the buzzer of possible disqualification.) As he kept struggling, Monk was bubbling over with impatience—this being our potential first look at live mammaries—and without realizing it, he said out loud, "C'mon already!" The girl screamed, "Oh my God, is there someone in there?" With that Throb and Kevin marched us out onto the roof and launched us fifteen feet down into this big leaf pile. Then they threw big buckets of water on our heads as they all stood up there laughing, watching us trying to get up, falling back down and spitting leaves out of our mouths. "Stay outta here, LITTLE DICKS! Next time you go off the side with no leaves."

Looking back, Throb was a genius. He had created a situation where he was Bill Graham, Mick Jagger, and Hugh Hefner all rolled into one. He was the promoter, lead singer, and owner of this twenty-four-hour bacchanal and he didn't even have to leave his own doorstep.

I was just a little jock kid running around watchin' all of this and never had any ideas about actively taking part in it, but I certainly enjoyed surfing the chaos. It would be a little while yet before I had my first beer, toke, snort, or titty touch but the party bait had already been dangled, and when the time came, having seen what I'd seen, I bit down on that chum as hard as I could. The umbrella rig of drugs and booze would drag me through the seven seas and back again but it was the music that really held me spellbound.

It was a siren that lured me outta my childhood, perhaps a bit early (I started playing in bars when I was sixteen) and into a world of freaks and felons. Jesus partied with tax collectors, thieves, and whores so I was comfortable with it.

When you tell people you wanna be a rock star when you grow up, they usually give you the same look you might get if you said you wanted to be center fielder of the Yankees or president of the United States. Nobody tries to quell your enthusiasm but you're immediately tagged a dreamer. Then you get a little older and you're seen by certain people as a loser with delusions of grandeur. Then when you're older than that, say around thirty, just a loser. I never felt like that. One reason is that The Knockout Drops always had a die-hard following and the affirmation from that kept me going, but the other is that I had tangible evidence that it could be done. Our new next-door neighbor arrived in the summer of '78. He was a real rock star. No shit.

. . .

It was late afternoon in August and I was trying out Rod Carew's batting stance to combat my brother Kevin's rising fastball, which I hadn't been able to hit all summer. Predinner wiffleball was customary in the Campion clan and it was played with the kind of passion that other families put into camping or skiing. We were wiffleball people. Ol' Rod's mechanics seemed to be working for me 'cause I had connected hard on two pitches in a row when, of course, the next pitch came screaming in at my head, which was also customary if the pitcher was giving up too many hits. I could hear that ominous high-pitched whistle as the hard plastic grazed the side of my head and thumped into the lawn chair that we had set up for a strike zone. "That's a strike," he yelled from the mound. "No it's not . . . it hit me," I told him. "Serves you right for crowdin' the plate. All right, bases loaded," he said, pushing aside the long, wavy, dark hair from his face and getting into his pitching stretch.

Then he started imitating the old Mets commentator, Lindsay Nelson: "Oh, Seaver's gotten himself into a jam here and if he doesn't start keepin' that ball down and throwin' strikes it's gonna be a long inning followed by a short outing." His Lindsay was spot on and I always loved when he did it 'cause it made the game a lot more dramatic and fun, as if we had real announcers. He fired the next pitch in, and as it hit the chair, we were both suddenly transfixed by a mammoth eighteen-wheel truck that screeched and revved as it tried to make the narrow turn into the driveway next door.

As the truck backed out and came forward again, repositioning itself for the turn, out popped four roadie guys all with long muppet hair, pale white skin, and English accents, hollering at one another. "No, mate, turn it 'round again. You're not gonna make it," I heard one of 'em yell. They ran around the truck like Oompa-Loompas, seemingly busy but not really doing anything as the truck huffed and puffed exhaust, idling louder than bombs.

One roadie, who I guess was the leader, started barking commands. He had that birdlike pointy face with the stern, steely eyes that people in charge often have but some of his authoritative swagger was lost by the ringlets of Cowardly Lion hair that fell to his shoulders. "If you continue like this you're going to take out the FUCKING mail bin," he screamed up at the driver, a wide-eyed rotund-looking fellow, also with rocker hair, who had the expression of an eight-year-old being told to land a 747. He just kept frantically turning the wheel and looking behind him, which I couldn't understand because there was no back window in the cabin of the truck. Kevin and I watched them over the fence, the way kids do, with our noses between our curl-fingered hands.

Actually Kevin wasn't a kid. He was going into his sophomore year at Notre Dame. I was twelve. Kevin and Throb were a year apart to the week—Irish twins. Kevin was the younger of the two. Throb was a straight-up stoner fuckup. Kevin was a stoner, too, but got good grades and knew how to play the system, the system being do well in school and be left alone by my dad, so he could do whatever he wanted. Throb got caught for everything he ever did and even took the blame for things he didn't do. Kevin never got caught. I aspired to be like Kevin but my nature led me to be like Throb, a bull in the china shop of life.

They finally got the truck into the driveway and up toward the house, an old white-brick place that was built in the late 1800s and, to me, looked haunted. It was the kind of Gothic house where every time I walked by at night I'd look up and expect to see a raccoon-eyed little girl ghost in a white dress walk past the second-floor porthole window.

Our old neighbors, the Shamans, had moved out earlier in the summer, but we hadn't heard anything about who had bought it and were taken a little off guard by all this.

"Who are these guys?" I asked. They didn't look like a family. "I dunno," my brother replied, "but they're not from around here, I can tell you that." Then a sparkling new Mercedes appeared, its shiny wheels slowly crunching its way up the blue gravel. The doors flew open and another guy with the same shoulder-length hair and bangs, about thirty-five, walked out onto the lawn to greet his minions, accompanied by a big-busted chick who was the spitting image of Daisy Duke. Kevin and I instantly turned to each other and shot that knowing look guys salute each other with when they see a hot girl, but he pulled his back quickly remembering I was only twelve. She was fuckin' gorgeous. Even a dead man could see that.

"Holy shit, it's Richie Blackmore," Kevin said, his jaw frozen open, his eyes wide in disbelief. "Go inside and get Bob quick . . . QUICK!!!" I needed to know who this guy was who could send my otherwise cool and unflappable brother into a state of hysteria. I knew a lot about music by then from my nights with the radio, but for some reason this name escaped me. "Who's Richie Blackmore?" I asked. "He's the lead guitar player of Deep Purple. . . . Ya know, *dun dun da . . . dun dun da da . . . dun dun da . . . dum dum . . .* 'Smoke on the Water'? He's one of the biggest rock stars in the world! Never mind, just go in, find Throb, and bring him out here fast . . . and get Donna and Eileen too! . . . You know what, just go get everybody," he commanded, never taking his eyes off our new neighbors.

All six of us stood in the middle of the yard watching Richie's crew move him and his new nineteen-year-old bride, Amy, into their new house. I put Billy on my shoulders so he could see. There was nothing out of the ordinary happening, just people lugging boxes and shit, but because of who he was, we looked on as if it were a lunar landing. Then the screen door cranked open and Mom yelled out, "Dinner!"

She had the fondue all set up when we got into the kitchen. This was my favorite dinner of 'em all 'cause you got to skewer little strips of beef with a long metal fork and deep fry them in a copper pot of oil, suspended over a small flame from a can of Sterno in the middle of the table. The dinner table was abuzz with speculation about our new neighbor.

"Why would a rock star like him buy a house in Huntington? What's out here for him?" Donna asked Mom. "Nothing. I think that's the point. When he's away from that stuff he probably just wants some peace and quiet," she answered. "Good luck living next door to us," I said matter-of-factly. "Yeah, man, did he pick wrong . . . musta had a lousy Realtor," Kevin said. I speared a primo piece of raw meat from the pile, fried it up to perfection, and as I was pulling it out, Throb clamped down on my fork with his, like an expert swordsman, knocking my piece off and stuffing it into his mouth quickly. "Take that, little dick . . . ha ha HA!" "Bobby, would ya let him eat his dinner, please?" Mom said.

We kept eating, and as usual, we heard my dad's car come rumbling up the driveway about halfway through the meal. He careened through the door, singing a Hank Williams song, dead drunk. *"Gonna build me a doghouse forty-five miles long,"* he sang, plucking a rocks glass from the cabinet then beelining it to the freezer for some ice. He opened the door and an avalanche of frozen peas, waffles, and Wammies (a brand of Popsicle) tumbled out on him. He made a heroic effort to catch each one, dropping them all. "Goddammit, who booby-trapped this freezer again?" he yelled in frustration, because this happened every single night when he got home from work, and I'm not exaggerating.

He was looking kinda disheveled in his suit, wearing one of those hats that made him look like a G-man from the Hoover era, bobbing and weaving a bit, with slurred speech. "Bob, I told you no more bar car on the train. Wait till you get home to have a drink," Mom told him. "Look at you, you're drunk." My dad's an old sandlot football player and he knew in a situation such as this that the best defense is always a good offense. So his reply was, "How dare you accuse me of such a thing, and in front of my children! I am not drunk . . . haven't touched a drop. . . . Murphy and those guys were all drinking on the train and asked me to join them and I said, 'No thanks, guys . . . I promised my wife I'd wait . . .' but I'll tell ya what?—I'm gonna get good and drunk now because my own beloved wife doesn't believe me . . . and that hurts."

She walked across the kitchen and gently removed a note that was tucked into the ribbon in the front of his hat and read it to him. "It says here, 'Conductor, please wake this man in Huntington. HE'S DRUNK!'"

When it was time for bed I kissed my mom and dad good night and went up the stairs but stopped on the landing to spy on them a little. Dean Martin was coming out of the stereo, singing "Volare," while they sat close on the love seats in the living room having martinis, talking low, and laughing.

"Honestly, Bob, did you really think you were gonna pull that one off? I'm from Woodside too, ya know. You don't think I can tell sober from drunk? I'll have to thank Gene Murphy for tipping me off with that note," she said, cracking up. "Yeah, Gene's a pistol, isn't he? I'm gonna have to come back at him hard with something to even the score for this one," he said, laughing just as much. I watched for a little while longer until Mom laid her head on Dad's chest, both of them smiling off into space, letting Deano do all the work.

I went to bed that night excited by the world. I had a real life rock star living next door to me! *I wonder if we'll get to be friends,* I thought. *Holy shit, I wonder if he knows Mick Jagger!* Then I got depressed. I had to get a haircut the next day. *"Shit,* I hope I get to meet him with my cool hair first," I said out loud, looking at the whale on the ceiling.

I fished out my trusty transistor from its hiding spot at the foot of the bed and dialed up my favorite deejay, Scottso. "This is Scottso Muni here on WNEW and I don't even think I have to introduce this song anymore. You'll know it when you hear it, folks." Then that unmistakable riff filled the little white earpiece. *"Dun dun da . . . dun dun da da . . . dun dun da . . . dum dum."*

Chapter Two

Vicious Freaks

Vicious freaks is a term of endearment I use to describe all those who dance on the edge of their own madness. In this life I've always had a passion for three things: rock 'n' roll, booze, and vicious freaks. I love the gals too, but, fellas, lemme tell ya, you'll never get any of them if you go around beating your chest and sayin' stuff like that. Wait a minute. I think I just did. Anyway, I've always loved freaks because they seem to live carefree outside of the usual social confines. For me the environment of a dive bar, out in the middle of nowhere at three A.M., singing and telling stories to a bunch of cock-eyed twist-offs, is like my warm embryonic fluid.

When I was a kid all my friends were into the typical icons of the day like Fonzie, the Six Million Dollar Man, and Evel Knievel. I liked Tiny Tim. He was fuckin' vicious. I liked Rip Taylor too. His whole act was to run out onstage, all gacked up and gay, and just throw confetti around everywhere (nice work if you can get it). I died laughing every time. I just loved him. Chuck Barris was great as well. He reminded me of the people at my parents' parties. He'd be on TV, hammered and just not givin' a shit. He was the television "pie-eyed" piper to vicious peoples everywhere and created *The Gong Show* solely for the purpose of showcasing them.

Huntington was founded in 1653 and it's situated on the north shore of Long Island, about an hour from New York City, with a bay, a harbor, and a hauntingly majestic nineteenth-century lighthouse sandwiched between them. I've always had a thing for that lighthouse, and whenever I felt troubled, I would go down and sit at the end of a jetty gazing at it, casting my problems upon its surrounding rocks. Goddamn, do I miss that. Now I live in Manhattan and go to the twenty-four-hour Duane Reade to wander the aisles when I can't sleep—not nearly as poetic.

It was a beach town with lots of nautical culture and about thirty-five bars within a quarter-mile radius. If I was from an alcoholic family, then Huntington was an alcoholic town, for sure. My folks definitely chose the right place to jam the Campion flag in the sand 'cause we didn't stick out at all. There were lots of big families there and everybody drank like us. Some of that can be chalked up to different times, but mostly it was (and still is) a town that loved its liquor. Wherever you have that kind of setting, with that many saloons, you're gonna find vicious freaks, and Huntington was laden with them.

Like Mr. Schankler (pronounced skank-ler), our eccentric millionaire, who would bomb around the streets of Huntington in an old fire engine. He had these flaring black holes for nostrils and Marty Feldman eyes that looked gigantic behind plastic-rimmed glasses. When talking he gasped for air, his nose occasionally whistling, due to a severely deviated septum. Actually he talked and he honked, but his honk sometimes sounded more like a quack—kind of a honk-quack. The point is you could only catch every third word of what he was saying, but God forbid you told him you couldn't understand him. He'd fly into a rage. "What the hell's wrong with your . . . awnk . . . ears, kid? . . . awnk . . . sssp . . . awnk . . . take the cotton . . . awnk . . . out of 'em . . . ssssp . . . for chrissakes." I think he'd been told one too many times that his speech was indecipherable.

One time I asked him why he didn't just get his septum operated on because he was always complaining about it. He told me he was afraid it might change the sound of his voice, which to me sounded like a wild boar being fist-fucked by a toothless hillbilly. I said, "I think you should get it fixed. You'll breathe better and it's not like you have to sing at Carnegie Hall or anything like that." He snapped at me, "Hey, any asshole can sound like a fuckin' normal . . . aaawnk . . . person." I tend to agree with him on that one, any asshole . . . awnk . . . can.

His family owned a patent on something like belt buckles but the rumor was that his brothers bought him out because he was too crazy to work with, leaving his days free for harebrained scheming.

One day I ran into him at the beach as he was looking across the Long Island Sound to Connecticut, his eyes squinted, his hand on his forehead acting as a temporary visor to shade the sun. "What's up, Mr. Schankler?" I asked, knowing that he was plotting something. "I'm gonna build a bridge . . . awnk . . . but not one for cars or trucks or buses . . . awnk . . . mine's gonna be a footbridge but not for feet either," he said, wide-eyed. "Not for feet?" I asked. "No . . . no . . . not allowed to walk it . . . not on my bridge . . . aaaawnk . . . I'm gonna freeze the whole damn thing and everybody'll have to ice-skate! Whattya think of that? That'll separate the men from the boys, eh? Heh heh heh . . . AAAAAWNK . . . AWWWWNK!" he said, with the same sense of pride and delight that my seven-year-old brother had when he showed me his Lincoln Log fort. The one difference was that Hank Schankler was fifty-seven.

"It'll be magical . . . MAAAAGICAL . . . awnk!! And people around here really need the exercise. Have you seen these fat fucks around here lately? Everyone's a fat fuck . . . aaawnk. . . . Even the kids . . . have you seen that Barcosi kid? Whatta fat fuck . . . awnk . . . ssp . . . What's he, mainlining pizza pies? What the hell's his mother feedin' him? Aaawnk . . . I mean have a little pride for chrissakes (the kid was five). And look at this fat fuck," he said, pointing at his handyman and sidekick, Luther, who was rigging up his sailboat for him on the beach next to us. "Eat another Yodel, you fat fuck . . . sssp. . . . I knew him when he was a skinny fuck . . . sssp. . . . Now he's a fat fuck," Mr. Schankler said, teasing Luther. "Easy, Hank, or I'm'a have to drown you once we out there," Luther replied playfully. "Go ahead and try. Everyone knows your kind can't swim," Mr. Schankler said, winking over at me, knowing his comment would rile Luther, who was a heavyset black guy in his thirties, a really warm-hearted dude with a cool-lookin' afro like Dr. J's (when he was in the ABA), overweight, but not fat.

Luther threw down the rudder, grabbed him, and raised him up. "That's it, old man, it's drownin' time," and he dropped him into the shallow water in his khakis and button-down shirt. "Just for that, Luther, I ain't gonna let you skate on my ice bridge when I build it . . .

aawnk . . . slurp . . . ssp . . . awnk . . . and you can't play poker with us at my house tonight either now." "Good, you mean I don't get to hear you sound the siren on that goddamn fire truck every time you win a hand? I think I can live without that," Luther retorted, he now winking over at me and smiling as he helped Mr. Schankler out of the water.

"Tell your old man to call me if he wants to play with us tonight, Chrissy," Mr. Schankler hollered to me as I was digging my bike out of the sand. I yelled back, "OK," knowing my dad wouldn't wanna play. He got a huge kick out of Schankler at cocktail parties when he'd get loaded and horrify people, but could only take him in small doses.

When it snowed my friends and I used to do a thing called bumper skiing or "skitching." We would hide in the bushes by a stop sign, wait for a truck or a school bus to come (anything with a bumper that could accommodate three or more people), then we'd crouch really low so the driver couldn't see us, latch onto the back bumper, and ride it as far as we could. Whoever could hang on the longest without getting bumped off won. Some winter days we'd choose this as our mode of transport both to and from Finley Junior High School rather than taking the bus. It was an all-out pisser to do.

We were all forbidden by our mothers to skitch, obviously, because it was too dangerous. Sometimes we'd be going up to forty miles an hour, shittin' in our pants, gripping one of these big vehicles like our lives depended on it (because they did) and without being able to see we'd get to a part of the street where the snow turned back into pavement. The rubber from our boots would then catch the cement and throw us ten to fifteen feet, splattering us back down onto the road or into a hedge. Whenever that happened our gloves would stay stuck in the bumper and we'd watch, helplessly, as they disappeared with the taillights, knowing we were most assuredly busted when we got home. How many times could we say a dog made off with them?

If a driver saw us from the rearview usually he'd get out and chase us off, which provided a lot of the excitement. "I know all your parents and I'm calling them all," we'd often hear as we high-stepped through a foot of snow in someone's backyard, knocking one another down and subsequently falling over one another. We'd be laughing so hard it would sometimes render us breathless and we'd have to hoist one another back up to run for the safety of the tree cover under the rusty-layered horizon of winter dusk.

Schankler was the only one who wouldn't give chase. Instead he'd scream out the window of the fire truck, "Hang on, boys! I don't wanna see any of you pussies lettin' go or Luther here is gonna come out and kick your asses for me!" Then he'd floor it, going full speed around hairpin turns, fishtailing into the oncoming traffic of the main roads, cars screaming past our ears from the other direction, this mad-man sounding the siren and cackling, throwing empty Bud cans out at us. "HA HA HA . . . awnk . . . sssp . . . awnk!!!" He looked like a maniacal Mr. Magoo behind the wheel of that thing and I don't even think he had a license due to his poor eyesight.

We all loved Schankler but he was only one in the assortment of VFs the town offered.

Another favorite of mine was a guy everyone called Loyal. He got his name because when he met you he'd profess to be your friend till his dying day. He had a whole speech that sounded like the warranty a salesman gives at the point of purchase. "What's your name again? Chris, is it? OK, Chris, it was very nice to meetcha and now that we know each other I want you to know that you have a friend in me for life. That means I'll stick by you through anything. I'm not going anywhere."

This is what he told me the first time I met him on Stinky Cor-ner (the name my little brother, Billy, assigned to the corner of Main Street and Route 110 in Huntington Village because he thought it smelled like pee). This was where all the freaks, like Loyal, hung out. They'd sit out there, banging on tambourines, dancing, singing songs, and engaging passersby. Occasionally the old Italian guy from Little Vincent's Pizza would come out and shoo them from his door with his big wooden pizza flipper, sometimes thwacking one of them across the ass with it and emitting big clouds of pizza dough dust. He'd let out a huge laugh when he nailed one of them but it was just to keep them from blocking the entrance, not to be mean spirited.

"Really? You'd be my friend through anything?" I asked. "Even if I committed murder?" "Yes, even if you killed someone, yes. As-suming you had cause, yes. No friend of mine would ever kill someone without cause. I know this for a fact because all my friends are nourished enough by my friendship not to wanna do something like that because I make sure they're all happy. That's what friends do," he said. "What if I killed you?" I said, being a wiseass. "Would you still be my friend then?" He took a moment to think. "Yes . . . if you had cause . . . yes."

Loyal was a lanky guy with a big Adam's apple, short brown hair, bulging blue eyes, and a hook nose, about twenty-eight years old. There was nothing in his appearance that would give him away as a VF. He wasn't mentally ill or homeless, just a little off, acutely sincere, and he really, *really* believed in friendship. He was a permanent fixture in Huntington Village and any time you'd stumble upon him he'd be laying down his philosophy to some unsuspecting person walking out of a store or window-shopping. He had more than a few oddball idiosyncrasies but the one I especially loved was that he would forcibly overpay for things. He was known for it.

I was lucky enough to be behind him on line at DiRaimo's Pizzeria one early evening and he said to the kid at the register, who was straight off the boat from Italy, "How much for that stuffed slice?" "Two . . . a . . . seventy-five, sir," the counter guy told him routinely. "I'll tell ya what. I'll give you three bucks for it," Loyal replied, dumbfounding him. "Ah, no, eet's okay ah . . . justa two a seventy-five, please." "No . . . not gonna do it. You guys are selling yourselves short on this one and I'm not gonna participate in it and have you guys believing you're not worth more. Someone's gotta step up here. This is delicious pizza. I come here all the time and it's always excellent and so is the service and I just wouldn't be able to live with myself if I walked outta here with that extra quarter. Please . . . *PLEASE* take it. "No, sir . . . I'm not . . . ahhh . . . permitted to take it. . . . please . . . ah . . . no," the kid said, pleading with him to take it back. (Keep in mind this all happened in the days before the omnipresence of fuckin' tip cups.)

This went back and forth about five times and the line behind me was now getting pretty long. It was around dinnertime and people were growing really impatient with this little Abbott and Costello routine that was going on at the counter. They were hungry and just wanted to pick up their pies and get home to their families, but Loyal was having a crisis of conscience over this quarter. "I just can't do it. The pizza's too good. It wouldn't be fair," he kept saying. Someone from the back of the line yelled out, "C'mon, Loyal, we all wanna eat, dude! He doesn't wanna take it."

Finally the young Italian guy caved under insurmountable pressure from the crowd and gave way, accepting Loyal's quarter. "Thank you, sir. You are nice man," the kid said, shaking his head a little and holding the quarter up for all to see. The place exploded with applause! I leaned in to place my order and before I could get the words out Loyal turned around and said, "Say, I didn't catch your name." "Pasquale, sir." "Pasquale, eh? Hey, Pasquale, did you know that now we're friends and that we're always gonna be friends and what that means is . . ." I turned around to leave and the line was already gone.

One of Loyal's best pals on Stinky Corner was the mad violinist, a portly gypsy fellow, with dark features, who would magically appear out of nowhere in a full tuxedo, and start serenading you with a violin. He could be seen around town at any time of night or day doing this.

One time I was making out with my high school girlfriend at two-thirty in the morning in the parking lot of the graveyard (a romantic place, I know) and he popped in front of the driver's side window and started playing the Moonlight Sonata. How he ended up there is anybody's guess. He was a big mystery because he never spoke. No one even knew what nationality he was or if he could speak English. He just played. He was like the David Carradine character in *Kung Fu*, only he drifted with his violin and played it wherever necessary, not even busking, just playing it. He'd do a little jig with it too, which brings me to my all-time favorite Huntington vicious freak, Walkin' Willie.

Walkin' Willie appeared on the scene when the Sony Walkman came out. He was one of those fuzzy little guys who went bald on top but just let the rest of his hair grow down to his shoulders (giving him the look of a science teacher). He had these intensely dark eyes and would stride the streets of Huntington with a sense of purpose like he was late getting somewhere. We all fell for that for a while till we realized that he had no destination. But that's not what made Walkin' Willie a legend of the game. He was famous for his dancing.

He'd make like he was crossing the street at the intersection with his usual sense of urgency; then when the light turned green he'd freeze right in front of your car. The only way to get him to move was to beep your horn. When he heard the sound of the beep it activated his Walkin' Willie dance! He'd boogie-oogie-oogie, his hands pressed to his ears sealing in the smooth sounds of the Walkman, letting the music translate to his feet, and then the once-burdened look on his face would burst into one of unmitigated joy! He'd squat and pop up, turn, then stare you down through the windshield like a dance floor lothario. For his showstopper he'd grab hold of your bumper and start humping it like a Labrador no longer able to contain his red rocket. I've lived almost forty-two years on this planet and it is, without question, one of the greatest things I've ever seen.

I remember being out with my dad the first time Walkin' Willie happened upon our car at the crosswalk. The light changed so my dad beeped to get him to move and he started his spastic dance. "What in the HELL is this asshole doing?" he said angrily and went to lean on the horn again. "Dad, no, don't beep the horn. You'll reactivate him," I said, trying to educate him to the ways of Walkin' Willie. "I'll what? I'm gonna flatten him like a pancake if he doesn't get out of the way. What's he doing now, trying to put the stones to our car? Your mother drives this car!" he said, as Willie humped the shit out of our bumper. "His dances only last a minute. If you beep again he's gonna start a whole new dance," I said, desperately trying to explain it to him. "Ho-lee shit, only in this town," he remarked, rubbing his temples as he watched Walkin' Willie follow through with his final thrust and then scurry off. My dad shook his head as we pressed on with our errands.

It was early Saturday night and the streets of Huntington were packed as usual with throngs of noisy people as we drove through, every few feet a tavern door abruptly swinging open with the raucous sounds of some sweaty rock band trailing the buzzed bar-hoppers out onto the sidewalk.

We pulled up in front of Carvel, where my dad gave me a twenty, instructing me to go in and buy eight Brown Bonnets for the family. Right as I was about to yank the Carvel door open, I saw Loyal through the window talking animatedly with his hands to the man behind the counter and a couple of pissed-off people behind him waiting to order. Then Schankler and Luther pulled up to the light in front and revved the engine of the fire truck to a bunch of young bucks in a convertible black Mustang that had already been sitting there. The Mustang crew answered with an engine rev back and when the light went green they took off drag racing all the way down the street and around the bend. In that moment I can clearly remember thinking only one thing: I love this fuckin' town.

Chapter Three

Not a Rebel

Childhood gave way to the teenage years and with them came the usual changes; pubes made a stealthy entrance, sweaty underarms weren't far behind, then my first terrifyingly gratifying nocturnal emission (I've only had three to date but I'm still holding out hope for more). I got to second base with Nancy O'Dwyer after the Sadie Hawkins dance (behind Friendly's), didn't have too bad a zit problem but always managed to have the worst one on yearbook picture day. I smoked pin joints with the boys before homeroom now and again, snuck a few shots from the old man's liquor cabinet, Laser Floyd, blah blah blah blah. I think you're all caught up now. Hey, no one knows what happened to Jesus from age thirteen to thirty-two. I think I summarized well.

I continued to monitor my rock star neighbor pretty closely, but it was slim pickins as far as making mano-a-mano contact. Every once in a while he and his wife, the lovely Amy, would come over and sit on our deck with us after dinner, but she would do all the talking. She was a real chirper. He would clam up and look about as comfortable as a perp sitting under a police interrogation light. I don't think he wanted to be there. No matter how hard I tried, I couldn't pry my fourteen-year-old eyes from his wife's glorious rack. Those turkey-timer nipples of hers saluted me at every turn, poking through her tight T-shirts, sucking me in like tractor beams. I don't think he liked that either. He'd turn his head quickly sometimes to catch me looking, like a pitcher throwing over to first base, but I got back to the bag safely most of the time.

The person he would talk to was my mother. She has always had a way about her that invites everyone to seek her counsel. People just tell her things. Everywhere we went, especially the supermarket, someone would come over to her and grab her forearm. "Do you mind if I steal your mom for a minute?" and then start bleeding about their husband or wife or kids or job. She'd stand there with her arms folded, listening, and then dispense some quick advice or tell them to call her. The conversation always ended with Mom saying something; then they would have a big laugh (my mom has an uproarious laugh that could quake the cereal boxes off the shelves), and the person would walk away with a smile of relief. She's quick with a joke like that.

One time Mom was helping Mrs. Markham with a problem in the frozen foods section. Mrs. Markham was spewing about something with a box of Jolly Green Giant peas in her hand, and by the time she was through, the peas had thawed, so she had to throw them back and grab another box. "What was that about?" I asked in an annoyed voice. "She just needed to talk. She's going through some stuff. Sometimes people just need to vent a little . . . nothing for you to worry about," and she tousled my hair, continuing to search the aisles with the grocery list in her hand, as if the whole thing hadn't even happened.

One afternoon I was in the backyard pitching some wiffleballs to Billy and Mom was on the deck watering her plants when I saw Richie duck through the hole in the fence. "Pat, have you got a second?" "Sure, Rich, come on up," she answered in her usual buoyant way. They sat on the deck talking for like an hour. My eyes kept wandering over from the pitcher's mound, desperate to hear what they were saying. "Pitch it in, come on!" Billy whined. I couldn't concentrate and kept hitting him with the ball until he got totally exasperated. "Screw this, you suck," and he flung the bat at my feet, got on his BMX bike, and peddled off.

They wrapped up their little conference right as I got the nerve to go up there. Actually Richie saw me coming over and bolted. I asked my mom what they'd talked about. "Not much," is all she said. "Whattya mean not much? He was up here for over an hour, how could that be not much?" "He's just going through some stuff," she said casually as she watered more plants. This set me off. "Oh my

God, stuff . . . it's always stuff . . . well, I wanna know his stuff. What stuff are we talking about? Rock star stuff?" "It wouldn't be right to tell you," she said, an answer I knew I'd get. "Well, did you ask him what I asked you to ask him?" I asked. "What was that?" she asked. "If he knows Mick Jagger. Did you ask him if he knows Mick Jagger?" I said, all hopped up. "No," she said. "Why not?" I probed, with frustration. "Because the conversation didn't go that way," she said, still watering. "You gotta make it go that way. You change the subject. You say, 'Hey, Richie, oh by the way, I've been meaning to ask you, do you know Mick Jagger?' How hard is that?" I told her, thinking I was making a good point. "It's not hard if you wanna look like a moron," she said, unaffected. "He was talking about some problems he's having and it would've been rude to ask him something like that. The reason he likes talking to me is because he knows I could give a rat's ass whether or not he knows Mick Jagger. He gets that kinda thing everywhere he goes. It puts him in a bubble and who wants to go through life in a bubble? Next time he's over, you ask him." "You're the only one he talks to," I said. "Yeah, that's because I'm cool and you're not . . . HA!" she said, laughing loudly. "Next time he's over, if the timing's right, I'll ask him." Eventually she did, and he does.

I got an opportunity to talk to him a few months later. He'd just gotten off a tour with his band, Rainbow (Deep Purple had broken up by then), and he was in his yard, kicking a soccer ball around by himself, looking exhausted. He was a really good player and even played with local teams sometimes. At the time I thought soccer was a wimpy sport, played by pussies whose mommies wouldn't let them play football, but I feigned interest just so I could go over and kick it with him (terrible pun, I know).

"So you play American football, then? I've seen you walking into the house in all your armor," he said, booting the ball over to me. I felt like he was using the word *armor* sarcastically, so defensively I came back with, "Yeah, I've seen you guys out here after your games too, kickin' the ball around in your hot pants," and I kicked it back to him. "Nice one, mate," he said, chuckling. "Well, have you ever played . . . ummm . . . soccer?" he asked, adjusting to the American vernacular, obviously bothered by having to do so. "No, soccer is for puss . . . ummm . . . requires different skills. I like to hit people. You can catch a real buzz off of knocking somebody outta bounds into a water cooler," I said, trying to impress him, but I actually do stand by that. You can. I have and it's great.

"You're a bit of a ruffian then, yeah?" he said, smiling, knowing I was talking big. "No, not really," I said, stopping the ball under my toe. "I wanna be a rock star like you. You got any advice?" His face changed on a dime. He looked like I'd just asked him if he'd smuggle sixty balloons of heroin up his sphincter across the border for me. "No, mate, no advice, just know it's not all what you see on the telly. It can be a bloody hard life," and with that he picked up his ball and went home. Or I should say, he moped back toward his house, where his stunning young wife and her three gorgeous friends lay poolside in string bikinis, and his lead singer, Joe Lynn Turner, was tightrope walking along the water's edge, rockin' a banana hammock. Needless to say, that little scene disrupted the scared-straight effect he was going for with his parting line. I was grateful for the convo, though. I'd finally established contact. Richie was a good guy.

I bragged to all my buddies on the school bus the next day about how we'd kicked the ball around and me telling him I wanted to be a rock star, but changed the ending to him saying, "I've heard you singing in the shower through the window, mate, and you're quite good. You've obviously got the talent. Now go for it." And, of course, I had to throw a little relish on the embellish by joining him poolside for some beers with the ladies afterward. My friend Monk said, "You had a beer with him?" "Oh yeah, over in Europe people our age drink with the adults. It's common," I said, with a newfound worldliness in my tone. I never did tell them the truth. It really sucks to have to come clean about it now. I've scattered alotta little white lies across the decades (alotta big fuckin' fat ones too).

Despite Richie's attempt to veer me toward another vocation, my dream of rock 'n' roll stardom was in full bloom and it was time to do something about it. I had gotten a cheap acoustic guitar with nylon strings for my birthday. I'd been noodling on it for a few months, but I wasn't really getting anywhere on my own so I thought it would be a good idea to get some lessons if I was gonna be good enough to start a band.

A friend of mine at school, Robert Kresper, recommended his

teacher, a guy named Roy Stevens. Knowing I was a spaz when it came to learning anything, I asked him, "Is this guy really patient? 'Cause I'm not really a fast learner." He said, "Oh yeah, Roy specializes in teaching little kids the guitar so his style is to go really slow with you till you get it." "Perfect, 'cause I'm pretty retarded," I confided. "That's good, two days a week he teaches them too, so you won't be the worst he's seen," he said jokingly. "It's not a competition, Rob," I said, secretly nervous that I would suck and that it would get back to him.

Roy was a straight-up, soft-spoken, tree-huggin', herbal-tea-drinkin' hippie, who drove a VW bus and looked like he'd stepped right out of the year 1967. He had shoulder-length black hair that he wore in a ponytail and you couldn't find a nicer, sweeter, more gracious, and caring guy on this planet. His patience was only exceeded by the love and passion he had for his profession. I couldn't stand him. Actually it's not that I couldn't stand him, it's that I don't know how to get on with people like that, all sincere and shit. He was this cuddly ball of earnestness—very pious too. It was fucked up. I like to joke around when I'm doing anything and he was pretty humorless. It made our conversations uncomfortable.

During one of our lessons he was showing me the chords to "Maggie Mae" and I looked up and said, "Have you seen the cover of Rod Stewart's new album? It looks like they pumped all that giz out of his stomach and into his hair." I utilized that urban legend for my punchline to be cool and to maybe get a laugh out of him. There was an awkward silence, and without taking his eyes off my fingers, he said calmly, "You know, Chris, that's a rumor that's been going around for a few years now and I don't like to participate in stuff like that. Rod's a great artist and deserves better. Now let's see if we can't get you to do that A chord properly." He was right, of course, and the joke wasn't that funny, but what the fuck? Who was I getting lessons from, Gandhi? In that moment I knew our days were numbered.

He would come over on Monday nights at eight-thirty and I hated the time slot because it cut into *Monday Night Football* that my dad and I watched together religiously. Because I couldn't relate to this guy on any level, I started getting high right before the lessons.

I'd purchased a little pot one-hitter at Amber Music (our local headshop–record store) and would dig out a few bat hits, fire them up, and blow them out the window just as his VW bus was rumbling up the driveway. I was as high as a runaway satellite every week during the lesson and then one night I stumbled across a way to fuck with my saintly guitar instructor.

Roy had this very high-pitched, pristine voice that in a choral context probably would've rendered him a first soprano, unusual for a thirty-five-year-old man. He could've auditioned for the Vienna Boys' Choir and gotten in, that's how liltingly unblemished it was.

His style of teaching was to sing the song you were learning while you played it and stay on whatever line or phrase that was giving you trouble till you got to the next chord change. One week he was teaching me the Jethro Tull song "Aqualung" and I couldn't configure the next change. We were on that famous line in the song, "Snot is running down his nose." My fingers were fumbling as he just kept singing, "*Snottttttttttttt . . . snottttttttttttttt,*" trying in between to get a breath, "*ottttttttt . . . snottttttttttt,*" in that piercingly high tone.

I was dying laughing, but only on the inside, like a true Karate man. I couldn't let him see that I thought it was funny or he'd stop doing it. Every week I'd purposely get snagged on that part of the song just so he'd sing it again and again, which meant that every Monday night, around eight forty-five P.M., from the Campion living room, all you could hear was Roy Stevens singing, "*Snottttttttttttt . . . ottttttttttt . . . snotttttttt,*" for probably what seemed like an eternity but in reality was only about five minutes. To those that had to listen to it, namely my family, that was a long-ass five minutes.

After four or five Mondays of this we were in the middle of my lesson and again we started strumming through the song as my dad was sitting down to *Monday Night Football* in the family room. I could hear Howard Cosell doing the pregame setup through the glass doors that separated the two rooms. "I'm not afraid to say that I'm as excited as a schoolboy for this contest tonight between these two storied AFC franchises, the Miami Dolphins and Oakland Raiders, as I pass it over to my two esteemed colleagues in the booth, Frank Gifford and Dandy Don Meredith."

We got to that treacherous part of the song where, for the life of me, I just could not remember the next chord change as Roy caterwauled, *"Snottttttttttt."* While he was singing that word my dad muted the TV and from the other room yelled, "Jesus Christ, Roy, can't you see that he's busting your balls? I mean, really, how many more weeks is it gonna take till you figure it out? I mean, come on . . . ?"

Years later I would tell that story to Ian Anderson backstage at Jones Beach Theater when we were opening up for Jethro Tull. We were standing by the craft-services table after sound-check and he did a spit take of his drink, nearly throwing up a lung, laughing.

That was the last guitar lesson I ever took. I figured out that I really didn't wanna play it anyway. Mick didn't play guitar and neither did Roger Daltrey, Robert Plant, or Jim Morrison. I wanted to be a lead singer. Besides, once I got into a band I didn't wanna have to fuckin' carry anything.

.   .   .

I wouldn't describe my teenage self as cool. I was a loud and un-self-conscious jackass who partied heavily on the weekends and would do anything for a laugh. That won me a lot of friends, 'cause let's face it, people are bored a lot of the time, and they like a guy who can come in and stir the pot—but I wasn't cool. So when Pete Zendowski, the coolest kid in school, called me up and asked me to be the singer of his band, I could already feel the cool wash over me before I even hung up the phone.

Pete was my neighbor down the block and a year older than me. He was Huntington High School's hotshot ax-man and had been playing in a band for a couple of years by then, in bars and everything. He hung out with a much older crowd of musicians, dirtbags, and drug dealers who were out of school already. He had that air about him like he thought everything connected with Huntington High was just Romper Room shit. You know the type—he was a tall, thin, good-lookin' guy with long, wavy, light brown hair and an acerbic wit—a consummate wiseass.

I got the gig because of the legacy of my brother Hollywood Bob, whom Pete used to sneak in to see play with Old #7 at Chelsea's Bar. "Dude, if you're even half of what your brother is we can't miss. See you tomorrow in Braxton's basement at four P.M. sharp," is how he ended the call. The Braxton he was referring to was Buddha Braxton, our drummer, who'd earned that nickname by having the appetite of a competitive eater and, of course, because he looked like Buddha.

We started rehearsing in Buddha's basement every day after school. We'd sneak a few beers in and hide 'em behind his drum kit, then smoke a little weed to get in the right head, and start plowing through the cover songs we'd chosen for our set. I'd belt it out behind center mic with my eyes closed, disappearing into my rock 'n' roll fantasy—legions of screaming chicks were adoring me, but I was unfazed because I was so used to it. I'd look at myself in the huge mirror we had set up across from us, posturing like Mick, slinking around the stage, elongating my body to look more sinewy in my sleeveless concert tee. My transformation into a cool guy was *at hand* . . . but then Buddha's mother would walk in and my rock-star daydream would come to a screeching halt. Mrs. Braxton had been my teacher at Huntington Elementary, and every time she'd entered the room I'd be back in the fourth grade.

I remember her surprising us one day with a tray of drinks as I was chicken-stepping in front of that mirror, another lift from Mick's repertoire of moves. "I thought you boys might like some ice tea and I'm gonna have to run the dryer, if that's okay? Hello, Christopher. Nice arms, what are you doing, push ups before bedtime?" she asked, squeezing my arm. "Uh, no . . . um . . . I'm cuttin' alotta people's lawns these days so I think it's from that. Ya know, pushing and pulling the lawn mower. Do you need a hand with those laundry baskets?" "No, I'm good. You boys have your fun," she said as she walked away with that aren't-they-adorable-in-their-little-band look on her face. I was just glad she didn't know I was stoned.

Our set was an eclectic mix of rock. Pete loved the Grateful Dead, so there were a lot of Dead songs in there. I had to have my Stones, so the Stones were well represented. Buddha was a Van Halen man, so there was some of that. Our bass player, John, couldn't get enough of The Police, so we learned a bunch of songs off of *Regatta de Blanc* and *Outlandos d'Amour.* We all loved The Doors, The Clash, and were starting to get into a new band called U2, who'd just released the album *War*, which had us all excited. We also played The Who, Kinks, Bowie, Elvis Costello, The Beatles, and, of course, what would a high school band be if we didn't play "Sunshine of Your Love" at least fifty times a week?

Pete was a real taskmaster and would have us go through each song four and five times to get it right, but he wasn't a dick about it. At one of our afternoon practices we were trying to work up our own epic version of The Beatles song "Dear Prudence." We kept stalling out and wanted to move on to something else, and he said, "Hey, if you guys wanna look stupid then I'll gladly look stupid with you. We're a band. I mean, I really don't give a shit but I'd rather not. If we do it one more time then we probably don't have to worry about it when we play it at the gig." At the same time we all did a double take and said, "Gig?" "Yeah, I got us a gig at Bridget Calhoun's graduation party. I haggled her cheap-ass old man into payin' us two hundred bucks too. He wanted to pay us only a hundred but when I told him we'd bring the sound system he caved," he mentioned, in the most casual way possible, futzing with his distortion pedal.

Two hundred dollars was a king's ransom to five guys in high school in 1983. "Shit, that comes out to forty bucks a piece!" Buddha shouted, rolling out on his drum kit and punctuating it with a rim shot.

This would be the night of lunacy I'd been waiting for my whole life. It was gonna be the bash to end all bashes with me at the helm of my hometown's teenage wasteland. It was the party where I would, for the first time, trot out the new and improved version of me, no longer the slapstick party boy but an enigmatic, cooler-than-thou lead singer.

I had read *No One Here Gets Out Alive, On the Road, Catcher in the Rye,* and *Fear and Loathing in Las Vegas* in succession and the ideas I had taken from these books had cocked and loaded me full of rebellion and a new nihilism that was impermeable to the outside world. A spell that could only be broken when I'd hear my mom call, "Dinner!"

I was seventeen that summer and determined to roar through this world like an antiauthoritarian cyclone, sexy and sleek even when I spit. The look I was going for was late-sixties Mick. I was rake thin and had brown tousled hair so I didn't have far to go. I just grew it out a little.

Pete named our group Given Hallack after a phrase that was supposed to mean blow job in some sort of Turkish slang. One of his scumbag friends, Johnny, who was of Turkish descent, laid that one on him at a party we all went to after rehearsal one night. He yelled over to us by the keg, "Hey, whatta you guys think of Given Hallack? It means oral sex in Sanskrit or some shit." Buddha was kneeling down, tilting his cup, as I was filling it up slowly with foamy beer, and we all looked at one another and collectively said, "OK." It sounded cool to tell people even if we didn't know for sure that's what it meant. Johnny wasn't exactly an expert linguist, even if he did claim to be one-quarter Turkish.

We had our name and now it was time to play the show. In my mind this was the event that was gonna solidify my rock 'n' roll legend, first here in Huntington, then the world over. I couldn't have been more pumped. Another reason I was idling high was that I knew Kim Pearson was gonna be there. I'd had a silent crush on her for the longest time but never got the feeling I had a legitimate shot. She hung with Pete's crew, was a bit more mature, and used to roll her eyes at me when I did stupid shit, like the time I whipped a peanut butter square across the lunchroom at Monk and missed him, knocking her milk into her lap. That was the old me. She hadn't seen Mr. Disassociated Artist yet. She was gonna like him.

Kim was a real beauty with sandy brown hair, olive skin, and big hazel-green eyes with just a hint of melancholy in them. She was shy in a group setting and was known as a tough nut to crack. At rehearsal I asked Pete about her. "Did you ever try to get anywhere with her?" "Briefly but I think she's a vee, and as you know, I want no part of that," he said, looking down and tuning his guitar. "What the hell's a vee?" I asked him. "A virgin, dipwad. If you're gonna do her then I suggest you get out your hammer and sickle 'cause you're gonna be there a while," he said callously. "I just wanted to know what she was like. I don't need my sickle, dickhead," I snapped, not liking how he'd objectified her. "Suit yourself but there's gonna be a ton a chicks at this party, and you'd be a fool to fixate on just one," he said, and then riffed out on the guitar.

As you can tell, Pete was already a stick man. I had only crossed that golden threshold once, which is a whole other story. It involves me passing out drunk on top of this girl, while we were in the act. It was at a Halloween party and I'd needed a costume last minute so my mom had found this old white wedding gown in a closet and I slapped it on. I woke up with the girl giving me postcoital kisses, not knowing I'd been asleep. So essentially I lost my virginity dressed as a bride on her wedding night. I had a more romantic vision of what it might be like with Kim if we ever got to that point. At the very least I planned on being awake for it.

We got to Bridget's house early to set up the P.A. (the sound system) and have at the keg to get a good glow going before we went on, a time-honored tradition.

After drinking our body weight in Meister Brau we took the stage (a patio) with an incendiary version of Elvis Costello's "Mystery Dance." The girls all danced in front of us while the guys looked on expressionless, their eyes red and intense like laboratory rats, but when we finished a song, they'd yell out something specific like, "YEAH!" to let us know they liked it. In between tunes I'd take huge pulls from a bottle of Jack Daniel's that Pete had stashed by his amp, making sure everyone could see so they'd think I was like Jim Morrison. I was carrying off the cool-guy persona beautifully, conducting myself very professionally, all the while getting more and more bombed.

We played a couple more songs and then out of nowhere a policeman appeared in front of me with a very stern look on his face, trying to tell me something above the volume of the music.

He was a mountain of a guy with a military-style haircut, about forty years old. "Sorry, Officer," I said to him over the microphone with two hundred stoned teenagers hanging on my every word, red keg cups in hand. "I couldn't hear you. What'd you say?" "I said, tell the band to turn down," he replied forcefully. "Oh, I'm sorry I couldn't hear you before. My ears are a little blown out from the amps," I said apologetically but visibly insincere. I turned to the crowd and over the mic I asked, "Is there a Vern Brown here?" Everybody started to laugh and the cop got really pissed. "Hey, wiseass, I said TURN DOWN, not Vern Brown. How would you like to take a ride in a SQUAD CAR? Any trouble understanding that?" he said, meaning business. I looked at him dumbfounded and said into the mic, "OK, got it now." He said, "Good" and started to walk away, shaking off his annoyance. Then into the mic I said, "Is there a Todd Carr here . . . Todd Carr . . . has anyone seen him? TODD CARR?"

He was in the middle of the lawn on his way back to his patrol car, heard this, and came storming back over right as we were going into the epic Doors song "When the Music's Over."

He started chasing me around the patio, creating this rock 'n' roll Benny Hill–type situation. I kept on singing and every time he thought he had a hand on me I'd move with catlike quickness behind one of my bandmates or I'd jump up on a flower pot so he couldn't get hold of me. He was getting more and more heated, and though it probably looked more like something out of a Marx Brothers movie, to me it was The Stones at Altamont Speedway or Morrison being arrested onstage in Miami. I was going to wring it for all the drama it was worth.

He finally got me cornered where I had nowhere to go. We were in the intense middle part of the song and right as he was about to snatch me up I dropped to the cement in all my Morrisonesque glory. I could feel the intensity radiate out over the freshly cut lawn, the wet blades of dead yellow grass spattered onto the patio by the lawn mower adhering to the side of my cheek, as I laid there staring at people's sneakers, and seeing six-packs dangling down from their thumbs, bouncing against their swaying pant legs. *"Cancel my subscription to the resurrection,"* I sang with my eyes closed. *"Send all my credentials to the HOUSE OF DETENTION,"* I crooned, crescendoing on the last line and glaring at the cop as I sang it for full ironic impact. Everyone on the lawn cheered. I couldn't have planned this any better. *I hope he arrests me onstage,* I thought. *That'll look fuckin' great! I'll get laid for the rest of the summer off that one alone. My dad will freak a little bit but it'll be worth whatever sentence he hands down,* I mused, foreseeing the future nostalgia. It was already the perfect legend for retelling.

The music had come to a sudden halt but with my eyes closed I couldn't tell if he'd pulled the plug or if the band was pausing 'cause there are a lot of stops and starts in the song. Then I felt the policeman yank me up off the ground by the scruff of my neck. He spun me around and peeled a half-eaten, mud-and-mustard-soaked weenie off the back of my black sleeveless T-shirt and held it up for all the crowd to see. Explosive laughs were heard around the yard. "This yours?" he asked, both of us knowing he had just shattered my rebel image that I'd worked so feverishly to create.

What to do now? I thought. I couldn't let it end this way. Then it came to me. "Yeah, I was looking for that. Thanks," and I took it out of his hand, held it up to the violet bug zapper light, and scarfed it in one bite!

The party erupted in awestruck cackles and disbelieving "Eeeews!" That hot dog had been on the ground getting trampled all night. It had its own identity of sorts. It was bunless and had been pointing straight up out of the beer-soaked dirt, so we'd spent the whole night referring to it as the "magic mud penis." Whenever someone crossed over the patio to get to the keg I said into the microphone, "Be sure to step on the magic mud penis. It's a lifetime of good luck if you do."

The cop stared at me, squinting his eyes, trying to fathom why I'd gone that far. I smiled back defiantly, still chewing a little, as everyone stayed glued to the action. He walked around and examined me closely. It felt like I was being inspected in front of a boot-camp cot. I kept chewing and made sure not to flinch. I thought for sure he was gonna knock me to the ground and slap the cuffs on me.

He came right up to the side of my face, his nose practically touching my cheek. I could smell his coffee breath as he panted angrily. We hung like that for a minute and then something unexpected happened. He started laughing. And I don't just mean laughing. I mean REALLY LAUGHING! I guess it was a time-released thing, but when it finally hit him that I'd eaten this disgusting, ashed-on, beer-saturated, mud-caked nub, he fell apart. Summoning his breath, he said in his thick New York accent, "Look, I don't wanna shut yas down. I was at Woodstock, for chrissakes. Just take it down a notch. Do yas know 'Jumpin' Jack Flash'? I love the Stones."

We played "Jumpin' Jack Flash" and while I was singing it and chicken dancing, like Mick, I had one of the first great epiphanies of my life. As I watched the cop bop and smile, giving me the thumbs-up, while eating a fresh hot dog someone had just handed him off the grill, I realized I wasn't supposed to be cool. It's not in my nature. And I wasn't a rebel. Rebels either stand for something or they stand up against something. I was never gonna be that. I was an incorrigible fuckup, which was even better. I liked to get so drunk I couldn't stand up, period.

My syllogism was this: Everyone loves a clown. Everyone loves booze. Therefore, everyone will love a boozed-up clown. But as a budding teenage alcoholic, I didn't know that my formula was flawed. There's a thing called real life that I was afraid to confront and live in.

In the car on the way back from the party, I remember the world slipping in and out of focus as Mark Knoppfler sang, *"Get yer money for nothing and yer chicks for free."* It was so loud I could see the Blaupunkt speakers pulsating back and forth as I lay there with my head against the passenger side window of Kim Pearson's car. She was steering us down to the beach and I was trying not throw up.

"I can't believe you ate that thing . . . the magic mud penis. I probably stepped on it eight times before you guys even started playing. Are you all right? Why did you do it?" she asked. "I don't know but whatever power it had it's in me now," I shot back, sticking my head out the window for some fresh air. "That was so gross," she gasped. "Yeah, well, it had to be done," I said, not really wanting to explain any of it. "No, it definitely did not *have* to be done," she said, laughing. "I'm kinda fighting something off here. Can we find another subject maybe?" I said, sticking my head farther out the window.

"Do you always drink like this, 'cause every time I see you at a party you're drunk," she said bluntly. "Well, every time I see *you* at a party I'm drunk too so we're even," I slurred. "Uh . . . that doesn't even make any sense," she said as she giggled. "I know. I'm sorry. I just don't feel so well right now. Do you wanna take a walk on the beach when we get down there?" I asked innocently, pulling my head in from the window and cracking a beer. "Yeah, that'd be nice. If you don't feel well, why did you just open another beer?" "Ummm . . . 'cause it was in my hand?" I said, thinking that was a good answer.

"Are you ever serious, Chris? I don't think I've ever seen you in a serious moment. I mean, are you ever not fucking around?" she asked, really wanting to know. "No, not really," I said, doodling with my index finger on the dusty dashboard. "Funny you should ask that, though. I tried being all serious tonight but it just wasn't me. I don't think I'll be trying it again any time soon either. So, the answer is no. I'm never serious. I don't think it's in the cards for me to be," I said, meaning it. "I think that's really sad. You're a funny guy but I think that's really sad. I don't even know why but it makes me wanna cry," she said, choking up. "Shit, this is going well. How close are we to kissing?" I joked, out of reflex. She hit me hard on the upper arm. "That was your shot at a serious moment, asshole."

A full moon was up over the bay and shone down on the Huntington lighthouse as the moorings bobbed and clanged an unwitting symphony. The water lights flickered, and under a dome of stars Kim and I did what drunken teenagers on a hookup do. We talked about our dreams, stared into each other's eyes, fooled around, drank some more beers, listened to the radio, and talked about our dreams some more. She wanted to teach special ed. I wanted to be the next Mick Jagger. I told her that I'd hire a bunch of mongoloids as roadies. She thought that was sweet.

She had to pull over on the way home for me to get sick on the side of the road. She put her hand on the back of my neck and caressed it as I sprayed the night's indulgence. When I got out of the car to go into the house, I went to give her a peck on the cheek 'cause I didn't wanna gross her out. She pulled my head in and French-kissed me good night anyway, a profound gesture from a soulful girl. She'd be my girlfriend on and off for the next few years. That first real connection with someone is one that never dies, wouldn't you say? I made it up to my room feeling like a molecular rearrangement had occurred in me. I knew who I was. Then the bed started spinning.

Chapter Four

Meet the Drops

Given Hallack disbanded when Pete went away to college, leaving me in the lurch. It was just as well. I loved the guys but it was just a cover band. I'd started writing songs by then and wanted to get into an act that had material and a personality of its own.

My taste in music was changing too. I still had the foundation of my beloved Stones along with The Who, Bowie, Beatles, Neil Young, and so forth, but my sisters had both just returned from semesters abroad and brought back a whole slew of post-punk rock from the UK. They turned me on to records like The Jam's *All Mod Cons*, XTC's *Black Sea*, and Echo and the Bunnymen's *Ocean Rain*. These bands had such a blend of brashness, independence of spirit, and lyrical rhapsody that they made the old classic rock on the radio just sound tired to me.

I was so dumbstruck with passion for these albums that it gave me an insatiable appetite to find more of them on my own. I would soon discover the American version in bands like R.E.M., Violent Femmes, Hüsker Dü, and the group that had the greatest impact on my trajectory, The Replacements. Commercial rock radio didn't play this kind of music, so I started listening to a radio station on Long Island that did, WLIR, "the station that dares to be different," and different is what I wanted to be.

I was thrown out of J. T. Carringtons' bar one Friday night when the friend of my older brother Kevin, whose ID I had swiped from his wallet and been using to get into bars, happened to walk in. I'd been inside for a few hours and was completely wasted. He got flagged at the door so the bouncers corralled us for a face-off. This was in the days before pictures appeared on licenses in New York State. "Well, there can't be two Omar Gullicksons with the same age, height, and address in here at the same time, now can there?" the burly head bouncer said. "Now, I'm no super sleuth but I'm guessing one of you is lying." "One of us is, and if I were you I'd waste no time and kick him the fuck out," I slurred boldly, shooting a suspicious glare at the real Omar. With that, Omar grabbed me. "Gimme my license back, you little prick! I spent half the day at the DMV last week because of you!"

The bouncer bull rushed me out the door and I fell onto the sidewalk, yelling, "You'll pay for this! IDENTITY THEFT IS A CRIME, OMAR!" "If you're the real Omar, then why'd you just call him Omar?" the bouncer asked. "I mean IMPOSTER OMAR!" I shouted, looking past him into the doorway. "Go home, Chris," he said. "How'd you know my real name?" I asked. "Omar told me," he replied, giving me a hand up. "Oh . . . do me a favor and give this back to him and tell him thanks, will ya?" I said, handing him Omar's license. "Sure thing, buddy," he said, chuckling and shaking his head.

While I was dusting myself off and peeking back in the window trying to signal my friends to come out, I started singing Echo and The Bunnymen's "The Killing Moon" out loud to pass the time, something I always did. *"Fate up against your will . . . through the thick and thin,"* I bellowed, in a drunken and overly dramatic voice, trying to imitate their singer, Ian McCulloch.

This guy walks by and says, "Are you singing Echo?" I turned around. "Yeah, you know 'em?" "Know 'em? I fuckin' love 'em! I heard that song "The Cutter" today on LIR, what an awesome tune," he said. "Dude, come and meet the rest of my band. We're at the Rose and Thistle." "I haven't got an I.D.," I said. "Don't worry about it. I can get you in through the kitchen entrance. My name is Jimbo. I play guitar," he greeted me. "How ya doin'? I'm Chris." "I know. I saw you sing at Sparks one night last summer. You were fuckin' crazy! Was that Richie Blackmore in the audience watching you?" he asked. "Yeah, he's my neighbor," I told him as we tippytoed through the shrubbery and ducked under the side windows of The Rose and Thistle en route to the back door.

He was referring to a gig I'd done with Given Hallack when I got onstage and noticed that all the guys in the room had their backs turned away from us. I dialed it up a notch and started going ape shit, tumbling around and standing up on the drum kit because no one was watching, only to figure out, once I got up there, that their eyes were glued on Amy, who was hunched over in the back of the room in a low-cut blouse playing foosball. "We're looking for a good singer who's into the same kinda music we like. It's hard," he said, gently opening the steel door into the kitchen.

The musical landscape on Long Island in the mid-eighties was bleak with horrendoushair metal bands and synth pop drivel, so finding the right guys to play with was like stumbling upon an unexpected water source in the desert. I walked into the bar and seated at the table were Tom Licameli (guitar) and Phil Mastrangelo (bass). We formed the group that would eventually be called Knockout Drops.

Though we lived in the same town, I didn't know them because we were attending different high schools. Little did I realize at the time that we were about to embark on a twenty-five-year odyssey, through the bowels of the music business and across countless club and dive-bar stages. We were just teenage music heads, getting revved on one another's company, talking about bands, books, and movies we loved and sipping on some cheap beers. "Have you guys heard The Replacements yet?" I asked. When they said they hadn't, I pounded my fist on the table, knocking over everyone's drinks, "Oh, man! I just got one of those radios that can tape tapes. I'll make you all one."

The conversation ultimately devolved the way it always does with young dudes, to the ever-popular subject of the ladies. The waitress brought over a pitcher of beer, and as she was walking away, Phil said, "Jeez, I'd like to spaz out with her." I said to him, "Whattya mean 'spaz out'?" "I dunno, does it matter? Look at her!" he said, laughing loudly.

I liked Phil instantly—everyone who meets him does. He's a handsome Italian guy with a glint in his eye and a boisterously jolly laugh that he lets fly easily. His dad, Angelo Mastrangelo (love that name), used to be a working jazz musician and instilled in him a real sense of commitment to the music. I used to go over to Phil's house for dinner and wind up his old man to tell his road stories from the fifties and sixties. He had some juicy tales too. One night over the barbecue he laid a good one on me. He told me of how he was once in a band with Hal Linden of Barney Miller fame. "He was a nice guy, played the horn. Everyone liked him. Then one night our singer took sick and couldn't make it. Are you with me so far?" "Yeah," I said. "OK, so we're like, whatta we gonna do? Hal steps up and takes over in a moment's notice on lead vocals. Saved the day, right?" he said to me. "Right," I answered. "Great guy, right?" He put the question to me again, and again I said, "Right." "WRONG! He heard that applause and was a schmuck every day of his life after that. Don't let that happen to you, kid," he said, waving a cautionary spatula in my face. "Too late," Phil said, entering from behind us with hamburger rolls.

The rest of that night at The Rose and Thistle all we talked about was how hot all the chicks were in the bar, none of us getting lucky, of course, or even getting up from the table to try. And yet I consider it the luckiest night of my life. We made a date to get together the next day and jam.

At the first rehearsal I issued a half-kidding mission statement to everyone regarding what I wanted to be as lead singer. "I want to combine the sexiness of Mick Jagger, with the intensity of Jim Morrison, and the charisma of Al Jolson . . . ya know, without any of the racism." Tom chimed in, "I don't know about Mick but I know an easy way to fuse Jim and Jolson. You step up to the microphone and go: "Father? Yes, son. I want to kill you . . . MAMMY???'" We all died laughing. We used to do that as a piece of comedy in between tunes in our live set with me saying the lines and the band underscoring me with the song "The End." Not many people got it but we did it anyway 'cause it cracked us all up, a philosophy that endures to this day.

We rehearsed in Tom's parents' basement those first few months. Tom was our drummer at the time but soon switched to lead guitar when Jimbo left the band to go back to college (he was two years older). I'm realizing as I write this that Jimbo is fast becoming like Chuck from *Happy Days* in this story. I gave him a bit of a buildup back there because he brought me into the bar that night, but he wasn't actually in the band for that long. Sorry if I led you to believe there'd be more Jimbo. There isn't. We love Jimbo, though. He plays guitar in a band somewhere in South Carolina, I believe. Fare thee well, Jimbo!

Tom was way ahead of the rest of us both musically and technically, with a four-track studio all set up at home where he and Phil would demo their song ideas. If we were Hogan's Heroes he'd be the one who always had the headset on. Tom was also a nice-looking Italian American boy. We used to jokingly refer to ourselves as the McKnockout Wops. "Beautiful Italian music with jaded Irish lyrics" was our advertising hook. We never did launch that campaign. Perhaps, one day, we will.

When Tom and Phil were done demo-ing a song, they'd hand off the tape to me and I'd go home to work up lyrics and a vocal melody. I'd stay up all night listening and singing to it on the boom box in my bedroom at a low volume, just rewinding, humming, and feverishly jotting lyrics in a notebook. I took such joy in the responsibility of coming up with lyrics and would ask the Holy Spirit to help me pluck the right words to match the mood of the tune. I'd come in the next day, shot out of a cannon, manic, and raring to try it all out. Sometimes I'd scrap what I had and aimlessly voyage behind the microphone, spitting out whatever came to mind. It was an unbridled feeling I'd never experienced before, skydiving through the blackness of my imagination, and having it yield something beautiful or ugly or irreverent.

We'd bring down some beer and stay in that basement for hours upon hours, laughing, talking, drinking, but mostly just crankin' it up. We'd be shot and dripping with sweat by the time we finished, the jam room smelling like the rowing chamber of a Viking vessel, but we'd be back early the next day to do it all again to the point of exhaustion. That's how much we loved playing together.

The basement was both a tree house for our friendship and a womb for our gestation period as a band. We recorded a five-song demo on Tom's four-track and we were born. It was time to go get a gig!

We started out playing some backyard keggers, handing out that tape to anyone and everyone. It was great because when we played these parties we would mix our material in with copy tunes but once the tape had gotten around a little, people started requesting our songs over the covers, a big step. I remember this really stoned kid, Marty, came up to me as we were breaking down after one of these things and said, "Wow, I didn't know you guys did originals." And I said smugly, "We do our own songs, Marty. We call them songs. Only guys in crappy bands call their material originals." How's that for an atti- tude? HA! As you can see, I was proud of what we had going and by the way, it's true. If someone tells you that their band does "originals," don't go to the gig. It will suck.

We had our following in place and got our first big audition gig at a place called The Tuscaroo Lounge, which was the bar in the local Howard Johnson's. The whole summer was riding on this night, 'cause if we did well, they promised us we could play there once a week until school started again. We promoted the hell out of it and packed it with all of our friends.

The night started off well with us getting shit-faced at the bar and Phil fighting the bouncer. A speaker had come loose from the ceil- ing, falling, and doinking his girlfriend on the head. The bouncer was standing right there, and when he did nothing to assist her or even acknowledge that the accident had occurred, he and Phil ended up tussling. It was just a scrum, with all of us in the middle, and only a couple of real punches thrown, but it was enough to set the tone for an exciting evening. Two minutes later we were onstage rockin' out. I could see that the dustup before the set had gotten the crowd a little on edge so I led the room into a sing-along of "All we are saying is give peace a chance" over the mic and instructed all to look over at the troglodyte bouncer while singing.

The Tuscaroo was your basic hole in the wall with a bar to the left of the stage (if there had been a real stage) and the band cramped into the back of the room. Through the double doors was Howard Johnson's restaurant. I treated it like Madison Square Garden, hopping around frenetically, swinging from the cross planks in the ceiling, and yelling into the microphone "Thank you!" after every song. I was sustaining my buzz by drinking beers just as fast as people could hand them to me, but I was on my game—hammered, but not too sloppy.

We were all wearing our best thrift-store gig attire, looking like a

Salvation Army version of the British invasion. The place was totally jammed to capacity (which was about one hundred). Kim and all her girlfriends were in front of us, dancing with Loyal. I was surprised to see him in there, so after one of the songs I said into the mic, "How ya doin', Loyal?" "It's just nice to be amongst friends," he said shyly. "Had a feeling you'd say something like that . . . Loyal, everybody!" I announced, and everyone cheered him. Kim smiled at me and we shot each other a knowing look. She loved Loyal too.

She was luminescent with a little bit of a sunburn on her face, a flower in her hair, and a summer dress on that hugged her perfectly. She was a staggering beauty but her heart is what made her truly breathtaking. She sanctified that shit hole of a room just by being in it, a fact that she herself didn't know. Goodness is like that.

We'd played a high-energy set and the register had done a titanic ring on drink sales so now it was time to go see Lenny, the booker, for the thumbs-up or -down.

Lenny was a true vicious freak, a middle-age Italian guy with raccoon eyes and a Ramones haircut that his face was way too old for, but we looked up to him because we'd heard him talk about being on the road. We found out later that it was really just one road. . . . the L.I.E. (Long Island Expressway). He lived in his grandmother's basement across the street from the bar and after our sound checks we'd be outside and see him kiss her good-bye. She'd hand him a sack lunch and then he'd jump on his Harley for his four-and-a-half-second commute in to work. On the back rode an eight-foot-tall inflatable Godzilla with hands he would interlock around his waist, like it was his girlfriend. He would ride noisily into the parking lot, revving the engine; he'd turn off the bike and unfasten Godzilla; and maintaining his tough face he'd walk by us into the bar as if there weren't anything at all strange about it.

Lenny had an encyclopedic knowledge of rock 'n' roll. You could ask him a question on anyone from Jan and Dean to Foghat to the Sex Pistols, and he would give you every detail about their career. He was impossible to stump. We didn't know all of this at the time of our first meeting, but we did know that he was the guy who could give or not give us the gig. We walked into his office in the back of the lounge as he was playing a game of Space Invaders.

He turned around and paced in front of us, formulating his thoughts, and then started speaking. "Yas got a good sound, yas do. And what's good is your lead singer, here, reminds me of a young Eddie Money . . . only without the . . . uh . . . thing . . . ya know that thing?" he said, pointing at his face and pushing his tongue to one side of his mouth, distending his cheek. He started talking through it, trying frantically to illustrate what he meant. "Makes one side of his face frozen . . . looks like he's singin' tru a set a testicles on one side of his mouth. Whattya call that again? A guy told me once what it's called . . . um . . . I'll think of it in a second," he said, his eyes rolling up into the atmosphere to find the term. "It doesn't matter anyway . . . oh . . . wait a minute . . . BELL'S PALSY! That's it! Hallelujah, that woulda bothered me all night. Thank God, you don't have that," he said, looking at me intensely. "You know how he got that? He got shot in the face. Yeah, he was a cop or somethin'. Didn't stop him from rockin', though, right? RIGHT? NOT EVEN A BULLET COULD STOP HIM . . . HA HA HA! And that's how yas gotta be if you wanna make it. Yas gotta stay together and keep goin' no matter what," he said, his voice going from atomically loud to a whisper in an instant, giving his address a dramatic nuance that had us all sucked in.

"And I'll tell yas another thing. Any record company guy worth his salt is gonna pick RIGHT UP on the way your lead singer, here, drinks. Don't think I didn't notice you up there suckin' 'em down like they was mother's milk," he said, staring me down. He paused for a minute. "I'll tell yas what. I'll give yas Tuesdays but I'm warning YOU," he said to me. "Watch the drinkin'. It'll derail you from your dreams. I seen it too many times." Then he looked us over one last time, satisfied with his speech, and said, "Anybody got any blow?"

So there we were, baptized by Lenny into the professional world of rock 'n' roll, cautioned of its evils, then shaken down for drugs—a confusing and powerful message that none of us really thought about at the time. Still, I like to think that we did take some of ol' Lenny's advice to heart 'cause we've managed to stay together.

I was loaded every night that summer and would stay that way for the next sixteen years. I could probably count the number of nights I stayed in on two hands. I ended up snorting many lines with Lenny in that office, all off of the *Frampton Comes Alive* album cover, which never moved from the corner of his desk.

On our last Tuesday night of that summer at the Tuscaroo he invited me back to his lair after our set to count out our gig pay. We'd packed his joint every night that we played, and he'd become an ardent supporter of our cause. "I seen a few bands come tru here but I think yas actually have a shot at the real thing. You're all young and the songs are great." "Thanks, man," I told him. "No, no, I mean it. I think yas have a real shot."

Lenny then dumped a big pile of blow out on Frampton, obscuring his face. He chopped four fat rails, handed me a straw, took a big swig out of his Yoo-Hoo, and said, "But you really gotta slow it down with the booze, Chrissy. It'll rot your liver. Did you know that? That's what happened to my uncle. It killed him. He was the one that raised me, ya know?" "Really?" I said. "How old was he?" "Fifty-six," he answered. "Let's see, I'm eighteen now . . . ," I said, staring straight ahead, squinting my eyes, and counting on my fingers. "Shove over and give me the straw, wiseass," he said, almost knocking over his Yoo-Hoo.

Chapter Five

Vanillanova

The morning I would go off to college I awoke with an uneasy feeling. It wasn't the usual bilious uproar in my stomach or the immense pressure in my frontal lobe that, if left unattended, would surely blow out my temples. Those things I'd grown to accept and greet with a gastrointestinal moan and a pained yawn. This was that other feeling that only drunks and people suffering from amnesia due to a severe head trauma share—the terror of not knowing what the hell happened. Actually amnesiacs don't even share it because their condition is blameless, the lucky fucks.

There was no visible evidence in my bedroom that anything was wrong. I gave myself a quick once-over, starting with my balls, of course, then working my way up and down, to find that there'd been no injuries sustained (my grandpa used to call them whiskey dents). And yet I felt something had gone awry. Whenever that feeling was upon me, trouble always followed. That dark cloud hovered over my bed for half an hour. I took one last cowardly dive back under the covers trying to wish it away, but my sour stomach drove me from bed in search of some Alka-Seltzer. Once on my feet I had no choice but to put on a detective hat because clues started to pop up.

For one, I was naked and I don't sleep naked. And for two, where the fuck were my clothes if they weren't on the floor? I did the only thing I knew how to do in that moment; I checked my balls again. Still good.

I threw on some sweats and went downstairs, taking each step with heavier trepidation. I got to the landing, caught the waft of coffee, bacon, and eggs up my nose and heard the searing sizzle and crackle of the griddle. The Sunday-morning ambience of my warm and loving home sent me rushing into the second-floor bathroom for cold water on my face and some dry-heaving, which was brief but painful.

I sat down to the breakfast table not feeling my best but confident that I could soldier through an English muffin and some eggs. My parents knew I'd gotten in late, but I was always careful not to let them see me too banged up because my mom was a worrier.

She'd been hinting here and there that I should take a look at my drinking. I'd awoken on more than one occasion with her pelting me with holy water, speaking in tongues for the most part but ending her petition with "that he be safe and sober, Lord. Amen." After she left the room I'd rise to a fan design of pamphlets at the foot of my bed targeting teenage alcoholics with titles like, "Thinking About Drinking" or the incredulous "I Can't Be an Alcoholic! I'm Too Young, Right?" the latter coming with a pop quiz that I secretly took and failed miserably. I remember one of the first questions was "Have you ever gotten drunk and as a result forgotten what you'd done?" to which I answered out loud, and to myself, while checking the box for yes, "C'mon, assholes, at least gimme a fuckin' chance to pass."

The reason she had this literature handy was because the year before she'd successfully gotten my dad to quit drinking and was now an active member of a certain support group for loved ones of alcoholics (whose name I can't mention because it would be violating their bylaws and traditions).

I pushed my eggs around the plate, occasionally mouthing a forkful just to make it look good, while my dad read the paper. I still had that ominous feeling but I'd done the forensics in my head a few times and had come up with nothing out of the ordinary. My friends had dropped me off around three A.M. I'd stumbled in dead drunk, made a crazy double-decker sandwich whose contents I couldn't name (but I was tasting the unpleasant vapor of olive loaf in my burps), inhaled it mightily, and gone right to bed. That's all I knew. I kept eating, my mom kept cooking, and my dad continued reading but they were strangely subdued, and like I said before, we're not quiet people.

After a few minutes, Dad lowered the paper and broke the silence. "You have to stop coming between your mother and me like this," he said and started up reading again. What the hell did he mean by that? My mind was blank. He folded the paper down, abruptly this time, and said, "Go upstairs to our bedroom and maybe you'll have some luck piecing it together."

I ran upstairs, my heart racing. I went into their bedroom and there at the foot of the bed were my clothes, neatly stacked in a pile, starting with my sneakers on the bottom and my tightie-whities, the cherry on top. "OH, SHIT!" I shouted to the rafters, slapping my hand on my forehead. I'd gone to bed all right, only to rise a few minutes later in a sleepwalking stupor, go into my parents' bedroom, get naked, and climb into bed with them! Needless to say, it would take a legion of psychotherapists to help figure this one out but I'm content not to try. I'm just happy I didn't climb in there with half a stinger.

I went back downstairs and Dad said, "If you're gonna drink like that down at school then I'd get into the habit of locking yourself in your dorm room before bed or you might find yourself an unpopular guy." I was speechless. "Go get your stuff together and load it in the car. We gotta get on the road. We're supposed to be at Villanova by one."

Not much was made of the incident on the ride down. I was the fifth of six kids and my parents had been through many such mishaps. Comparatively speaking, my naked swan dive into bed with them only fluttered the Richter scale. "At least you didn't pee anywhere. Sometimes when people do that, they pee," Mom said casually. "Who peed?" I asked. "Oh God, your father used to come home and . . ." But before she could get that story out, my dad shook his head, giving her the sign not to tell it. "Nobody, I've just heard that some people do," she said.

Mom was excited for me to be going off to such an esteemed institution of higher learning. "How are you feeling right now? You're starting a whole new life! It is such a beautiful campus too. I just know that you're gonna love it. You're gonna love it, I just know. Are you excited?" I groaned a little, not really ready for the cheerleader speech so early in the ride, still feeling my oats from the night before. "Yeah, Ma, I'm looking forward to it."

Which was a total lie. I wasn't looking forward to it at all. I didn't even wanna go to college. I wanted to get in a van and go play music. What was I going to college for? It's not like I had any plan to use my degree. But everyone else in the band was going off to college and my dad was pressuring me by saying, "Get a degree first. Then you'll have something to fall back on," a phrase that I still hate more than almost anything else I've ever heard in this lifetime. People who have something to fall back on end up doing just that. I was ready to eat out of fuckin' garbage cans for the rest of my life just to be able to say I was a musician, but instead I was going off to college and relegated to only playing with the group on school breaks. I just went because I didn't know what else to do. That's some nauseating middle-class whining if ever there was, eh? But rock 'n' roll is a singularly strong intoxicant, and as any musician will attest, once you've had a taste of it you don't wanna do much else.

"You have to get excited! Take a little nap and when you wake up we'll be getting closer and it'll hit you. You have no idea how lucky you are. Growing up in Woodside I would've killed for an opportunity like this. Bob, this probably reminds you of the day you went into the navy, right? Do you remember how you felt that day?" Mom asked Dad. "Hungover," he said, adjusting the rearview, shooting me a sympathetic look through it.

I couldn't fall asleep. Then the ride got strange. Something really horrible flew into my head, that grabbed hold of me and wouldn't let go, like an angry Chihuahua with a newspaper clenched in its teeth. This wasn't just your run-of-the-mill intrusive thought that could be quickly dismissed, like "What if the car spins off the road and we all burn up?" This was something that rocked me to my core and left me feeling frightened and alone. It didn't pass, but lay in wait, poised to pounce on me at inopportune times for the next decade of my life.

Since that fateful day of my first Holy Communion I'd always been pretty tight with God. I included him in everything I did. On the football and lacrosse fields, onstage, whatever it was, I'd say a little prayer to the Holy Spirit to guide me and would feel fortified by that. I had lengthy discussions with him from my pillow that were not prayers but intimate conversations you would only have with your most trusted friend, venting all my hopes and fears, offering them all up to him, so that he could keep them and I wouldn't have to worry. I had the kind of unflappable faith that you only really get to enjoy in childhood before the world encroaches. God had my back. I knew that to be true. Then, out of nowhere, in the back of my parents' Subaru, droning down the New Jersey Turnpike, *poof!* Faith left.

As I looked out the window at nothing in particular this inner voice suddenly proclaimed, "There is no God." An irreversible paralysis washed over me. "It's all just man-made mythology," the voice prodded again, authoritatively. I tried to pray it away but it wouldn't stop. A permanent twilight took up residence in me that I would never say a word about, not to my friends, not to girlfriends, not to anyone. To this day I don't know what triggered it.

The rest of that ride I clammed up and pretended to nap. I wasn't about to tell my devoutly Catholic mom and dad that I had turned into a hopeless atheist in a matter of minutes, while they were dropping me off at college. I just said nothing and hoped the feeling would dissipate. It didn't. I felt true existential loneliness for the first time. I was consumed with the terror of my own expiration. The image of the little light cube that you used to see on the TV after you clicked the knob off, just before it turned black, was all I could see. That was how my life would end. Religious icons like Jesus and the Virgin Mary were pushed onto a shelf in the back closet of my mind, next to Santa Claus and the Easter Bunny. My insides churned. Faith was gone. God, my best friend, had vanished. In his stead was fear—a fear that I would never outwardly acknowledge. I tried to outrun it with laughs. It was still there. I tried to drown it with booze. It fuckin' floats.

We drove up to St. Mary's dorm, dropped my stuff in my room, and took a stroll through campus. My mom was right. It was really beautiful. The campus was lush—green and finely manicured, the regal old buildings adorned with ornate religious statues. There were rows of oak and maple trees everywhere whose leaves would start turning the following month. A lovelier place in autumn I challenge you to find. I put on a brave face and even managed to feign some interest as we searched for my orientation group. We found them in front of Sheehan dorm on the big lawn that faces Lancaster Avenue. They were out there doing some rah-rah shit that I knew I was gonna duck out on just as soon as my parents left. Then I'd find the closest bar.

We said our good-byes. My mom started crying. "Just be open to all this and remember that God is with you." That one hurt. The three of us hugged. They got in the car and pulled away. I followed them down through the parking lot, waving, and when they made the turn and were out of sight, I went behind Bartley Hall and wept. After a few minutes of sobbing I looked up and saw a sign that read WELCOME TO VILLANOVA. . . . A CATHOLIC UNIVERSITY. Then I quickly dried the tears on my sleeve 'cause some people were coming.

. . .

My first few days at Villanova were rough. It just didn't seem like my kinda place. The student body was comprised of preppy guys and gals, seemingly from Catholic and private high schools, the boys all looking like Alex P. Keaton, the girls straight out of a Benetton ad. I'd walk through the quad and see American flags draped outside dorm room windows. Springsteen's *Born in the U.S.A.* album blared from boom boxes as a bunch of budding Reagan Republicans played Frisbee and sang along to it. I'd stride through, wearing all black, with the Clash song "Straight to Hell" pegged on my Walkman—a stranger in a strange land, or so I felt. I have no problem with the American flag (I'm as patriotic as the next guy), and unlike some of my indie rock cronies, I actually love the Boss but it clearly was not my scene.

Villanova is about twenty minutes outside of Philly and the radio down there at that time was dominated by their hometown band made good, The Hooters, whom I despised. I must've heard their song "And We Danced" five hundred times that first week alone—each time inching me ever closer to smoking a fuckin' pistol.

I had a single room in St. Mary's dorm. I would lie on my bed all day long blasting records and drinking beers I bought from the package store down the street (that was the term down there for liquor store). Omar had given me his old license as a going-away present before I left, saying, "You're gonna need ID down there and because of you I have two now anyway. So here, asshole," and he stuffed it in my top pocket. I rewarded him by being arrested twice in the first month of college for drunk and disorderly conduct. Both tickets went to his house and he had to pay or warrants would be issued for his arrest.

I was deathly homesick. I missed the band. I missed my drunkard friends. I ached for Kim. I longed for the comfort of my alcoholic hometown. I missed my family terribly. I mourned the loss of God, a despondency that was inconsolable. I had a tough time adjusting to my new environs, to say the least. To say the most, I WANTED OUT! Then it all changed on a dime, or should I say, a dime bag.

About a week and a half into this nightmare I opened my door to go to lunch and saw Gary McLain saunter by me and move some stuff into the room two doors down. He was the outstanding senior point guard on what later that year would be our National Championship–winning men's basketball team. I was a huge fan of Big East basketball and had been watching him play for three years (while rooting for St. John's, of course). I walked over to introduce myself as he was shutting his door and noticed he'd thrown a towel down under it immediately. Within seconds the sweet smell of sinsimilla was filling the hallway. Gary was a burner!

I waited till after dinner, twisted up a fatty, and headed for his room. I knocked and he opened. "Whassup, chief?" he said. I pulled the joint from behind my ear and said, "I thought I'd bring you a little housewarming gift and introduce myself. I'm Chris." "What-ever do you mean, chief? I burn incense in here, that's it. That's it AND THAT'S ALL!" he said, looking paranoid and insulted. "I think I'm gonna have to ask you to leave," he said, pushing me toward the door. I felt ridiculous. We got to the door and he said, "But leave whatever it is you have in your hand with me. I just feel like it would be rude not to take it." I turned around and he was smiling ear to ear. "Aaaaaaaaaahhhhhhhh, you were shittin', dude! I saw you! HA! C'mon, let's torch it up!" I said, "I got some cold Buds in my room too." He said, "Bring 'em!" By the joyful way I ran down that hall and back, you'd have thought he said, "Fetch," to an eager-to-please golden retriever.

He took a big pull off the joint and talked through it with squinted eyes, trying to hold in the smoke. "So you're a freshman, I gather?" "You gather right, my smoked-up friend," I answered, as he handed me back the joint. "Where you from, New York?" he asked. "Yep, Long Island. How'd you know?" "I can tell these things. I'm a strong islander, too . . . born, bread, and buttered . . . Hempstead." "Yeah?

Huntington," I told him, pointing to my chest. "Yeah? How you likin' it so far?" he asked. "I can't fuckin' stand it," I said. He exhaled and let out a huge laugh. "HA HA HA HA. I knew you were gonna say that too!"

Then I went on a fifteen-minute rant about why I hated it. I said, "This place is full of uniform fuckin' robots . . . and these preppy Catholic chicks seem none too friendly either. I feel like I've been sentenced to four years of heavy petting and blue balls." By the end of my venting he'd fallen off his bed and was hyperventilating he was laughing so hard. "I'm glad you find my pain so amusing. . . . Someone should," I said, now half laughing with him. He took a tissue to his eyes and said, "Oh . . . no, chief, it's not you. You're just takin' me back is all. This is Vanillanova. It don't get more white-bread than this. I didn't like it at first, either, for all the same reasons, but it grows on you." "You like it now?" I asked sincerely. "Love it," he said definitively. "You're gonna love it too. There's no way not to love it." "Yeah, but you're a big-time basketball star; of course you love it," I volleyed back. "Got nothin' to do with it. I coulda switched outta here after my freshman year and gone alotta places other than this but I didn't. There's a spirit here and it just gets you," he said solemnly. "I'm thrilled to hear you say that because I could use some spirit right about now." He sensed that that statement carried more than just trivial weight but it was getting late and it was a conversation that neither one of us was up for.

He opened the door and said, "You're a freak, Spicoli. It's always harder for freaks to adjust down here but you will. I've seen it before. You play lacrosse, right?" "Yeah, I have my first practice on Tuesday," I told him. "You're gonna be right in your element on Tuesday. Trust me, I know some of those boys and they're freaks too," he said. "Did you just call me Spicoli?" I asked. "Yeah, you look like Jeff Spicoli from *Fast Times at Ridgemont High*," he said, like it was a given. "Get outta here, I do not," I protested. "You do. Don't be surprised if that sticks. Once I give a nickname it always sticks." He ended up being right about everything. Those guys were freaks, I did end up loving Vanillanova, and within two days I had six thousand undergrads calling me Spicoli, so maybe I did look like him. I don't know.

The reason I got into Villanova in the first place was because I was recruited off my high school team by the head lacrosse coach, Randy Marks. I didn't really have the grades, but he gave the admissions office a little shove and got me accepted. I had a B-minus average and due to a colossal hangover hadn't done so hot on my SATs. I think I scored about a thousand fifty but it's hard to tell because I've been lying about it for so many years.

I came in as a highly touted freshman and was given a warm welcome by the team at our first practice. I demonstrated that I could play, along with three other frosh phenoms: Kevin King, a fellow midfielder, who was from Maryland; Tom Ferguson; and John "Woody" Durham, a goalie and a big defenseman, respectively, who were both from Pennsylvania. I felt a kinship with my fellow freshmen instantly. They were funny guys and great players, but more important, they wanted to go get fucked up that night, an idea that met with my undying friendship.

After practice the upperclassmen got wind of this and took me, Kinger, Woody, and Fergie out to Kelly's Bar and got us all smashed. I walked into Kelly's and was greeted with the resplendent smell of stale beer and piss. I sashayed through the sawdust and sat on a deteriorating barstool patched up with electrical tape. I would practically collect my mail there for the next three years.

The older guys on the team, many of whom were from Long Island, were total mad dogs. I felt cozy in the bosom of my booze-swilling brethren. They operated on the fringe of Villanova campus life. They were anti-Villanovans as described by a sophomore midfielder from the Bronx, who everyone called Frankie Runs and Guns. "You can be an anti-Villanovan and still love Villanova, Spicols. We're just seen as outcasts because we don't fit the profile of most of the people that go to this school," Frankie said that first night in the bar. "How so?" I asked. "I dunno. A lot of us do drugs and we get arrested more, I guess," he said, throwing his head back, chugging an entire bottle of Rolling Rock. "Drugs? What kinda drugs?" I inquired with great interest. "We're big on EBH," he said, and burped loudly. "What's EBH?" I asked. "Everything but heroin." I had found my tribe.

I was soon to find out that Frankie Runs and Guns had earned that moniker not just from his lacrosse prowess but also because of his ninety-mile-an-hour midnight cocaine runs to dangerous cop spots in the Bronx in his black IROC, with a nine-millimeter pistol stashed under his seat. How do I know he went ninety and had a gun? I accompanied him, naturally.

Frankie Guns and I became close pals. He dealt coke to all the anti-Villanovans, both on and off campus, as well as some of the townies. Frankie was a classic Bronx guido with gold chains around his neck, six bucks' worth of cologne on at all times, and short jet-black hair always perfectly gelled back. He was simean in both posture and build, slick by nature—always two chess moves ahead of everybody—fun-loving as hell, but cross him and he turned into a fire-breathing sociopath. In these instances he made Tony Montana look like a kindergarten teacher. I saw him kick the shit out of more than a few people, but he didn't consider himself the fighting type. In fact, he hated that type and would beat them senseless when he encountered them. He was Alpha Alpha Alpha and I don't mean the fraternity.

His sidekick was a monster-size defenseman named "Double D," not a drug user, just a big drinker with a hearty laugh and a nose for mischief. I teamed up with these guys that first year, and we did everything together. Double D became my Ed McMahon. He was a great guy to have around if you wanted to feel funny. He had a big blond box head and laughed at everything. He was another guy with a pussycat disposition, but with Frankie we would invariably get into a scrape. I'd turn around to see him throwing someone into a wall, but he always did it with a smile.

Lacrosse is a sport that attracts lunatics. Don't get me wrong. It's a beautiful game, created centuries ago by Native Americans, and requires great athleticism and skill. But let's face it, it's also a bunch of guys running around, wearing very little padding, relentlessly hacking away at one another with metal sticks. At least, that's why I loved it. There wasn't a day that went by freshman year that I didn't thank the God I no longer believed in for lacrosse. It saved me at Vanillanova.

· · ·

My dorm was situated right in front of an active monastery (the building itself used to be one too). There was a cafeteria downstairs and the monks would emerge from the cloister around noon to eat with us. They'd shuffle through in their brown medieval robes and grab

71

their trays, beleaguered expressions on their faces that I attributed to sexless claustrophobia, in league with daily overdoses of religiosity. There were some priests among them. I figured, being surrounded by so much cleric, why not have a chat with someone about my little crisis of faith? Life without God really sucked.

I befriended one of the monks one day. He was eating by himself and I noticed him eavesdropping on our table as I was regaling my dorm buddies with a story. I surreptitiously motioned to them that I thought he was listening in and abruptly tacked away from the real subject. I raised my voice to an exaggerated level, just beneath shouting, and ended with "AND THAT'S THE LAST TIME I LET ANYONE RUB HAMBURGER MEAT ON MY BALLS!" Everybody howled at that and then got up from the table to go to class.

I hung there, eating a grilled cheese, dipping it in tomato soup, just staring off into space, one of my favorite activities. The monk slid his tray over next to mine. "Funny story," he said. "Well, it's a cautionary tale. . . . Chris Campion," I said, extending my hand. "Brother Gerard," he said, accepting it. "Do you always say such shocking things?" he asked. "I don't know. Do you always listen in on other people's conversations?" I batted it back to him, more fiercely than I'd intended. "I was at the mercy of your volume level," he stated. My normal tone *is* pretty loud and I thought that was a valid argument. Besides, he was a fuckin' monk. His opportunities to hear genuine irreverence in the world must have been so few that I didn't fault him for listening. "You're right, Brother, gotta get a handle on that."

He seemed like a wise and sensitive soul so I said, "Listen, Brother, I'm having a bit of a crisis of faith and I don't wanna get into it here with so many people around. Do you think I could swing by sometime and bounce it off ya?" He asked, "What's the crisis?" I said, "Ah, well, it's kinda complicated but the gist of it is that I don't believe in God anymore and I'd kinda like to get back to believing, ya know? . . . 'Cause . . . uh . . . life really sucks without him and I'm having crippling panic attacks about the thought of . . . ya know . . . not being anymore . . . like death but not just death . . . being dead and gone . . . like really gone . . . ya know, like sputtering out and then nothing . . . and questioning that . . . ya know? . . . Always questioning and going over it in my head . . . and trying to figure it out . . .

which causes more panic because I can't figure it out and then I get more and more terrified about death . . . and then, ironically, I start praying to God . . . who I don't think is there anymore . . . which ends up making me feel worse 'cause . . . ya know . . . there is no God . . . um . . . no offense . . . I know you got the robe on and it's your life's work and all . . . but I can't . . . right now . . . convince myself that there is one . . . but I don't wanna get into it now. There's too many people around."

He said, "Come by tonight around seven and we'll talk." "Great, Brother. That's great. I'll try not to drink till then," I said, realizing that my confessional vent was still open and a piece of unintended honesty had slipped out. "Why, will you have trouble staying sober until then?" he inquired with an alarmed look. "Well, what time is it now?" I asked him, trying to joke it off. "One-thirty," he answered. "Let's make it six . . . better make it six. . . . Can you do six?" He just nodded yes. "Okay, see ya then," I said, and hightailed it outta the caf- eteria, feeling like a moron but relieved I'd made the appointment.

The monastery was a really weird place. Walking in there was like going through a porthole to the 1500s. It was eerily quiet, with stained-glass windows and a Gothic vibe that I found more unnerv- ing than comforting. Everything there was geared toward the con- templative life, and it seemed like the right place to go in search of some answers. I took solace in the knowledge that Brother Gerard was so steadfast in his resolve that he'd incarcerate himself in a place like this.

I gave a gentle knock to his already open door and there he was, looking especially monkish, seated in an easy chair, reading a big leather-bound religious book. It was pretty worn out and I could see it was written in Latin. I felt bad I was carving into his monk leisure time. His room was cramped and only essentially equipped, as ex- pected. He offered me a beer out of his minifridge, something I hadn't anticipated. "Please," I said.

We chatted, casually at first, and then he asked, "Christopher, are you aware that you're attending an Augustinian university? Do you know who Saint Augustine was?" "Ummm . . . I've heard of him," I answered, which was total bullshit. "Did you know that he was a drunkard and a womanizer for the first half of his life?" he stated.

"Wow, my kinda saint!" I said. "Did you also know that he struggled with his faith his whole life? But he committed himself to God. He put his intellectual questions aside and decided to dedicate himself to believing no matter what. The lesson there is that faith is something that can't be attained through rational thought. Faith is dark—you must take a leap," he said, taking a sip of his beer. "So, what you're saying is that if I keep punching and want it bad enough, that faith will come back?" I said hopefully. "Yes, in a sense I am. It won't come back to you as it was before all this happened, but it will be stronger and you'll have a deeper understanding of it. It'll take on more meaning and spur you on to great things, namely helping others in need, the greatest thing any of us can do."

"Fuck it. I'll try that," I said excitedly. "What?" he said incredulously. "Oh, I said screw it. I'll try that," I said, realizing I had cursed in front of a monk. "No, I heard the fuck part. I didn't get the second half of it. Did you say 'why rat'?" he asked. "No, I said I'll try that. Why would I say 'why rat'? I'm not here to rat on anybody," I said, laughing. "Exactly, that's why I found it so strange." "All right, Brother, next time I come here you be Abbott and I'll be Costello," I said, opening his door. "Remember what I said, Christopher. You're a diamond in the rough." "Thanks, Bro," I said, shutting his door, leaving him in his easy chair, drinking his beer.

I took the good brother's advice and I leaped. Into what, I didn't know, but I kept on leaping. Leaping is good. It's better than staying put and panicking.

. . .

The lacrosse team took an unsanctioned trip down to Fort Lauderdale in February of '85 for spring break. I was excited about going 'cause the hype on Lauderdale was that it was a round-the-clock drunken, lawless, Sodom and Gomorrah fuck about with all the fixin's—a veritable Eden for young men. On the flight down Frankie Guns said, "I heard girls just walk up to you and grab your dick." Double D nodded in agreement. "Yeah, they grab your dick, Spicols." "All right, we'll see," I said. Somebody had to anchor it down with some skepticism or I feared that conversation would give way to a spontaneous circle jerk under our food trays.

We flew but the rest of the guys drove down in Winnebagos and parked them right on the strip next to the ocean, giving us the primo beachhead for attracting girls. Frankie, Double D, and I grabbed a cheap room in one of the hotels for a place to crash.

There was an endless flow of booze, blow, hallucinogens, sunshine, beautiful girls in bikinis, and to top it off, we were lacrosse players from Villanova. Unlike the rest of the frat rabble walking around, we had an identity. I was resistant to all things "college," but if ever there was a time to invoke that when-in-Rome thing, this was it. And for once I could feel normal about drinking as soon as I woke up because everybody did that on spring break. I never lost my buzz once in all the time we were there.

Frankie had us amply stocked with his Bronx rocket fuel and would pack our beeks with blow before we hit the strip. I had watched him put Ziploc freezer bags of it in his suitcase, packing it just as he'd done his socks and underwear. "You're just gonna put it in there like that?" I said. "Yeah, they're not gonna check. I'm a fuckin' college kid. Do I look like a criminal?" he snapped. I hadn't the heart to tell him that he did.

Kim and I had broken up so I was a free man, not that it would've mattered. Cheating on your girlfriend while away at college didn't seem like such an egregious offense to me. That argument hadn't played well the month before when I'd gotten caught and she'd broken up with me over the phone. I knew we wouldn't stay broken up but that thought didn't enter into the equation at the time. I was in Lauderdale to play the field—and the field was rife with wanton nubiles! But I didn't seem to be getting any of them. I had a theory as to why.

Just before we left Villanova I'd torn up my knees on our stadium's artificial turf. The turf burns were long, deep red, and infected with pus pouring out—with festering chunks of green from the turf woven into the scabs. My legs were grotesque! I kept having to field questions about them. I felt like the fuckin' Elephant Man. One afternoon about three days into the trip I was chatting up this gorgeous gal from the University of North Carolina over by the Winnebagos and really hitting it off with her, only to have her look down and say, "Eeeeeeew, what's that?" and recoil in horror. About twelve guys from the team had been watching this little passion play and when

I lost her off the line they burst into hysterics. My buddy Rip said, "Spicoli, you better do something to cover those up or you're going home oh for Lauderdale."

I grabbed Double D and Frankie and went down to Cunningham's Pharmacy on the strip to get some oversized Band-aids. We got in there and realized that we were all wearing bathing suits and none of us had money. Rather than walk back to the trailers, Double D encouraged me to shoplift them. "Here, dude, shove 'em down your bathing suit. No one's gonna wanna go get 'em down there even if they do see you. Just walk out." I casually started walking out with this clunky box shuffling around in my drawers. It looked ridiculous, like I had a parallelogram for a penis. The store manager grabbed my arm and said, "What's that?" motioning to the tumbling box inside the front of my trunks. That's when we came to the realization that Lauderdale wasn't as lawless as all that.

I broke loose from him and started running for the door. Two of the stock boys began to give chase and Double D threw a nice block, taking one of them out. *Only one guy to beat*, I thought. He circled around the other aisle trying to head me off at the end of the row. He got there first but I deeked left and broke his flimsy attempt at a tackle. Frankie Guns boxed out the store manager as he tried to get back into the action. The door was in sight! It was clear sailing from there! Then the nice old lady behind the counter got in front of the exit. She was plump with gray hair and glasses. Do I barrel her over to get out? Could I do it? I galloped up a full head of steam as she bravely extended her wingspan, making it impossible for me to get by her without a collision. "Get out of the way, lady!" I yelled. She wouldn't. She was a *real* company gal, this one. I put my head down, ready to go through her but looked up one last time to see where she was, a fatal mistake. I saw her courageously standing there, her arms outstretched, and I pulled up. I couldn't go through with it. This was probably somebody's grandma.

They detained me at the pharmacy until the cops got there, which took all of three minutes. The old lady turned out to be not so nice after all. She reached into my crotch with delta force and yanked out the box. "Gimme those Band-Aids back, you dumb son of a bitch." I should've flattened her when I had the chance.

They threw me in the back of a squad car that already had another guy in there. We sped off for the police station. "Hi . . . name a Cal," my fellow passenger said, reaching his cuffed hands up to bump mine in lieu of a handshake. "Uh . . . Cal Ripken?" I answered. "No, I mean MY NAME is Cal. What's yers?" "Chris, Cal. Name a Chris," I said, not really in the mood to talk. "Hi, Chris." Then the arresting officer yelled back, "This isn't a social club, y'all. Pipe down back there!" Cal was beyond a redneck. He was like a radioactive redneck. He had it all goin' on: the sun-scorched face, a Cat Diesel hat, five-days' growth, enough dirt under his fingernails to mulch, blue eyes like a Malamute, and I don't wanna speak for him but I'm assuming no dental plan.

"Do you like niggers, Chris?" he asked. Now, how does one answer a question like this? If you say yes, then you're saying that it's okay for him to refer to black people as niggers, and if you say no, then you're agreeing with him, obviously not an option. I chose to give a long answer hoping it would end our dialogue completely. "If you're referring to those in the African American community, then yes. I'm very fond of them. Yes." "Well, I hate 'em," he said, breathing his canine breath all over me.

He started getting more belligerent. "I think the only good nigger's a dead nigger." "Well, that makes no sense at all because how can somebody be *good* to you if they're dead?" I said. "It makes perfect sense cuz they're better dead than alive. You git my meanin' now?" he said, getting angrier. "No, I don't. Because there is no meaning in what you've said. How could someone be *better* dead than alive? There's no plausibility to your argument," I said. "I ain't makin' an argument. I'm makin' a statement. That niggers is . . . Oh, I see what yer doin' now. Yer a smartass college boy, aren'tcha?" he said in an accusatory manner. Now I was pissed. I was no college boy. Or maybe I was but I didn't want him calling me that. "Well, you're a hateful, dumb fuckin' hillbilly!" I said, blowing my stack. "I said pipe down back there, y'all!" the cop yelled again. "When we get into that holding cell, yer mine," Cal threatened me, his stank breath causing me to wince and jerk my head away.

I didn't regret saying what I said to him, but I was starting to shit my pants because now I was gonna have to fight him. He was pretty big, not huge, but brawny. I was a wiry nineteen-year-old kid. He was about twenty-eight. I was trying to devise a strategy as the cop led us into the cell but I was coming up with nothing. I figured I'd just punch away and hopefully they'd separate us. The back of my neck was tingling I was so nervous. That wasn't made any better when he got in really close as the officer stopped us short and his nose went into the back of my head, and he whispered, "Yerrrrr mine." I was petrified.

We rounded a corner and the cop opened the door to the cell where three gargantuan black guys sat on a bench, staring up at a TV. He slammed the cell door shut, sending a condemning clang down the corridor. We stood there not saying a word as our eyes drifted immediately up to the TV. All you could hear for a minute was the sound of the local news. Then I turned to the three large black men on the bench and said, "Say, fellas, I was wondering if you could settle a little argument that Cal here and I got into on the drive over. It won't take but a second. You see, he says that the only good nigger . . ."

Cal ended up with a black eye. I ended up with the TV controller in my hand while they took turns kicking the shit out of him.

.   .   .

My junior (and final) year at school was a hodgepodge of lies to my parents, arrests, freak-out excursions, and gigs at colleges with the band. Notice I didn't say anything about classes.

One of my best friends from home, Paul, was now attending 'Nova. He was a star attack-man on the lacrosse team, a vicious freak incarnate, and a heroic lush. Paul was a stocky guy with dark curly hair and a boyishly handsome face. He would drink until that cherubic face swelled up and turned purple from alcohol poisoning and continue boozing until it reverted back. It was a miracle of modern science. He would also nod out, causing his head to bob up and down intermittently, giving him the look of some sort of narcoleptic Oompa-Loompa. He'd somehow party through that back to normalcy as well. He'd hit on chicks with his head going lifeless then snapping to, as if being yanked by a puppeteer, and go home with these girls, to the astonishment of us all. You'd think in that condition he'd fall over easy but he didn't. I'd get up a full head of steam in the bar, buck him, and he still wouldn't budge. What can I say? That's how we grow 'em in Huntington. One of our best friends on the lacrosse team, Rog, another freak in sheep's clothing, aptly nicknamed him, Sir Bobs Alot. That is how we'll now refer to him.

I was no longer playing lacrosse. Due to the ravages of my unstoppable daily intake of beer and vodka my skills had diminished to the point where I couldn't even catch a ball. My hands shook badly, causing the stick to tremble. It's pretty sad even now to think about it, but at the time I'd convinced myself that I just didn't feel like playing anymore. Besides, I was now gigging with the band on certain weekends and would have missed games anyway. We'd worked really hard that summer and gained quite a following at home. We were all miserable not playing music during the semester, so we decided to get together and rehearse as much as we could and book more shows during the school term.

I moved into an apartment off campus with Frankie Runs and Guns and Sir Bobs Alot. In his haste in securing the place by phone, Frankie hadn't realized that the apartment was about fifty yards away from the Radnor police station. We were not the sort of people who should've been living so close to a station house, and it proved our undoing time and time again. We'd had a bar brawl at a popular Villanova joint called Smokey Joe's that got written up in the local police blotter with the headline "Bad News for Villanova Students." Woody clipped the first half of that and posted it on our door. From that day on our apartment was known to all as BAD NEWS. There would be a few more noteworthy clippings before the year was out.

Frankie tricked out his room with a waterbed that spanned two-thirds the surface area (replete with leopard bedspread), a ceiling mirror (one on the headboard too), and a wall-size exotic aquarium. "You gotta give chicks the whole experience," he said, screwing in the ceiling mirror. "What experience is that—the under-the-sea strip-club experience?" I said. "You don't know nothin', Spicoli. Have another beer, why don't you?" "Thanks, I will," I said, not caring about his insult. "Get me one too," he said. Sir Bobs Alot and I shared the other bedroom, which consisted of two mattresses thrown on the floor, separated by a pile of clothes in between them.

Being from the Bronx, Frankie knew nothing about fish, or wildlife in general, and when we took him to the King of Prussia Mall to talk to the guy at the pet store, he was impossible. We had a crunchy-granola sales kid who kept trying to explain to him that he couldn't have all these predator fish in the same tank. "Why not?" he asked. "Because once the feeders run out, they're gonna eat each other," the kid told him. "Good . . . I want Armageddon in my tank. Let only the strong survive." Within a week the fish were all swimming around off kilter, looking like aquatic mutants with partial fins and half their heads bitten off. Within two weeks we were taking him back to the store because they were all dead.

We opted for a more harmonious ensemble this time. We returned to the apartment and threw them in the tank, watching them wriggle out of the baggies, and assume their colorful new habitat. Frankie left the room to go get the fish food he'd left on the kitchen table as Sir Bobs Alot yanked an errant nylon string off of my black-and-metallic-blue-checkered pants. He threw it in with the rest of fish and winked.

The string looked iridescent in the light of the water. The pump thrust it into motion, giving it lifelike animation—and making it look like it was swimming alongside the other fish. Frankie came back in the room, looked at his pride and joy of a fish tank, and said, "Who's this little fella?" tapping on the side of the glass, pointing at the nylon string. "It's a sea worm, Guns," Bobs said casually. "Sea worm? I don't remember buying no sea worm," Frankie said, perplexed. "You didn't. The guy in the store felt bad about what happened to the other fish and threw him in as a gift. We weren't supposed to tell you till we got home," Bobs said. "What does he eat?" "Just the powder stuff but make sure you feed him every day," he told him, really laying it on. "Yeah," I said. "They don't look like it but they eat a lot." "I'll feed him right now. Hey, little sea worm. Supper time, buddy," Frankie said tenderly, tapping on the tank and nuzzling his nose up against it to get a better look. He fed and cared for that sea worm all semester, loving it as I'd never seen him love anyone or thing before.

Our apartment building was half students, half young professionals, and a couple of families on the ground floor. It was a fairly nice place. We struck up a unique friendship with the two superintendent/janitors in the building, a pair of crazy ex-con African American alcoholics named Mac Smith and Wink.

Mac was pint-size and after a couple of drinks, his eyes would go in two different directions. The first day we met him, he ripped off his shirt and told us the story of how he'd won the 1971 Philly Golden Gloves in the bantamweight division. "You might not think it to look at me but I could whup yo' ass!" he said proudly. He had two missing teeth in the front so I asked him, "You lose those in a fight?" He said, "Yeah, the one with gingivitis."

. . .

Mac and I were getting drunk together one weekday afternoon at the kitchen table, something we did a lot, and I made the mistake of asking him what he went up for and got a three-hour she-said-she-was-eighteen explanation from him, claiming his innocence. I finally got him off the subject and Sir Bobs Alot walked in and said, "Hey, guys, you know that high school chick, Julie, who lives on the ground floor? Her parents are away so she's having a party and invited us down to drink some of the keg she has down there before we go out." This prompted Mac to utter a line that would be quoted many times for the rest of that year. He said, without any hesitation, "Them girls is downstairs . . . the PO-lice station is over there . . . AND MAC SMITH IS STAYIN' RIGHT HERE!" pointing to the floor between his feet.

Wink was only a little bigger than Mac in size and looked like Linc from *The Mod Squad*. He wore these funky hats, off to the side, with a huge 'fro underneath. He could've been an extra in the movie *Carwash*. He always wore mirrored shades to cover up his glass eye (hence the name Wink). We would make him pop it out at parties. He never wanted to do it but we'd beg him relentlessly until he did. One time I accidentally dropped it in this girl's drink and she almost fainted (all right, I did it on purpose). We asked him how he lost his eye but he wouldn't tell us, saying, "Y'all are nice boys. You don't wanna hear about that. It's messed-up stuff. That's all behind me now. Just stay nice boys as you are and that kinda thing won't happen to you." We got it out of Mac one day that he was in a gang fight in inner-city Philly when he was a teenager and lost it to a knife. Wink had a gigantic heart.

They were being paid next to nothing by our magnanimous land-lord and repaid him by spending most of their time getting wasted with us in our apartment. The five of us became a tight-knit posse. It was me, Mac, Wink, Sir Bobs Alot, and Frankie Guns, galvanizing the Main Line on a nightly basis.

We used to take them to Villanova parties and people would be just mortified. One night Bobs was taking this gal, Debra, to a dance on homecoming weekend and she invited us to the party beforehand at her sorority house. These were all wealthy coeds, many of them legacies, so there were a lot of the girls' parents in attendance. We were grabbing a beer from the bar and I asked Bobs, "Have you seen Mac and Wink?" He said, "No, I thought they were still with you." Debra came running over. "Uh, guys, you wanna do something about your friends? They're doing blow over there off the glass table in the living room in front of my mom and dad!" We looked behind and saw Mac chopping lines on the table, motioning to everyone with a rolled-up dollar bill, offering it around like hors d'oeuvres, as Wink twiddled with the knobs on the stereo trying to get a funky radio station to come in. Bobs looked at Debra and said, "I'll handle this." He screamed across two rooms, "Hey, fellas, where's your manners? Move that shit into the bathroom," which they immediately did. Having amended the situation he turned back to Debra for approval. They didn't end up going to the dance.

Frankie's little cocaine ring had grown from just servicing students and a few other people we knew from the local bars to a small regional business, which made our apartment an oasis for every jonesing Jack and Jane in the area. It was total chaos at all hours. There was one gal in particular who buzzed around our place constantly. Her name was Constance, so we dubbed her "Constantly Conscious Constance from Constantinople," later shortened to Constantly Constance, then bagged altogether because nobody could say it when they were drunk.

Constance was a redhead, freckled and fearless, prone to crying jags, laughing fits, run-on sentences of mirth-filled ludicrousness, and every once in a while would accidentally wake us whilst doing her Jane Fonda tape. She had the decorum of a wrestle-mania fan, knowledge of great literature (she could quote Dickens all day long), and a cocaine habit that made Rick James's look like a few harmless bumps. In fact, she would've been perfect altar material for him but she probably would've ended up scaring him off. It also looked like she and Mac shared a dentist. She could be an annoyingly shrill presence but I had a soft spot for her. After all, she was a vicious freak, the only criterion for my friendship.

We used to tease Frankie Guns that she was his girlfriend. Bobs would say to him, "Where's Constance, Guns? She's your girlfriend, right? Or are you two kids just foolin' around?" He'd fly off the handle immediately. "She is *not* my girlfriend." "OK," Bobs would then say, backing off, "but I'm not sure she knows that." "She knows . . . she knows," he'd say.

One afternoon we walked into the apartment after class, saw the bathroom door cracked open with the shower going, and yelled in to him, "Frankie, that you?" "Yeah, in here," he called back out. We rounded the corner and he was in there casually shaving with her on her knees blowing him. "Jesus, dude! Give us some warning, why don't you," I said, genuinely pissed. "See, she *is* your girlfriend, Guns. I knew it," Sir Bobs Alot said. She looked up. "I am not. I'm just bored. Has either of you guys seen my Jane Fonda tape? I've been looking all over." "I think I saw Mac and Wink doing it last," I said sarcastically, still trying to shake the shock of seeing that ape being knobbed. "Oh, good for them," she said, and went back to her business with the same nonchalance another person might have for picking up where she left off knitting. "Hey, Constance, when you're done, do us all a favor and shave his back too, wouldja? We feel like we're on safari around here living with him," Bobs said, cracking a beer and throwing me one.

Frankie stepped out of the bathroom, half shaven, with a chubber, and in an ultra-serious tone said, "Listen, you guys, I noticed the sea worm isn't eating very much; do you think we should bring him in? "Nah, he eats. You just don't see it 'cause they won't eat in front of people. They're shy like that," Bobs reassured him. "Yeah, but I mean I've never seen him eat nothin'," Frankie said, still concerned. "They won't even eat in front of other fish sometimes, that's how shy they are. They're known as quite bashful, even in the deep. The guy in the store told us that," I said, laying it on perhaps a bit thick and drawing a look from Bobs that I was pushing it too far. I had to take his direction. This was his baby. Frankie tapped some powder food in through the top of the tank right as the nylon string was propelled into the powder cloud by a current. "Holy shit! You see that? Musta heard me talkin'. Good little fella. Good little sea worm. You see? He'll eat in front of me."

I was halfheartedly attending classes, doing the college thing, but my mind wandered during lectures and I would end up working on songs in my head rather than listening. Phil, Tom, and I had circulated our demo tape around and the response we got was overwhelmingly good. People were making one another copies and creating the demand for us to go gig in these areas. Tom was attending the Berklee College of Music in Boston, so our first string of gigs was up there. Without telling my parents, I went AWOL from 'Nova for a week to go play some rock 'n' roll.

Our first show was in the college auditorium, which was awesome. The place was packed with kids—mostly aspiring musicians—and studio rats (producers, engineers, techs, etc.). They were a fantastic audience, energetic with good indie-rock sensibilities. Boston has always been a great music town, spawning bands like The Pixies, The Lemonheads, Throwing Muses, Buffalo Tom (whom we're very proud to call friends), and a lot of other groups that had our respect. It felt great to be up there and playing in the midst of that scene. We rounded out the week gigging at a small place called The Ratskellar and then The Channel, a big joint that was a coveted club to play at the time. We drew really well everywhere and every place wanted us back. The trip was a huge success.

Playing in Boston was a pivotal experience for me. For the first time I was playing in front of audiences that didn't know me at all. At all the shows that preceded these, there were enough friends in the audience that I never really knew if we were good or if they were just being our friends. Our success that week ignited a spark in me that never went out. It's an incredible feeling to turn on total strangers and give 'em a good time. We spent the whole week rolling out of bed, working on tunes all day, and performing at night. It was the life I wanted. I knew I was a fraud at Villanova. It was a great school but the only thing that sheepskin was gonna be good for was wiping my ass if I didn't have enough money for toilet paper, an economic condition I'd find myself in all too often in the coming years.

I got back to 'Nova, resumed my life there, and was thoroughly depressed. I couldn't function anymore at all. Rock 'n' roll had whet my appetite again and this time there was a sense of utility to go with it. We'd felt like we were a touring band there for a second, working on our craft and getting paid to do it.

The apartment was now officially twenty-four-hour bedlam with Frankie's blow business thriving and a never-ending party going on. I stopped going to classes altogether, partied 'round the clock, and felt guilty all the time. Guilt is like sour petrol for the alcoholic engine. It's fuel—but not the fuel you want. I would drink to silence my conscience, which was telling me I was burning my old man by not attending school. The alcohol would then paint me into a corner of self-loathing and self-pity, and when I emerged—or should I say, came to—I'd feel more racked with guilt than ever. This became my life—a daily cycle of using the drink to laugh and tolerate myself. Underneath that plastered-on smile was misery and confusion—a liquored-up perma-grin I'd wear long after I left Villanova. That's just the kind of booze hag I am.

Mac could see right through the mask. "You ain't fooling me and you ain't fooling Wink neither and he's only got one good eye," he told me over beers at the kitchen table, where I was now getting drunk with him every day while my roommates were at class. "You don't belong here with these kids. I seen them faraway looks on your face. Reminds me of guys in the joint," he said. "I dunno, dude, this isn't such a bad place. I gotta get my shit together and start going to class again," I told him. "You ain't gotta do nothin' of the kind. You gotta git up on outta here. God gave you gifts and you're not usin' 'em. You're screwin' God and yourself if you don't use them gifts, that's what they there for. Gotta use them gifts," he said, taking a slug out of the Jack Daniel's bottle to chase his Budweiser. "Maybe you're right," I said. "Goddamn right I'm right. You're never happier than when you sing them songs when everyone's around . . . telling them fucked-up stories of yours. You oughta be doing that too. You is a funny motherfucker and I never think white folks is funny, but you and Bobs is funny motherfuckers. Do you know why you funny? 'Cause you is a crazy motherfucker and everybody relates to crazy. Black, white, purple, octaroon, makes no matter. Funny is funny when you a funny and crazy motherfucker." "So what are you saying that I should be a stand-up comic too?" I asked him. "I'm sayin' you should go off and be a crazy motherfucker on a stage . . . whatever that is. You got no business being here. When's Frankie Guns gittin' home? I'm itchin' for a taste."

After my father-knows-best talk with Mac, I did some hard thinking. As much of a lunatic as he was, he had imparted some wisdom in there somewhere. I needed to leave school when the term ended and go pursue my dream. I was a month and a half behind in all my classes and knew it wasn't humanly possible to catch up. Sir Bobs Alot told me that if I could convince the school shrink that I was having a nervous breakdown that they'd give me all incompletes, refund my dad's money, and grant me a leave of absence from school. We stayed up all night drinking, doing blow, and working on my crazy profile.

"Tell him you're suicidal," he said. "No, then he'll call my parents right away. We gotta pull back on it a bit," I said. "Then tell him you're homicidal," he said. "What, now you got me tellin' the truth in there, asshole? Come on," I said, kidding. "Tell him you think you might be gay. I've seen you puttin' on eyeliner before your shows, you pussy. You're halfway there already, if you ask me. It's a layup!" he said, thinking that was it. "All that's gonna earn me is a couple of pamphlets on how to live my new homo life. Come on, dude, you're better than this," I said, carving out a couple of lines on a Michelob mirror we'd stolen from the Erin Pub. "I dunno, take Constance in there with you as your girlfriend and let her do all the talking. You're a shoe-in then," he said, laughing. We looked at each other for a long second. *Bingo!* That was it.

The next day I went in to see the on-campus counselor that V.U. recommended, Constance in tow, the two of us looking sleep deprived and manic as all get out. The therapist turned out to be a forty-five-year-old woman named Dr. Balamuth. She had dark hair and wore glasses, with everything from the shrink cliché present and accounted for: the notepad, matching leather couch and swivel chairs, big diploma up on the wall (UPENN, I believe), and that look on her face like she'd heard it all.

Constance got the session rolling by telling her that I was morbidly depressed—that every night she came over at seven-thirty, caught me jerking off to Miss Piggy on *The Muppet Show*, and that

I sobbed inconsolably afterward. I cosigned her story with a sheep-ish look, shifting uncomfortably in the big leather chair. "Why do you suppose you do this, Christopher?" Dr. Balamuth asked. "I don't know, I think it's the voice. Most of the time I have my eyes closed but I gotta admit I like felt a lot too. It's so soft and delicate just like the world we live in," I said, gazing into space, trying to give off an air of feeling things too much. "Yes, but why the tears?" she asked, her pen dangling out of her mouth. "Well, that's Kermit's girl. I'd never mow another man's lawn . . . or a frog's. It's probably guilt." I told her, still holding a straight face.

Constance was perusing the bookshelves in the office. She started asking Dr. Balamuth questions and answering them herself in rapid-fire succession. "Who do you like better, Freud or Jung? Whattya think of penis envy? I think it's alotta bullshit. I don't want some mini elephant trunk swingin' back and forth between my legs. You can keep that, thank you very much. Do you think Carl Jung and Sigmund Freud were both mama's boys? I do. I wouldn't seek the counsel of some pussy who couldn't say no to his mother. I have no respect for that and I see it all the time with the guys I date," she said, finally coming up for air.

"Constance, do you go to this school?" the good doctor asked. "Me, nah. I just go where the wind takes me," she said, again look-ing at the books. Dr. Balamuth turned to me for an answer. "Allow me to introduce myself, I'm the wind," I said, knowing the jig was up. "Constance, can you excuse us, dear?" the doctor asked, opening the door. "Sure, but I'm warning you. Have plenty of Kleenex avail-able. . . . He's a crier," she said, exiting like a hooker who'd just rolled a john.

Dr. Balamuth shut the door, turned around, stared me down, and with a pissed-off tone said, "What the hell are you doing?" "I think I'm having a nervous breakdown," I said. "I drink all the time. I'm consumed with the fear of death and dying. I don't really believe in God anymore, though there seems to be a little ember still burning be-cause I pray and feel a little twinge from it sometimes. I'm profoundly unhappy here. I'm in a band. That's my joy," I said, flabbergasting my-self. I couldn't remember the last time I'd told the truth. "Why not just say that up-front? Why the song and dance?" she asked, shaking her head. "I dunno. I thought I'd try lying first and see how it went. That's also one of my great joys. I like a good song and dance, don't you?" I said. "As a matter of fact I do, but I'd always rather hear the truth. I'm going to give you your incompletes and recommend that you try this," she said, handing me a meeting schedule for a support group for alcoholics. "Thanks so much. I'll check it out," I said obligingly, placing it in the shoplifting pocket of my coat, never to be retrieved.

"One question, which of you came up with the Muppet masturbation story?" she asked, giggling. "Ummm, that was mine but she went off the script a little bit and ad libbed the part about me crying after. Brilliant choice, I thought." "Yeah, that added a badly needed touch of realism. By the way, do you guys ever play around here? My husband and I love to go see live music," she told me. "We have a gig coming up at Twenty-three East Cabaret just up the road in Ardmore two weeks from tomorrow. You guys should come. I'll put you on the guest list," I said.

They ended up coming and we partied all night with them. Her husband was a construction foreman who worked up on the high steel in Philly. He was a revved-up madman. She turned out to be a vicious freak. It's always a blessing to stumble into a VF in a high place. Once they recognize the red light blinking behind your eyes, they'll always give you a leg up. At the end of the night she said, "I still think you should try going to one of those meetings. Who the hell knows? After tonight, I may join you."

Once out of the doctor's office, I met Bobs at the student center for lunch. "How'd it go? The Muppet thing work?" he asked, scratching his ass and grimacing hard. "It went perfectly. I'm in the clear. What the hell's wrong with you? You got the 'roids?" I asked him. "Nah, I think it might be a rash. It started up right after we got dressed this morning. I couldn't stop scratching my ass all through Mitchell's class." "Bummer . . . let's go grab a hoagie," I said, rounding the O in hoagie, imitating a Philly accent.

We got our trays and loaded them up with sandwiches and chips. As we were sliding through the salad bar section, Bobs yelled, "WHAT THE?" and pulled one of my dirty black dress socks out from the back of his white painter pants. "I knew a rash couldn't come on that fast. I've been walking around with one of your socks in my ass!" We both died laughing. "We gotta clean that room up and stop dressing off the floor," he said. "Gimme that," I said, taking it from him and submerging it in the blue cheese dressing. "Nice. Let's go find a good seat where we can watch this," he said.

We plunked our stuff down at a table right next to the salad bar. "Dude, I have some phenomenal news for you," he said, bursting with excitement. "The Chestnut Cabaret in Philly called. They said they're thrilled with the crowds you've been bringing in at Twenty-three East and are giving you the opening slot warming up for Mick Taylor from the Stones next month at the Chestnut!" "Holy shit! AGHHHHHHHHHH!" I hollered out, grabbing him by the shoulders and shaking him across the table. "The message was on the machine when I got up," he said, his voice vibrating from me shaking him.

Our excitement about the gig morphed into a spontaneous wrestling match. As we both got each other into headlocks, we heard a bloodcurdling scream behind us. We turned around and there stood a dark-haired girl with freckles, her mouth agape with confusion and horror, holding a ladle with my crusty black sock slung around it—hanging down. It was saturated in blue cheese dressing, dripping fist-size globules of gunk off of both sides onto her tray. A cafeteria worker was crouched next to her examining it and frantically trying to pluck it off with salad tongs. He knew that, if seen, it could set off a cafeteria-wide panic. "We're outta here. Let's go grab everyone and celebrate at Kelly's," Bobs said. We picked up our trays and walked past the girl who was damn near catatonic at this point. "Wow, looks like you went a little overboard with the fixins' there," I said to her. I can still see her traumatized expression to this day. I didn't worry about her too much at the time, though. I figured Dr. Balamuth's office was right next door.

.   .   .

The Chestnut Cabaret was a huge gig for us. Getting into the room was a pretty big deal to begin with because mostly national acts played there, but doing it with Mick Taylor, the lead guitarist for The Rolling Stones during what many (myself included) consider to be their greatest period was an unforeseeable coup. We were included in all the radio ads as the opener, and every time I heard it my heart stopped—the palpitations of excitement were volcanic. The only drawback was that the name of the band was Column 13 back then, a handle I hated and wanted to change.

I didn't have to attend classes anymore, so my only job for the last month of school was to promote the gig. Phil was going to the University of Delaware, which was pretty close to Philly, so the U of D students would give us double the pull for the show. We'd done some gigs down there over the past two years and had generated a big following. The stars were all aligned.

My last few weeks at Villanova were my happiest. I was living a lie, calling home and telling my mom and dad that I was gearing up for finals, and feeling awful about that; but the buzz in the air over the Mick Taylor show was so electric it squashed whatever guilt I had over it. I was still Spicoli but my identity had evolved. I was no longer just a drunken druggie fuckup. Our tape was being played regularly in every dorm room and off-campus house, and I got the feeling that everyone believed in me and was rooting for me to make it. They genuinely loved our music.

Sir Bobs Alot and I had taken up with two Villanova nursing students who lived on the floor below us. Every night we'd go out to the bars on the Main Line, get loaded while handing out flyers, and adjourn to the nurses' place for an after-party. They kept their house really clean and it was a welcome change to the degradation, disgusting mess, and madness that we walked into every night in the Bad News apartment.

We'd throw on New Order's *Power, Corruption, & Lies* album and dance with them till dawn, laughing, singing, and falling over the furniture. Then we'd bed them down, hearing the murmur of each other's giggly conversations with the girls and subsequent romps through the paper-thin walls. It was one of those magical three-week relationships that you only get to have when you're in college or your early twenties, where nothing is expected by either party and you're only there to have fun and be young, knowing that when the semester's over, it's over.

The girls' names were Shelly and Lucy, two blond Bettys from Staten Island, with great senses of humor and a mad capacity for drink. We'd wake up every morning to Mac and Wink chugging the Spaldings off of the living room table (Spaldings are what we called half-finished drinks). Lucy and I poked our heads out of the bedroom one morning and Wink said, "No need to wake up, y'all. Allow me to bus this table," and threw back a red wine leftover into his mouth with one hand and a half-empty beer with the other. He whistled as he walked to the kitchen with a bunch of empties. "I do like a clean room," he said.

The night of the show fell perfectly on a Thursday before everyone had to start studying for finals and was widely considered the last hoorah of the semester. We loaded into the club around four P.M., sound-checked, and then watched in awe as Mick Taylor did the same. He'd put on a lot of weight since his heyday with the Stones but could still shred on that guitar. From the moment he plugged in, the sounds that came out were unmistakably his. He riffed up and down the fret board, fiddling with the knobs on his amp. I closed my eyes and imagined I was in Keith Richards's recording studio at his house in France as Mick Taylor was about to do one of his takes for "Exile on Main St." As a fan it was thrilling—as a twenty-one-year-old about to take the stage before him, it was terrifying—making the whole thing terrifyingly thrilling. This was Mick Taylor from the Stones!

I was, of course, dying to chat him up but thought better of it when the Chestnut's manager told me, "He's kinda cranky. Don't ask him anything about the Stones. I already made that mistake. He doesn't wanna talk about it." I kept my distance, giving him his space.

I had arranged backstage passes for Frankie, Bobs, Mac, and Wink, and upon returning from dinner they were already in our dressing room partying. "Big night, my brutha," Frankie said. "You need a little blast to get ya goin'?" "Nah, I'm gonna wait till after. Where's Mac?" I asked him. "He saw Domino's going into the other dressing room and went in there to get a slice," he said. I ran into Mick's dressing room, wading my way through a densely thick cloud of pot smoke, and found Mac talking to Mick. "Who are you, then?" Mick asked him. "I'm Mac Smith, motherfucker. Who are you?" he said. "I'm Mick Taylor, the person performing here tonight," he told him. "I don't get care if you Sly fuckin' Stone, I'm a git me a slice of pizza," Mac said gruffly. Mick looked at me not knowing what to make of the exchange and then started cracking up. "It's right over there, mate, go and have at it," he said to Mac. "Thanks, partner," Mac said.

After Mac inadvertently shattered the ice, I got to talk with Mick for a few minutes. He was really gracious, not at all difficult as reputed. He told me about how much fun he was having being back out on the road playing and even offered up a little something about why he left the Stones. "It just got too crazy. I'm much happier now but I have the greatest of respect for them guys, ya know?" I said, "Well, I loved your contribution to the band. I'm a big fan of early-seventies Stones," and with that shook his hand, heading back to our dressing room. I stopped short and turned around to retrieve Mac as he was ripping his shirt off to show his boxer's physique to Mick's bandmates, wielding a slice of pizza in his hand, pantomiming punches. "C'mon, Mac, let's leave these guys to get their game face on," I said to him. One of Mick's bandmates interjected, "He's all right, mate. We'll have him back to you when he's done telling the story." Mac was a big hit in there!

The night couldn't have gone any better. It was a sold-out show with six hundred people going crazy as we played. At one point I looked side stage and saw Mick Taylor tapping his foot, grooving and smiling. I was in heaven. We played our most popular song at that time, "(You'd Look Good in) My Blue Bedroom," and the whole room sang along with us. We burned through our thirty-five minutes of allotted time and then Mick took the stage and wailed through some power blues. Me, Phil, and Tom abandoned the wings and instead got right up front, drinking it in like fine wine, random strangers coming up to us every few seconds, slapping us on our backs telling us, "Great set!"

At the end of the night Frankie had to go back to 'Nova to tend to some business and left with Mac and Wink. Me, Bobs, and the band caravanned it down to Phil's place in Delaware for a victory party with a big crew of people who'd gone to the gig. We got to Delaware around four in the morning and the party devolved into a lost weekend from there.

I hooked up with a Delaware cutie named Charlene, who became my unofficial girlfriend for the weekend. She was a sexy gal with big brown eyes and a zaftig body—voluptuous in every way. I get blood flow southward just picturing her. She said, "Two days is all I can give you. My boyfriend comes back from a rugby tournament Sunday night." Magic words if ever there were any. I'd be gone Sunday afternoon.

Sir Bobs Alot got hold of a big sheet of blotter acid that we took in eight-hour intervals all weekend. It culminated with him zipping himself into a sleeping bag Saturday night that he couldn't get out of after we'd all gone to bed. We heard him whimpering in the living room, but figured he was just goofing around or seeing some weird acid shit up on the walls. We found him the next day out on the sidewalk next to the road, still all zipped up in the sleeping bag with only his nose sticking out, cars whizzing past his head. Apparently he'd tried to inchworm his way out of captivity and over to the next house for someone let him out, but didn't make it. We unzipped him and with his eyes dilated to the size of kickballs, he said quite scientifically and in a monotone voice, "I counted one hundred ansd thirty-seven cars and not one of 'em stopped to help me." "Once again proving that people just don't wanna help acid-gobbling freaks who soil themselves in sleeping bags," I quipped, getting big laughs from the ten people standing out on the lawn.

Just before we left U of D we got a call. Frankie had been locked up for a DWI back at Villanova the night before, and we might need to bail him out. We jumped in Bobs' Jeep and gunned it all the way back. It was one of those rides after a wild weekend where there were no words left to be spoken. We'd freaked ourselves to exhaustion. We just ripped off the top, turned up the tunes, and let the wind blow our faces into funny shapes all the way home, hoping Frankie hadn't had any gack on his person when they pinched him. The residual effects of the acid teamed up with the rumble of the motor and the visual of the oncoming traffic, making my square of the windshield feel like a video game. Bobs and I stayed in our own heads the whole ride. Later that night he confessed that a few times he'd looked down, startled to realize he was driving.

We walked into the Bad News pad and to our surprise found Frankie already there, sitting with his head in his hands at the edge of his giant waterbed, facing the fish tank. We sat down on both sides of him. "You all right, man? We thought we were gonna have to spring you," I said. For the first time in the three years I'd known him, he looked like the fast lane had finally caught up to him. Or that he'd passed out in it and been run over repeatedly by a tractor-trailer.

He told us of how he'd gotten into a high-speed chase with the cops that lasted for two hours (a story that would make all of the local papers the following day) and how he'd eventually lost them on a side street, parked in someone's dark driveway but in haste had forgotten to take his foot off the brake. The third squad car that went by noticed the brake lights on and arrested him in front of some family standing in their robes, watching from their porch. He'd chucked the coke out the window earlier so he was in the clear as far as that went.

"Dude, I know it might not seem like it now but this is actually good news. You'd've been fucked if they got you with the gack. Now it's just a dee-wee," I said, trying to cheer him up. "I know . . . believe me I know. That's not why I'm depressed. Take a look at the tank," he said, with heaviness in his voice. "What? I don't see anything," I told him. "Exactly," he said, massaging his temples. He looked at both of us, exhaled as if he were about to drop the emotional bomb of bombs, and blurted, "THE SEA WORM IS DEAD!" "What happened?" Bobs asked. "I dunno. I think the Oscar might've eaten him. I haven't been home to put feeders in. You guys wanna take a ride out to King of Prussia right now and get another one?" he asked, looking about eight years old. "No," Bobs said. "I think we oughtta mourn this one first. It just wouldn't be right to replace him so quickly. Let's go hoist a few in his honor." Out we went to the Erin Pub and did just that. The joke actually backfired on us. The truth was that we'd grown to love that little fella every bit as much as he did, even if he was just a nylon string. Bobs and I found it a few days later, stuck in the filter, and for a brief moment contemplated telling him the truth but decided to just leave well enough alone. We never got another sea worm.

I left school a few weeks later, never to return. The siren call of rock 'n' roll was too loud to ignore anymore and I charged headlong into its unending night. I might not have been your typical Villanova student but I still have a deep affection for my almost mater. They have the best fuckin' cheesesteaks down there too. You can't get 'em anywhere else like that.

Chapter Six

Unemployable

D runks and jobs don't mix. There's really no mystery to that. There is such a thing as functional alcoholism, though. Some people get their load on every night and still faithfully make it in to work every day, God bless 'em. My forays into the working world were unmitigated disasters, each and every one.

I am, by nature, a bum. I have no good explanation as to why that is. My dad tried his damndest to instill a work ethic in me. He was born in 1931, the beginning of the Great Depression, and his generation had it beat into them that they should be grateful for the opportunity to work and respect the value of a dollar. When the men of his time turned eighteen, they either got drafted or enlisted for their obligatory time in the service. I grew up watching reruns of *Gilligan's Island* and by the time of my eighteenth birthday was a fully formed moron-dreamer. I don't wanna indict everyone my age with that statement. I'm only talking about myself, but when he lays claim to the men and women of the World War II and Korean War era as "The Greatest Generation," I'm not one to argue.

When I was a kid, Dad used to say things like, "There's no better feeling in the world than having put in a hard day's work," or when I wanted a five-speed Sting-Ray bike his answer was, "Anything worth having is worth working for." I did the arithmetic on that one easily by just deciding I didn't want it anymore—not having it was better than doing something strenuous to get it. All I ever wanted to do was fuck around and I didn't need material things to do that, a philosophy

I carried into adulthood, or my meager version thereof. My attitude was to let other people worry about that shit—let other people worry about having a car to drive, but "Dude, could you hook me up with a ride to the party?" It was my job to cut our lawn every week, so ours was the house on the block with the grass so overgrown it looked like we'd moved out. It took herculean prodding on my dad's part to get me to do anything.

Another of my glaring defects as it pertains to any job is that I have no attention span or anything in the way of stick-to-it-iveness. In addition to my titanic sloth and lack of concentration, I might as well mention that I'm a Class A spaz too—a techno-putz of immeasurable incompetence. Forget about asking me to operate anything with an engine or that takes any kind of know-how. It just ain't gonna happen. Even the most menial of tasks baffle me. So let's review my qualifications, shall we? I'm a drunk, who doesn't like to work, doesn't know how to do anything, and is incapable of learning how. But what I lacked in skills I more than made up for in absenteeism, which struck a nice balance for my bosses.

That's the package I brought to the job market, but none of that mattered one iota to my dad. Once I was back from Villanova and living at home, he was all over me to get a job. He didn't give a shit how I felt about it either. "If you're going to live here, then you're going to pay rent," he said.

My job search was slow out of the gate, not out of disdain for hard work but because I had to be home every day to intercept my report card in the mail. I hadn't told him about those incompletes yet. I was waiting for the right time that, in my experience as a lifelong fuckup, had a habit of never presenting itself when I had to fess up to something grossly negligent—a nice way of saying when I'd screwed somebody.

We'd already had our heart-to-heart about me not going back to 'Nova, which he wasn't happy about, but wasn't that surprised to hear either. What I chose not to address was how I'd bagged outta my courses, gotten his partial refund check (about fifteen hundred dollars), cashed it, and gone to Cancun, Mexico, with Frankie Guns. I'd taken the four hundred dollars he'd given me to buy a moped and blown through that too. My car had died on the highway, on the way back from visiting Kim at Cornell College, and I'd abandoned it on the side of the road (an act that carried a costly penalty from the commonwealth of Pennsylvania, which he got zapped with as well). He told me to get a moped just to get to and from class for the last month of school. There was no class to get to anymore so that was a quick and easy rationalization done over the bar at Kelly's. I, of course, told him I'd gotten one and even delivered a delightful story to him and my mom over the phone about how I'd innocently plowed into a fruit cart with a girl riding on the back, a tale that had them laughing hysterically. There were also court and lawyer fees he'd incurred for my alcohol-related arrests (one I had yet to go back down and appear for). Suffice to say, his investment in me as a college student hadn't quite panned out.

I hadn't intended to spend the refund money. My plan had been to buy a bunch of weed in Mexico on the cheap and sell it for a killing out of the hotel to all the spring break kids. I'd replace the money as we made it. Instead Frankie's grass connection never came through and I partied the money away. I kept a tidy ledger of all the dough I owed my father. I knew in my heart I'd never pay him back, but as long as I could convince myself that I was "gonna do it," I could live another day without being asphyxiated by my conscience. I torturously felt the hash mark going down every night from a barstool, as I bought the whole place drinks, but successfully drank and drugged my way to the isle of "fuck it." When you cut the ribbon on those kinds of wrongdoings, it's important to drink your way to a better feeling and deal with it later. In the Bad News apartment we had a motto: "Drinking might not be a way to solve your problems, but it's the best way to ignore them." It's a helluva catch phrase, but later always did come and I was never prepared to deal with it when it did.

I eventually hijacked the report card from the mailbox, stowed it away in my room, and began a slow, agonizing pregnancy of lies leading up to my inevitable birthing date of the truth, a predicament I'd know again and again as a born liar and a drunk. "Shouldn't we have gotten your report card already?" my dad asked every night at dinner. "Uh, I talked to Paul and he hasn't gotten his yet either. I think they're a little late getting 'em out this year. I have a lead on a job, though," I'd say, and sculpt another fine piece of bullshit to steer the conversation elsewhere. I hadn't been looking for a job at all. I got stoned and played wiffleball every day with my friends Larry and Kyle, who had the same faux job searches going on at their own houses. It's always nice being part of a team.

One morning in late June 1987, I was sleeping one off and heard my dad downstairs in his office, talking on the phone. "Yeah, Villanova registrar's office, please?" I lay there marinating in the guilty juices of my mendacity. He hung up the phone and I heard his feet hit the stairs with a strident purpose. I was like a prisoner on death row, stretched out on my bunk, counting the clacks of the guard's footsteps down the long corridor, signifying the end of my transgressive life. All right, maybe that's a tad dramatic, but I knew I was getting kicked out of the fuckin' house and moreover had to own up to the fact that I'd lied to and stolen from him. I loved my dad and felt bad for him that he'd raised a son of such weak character and cowardice. It wasn't his fault. I sat at the end of my bed and waited for the door to fly open.

"What the hell's the matter with you? Whattya think, I'm stupid? Is that what you think? What the hell were you doing down there for four months? Don't answer that. I already know what you were doing. Get your things together and GET OUT!" he screamed. I got up slowly. My dad was mostly a yeller and not one to get physical, but I'd never seen him so pissed off and could actually picture him belting me one in that moment. I tread lightly past him, picking up some clothes off the floor as if to pack but not really knowing what to do. "One last question . . . was there ever a moped?" he asked cautiously, but still with an angry tone. I had told him I'd left it down at school and would retrieve it when I appeared for my court case. I could tell that he was desperate for a yes so he could hold on to his last frayed vestige of trust in me. There was a period of interminable silence before the answer finally came back. "No . . . no moped," I said, wanting to cry.

Unceremoniously exiled from the nest, I moved in with the band in a ramshackle house by the train station. This was what we needed to do anyway. We were all gonna hold down day jobs, rehearse and gig at night, and record a fresh demo that would include all of our new songs. This was the one area of my life where I wasn't lazy. Passion breeds a strong work ethic. I did have to get a job, though, in order to carry my share of the rent, so it was sink-or-swim time. My idea of swimming was to sink over and over again and hope for a lifeguard on duty.

The first job I got, I was fired on the first day for drinking. I was making deliveries for a florist, and unbeknownst to me, this old lady peeked out her front window to find me throwing up in her azaleas as I was ringing her doorbell. Stinking of last night's booze (made stronger by the nips I'd taken that day), I handed her a bouquet of roses and slowly slurred, trying to sound out her name from the muddled work order, "Delivery for a Mississ High-nee-out?" "That's Hignecor, dear. Are you all right?" she asked sincerely. "Me? Oh, I'm fine. Thanks. They really oughta print on these tickets. It's hard to read another man's cursive," I said. "No, I mean you don't look or seem well," she said. "No, I'm OK . . . just a bit harried with deliveries. Enjoy the flowers," I said, backpedaling down her walk. No sooner than I was pulling out of her driveway she was on the phone narc-ing me out to my boss, calling me "peculiar" and "visibly drunk and undone."

I stopped off for a few shooters at the Shamrock Pub before returning to work, not knowing anything about the call, and got a few pats on the back from the daytime dirtbag crowd. My old drummer Buddha Braxton was in there, saw me in my uniform, and said, "You got a job, Chris? I didn't think you had it in ya." I said, "Gotta bring home the bacon, Buddha. We all gotta grow up some time."

I parked the flower-mobile in front of the store, got out, and was fired on the spot. My boss, Dave, a fat guy with a nervous disposition, was standing next to the car as I opened the door. He said sternly in his thick Long Island accent, "Jeeeezus H. Christ, you smell like a distillery! Chris, I'm sorry but we're gonna have to letcha go. We can't have ya drinkin' and deliverin' flowers, especially if you're drivin'. We've already gotten complaints." I said, "Dave, in all fairness, we never really discussed that when I took the position." His eyes nearly popped out of his head. "Discussed it? I didn't think we had to DISCUSS IT! What you're doing is against the law. YOU'RE FIRED, YOU FUCKIN' JACKASS! Here," he said, handing me fifty bucks cash, "take this for today, and please, *please*, don't come back," and waddled angrily back into the flower shop.

I reached back into the car and lifted out an undelivered bouquet of flowers. It was a really pretty arrangement and I gave it to Kim when she met me back at the Shamrock after my untimely dismissal. "They're beautiful," she said, her bright green eyes colliding with the gray light of dusk floating in through the window, setting them aglow. Happy hour and Kim Pearson was my favorite combination in the world. Individually either gave me buoyancy; together they produced the prodigious power of transcendence, no matter the circumstances.

"How'd it go today?" she asked. "It's over. Flowers aren't my thing. They ignite my hay fever something awful while I'm driving. I had a real bad headache at the end of the day so I told him to find some-one else," I said, grabbing and kissing her to halt any further inquiry. "Yeah, you need to do something manlier," she said, squeezing my biceps and giggling. She knew what had happened. She just didn't say anything. I loved her for that. I bought us drinks till the money was gone. Then she bought. I ended up keeping the uniform and wore it onstage occasionally. The shirt was way too big 'cause I think it had originally been that fat fuck Dave's.

Next I tried my hand at sales. I started working for a fly-by-night outfit called the Sunrise Meats Corporation. They were in the busi-ness of selling wholesale frozen steaks and seafood door-to-door. The pitch was to ring someone's doorbell and pretend that you were a truck driver making some drop-offs in the neighborhood and had some surplus to unload at cost. I was issued a drab gray jumpsuit with the name Pablo stitched onto it, which had me pretty jazzed. They also provided a truck that you got to take home with you at the end of the day, a perk that would prove my undoing.

For the first two weeks I was Sunrise Meats' golden boy, racking up huge sales. They thought I was a natural-born salesman but all I was really doing was selling to my parents' friends in my old neigh-borhood who were buying out of pity to "help out Pat and Bob's troubled son." I didn't care why so long as they were buying.

The sales manager up at the yard was named Mario. He had big circular dark eyes, black curly hair, and a thick push-broom mustache that ran all the way up his bulbous nose—his features working to-gether formed the look of a cartoon chef on a pizza box. He'd line up the sales team at the start of the day (about twenty of us) for a little pep talk. He'd pace up and down the line, clapping his hands and lecturing on how to sell better. "When you start giving your pitch, it's important that your eyes don't leave their eyes and be on your toes enough to realize that in all that time if their eyes haven't left your eyes then . . . what?" he'd ask, waiting for one of the salesmen to answer. "THEN THEY'RE TELLING YOU THEY WANT IT!" he'd scream with the enthusiasm of a charismatic professor. "Learn to read body language, my friends. If a guy looks over his shoulder and shuts the door behind him, then get his ass out to the truck and sell him pronto because that means he wants to make a purchase before his fuckin' wife puts the kibosh on it. Which brings me to my next point. STAY AWAY FROM THE WIVES, if you can help it. They're smart and they are supermarket shoppers. That equals INSTANT DEATH," he'd say, running his index finger across his throat. He'd follow his pump-up speech with a little *Hill Street Blues* thing at the end, saying, "And let's be careful out there, guys."

To say that he had a disinterested audience would be an exaggerated understatement. My coworkers were all beaten men in their forties and fifties, a lot of them with criminal records. They'd shuffle off to their trucks with about as much bounce as if they were heading to the electric chair. In fact, I think many of them would've preferred that to another day with Sunrise Meats.

The truck was a mini pickup with a freezer in the bed that I dubbed the "Meat Wagon." I even came up with a snappy little jingle that I'd sing in the bars as I was trying to peddle my wares. I'd dance through in my jumpsuit, donning my Sunrise Meats baseball cap, bellowing:

> *Meeeeat wagon, headin' on down the line . . .*
> *Meeeeat wagon, sellin' meats a prime . . .*
> *Meeeeat wagon, got salmon and steak in my trunk,*
> *Meeeeat wagon, buy it sose I can get drunk.*

It was a catchy number that netted me a few sales. The product itself wasn't bad either. They had Omaha Steaks and the like. Listen to me! The old pitch dies hard, I guess. Kim hated the Meat Wagon. I picked her up in it once and she saw that when the speedometer hit 40 mph the whole truck started quaking as if all four wheels were about to roll off. "I don't like you driving around in that thing. It doesn't feel safe and you don't make it any safer by being bombed all the time. From now on at the end of the day, drop it off at home and I'll drive us." I should've listened to her.

One night on my way home from Finnegan's Bar I decided to drive past my house and go to 7-Eleven for a microwave chimichanga, a foolish misstep in pursuit of drunken cuisine of the highest order. I nuked it in the store, got back in the Meat Wagon, and started eating it on the drive home right out of the wrapper. I only had to go about three blocks. After about fifty feet of driving I already had brown chimichanga sauce all over my face, and then it slipped out of my hand and onto the floor. I went to pick it up, never letting go of the wheel, and as I was wiping it off on my pants I found myself tilted up on an embankment and plowing into a telephone pole. The latch on the freezer popped open and all the boxes slid out (which I hadn't a clue about until the following day). I was only doing about twenty miles an hour but it was a pretty flimsily built truck and the thing was totaled. I somehow managed to drive it off the hill and back onto the road, getting it home with the engine huffing, puffing, and billowing smoke, the wheels misaligned and screeching. I went inside and passed out.

The next day our drummer at the time, Neil, a hepcat jazz aficionado with goatee, glasses, and a sardonic sense of humor (great drummer too) woke me and said, "Chris, is that your truck majestically parked over the stump in our front yard?" I rushed to the window. "Oh yeah. I forgot about that," I said, sashaying back to bed. "I was thinking about getting us one of those little garden gnomes but this is good too," he said, sipping a cup of coffee.

Sir Bobs Alot and my friend Carsy came over to help me. I called work and they dispatched a tow truck. Carsy, Bobs, and I rode behind it in Bobs' Jeep up to the yard. "Hey, Campy, I think I've spotted the scene of the accident. Look out to your right. Is that where you hit the pole?" Carsy asked. We all glanced over at the same time and there were white boxes strewn everywhere with about fourteen cats trolling around eating out of them. "Yeah, I think that's it," I said, resting my head on the dash. "Look on the bright side, at least you won't have to wear that ridiculous jumpsuit anymore," Bobs said. "I like the jumpsuit," I shot back. "Yeah, me too. I was just trying to find somethin' to say. You're fucked," he said, and the two of them laughed heartily. I half laughed, not having much of a choice. "Listen, don't be your normal fuck knob selves when we get up there. I've concocted a story that just might get me outta this and I don't need you guys blowing it for me," I warned them, deadly serious, but unable to keep a completely straight face. Who was I fuckin' kidding? I'd totaled the truck at three A.M.

We pulled into the Sunrise Meats depot where Mario and the rest of the bosses were waiting. I immediately went into a floorshow explaining the accident. "And then out of nowhere this kid on a bicycle pulls out into the middle of the road from a side street," I said, trying to captivate them with my storytelling. I started getting into intricate details about the bike. "There was a big orange flag on the back, flapping in the wind, and baseball cards tucked into the spokes." As I was getting more entangled in the minutia of the story, stalling and trying to figure out what to say next, Carsy and Bobs noticed the looks of disbelief on the bosses' faces and they fell apart laughing. I flashed them a murderous expression but it was too late. I could see the story wasn't going over. "So I swerved to miss him and hit the pole," I said, rounding it out anyway.

Mario shook his head. "At 3 A.M. this kid was out riding his bike?" he asked, obviously not buying a word of it. "Must be some insomniac paperboy, huh?" Carsy and Bobs were now doubled over, trying to hold each other up. "Chris, do us all a favor and just get the fuck out of here," he said, looking away from me and motioning with his hand for me to scat. As we were walking away, he called out to me, "It's too bad too . . . you coulda been one of the greats." I turned around to my little ginzo-Yoda sales guru and said, "I'll try to apply the wisdom you've imparted to me here elsewhere." "Yeah, yeah. You are one pathetic bullshitter, I'll tell ya that," he said, examining the crushed-in nose of the truck. And so ended my brief but illustrious career in sales.

Bobs and Carsy took me out for a consoling liquid lunch at Finnegan's, where, still in my jumpsuit, I mesmerized the bar with the story of my meteoric rise and fall through the murky world of Sunrise Meats. A little later on in an honest moment of reflection I asked Bobs, "Do you think I'm an alcoholic?" He answered swiftly, "Oh yeah, we all are. You're the worst, though. We're lucky to have ya." "Thanks, man," I said. "Don't mention it . . . and when I say don't mention it I mean *don't*. I don't want anyone finding out I admitted I'm an alcoholic. That's when they start circling the wagons on you," he said, chuckling then chugging. Eleven rounds later they dropped me off at my parents' house to break the news to my dad that he wouldn't be getting his five-hundred-dollar deposit back on the truck.

Only two weeks before I'd begged him for the money, promising I'd pay it back in weekly installments out of my commission checks. I'd had two prosperous weeks but he hadn't seen a dime. He gave it to me, saying, "I shouldn't do this, but believe it or not, I think you could do really well with this. One thing you know how to do is talk." When he said that I felt a brief glimmer of hope that I could repair things between us after the Villanova fiasco by doing well at this job. Plus he was a salesman and I knew it would make him proud if I did, even if it wasn't what I really wanted to do with my life. Remembering this made what I had to do that much tougher.

I broke the news to him and he didn't say anything at all. He just sat there, eating orange sherbet out of the container, watching the Mets game. I tried to massage him into talking by commenting on the game. "Wow, we're clinging to a one-run lead here, huh? Oh no, who's on the hill, Sisk? It's like waiting for the other shoe to drop with this guy every time," I said. He turned and said, "Kinda like watching you go through life." I knew enough not to even try to provide a rejoinder to that and kept mum. After a few unbearable minutes of watching him watch the TV I said, "Dad, say something." He looked up. "Whattya want me to say? You want me to ask you what's next? I don't wanna know what's next. I like to be surprised. Only you're getting so predictable that the surprise seems to have gone out of it. Go and visit with your mother and do us both a favor and don't mention any of this to her. Just tell her you're moving on to something else." I stood there feeling incredibly stupid and ashamed as usual. Then he said, "I'm asking you to lie. You should be thrilled. That's your thing, isn't it? Lying?"

I bolted from the house. I didn't wanna face my mom. I just

wanted to be back in Finnegan's and return to my natural state of fucked-upness. I walked back downtown at double clicks. Kim was in there when I got there. I stuffed my face with fistfuls of cheddar Goldfish from a wooden bowl on the bar, chugged pint after pint, and lost myself in her angelic face until I felt better. It took about twenty minutes.

.   .   .

On the home front—my new home, that is, with the band—things couldn't have been going better. Living together and rehearsing all the time had us musically tighter than ever. We were prolifically writing songs. We gigged weekly downtown in Huntington Village, pulling our usual big hometown crowd, and we had begun doing shows once a month in Manhattan as well. The followings we'd garnered from playing colleges like Villanova, Ithaca, Delaware, and Berkelee helped us draw big and sell out small clubs like the Bitter End on Bleecker Street with relative ease. Lots of these college kids we'd converted into fans lived in the tristate area and when home on breaks would come see us. The ones who'd recently graduated were getting jobs, moving into the city, and showing up to the performances faithfully with all their new work friends.

Before we knew it we were headlining and selling out big venues like the Cat Club, which held five hundred people. Other than me being employably challenged, always having to hit one of the other guys up for my share of the rent at the end of the month, our problems were few and our hopes many.

Legendary New York club owner Don Hill, who was our booker at the Cat Club in those days, said to me after one of our sold-out shows, "You guys keep this up and you'll have a record deal in no time." I shouted back over the loud overhead music, "Record deal? You mean like one of those deals from Columbia where for ninety-nine cents they send you an album a month for a year?" He said, "No, this is one where they pay you to record your music. Your pupils are the size of grapefruits, by the way." "I know, I'm shrooooooming," I yelled. "I know, you told me that already," he said, tapping his foot to Talking Heads' "Psycho Killer," while doing a pan-surveillance of the club. "Really? When?" I asked. "When you first walked in tonight and every ten minutes since," he said, putting his hand on my shoulder. "Come on, shroom-head, let's go do a couple a shots at the bar. I'm buyin'."

The Cat Club in the late eighties was a pretty wild place, a far cry from the Tuscaroo Lounge—our starter dive back in Huntington. It held all the glitz and glamour of a high-profile NYC rock venue, equipped with a big stage and lighting rig, expansive dance floor, and VIP tables in the back, but it also had that underlying vibe of degradation. There were plenty of nooks and crannies to do drugs in, and so long as you kept it in a dark corner you could do pretty much what you wanted. People did lines, smoked weed, and had sex everywhere in that place, and as the hour got later you had to be really careful where you tread in the dark or you might accidentally step on someone's cock or kick over their blow. I had both of those things happen while stumbling around in there. The guy whose blow I knocked over was the angrier of the two.

Don had the Cat Club catering to all scenes with gender-bending cabaret revues, metal nights, multi-band punk bills, and kitschy disco parties. He also hosted concerts for up-and-coming national acts like the Red Hot Chili Peppers. I saw them play and all they wore were sweatsocks on their dicks, which I thought was a fantastic low-budget high-concept look. The Cat Club was the downtown place to be so it wasn't unusual to see celebrities partying in there as well. I'm not one to get all aflutter about shit like that, but one night when we weren't playing I saw Johnny Depp all shit-faced at the bar. I think he was talking to Don. I didn't bother approaching him, though, because this was the *21 Jump Street* Johnny Depp of the eighties who, to me, was just another blow-dried perfect-haircut pussy churned out by Hollywood. He went on to become one of my favorite actors, starring as that most vicious freak of freaks, Ed Wood. See what happens when you judge people, kids? You miss out.

One of the most memorable evenings we had in there occurred during a blizzard. We were worried that we wouldn't have a crowd 'cause of the weather, but then people turned out in droves and brought with them that crazy storm energy. Have you ever been stuck in a bar somewhere with a bunch of people when extreme weather hit and you had no choice but to stay put? There's a phenomenon I've noticed when this happens. People get positively twisted and giddy, everyone giving themselves over to the collective we're-fucked-so-let's-get-fucked battle cry. I've watched many a hurricane, nor'easter, and blizzard from a barstool and I can tell you right now, t'ain't nothin' like storm drinkin'. This was one of those nights.

There was already about three inches on the ground when we arrived at the club, so we were just gonna take this one on the chin and chalk it up to being on the wrong side of the weather gods. The snow was torrential and would stay that way all through the night. Unbeknownst to us, loads of people from Huntington decided to make the trek in on the Long Island Railroad anyway. The city people had no problem because they didn't have to drive so, to our surprise and delight, the place was jam-packed when we went on.

The crowd was going ballistic from the opening number and maintained that energy all through the set. We closed the show with a revved-up version of the Velvet Underground's "Waiting for My Man," and I wrapped the mic chord around my neck and mock-hung myself at its climax. Phil dragged my dead carcass off the stage—in a macabre James Brown tribute—and I suddenly sprung to life before reaching the wings as the band spontaneously reprised the song, wanting to end it properly. We then banged through another verse and chorus and took it out like a runaway train. I stage-dived into the audience and they passed me person to person, depositing me at the bar. In one motion, with people still watching, I tilted my head back like I was being shampooed at a hair salon and the bartender poured tequila in my mouth as the band hit the resounding final note of the song, Tom drenching the club with distortion and feedback from his amp, as the band left the stage with the sound reverberating.

Later that spring we did a big outdoor show in Heckscher Park, which is Huntington's version of Central Park. The park is fairly large with a museum, a big pond, a playground, a baseball diamond, tennis courts, and a huge band shell/stage carved into the hillside. It's a beautiful place located at the very center of town. When I was a kid, the family would go to see jazz greats like Buddy Rich and Lionel Hampton play there. The closest thing they'd ever had to rock 'n' roll was Harry Chapin, who'd lived in Huntington, and was a major contributor to the town as well as being a celebrated international philanthropist. His big tune was the iconic seventies radio hit "Cat's in the Cradle." He'd do charity gigs down there occasionally when I was growing up. I loved going to see him. I was enamored of his singing, but it was his storytelling that really drew me in. He was a funny guy. It was a black day in Huntington when he died in a car crash on July 16, 1981—a black day everywhere, I believe. I was psyched to play there and carry on his tradition.

The entire town turned out for our show. It was a perfect evening under the stars, eight hundred people on the hill in front of us, standing there drinking beers out of coolers, and hollering up to the stage for us to play their favorites of our songs. "Play 'Blue Bedroom'!" we heard from all the way in back. We had officially become a big fish in a small pond. It felt good but I wanted more. I badly needed a record deal to validate my existence. With a record deal I could be my normal fuckup self and nobody would bat an eye. Without a record deal I was just another loser with a rock 'n' roll pipe dream, hopelessly unemployable, and unencumbered by that fact—a characteristic that bred resentment in certain working people. A record deal would be the equivalent of God thrusting his giant and mighty hand down from the clouds and stamping mine, announcing to the world, "This guy's okay." That's just a small indication of how much pressure I was putting on this deal thing to happen. It would haunt me every day of my life until it did. It was a vision quest, or in my case, a double-vision quest. I defined myself by my dream and how well I was, or wasn't, doing to achieve it.

Tom's older brother, Lou, was managing the band and doing all he could to get A and R (artist and repertoire) people from record labels down to see us. A and R men are the ones who sign bands. He'd get bites from them saying they loved the tape and were coming to the next performance. We'd get all gussied up and excited, and tell everyone that they had to be there to support us on our big night, but then the A and R guy would pull a no-show and once again our hopes would be dashed. This happened over and over and over again—to the point where we would no longer tell our friends if a record company was supposed to be at a gig. They wouldn't believe us anyway.

Around this time, in my fantasy-filled buzzes at the bar, I started telling people that we'd already been signed. I'd spin some made-up, cliché-ridden yarn about how the head of MCA, or the like, took us out to dinner and signed us on the spot. Then I'd go out the next night and some random person would come up to me and say, "Hey, Chris, congrats on the MCA deal! That's awesome," and I'd say, "Thanks, man." Then whenever we next ran into each other, I'd have to spin a tragic tale of how we'd been dropped. It's a lot of work being a liar and the level of difficulty increases when you can never remember your own script. Boastful lies were the quick salve for my self-loathing and the shame of not actually having a record deal.

My nightly blastoffs from a barstool was still making it impossible for me to hold down a day job. One of my best friends, Larry, had now started managing a bar-restaurant called Mother Magee's, right down the road from our house, which wasn't helping me any. Larry's nickname was Her-yo-yo because he put the attention-getting prefix "yo" before his every sentence. He was three hundred pounds with a round, simpatico face and a personality even larger than his torso. Picture an NFL tackle with a sunny disposition—he was always laughing and he drank tirelessly. He was tailor-made for running a shit-hole bar—and a glorious shit-hole it was! We played gigs in there that were a lot of fun but more important, knowing I had no money, Her-yo-yo graciously let me drink for free, an initiative killer.

One afternoon as I was descending into my head via Smirnoff, Her-yo-yo suggested I work for him at the bar. "No way, dude. Your friendship is too important to me. You'll end up hating me when I fuck it up," I told him. "Yo, are you outta your mind? I didn't mean have you really work. Yo . . . I've known you since we're ten years old, right? Whattya think, I don't know you're fuckin' useless?" he said tenderly. "Thanks for understanding," I said, and buried my nose back in my glass of vodka. "Yo, listen up, I have an idea where you can drink and get paid!" he said with a big smile.

He rented me a gigantic chicken suit and my job was to stand out on Route 110, in front of the bar, with a big sign that read EAT MY HOT WINGS! All I had to do was hold up this big advertisement for the passing traffic to see and I could drink all I wanted. No one would even know it was me because of the costume. It seemed foolproof.

The following afternoon I walked into the bar and didn't even joke around about it that much. I just went in back and got into the suit while Her-yo-yo was dealing with his lunch crowd. My start time was noon. I bopped in and out of the bar, sucking down rocks glasses filled with vodka continuously, and was hammered by two. I was belligerent by three from all the cars honking at me, yelling back to them, "GO FUCK YOURSELF!" By four, I'd gotten into a fight with a muscular Hispanic guy who claimed I'd scratched his El Dorado with one of my wings while frolicking in the road with the sign. Her-yo-yo looked out the window as he was serving a customer a drink and saw the guy beating me like a piñata with a broom handle he pulled from his backseat. That was the first day.

The second day I got so smashed that I passed out on the sidewalk from three to six, slumped over, cradling a bucket of chicken wings, with cars leaning on their horns, the drivers yelling, "WAKE UP!" as they motored past. The owner of Mother Magee's came by, scraped me off the pavement, and fired me. He said, "You're a helluva good singer, Chris, but I'm putting an end to your acting career right here and now."

I stayed in the suit and got blitzed with Her-yo-yo till four in the morning. "Yo, I really thought this was gonna work," he kept saying, refilling my glass with vodka. I was so bummed out I didn't even take off my chicken head. I didn't want anyone talking to me and no one tried. I just kept throwing booze back through my costume craw, looking like a suicidally depressed baseball mascot. What the fuck was I gonna do if I couldn't even hold a job where they let me drink?

It was now just Her-yo-yo and me in the bar. I finally took off my chicken head and got up to go to the bathroom. I had to walk bow-legged because the costume had chafed the inside of my thighs something fierce. I got to the stall, unhooked the pouch of feathers over my crotch, and let fly. After about thirty seconds I realized I hadn't heard the pitter-patter of pee that's supposed to accompany this kind of relief. Then I felt a warm sensation trickling down my legs, hitting the spot of both rashes at the same time. I looked down to see that, much to my horror, the pouch had somehow sprung back up and rehooked itself. I did nothing to fix it. I just stared into the mirror over the toilet, skunked outta my mind, one eye nearly closed, and continued pissing. I leaned in and pressed my forehead against the cold glass. It felt good. I pulled back looking at my reflection again and thought, *Her-yo-yo's right. This job really should've worked.*

. . .

My economic woes continued and I was now a penniless liability everywhere I went. Kim was growing tired of me because I was "never not drunk," as she put it, with the added bonus that she always had to pay for us when we were out together. The band was pissed at me because they were constantly covering my rent. I didn't like going home to my folks anymore because of the outstanding debt to my dad. Lou wasn't having any luck shopping our new demo. At this point, I'd say, my self-esteem was at an all-time low.

I spent all my time at Mother Magee's getting wasted and commiserating with the twinight—double-header—barflies, a term I coined for the old men who'd start drinking during the day and stay till closing. They were my tribe now. I'd stay out late enough to avoid my bandmates, knowing they'd be in bed by the time I got home, because they had to be up for work in the morning. I was a deadbeat vampire.

In the spring of 1990, Kim moved to San Francisco. Her aunt had died tragically in the earthquake and she went out there to help settle her estate, but as many have been known to do, she ended up falling in love with the city by the bay and stayed. I was devastated. I hadn't exactly been the model of virtue as a boyfriend, or a guy that a lot of people (in particular her parents) thought had much of a future, but, still, I didn't see it coming.

She got a job as a waitress at some restaurant on the water out there and fell in love with the chef. Feeling hurt and abandoned, I decided not to talk to her for a couple of years, except the odd late-night drunk dialing when I'd flog her with my apathy. It was either that or I'd let rip an expletive-filled, slurring soliloquy on her answering machine. According to those who heard it (her roommates), it was some of the most inane, foul-hearted wailing ever to violate human ears.

The only one of these calls I recollect fully was the last. It was a Sunday night after about nine hours of partying when Sir Bobs Alot broke the news to me that she'd gotten engaged to the chef. I listened intently to him, then calmly walked into his kitchen and called her. She picked up the phone. "Hello . . . hello? Well, it's two in the morning here, which means it's five in the morning in New York, so my powers of deduction are telling me it's you, Chris." I hovered on the phone not knowing what to say. A good part of me had believed that someday she'd come back and we'd be together again—a bigger portion than I cared to admit. Still, I was surprised by how hard I was taking it. "C'mon, just say something. What? Did someone give you the news? Aren't you happy for me? I know deep down you are," she said, talking to me in a voice that made me feel like I was four years old. A conflagration started in my stomach, moved up my body, through my windpipe, and exploded out of my mouth into the receiver. "HAVE A VERY NICE LIFE WITH EDWARD FUCKIN' SPATULAHANDS!" I screamed and hung up, never speaking to her again.

I truly loved Kim with everything I had, which if you were on the receiving end of it, wasn't much. I didn't blame her for leaving, though—a realization that felt even worse.

However, it did pave the way for some musically lovelorn laments. The Knockout Drops song "Wrong Side of Love" would be lifted directly from this scenario. Here's a little of how that one goes:

> *On a twisted Monday morning you and I woke up on the*
> *wrong side of love*
> *Another double fisted evening, a seeing-eye dog takes me to*
> *the wrong side of love*
> *and I never meant for you to wait around so long*
> *you were heaven sent, I guess God just got his timing*
> *wrong.*

I ended up getting with alotta chicks over the years as the author of that song, sensitive fuckin' guy that I am. I guess all *is* fair in love and war. Still, I always think of her when I sing it and those magnificent green eyes—the sparkling, cool green pools—lagoons of love I once called them, clumsily trying to impress her. They were full of mischief, moxie, and forgiveness—the looking glasses of my youth. She understood me. I got over Kim leaving a long time ago, but I still miss her sometimes. It's not a bad miss, but one I nurture as a keepsake—an infrequent pang that's triggered by a memory and fades with a smile. I think it's true what they say about first love. It is indelible. It fools you by having a vanishing adhesive. You go through your life thinking it's gone but it never really is. It returns when you least expect, while in a car or on a train—whenever your heart desires itself to be unhinged.

Losing her was rough but I was about to be without a band if I didn't get my shit together and start paying rent. Tensions at the house were mounting and I was now ducking out on rehearsals because the money I owed them was casting a pall over the practice room. I'd hide in the cloakroom up at Mother's when they'd come by looking for me. "Are they gone yet?" I'd ask Her-yo-yo, poking my head out from the coats, blowing one of the sleeves out of the way of my mouth. "Yeah, they're gone," he'd say, shaking his head. He was getting fed up with me too, but he wasn't nearly as sick of me as I was. I had to pull out of this rut. Enough was enough.

I started working for a landscaping company that was owned by a friend of the family. I figured the only way I stood a chance at hanging on to any job was to have that kind of buffer. The owner's name was Jim, a great, easygoing guy who liked to party himself. He had once been a total wild man but was now married with two little daughters and took that obligation very seriously, as one should. Jim knew what he was getting when he hired me but did it as a favor to my dad, plus he needed somebody. I showed up every day willing to do whatever it took, an eagerness solely derived from not wanting to be a piece of shit anymore.

I kept my head down and worked hard, always hung over, but sucking it up. The job was primarily cutting lawns, weed-whacking edges, and trimming the hedges of all Jim's accounts, which were many, including my parents' house. A few times I caught my dad staring out the window at me cutting the lawn with an expression on his face like, "I spent all that money sending him to college for this?" Jim handled the big projects like landscape construction, putting in sprinklers, and stuff like that, so it was rare that we worked together. Before I knew it, I'd been at the job for three months without being fired—a personal record—shattering my previous one of two weeks with the Meat Wagon.

My coworkers were two compact, adorably rotund guys from El Salvador, Hector and Nestor. They didn't speak any English, but loved to laugh. Nestor would make a big thing of huevos rancheros and other dishes that we'd all share every day at lunch. He doled them out in individual pale green Tupperware bowls. Everything he made was delicious. He wanted to be a chef someday, eradicating my emotionally misguided and irrational resentment toward all chefs everywhere. I brought an unexpected skill to the job by being able to speak Spanish fairly well. I'd taken five years of it in school, and after being around those guys for a time, got pretty good at it. I acted as Jim's translator. He didn't understand a lick of Spanish and wasn't in a rush to learn.

Hector and Nestor, on the other hand, were dying to learn English. We had a lady on the route that used to sunbathe in a bikini by her pool while we were cutting her lawn. She was about thirty years old, a blond, yummy mommy by the name of Nancy. One day Hector was looking over at her and asked me, *"¿Cristobal, como se dice mujer en inglés?"* ("How do you say *woman* in English?") I sat there with a weed-whacker in my hand and goggles on, mouthing the word "WO-MAN . . . now you try." "WO-MAN," he repeated back to me, walking away smiling, still muttering it to himself, "wo-man . . . wo-man . . . woman." I couldn't have loved these guys any more. They were a fuckin' pisser.

They were always trying to improve their vocabulary. One day I was in the trailer, taking a few pokes out of my one-hitter before lunch, and Nestor picked up the ripcord for the push mower. We needed it to pull-start the mower and it was always getting lost. He held it up. *"¿Cristobal, como se dice?"* I was a little stoned and decided to have some fun with him. "That's called a masturbate, Nester . . . a MASTUR-BATE," I answered. "MASTUR-BATE . . . *sí*, OK. *ES UN* MASTURBATE," he yelled over to Hector, holding it up for display. The weeks went by and every once in a while I'd see them talking and suddenly hear one of them say, *"¿donde está un* masturbate?"* and I'd crack up to myself.

We had a house on the schedule that I hated going to every week. The lawn was gigantic, with hills, and was a pain in the ass to cut—but not nearly as much of a pain in the ass as its owner, the admiral. He was a retired naval officer, a silver-haired son of a bitch, who nitpicked every little thing we did. We didn't help our cause much by running over his gas cap with the mower every week. "Welp, they did it again! Who's gonna be paying for a new one 'cause it sure as shit isn't gonna be me? You tell Jim to call me. And try to get those spics under control. They're scalping the shit outta the lawn down by the mailbox. It's all yellow down there!" he yelled at me once. He had gripes like that every week.

I was in a particularly good mood this one Friday afternoon—a mood I didn't think even the admiral could bring down. The sun was shining, it was payday in front of a three-day Memorial Day weekend, and his was the last house. The only drawback was that I had to collect money from him and he was a relentless, bitching tightwad. I knocked on the door and he came out wearing his admiral's baseball cap and usual scowl. "Afternoon, Admiral. Do you have any money for us?" I asked him, a small lump developing in my throat. He replied with relative ease. "Yeah, I have my checkbook right here," he said, pulling it from his top pocket and putting on his glasses. He started making it out. "You know, you guys have been doin' all right the last couple of weeks," he said, much to my surprise. I couldn't believe it but I was actually beaming with pride in this moment, getting a little pat on the head from the admiral, a man of such import and stature. True, he was also an unapologetic racist and bully but that didn't take anything away from the fine job we'd done. Could it be that I was changing? Maybe my dad was right—maybe there was no better feeling than a job well done.

Right as he was about to rip off the check Nestor came charging up the driveway in a panic, calling to me, *"¿Cristobal, donde está el* MASTURBATE*?"* pantomiming the motion of pull-starting the mower, flailing his fist from his crotch up to his shoulder repeatedly, to illustrate what he was looking for. "Uh, go back to the trailer, Nestor. I'll be with you in a minute, amigo," I said, urging him with a face to cease and desist. *"OK, pero no* MASTURBATE . . . *tal vez la* MASTURBATE *está en el* trailer?" he said, throwing his arms up in the air, defeated. I turned back to the admiral. He pushed his glasses to the edge of his nose and with an alarmed look, said, "Correct me if I'm wrong here, and I hope to God I am, but was that little Chicano just asking you for permission to jerk off in the trailer?"

· · ·

My landscaping job gave me some stability and self-worth, but I hated it nonetheless. I wanted to entertain people for a living, not blow leaves outta their gutters. "The record deal in the sky," as Neil called it, wasn't materializing. I wanted us to buy a van, get in it, and go play everywhere till we found it but we had no booking agent, money, or structure in which to make this happen. I knew we weren't gonna set the world on fire from that veritable crossroads of the music business, Huntington, Long Island. I wanted to move into the city but was handcuffed by my remaining debt.

We played in New York City every weekend, but I wanted to be playing more so Tom and I got a weekly acoustic duo-gig down at a place called Top of the Town in Huntington Village. This was a cool little lounge up a long flight of stairs, owned by my older brother Hollywood Bob's friend Jack Palladino. It had that old-school night-club feel to it. Jack owned a couple of other bars in town, as well, and was a big supporter of the band. He wanted us to make it as much as anyone.

We played every Wednesday night and developed a nice weirdo following of fellow musicians, spoken-word dudes, and would-be entrepreneurs. In other words, people who go out on a Wednesday night in the dead of winter—drunks with dreams and lonely bullshit artists. It was here that I first discovered a penchant for talking between songs. The gig itself was a lot less formal than with the full band and it was a great way to kill time and get to know people.

About a month in, Jack approached me and said, "You know you guys have been doing well, here, and I've got to tell you because you may not know this but a lot of people come up to me and tell me that they're here just as much to hear you talk as sing." "For real?" I said. "Yeah, they like the banter between you guys when you're not playing. Tom's a great straight man. All he's gotta do is look horrified when you start talking, which is easy 'cause everything you say is so fucked up. He does it well. You should try to develop it into something. You could be the modern-day Smothers Brothers," he said, with an encouraging tone. "Dude, we're musicians not comedians. No thanks," I said.

Top of the Town was a notable venue for a number of popular comics, who generated a lot of revenue for Jack's business. Comedians like Jackie "The Jokeman" Martling, from *The Howard Stern Show*, played there regularly. We hadn't been aware that we had this dimension. The truth of it was that Tom actually was uncomfortable with my drunken babblings. The looks of bewilderment he'd give me when I was trapped in one of my cosmic tangents made for unintentional comic payoffs.

Top of the Town had wraparound picture windows overlooking Stinky Corner. One of the regular bits we did was me going over to the window with the microphone and doing commentary on what was happening down there. It was a Lettermanesque segment we called, "What's happening on Stinky Corner?" There was always a lot to choose from, it being the vicious freak hub of Huntington. The audience was a local crowd so people knew the players to whom I was referring.

One Wednesday I strolled over to the window as Tom was tuning up. "Whoa, what have we here? We got Loyal out there banging on a tambourine and talking to some lady who's looking at him kinda funny . . . probably giving her the terms of his friendship, as he's known to do. And here comes Walkin' Willie making the scene. As most of you know, he's a big star here on Stinky Corner. Oh! You might wanna join me at the window for this one, folks. Walkin' Willie is humping the front end of a cop car!" The entire bar busted outta their seats and lined the windows to watch the Walkin' Willie spectacle unfold. We had some great nights in that joint but it wasn't getting us any further in our quest toward a record deal.

True to form, I started losing the handle on my landscaping job. I'd go on unholy benders after our weekend gigs in the city and not make it back to Huntington till Tuesday or Wednesday. I was running out of excuses with Jim. Once as a preemptive measure I snuck up to his house at four in the morning, and put a note on his door saying I wasn't gonna make it in the next day because I'd hooked up with a beautiful girl who was kidnapping me to Niagara Falls. I was trying to appeal to his old hell-raiser side to get out of work. Why I chose Niagara Falls as my exotic locale is still a mystery to me. There was no girl, obviously. I'd just been up for two days doing blow and knew I wasn't gonna make it in. He appeared standing over my bed a few hours later, note in hand. "Get in the truck, fuck nuts" was all he said.

When I did show up for work I was accident-prone. I'd run over people's flower beds with the mower or weed-whack potted plants. I was just a wreck. The worst of these incidents occurred early one Saturday morning while cutting the lawn of an estate in Lloyd Harbor.

We usually didn't have to work on Saturdays but it had rained during the week and we were behind schedule so everyone had to come in. I was a stumblebum from the word go, showing up drunk, running on no sleep. I told Hector to drive the truck. At least I had that much sense. Lloyd Harbor was a bit of a ride so I took advantage of the time by blowing bat hits out the window to settle my stomach and ready myself for the day.

My whole life I've suffered from a terrible phobia of insects. If a housefly landed on my forearm I'd jump ten feet. The guys on the job knew this and would have a good laugh watching me react like a frightened little girl if a bug got near me. On this particular morning I was cutting the lawn in back of the house—a lawn the size of a football field. I was still pretty drunk but the hypnotic rumble of the big Bunton mower and the weed I'd smoked had me in a robotic state of comfort. I walked behind it, row after row, content with the monotony.

The Waspy asshole who owned the house was sitting out by his pool, reading the paper, having breakfast with his wife and young family, two blond toddler girls and an infant boy in a carriage. He was wearing a pink Polo shirt, white tennis shorts, and a pair of Ray-Bans. We saw him every week but he never talked to us and wasn't very friendly. He had a palpable condescending air. He'd once asked Jim if I was "OK?" because he found it strange that I would sing loudly while cutting his lawn. "He asked me the question carefully, like I'd hired you out of a mental institution," Jim said to me, laughing his ass off.

I was cruising along behind the Bunton with my shirt off, bagging some rays, and starting to feel like my buzz was manageable when I came to a part of the yard where I had to duck under a big tree branch. It snuck up on me and I got tangled up in the leaves. When I emerged on the other side I quickly looked over to the pool area to see if this guy had seen my little gaffe. He hadn't. I resumed cutting.

Out of habit I began singing a song, The Replacement's "Bastards of Young." *"We are the sons of no one bastards of . . ."* and I looked over at the guy and stopped myself, remembering his convo with Jim. I was pissed off that he was stifling my favorite pastime. I loved mowing a long field and just singing away, at the top of my lungs, working on new melodies and lyrics or just belting out one of my favorite songs in the sunshine. How could this guy not understand that? It's not that unusual, is it? While I was batting these thoughts around in my head I looked down to shift gears and there, nestled ominously in the middle of my chest hairs, was a giant, prehistoric-looking, brown insect staring up at me. I could see his hateful black alien eyes and festering mouth, two big clamps protruding from it, and oozy bug stuff dripping out. His foot-long antennae were grazing my chin. I freaked out, screamed, and swatted him off, doing what must've looked like some sort of epileptic Apache rain dance, running in place frenetically and spinning, running my hand over every contour of my body, inspecting it for others, all the while continuously yelling up to the sky, "Ahhhhhhhh!"

I watched him fly away but turned around to a bigger problem. When I let go of the mower, I'd accidentally thrown it into high gear and it was headed full steam right for this guy and his family. None of them had any idea the machine was now unmanned. He was eating a croissant behind *The Wall Street Journal* and the rest of them were turned the other way. If I didn't get to it in time, the Bunton was gonna take them out.

These commercial mowers go pretty fast at full speed, as my landscaper brethren out there will tell ya. I sprinted like a madman after it, my heart beating out of my chest. It was about thirty feet in front of me and was almost upon them. When I realized I might not make it in time, I yelled, "Look out!" They all turned around and the father bailed them out to safety. They dove out of their chairs and rolled over in the grass with the father covering them. The mother yanked the baby carriage out of harm's way. I got to the mower just before it hit the table. The machine idled for a second. I exhaled, relieved the disaster had been averted, and said, "Sorry about that, folks. It's OK, you can come back and enjoy your breakfast now." Right as I said that the mower jerked back into gear, bulldozing the table into the pool. Pitchers of orange juice and bowls of cereal smashed against the cement, the other contents of the table were ground up noisily by the powerful blades of the Bunton, shards of glass ricocheting everywhere. When it was over, all we saw were muffins floating atop the water, and the mower, table, and umbrella shipwrecked underneath. The guy looked at me with fire in his eyes. "WHAT ARE YOU, HIGH?" I looked away 'cause I didn't want him to see that I actually was. We both stood there at pool's edge gazing down at the table and the mower doing a do-si-do at the bottom of the pool. Amazingly the motor was still running. They're good machines, those Buntons.

I didn't wait for Jim to fire me. He was such a good guy that I didn't wanna put him through that scene. I pulled a Nixon and quietly resigned—and by resigned I mean stopped showing up, deciding to go out in cowardly fashion.

.   .   .

I kicked around Huntington for the next two years, getting jobs and losing jobs the same old way. Phil took a real job in the city and left the band. We pressed on getting a few different bass players but the group had largely lost its mojo by then and I wasn't carrying my load financially, so we gave up the house and Column 13 was no more. The dream was over, or so I thought at the time.

I had to move back home, which was not a fate worse than death, but a regret-filled suburban purgatory that wasn't what you'd call a life. There's a great Paul Westerberg line from the song "Here Comes a Regular" that goes, "I used to live at home now I stay at the house," which pretty much sums up what it was like. There's no worse feeling in this world than that of being a failure, and when I lived with my folks again after being out on my own for a while, I got to experience that feeling 100 percent of the time. At least when you're out in the world on your own not succeeding, you get to return to the solace of your own place and veg in front of the TV. When you live back in the place where you grew up you're surrounded by the memories of a once-promising life. Everything in my old room mocked me, even my *Some Girls* poster.

I'd lie on my bed and hear my mom call, "Dinner!" but instead of that inspiring a good feeling (my mom's an awesome cook), it meant an hour of cross-examination from my dad as to what my plans were.

I didn't have any plans—I didn't know how to get any—and what's more, didn't really want any. I was immobilized in the quicksand of self-pity. I would sit and stare at the seventies faux-wood paneling in my bedroom, recognizing it as the remnant of a bygone era and identifying myself with it. I was stuck. I'd always relished being a dreamer but now I just felt like an unparalleled dumbass, incapable of the one thing you're called upon to do in this world and that is to take care of yourself.

To think, I'd once had the audacity to make fun of Lenny for living with his grandmother and working at the Tuscaroo. That was a sweet fuckin' life compared to anything I might hope for now. He had a motorcycle and a job that he loved. I should be so lucky. What the fuck did I have? I had car crashes, arrests, an estranged family that I lived with, an ex-girlfriend who moved to California just so she didn't have to bear witness to my train wreck of a life, and a whole bunch of songs that no one was ever gonna hear. Let the pity party begin!

Right around then I ran into Harold, a guy I went to high school with, at the deli. He'd been a slow kid in school, taken all remedial classes, and spoke with a really bad stutter. He was in blue-collar work clothes heading out the door. "Hey, Harold, what's the good word, my man?" I asked him. "Oh, hey, Ca-Ca-Ca-Chris! I'm just headed off to wa-wa-wa-work at the m-m-m-m-marina. S-S-S-Still got the band goin'?" he asked me. "Nah, I'm not doing anything anymore, Harold. You look like you're doing great, though, dude. Do you live around here now?" I asked. "Yeah, I just g-g-got an apart-m-m-ment on Creek Road oh-oh-over here. Ya-ya-you n-n-need a job? I m-m-m-might be able to-to-to ga-g-get you one with us," he stammered. "No thanks, Harold. You're gonna own that place one day and then I'll come work for you so long as you know that at some point you'll have to fire me," I said, chuckling a little. "You la-la-look so d-d-down, Chris. You used to be so . . . f-f-funny," he said perceptively. "Well, I'm hoping it all gets turned around with this Devil Dog," I said, waving the snack in the air. "Ta-take it easy, Chris," he said, smiling. "Later, Harold."

Harold could take care of himself. Why couldn't I? He'd been dealt a rough hand. I'd been given everything one could ask for. The reason he could cut it and I couldn't was that Harold had a little something called humility, the most honorable of human virtues. I knew all about humiliation but felt impervious to it—it was an emotion that better served people who gave a shit. But did I understand the concept of true humility? Never heard of it.

I walked out of the deli chomping on that Devil Dog and went straight across the street to the Shamrock to get bombed. Running into Harold had set me off. Did I think alcohol might have something to do with my life seemingly going nowhere? Maybe. I mean, it was possible, but why blame a beautiful social lubricant like beer for my many problems? I didn't think that was being fair to booze. Despite having this jumble going in my head I walked into the Rock with a cocksure grin. I had no money, naturally.

I ran a tab with Eddie the bartender that I had every intention of paying, but we both knew I wouldn't. Eddie was an excellent bartender. Like most of them he had an acute deftness for human surveillance. "You see that girl talkin' to her boyfriend over there? I'll bet you a drink that she starts cryin' any minute. Her boyfriend's breakin' up wit her," he said. I looked over and saw them in a booth at the back of the bar. To me it looked like they were just hanging out, passing the time. "Are you sure? That's like thirty feet away. How can you tell?" I asked. "You stay in this business long enough and nothin' ever gets by ya. It's all body language," he said proudly. I thought to myself, *Shit, I should really introduce him to Mario over at Sunrise Meats.* As I came out of that daydream I heard, "Fuck you, I'm outta here!" The girl from the corner went running past Eddie and me, crying. He flashed me a look. "What did I tell ya? Am I good or am I good?"

Eddie was about forty years old. Every day he wore stonewashed jeans buckled way too high up over his waist with a tightly tucked-in Hawaiian shirt. He had a classic mullet hairdo and was rumored to use Man-Tan, that rub-on tanning shit for men. I never confirmed this but I did notice that some days he looked more orange than others.

I'd learned by this point that if I could be funny in a bar during the day I never had to pay for a drink. People, especially bartenders, are so bored during those hours that if you can entertain them you'll be doing backstroke in a bevy of bevies just as fast as you can say, "Guinness, please." But you gotta go in there with your best stuff. Self-effacing humor goes over well because misery loves company— and daytime drinkers are, by and large, miserable, whether they know it or not. So I would go in there and light up Eddie and the other twinighters with a few stories of my pathetic existence at the house. It came naturally to me because my life really sucked, giving me a full arsenal. "Whattya got for me, Chrissy? How's it goin' over at the house?" Eddie asked, being my straight man. We'd done this for his day crowd once before. "Funny you should ask, Eddie. Not so good . . . not so good."

"You see this bandage on my elbow?" I asked him. "Yeah," he said. "Lemme tell you all how I got that," I said, pulling in the whole bar (all five of them). I said to Eddie, "Remember last time I was in here how I told you my dad's been getting really pissed about me losing my house keys?" He said, "Yeah, I remember." I then turned and addressed everyone to fill in the back story. "Lately I've been on a bad streak of going out, getting my load on, then losing my keys. Night after night I've been waking him up at four in the morning, leaning on the bell, all drunk, yelling, 'DAAAAAD, C'MON, LET ME IN!' He comes down in his robe, snarling, half asleep still, and just mega- pissed off. The other night as my friend Larry's picking me up to go out he stops me at the door. He says, 'Here,' and he hands me an extra set of house keys. He says, 'If I have to get my ass outta bed one more time because of you, you're outta here.' And I could tell he was serious so I stuffed the keys into the top pocket of my jacket and buttoned it. I'm petrified to lose these keys but they're in a safe place so no wor- ries, right?" I said, looking around to make sure everyone was fully invested in the story. I carried on.

"Long story short, I get all shit-faced at Finnegan's, skip with some girl the likes of whom I could not pick out of a police lineup if my life depended on it, but if vague memory serves she'll probably end up in one. I mash with her in the driveway for twenty minutes or so. It's going nowhere, so I get out and she takes off down the driveway like a rocket . . . with my jacket in the backseat . . . AND BOTH SETS OF KEYS!" I said with a crescendo. "OH NO!" Eddie yelled. "So what did you do?" "Be patient, young man, and I'll tell you, for the best is yet to come. Howzabout another libation? What say we kick it up a notch with some Jameson's?" I asked, but really commanded. He filled my glass to the top with brown and I continued the story.

"Well, I can't very well ring the doorbell or I'm done . . . fineeto . . . it's over, right? So I decided to scurry up the drainpipe and through my sister's open window like the second-story man that I someday hope to be. I felt just like James Caan in that movie, *The Thief.* I get about three-quarters of the way up and all of a sudden I feel the pipe bend back a little from the house. I'm like, it's okay. Stay calm. You're almost there. Then it really starts to go. Now I'm suspended off the house, twenty feet up, with about four feet left to go. I can either jump for the roof and maybe make it or drop into the pricker bushes below. I think on it for a second but there's not much time because the pipe is pretty flimsy and goin' fast. I realize that there's no way I'm gonna physically make it to the roof at this point so I let go, AAAAAAAAAHHHHHHH!!! And I land back first into the prickers. They're up my nose, in my eyes, I'm spitting 'em out of my mouth along with some blood. I see a light go on in the kitchen. My dad pops his head out, sees me in the bushes, and yells over, "DID YOU TRY THE DOORKNOB? IT WAS OPEN THE WHOLE TIME, ASSHOLE!" Eddie and the boys erupted. "Ha! He's right. You are an asshole," Eddie said, speaking for everyone.

Those boys and Eddie kept slappin' my back and fillin' my glass for the rest of the afternoon. A compelling bar story is better than currency. People are grateful to you for giving 'em a good time. It sounds calculated, I know, but I needed to drink in the same way I needed to eat or breathe. Some people suck cock for crack money. I told stories in bars for hooch. There's really not much of a difference but it did have an old-fashioned and wholesome charm to it, or at least that's what I told myself. I still felt like shit about it, though. Having money would've been better.

As I was getting ready to leave, Eddie topped me off with some more whiskey. Still laughing, he said, "Listen, don't worry about the money, Chrissy. Stop by and see me anytime. I'm here every day during the week. I'll take care of ya." "Sure thing," I replied, one of the rare promises I knew I'd keep. I staggered home at seven o'clock just in time for dinner, "after a hard day of nothin' much at all," just like the regular Westerberg sings about in that song. I blew into the kitchen to find my folks and Billy already seated at the table. I had the same glow on that my dad used to bring through the door with him when I was a kid, giving the scene an odd familiarity, the one difference being that he came through the door as the breadwinner. I was a breadloser, if there was such a thing.

My little brother, Billy, now a senior in high school, was playing in a band, and having a blast. He was a rising star in the town. It was like watching a home movie of myself from five years earlier. He'd be in and out of the house like a shot, running around excitedly, singing everywhere, toting his guitar, his bandmates beeping the horn in the driveway, urging him to hurry it up. "Where ya goin', Willibee?" I asked him one night as he was taking a G.I. shower in the sink, his buddies honking for him outside. Willibee was a nickname I'd given him as a kid that used to send him into a white-hot rage, but by this time he'd gotten used to it. "We got a gig down at the beach, wanna come?" he asked. I mulled it over for a second. "No thanks, dude," I said. I just couldn't be that guy. You know the one? The twenty-three-year-old loser who has to latch onto his little brother's high school scene because his ego can't cut it in the real world. Then he gets into a disturbing codependent relationship with some pretty high school girl with rock-bottom self-esteem and ends up marrying her, popping out two sad-faced little ones, and working at the gas station? Besides, I'd already been fired from the gas station. I couldn't handle all those cars coming in at once. I loved the smell of gas, though.

I was drowning and needed someone to throw me a rope—that lasso came from my brother Bob's guitar player from The Old #7 days, Dad Nud. Nud owned a successful house-painting business in Huntington and let me work for him on the condition, he said, "That I put a band together and start playing again." He was away from playing music for a while himself, and I'd brought him out of retirement to play with us back when Tom and I were gigging at Top of the Town. He didn't wanna do it at first, but after some chiding he agreed. He had a southwestern sound and played these haunting dustbowl ballads and countrified rock 'n' roll songs he'd written. He was a big hit down there. He later went on to form a group called The Last Hombres with Levon Helm from The Band, putting out records and touring all over the country, but at this point he just had the painting business.

His crew called themselves The Paint Dogs and a bigger collection of riotous booze bags you won't find anywhere else in the blue-collar world. They prided themselves on being able to drink hard and work hard. I felt right at home with them from the get, except for the work part but they all understood. They gave me tasks I could handle like going to get the lunch order (no one ever got their change back) or monitoring the big buckets of paint as they sprayed the outside of a house, making sure they didn't run dry (they often did while I was throwing a Frisbee around), spotting them on ladders (I did that one pretty well but was told I talked too much), changing the radio station (I got yelled at for singing to it too loudly), important stuff like that. They drank beers as they worked but were known as the best painters in town, securing all the biggest contracts.

The Paint Dogs version of Semper Fi was "Just make it in." No matter how hungover you were, even if you were still fucked up, all you had to do was make it to the job site and somebody would pick up your share of the work while you slept it off, usually wrapped up in a tarp out of the view of the customer or Nud, if he was around (though he knew about everything that went on and turned a blind eye). It was my dream job.

Every Paint Dog had an I'm-just-working-here-for-now-to-get-my-life-back-together story. They'd flunked out of college and were gonna go back, or were trying to save money to go into business, or had gotten a degree and were interviewing for Wall Street jobs in the city. This job was a holding pattern for everyone but it was easy to see that none of them really wanted to leave. These were all funny bastards who enjoyed one another's company. I actually felt comfortable with, and fortified in, my employment for the first time ever.

My lifelong pal and co-fuckup, Monk, was already a Paint Dog by the time I started working there. In keeping with Paint Dog tradition, he'd flunked out at the University of Virginia and was planning on returning. The crew took long lunches and would often engage in sociopolitical discussions of the day like the upcoming Bush-Clinton presidential election or "Could you really see Sharon Stone's snatch?" in the movie *Basic Instinct*. Often these topics would come straight out of the newspaper. My foreman, Curly, a former Navy Seal and savage boozer, with a perverse sense of humor, was reading an article about Lee Iacocca and posed the question to all of us. "Would you blow Lee Iacocca for his annual salary of two-point-two million dollars?" This later became known as, the "Lee Iacocca test" and would be put to all future would-be Paint Dogs as an initiation question during their job interview.

We went 'round the horn and everybody gave macho responses like, "You'd have to kill me first," or "Do I get to kill him afterward?" The one who gave the best answer was Monk. He took a bite out of his sandwich, swallowed, and said in an even voice, "I'd have to be really drunk." Curly yelled out, "WE HAVE A WINNER!" everyone agreeing that there wasn't anything that booze couldn't make tolerable.

I stayed with the Paint Dogs for the better part of a year and became one of them. We had our own language for things. An electrical hand sander was called a "little man," named after NHL great Stan Mikita, who was nicknamed the Little Man and had the same surname as the brand. A five-in-one-tool, which was a small utensil used for scraping, gouging, and opening stuff, was referred to as the "wonder tool." If you were being "I and O'ed," that meant that you were talking too much, disrupting the job, and would be exiled to another part of the house with more work than you could handle (*I and O* standing for "isolated and overloaded"). They tried that one on me but quickly realized it was better to keep me with the group. I couldn't paint worth a damn.

I still wanted to play music but didn't wanna leave the safety and security of the life Nud provided. Where else could I have little to no utility and still be employed? This attitude had me decorating a different kind of rut, one of settling. This, to my shock, didn't sit well with my dad. His view on it surprised me at the kitchen table one afternoon. "You know, when you were playing with the band, you had a drive that I respected. I didn't agree with you for leaving school but I do acknowledge your talent. You got something. I can see that. Your mother really sees it. She talks about it all the time," he said, filling up his coffee cup, patting me on the shoulder. "She does?" I said, holding back tears. "Hell yeah. Forget about Villanova. What's done is done. You're not a goddamn housepainter, I know that. Your dream is out there. Now stop feeling sorry for yourself and go back out there and try and get it, like you were doing before," he said, exiting the kitchen with his coffee. I waited till he was in the next room and went into the bathroom and sobbed heavily. Forgiveness is a mighty powerful thing in this world, no matter what side of it you're on. I do believe that to forgive is divine and to be forgiven . . . well, that's just a fuckin' relief. I wish I could give everyone in the world the feeling I had in that moment.

After my dad's unexpected pep talk I was like Popeye after he eats the spinach. I got right on the phone to Tom Licameli, and when he answered I delivered that famous line from *The Blues Brothers*, "We're puttin' the band back together!" He laughed and said, "I've been waiting for this call. When do you wanna meet?"

Tom and I got together that night and wrote two new songs, "The Dropout Song" and "Burning Bush Chronicles," the opening lyrics to the latter were:

My first day
Back from Hell
Can't you tell
That I've changed?

We called Phil and he was in too. We rehearsed with him the following day. "What should we call ourselves?" Tom asked. We were huge fans of the book *A Confederacy of Dunces* and in it the term "knockout drops" is used by one of the characters who is accusing a tavern owner of watering down drinks and dosing them with liquid downers. I cared nothing about the literal meaning of it. I just thought it sounded cool. "How 'bout Knockout Drops?" I said. We looked at one another and knew it was right and that's still our name today. Not soon after, we played our first gig at the Bitter End. We sold it out and were on our way once more into the black-hole abyss of the music business. "Back where we started. Here we go round again," to quote one of my heroes, Ray Davies.

The Paint Dog job ended on a high note. We were painting a beautiful old Victorian on the water that was owned by a retired couple, the Rasmussons. They weren't just painting but restoring this house to its once-proud grandeur. Every day Mr. Rasmusson would come by and bust Nud's balls about every last little thing. He was a cranky, hunched-over, old fuck with the kind of stately looks you might see on a Gold Bond powder commercial. He caught me and Curly sunning ourselves on his dock, drinking tall boys, one day at lunch and always looked at us suspiciously after that. His wife would give us the once over too. She looked at me with my long straggly hair like I was dipped in shit.

They were staying somewhere else while the work was being completed for the most part, but once the master bedroom was done to perfection they'd occasionally stay overnight, it being the only finished room in the house. There were a lot of different contractors coming in and out all the time and I noticed that the door was always left open. I made a mental note of it—and pulled that note from my files at about four A.M. in Finnegan's a few nights later. Monk and I had a couple of girls on the line and, being the lame-os that we were still living at home, had nowhere to take 'em.

"I have an idea. Let's take 'em to the Rasmussons' and we'll tell 'em it's our house! Whattya say?" I proposed, pretty drunk. He had the exact same expression on his face as in the first grade when I convinced him we didn't have to go back inside after recess. The teacher stood out on the playground in the rain waiting for us to come in but we just hid behind a leaf pile laughing and watching her hairdo get mussed. Our parents ended up having to come up to the school to get us and I was forever after vilified in his house for being the one who got him in trouble—always the Tom Sawyer to his Huck Finn.

"Dude, I dunno. Curly will have our ass for this, not to mention Nud," he said, erring on the side of caution. "Get outta here. I work with Curly every day. If he were here right now, he'd be asking me to do this. He's a complete lunatic. And you know what to do if Nud fires you? You just keep working like nothing's happened and he just forgets about it," I said, pleading my case. "All right, let's do it!" Monk said, slamming his drink drown. "That's my Skunker!" Skunker was the nickname on top of his nickname.

The girls were two gum-snapping sisters with high hair from Dix

Hills named Cassie and Dolores. They were C.W. Post students who loved Mariah Carey. We heard her version of the Jackson 5's "I'll be There" in the car on our way to the Rasmussons'. "Oh, Cassie, turn it up! She's from Long Island, ya know," Dolores turned around and told us. It was ear-splittingly loud, distorting to an unintelligible level through the tiny speakers of their Chevy Citation. Skunker and I looked at each other with matching Cheshire grins and sang with the girls, "I'll be there . . . I'll be there. . . . Just call my name . . . and I'll be there."

We pulled up to the house. "Oh my Gawd, this is your guys' house?" Cassie said in disbelief. "Yeah, for now anyway. We buy 'em and fix 'em up, then turn 'em over for a profit usually, but we're thinking of keeping this one and maybe moving into it for a while. Whattya think, ladies, if we move in, will you come by and cook for us? We're slovenly bachelors," I said. "Oh, we'll cook for you. Don't you worry about that," Dolores said.

We threw on WLIR when we got inside and they were playing a block of Depeche Mode songs. The opening synthesizer riff to "Just Can't Get Enough" came on and the girls went crazy. "Come on, let's dance," they both said. We cranked up the tunes, drank beers, and danced all night. Skunker started pulling these Gene-Kelly-from-*Singin'-in-the-Rain* moves out of his ass, dancing up ladders and incorporating tools from the job site, taking dry rollers and rolling them up and down the girls' bodies as we danced—like it was some Paint Dog aphrodisiac. I boogied over to him. "What the hell are you doing?" I said. "I dunno, but they seem to like it," he said, handing me a clean roller out of a paint tray.

He disappeared down to the dock with Dolores and I stayed up at the house with Cassie. "I'm hungry," she said. I suavely sauntered over to the fridge, pulled out some leftover Chinese from that day's lunch, and discovered all these diner butters in there. I started pulling them out of the foils one by one and hurling them up at the ceiling. "What are you doing?" she asked me, giggling. "I'm gonna stick them all up on the ceiling in the form of the Big Dipper and make out with you under it," I told her. "Gimme a few. I'll help. Should we be doing this? It looks like they just painted," she said. "Don't worry about it, baby. They're on my payroll," I said, like a modern-day swashbuckler, scooping her into my arms and kissing her. "Oh yeah, well how do I get on your payroll?" she said, kissing me sweetly. "Oh, shit, are you a hooker?" I joked. "Ass!" she yelled, smacking me in the shoulder. "Whattya say we go up to the master bedroom? I've got another big dipper up there I wanna show you," I said, grabbing a six-pack from the fridge and slinking up the stairs, her trailing me with her finger in my back belt loop.

I woke up bare ass with her, spooning, with Curly standing over us. "You're in a lotta trouble, son, if we don't act fast. Nud's in the van with old man Rasmusson headed this way. We got approximately eight minutes to get this place cleaned up and ready for inspection," he commanded in a military tone. "Oh, duuuude, I'm so sorry," I said, my eyes not all the way open, hungover. "No time for that now. We've got a situation here. Did you use a condom, soldier?" he asked weirdly. "What?" I said. "It's okay. She looks clean. Morning, ma'am," he said, tipping his baseball cap to Cassie. He threw me the keys to the paint van. "Get her home and get back here in your work clothes, STAT!" he said. He then ran out of the room, yelling to all the other Paint Dogs, "We got a code red here, gentlemen . . . CODE RED!"

"I thought you said you owned this house. Who are these guys?" she asked, annoyed. "They're my crew. Old man Rasmusson is a potential buyer of the house," I said. I looked up and Curly was standing in the doorway having heard that last exchange. "Nice," he said to me, smiling. "Uh, Mr. Campion, sir, I think it's in your best interest for you and the young lady to vacate the premises and let us get the place spit spot. I don't want to rush you, sir, but time is of the essence," he said, loving the charade. "OK, man, we're outta here." We pulled out as Nud was pulling in with Rasmusson.

I dropped her off, swung home for my clothes, and got back to the job as Nud was still going around with the old man. Curly and company had gotten the place looking decent so that nothing was noticeable from our little party. Luckily for me Rasmusson had started his appraisal of the work on the outside of the house. I was in the kitchen mixing some paint when they came in. "Well, Nud, you and your boys seem to be doing a fine job," the old man said. "You're a little slow but good work takes a little longer, I find." "Well, thank you, sir. We're proud of the work we do," Nud said obligingly. I kept my head down, knowing the old man didn't like me. "What in Sam Hill is this?" old man Rasmusson said in disgust. "Sir?" Nud asked. "It feels like a bird just crapped on my head!" he said angrily. I turned around and one of the butters from the ceiling, which I'd completely forgotten about, had come loose from the ceiling and dropped in the middle of his forehead and was dripping down off the end of his nose. "THERE GOES ANOTHER ONE!" he screamed, this time it landing on his shoulder. All three of us looked up simultaneously and saw the constellation of diner butters in the shape of a horseshoe on the ceiling. The two of them then turned their stares to me. I just looked down and kept stirring the paint, saying nothing.

When the old man left, Nud signaled me to meet him in his van for a talk. "Nud, listen, I am so sorry . . ." Before I could get my apology all the way out, Nud was already laughing. "Don't apologize. I fuckin' hate that cheap old fuck. He had that comin'," he said. "Oh, I thought you brought me in here to fire me,' I said, surprised. "You'd like that, wouldn't you? So then you could kick around town some more, feelin' like a loser, drinkin' up a storm. I'm not gonna do that for you. I'm goin' you one better," he said cryptically. "One better?" I asked. "Yeah. I'm kicking you outta town," he said. "What?" "You heard me. I'm kicking you out of town. You got your band back together now and you don't need to be here anymore, so I'm kicking you outta town," he said, dead serious.

"I'm not sure I get it,' I said. "It's easy. I already cleared it with your sisters that you can move in with them and stay on their couch in the city till you find a place. It's time for you to leave here. You're by far the worst worker that's ever donned a Paint Dog uniform, but I knew that when I hired you. You're not supposed to be in these jobs. I'm not either but this is what I gotta do for now to support my family. Go to the city and be an entertainer. Do it in the subway, on street corners, in the canteens, wherever they'll let you but don't ever get a job again. You're not cut out for it. Go sing and tell your stories. That's what you're good at and someday people are going to wanna pay to see it, but you have to get out there and do it and don't stop doing it until that happens. It was nice havin' you around. You were great comic relief for the crew for a while but it's time for you to go," he said, counting out cash from an envelope. He then said with convincing authority, "In my hand is five hundred dollars that I'm giving you to leave town. Now go sing and never get a real job ever again." And I never did. The following day I embarked on a seven-year journey as America's guest.

Chapter Seven

"Christened by a Crackhead"

I got into the city around four o'clock and threw my overstuffed duffel bag on the floor next to the couch I'd now call home to my hangovers. My older sisters, Donna and Eileen, were still at work so I decided to hoof it over to St. Marks Place and buy a new gig shirt with some of that Nud money. I figured I might as well get something with it before nightfall because it would start to evaporate pretty quickly in the bar. I've never been able to keep a dime in my pocket. My sisters lived on Tenth Street between Fifth and Sixth, so it was an easy walk. As I strolled past the Astor Place subway stop, I saw a bunch of guys playing music on the concrete island that separated the traffic. They were a three-piece band with a little trap kit, a stand-up bass, and an acoustic guitar. They were good, sounding to me a little like the BoDeans. I wanted to jump up there with them.

The energy of the street was invigorating. There were artists, NYU students, junkie panhandlers, black, white, Asian, Indian, Latino, and Middle Eastern folks all meshed together, coexisting happily, seemingly immune to the prospect of racial tension—as if to say, "We are all New Yorkers first and fuck everything else." I was walking faster than usual. I wasn't in a hurry or anything. I'd been sucked into the riptide of the sidewalk traffic and had unknowingly sped up to its pace. I imagined that I was running back a punt in a football game, weaving through oncoming pedestrians like they were would-be tacklers, trying to anticipate openings; and when I saw them, surging through the seam, speed-walking up the outer edge of the curb, envisioning it as the sideline.

There were dazzlingly beautiful women everywhere of all shapes, sizes, and colors. I almost died of sugar shock. And these weren't just gals that were cookie-cutter pretty. I'm talkin' exotic, sizzling, and what's more . . . everywhere! I was a complete swivel-head the whole way over, meandering aimlessly into the crosswalk against the light at University Place, entranced by the three chicks in front of me. A big black lady saved me by grabbing the back of my collar. "Watch where you goin', baby boy! Them pretty girls ain't goin' nowhere. Gonna git yourself killed," she said, laughing heartily. I was taking long pulls of the sweet early-summer air and could feel the blood coursing through me, blowing sparks from my fingertips. It was a good day.

It wasn't just the gorgeous gals that had my spirit soaring, though they are always a welcome component. This was something different. It was a feeling I hadn't known in a while, the one of possibility—the atmosphere was telling me that something could really happen here because this is where it all happens—cue the Sinatra song. I'd hung in the city a lot over the years, gigging and whatnot, but I was seeing it in an entirely new light on this particular day. It was no longer a place just to rip it up and leave. This was home now. It was, indeed, a new beginning. And the cherry on top of this new lease on life was that I had a gig at The Wetlands that night—a perfect inaugural evening to kick off my conquering years—I was here to *succeed* and it felt as though the sunlight was finally gracing both sides of my face.

I was headed for Trash & Vaudeville, a store where I'd found some cool, cheap threads a few months back. It was famous for outfitting a lot of bands that I loved from the late seventies, CBGB's era like Television, Talking Heads, and The Voidoids. Still playing the punt-return game in my head, I crossed onto St. Marks and nearly plowed into a guy who was having a rather intense conversation with himself. This was long before those phone earpieces that you see every other asshole in the street talking on nowadays. I can't tell who's crazy anymore, having gotten it wrong too many times to count. I see a tattered guy talking aloud with no one there and hand gesturing . . . figure he's crazy . . . he walks by . . . earpiece. I see a business guy . . . doing the same thing . . . figure he's buying low, selling high . . . he walks by . . . no earpiece . . . and up close he's the three faces of Eve in a fuckin' cashmere coat. In 1993, we knew who the crazy ones were.

"Listen, could we not do this here? I mean come on. You're gonna break up with me out here in the street? You know what? Fine. I don't care anymore. I've had it!" he said, looking and acting like Richard Dreyfuss in *The Goodbye Girl*. I was mesmerized by his passion and stood three feet away thoroughly invested in the scene. I just wanted to see how it turned out, really. He started up again. "Oh, come back. How many times are we gonna have to do this? You know you take a little piece of me every time you . . ." He stopped abruptly and turned to me angrily. "DO YOU MIND?" "Oh, I'm sorry, dude. I guess I was daydreaming," I said, totally embarrassed, as if I'd really been caught eavesdropping. "Yeah, well do it somewheres else. I'm kind of in the middle of something here," he growled. "Yeah, of course," I said. I debated inviting him to go get a drink, thinking it might be highly entertaining to get his story, but thought better of it. There's a difference between being a vicious freak and a combustible schizophrenic. That poor soul had obviously crossed the line. Besides, he wasn't that friendly.

I met a cute girl named Amy in the store who helped me shop. "I'm in here to get my roommate a T-shirt for his birthday. He loves this store," she said in passing. "Your roomate's a guy? Any hanky panky?" I said, feeling her out. "Noooo. Oh God, no, he's gay. He's got a Bette Davis obsession," she said. "Shit, who doesn't? Lemme guess, he loves her eyes?" I said, flirting. "He wants to be her," she said, giggling and flirting back. "Again, who doesn't?" I said, playing it cool by walking away. We browsed on opposite sides of the store for a minute and then she came back over to me. "What are you here for?" "I'm looking for a good Bette Davis shirt but not because I'm obsessed with her or want to be her or anything . . . just 'cause I think she's cool," I teased, holding a pink T-shirt to my chest that had stenciled on it BETTE DAVIS EYES and a picture of her smoking a ciga-rette. "Whattya think? Yes? No? Yes?" I asked her, goofing around. "Absolutely, that's you," she said. "You know I got to see her up close once," I told her. "Get outta here!" she said. "For real, I did. She lived in my town," I told her. And it was true. Bette Davis and I once had a close encounter.

She lived in Huntington for a few years in the early eighties when she was an octogenarian recluse. It was a pretty big deal when she moved in (I was fifteen). My friends and I were told to respect her privacy and go nowhere near her property. She lived in a small house that was built right up against this seawall that we used to walk on at the beach. We honored that for a while, but then one night when we were really baked, we decided to have a look-see. As we were walking by, from the beach we thought we saw the shadow from her rocking chair being thrown up on the wall with her in it. It was hypnotically creepy. I said to the fellas, "We gotta go up there and look in. C'mon, something to tell our grandchildren."

She had a big picture window in front that ran right up over the seawall. The drop to the beach was twelve feet or so. My stoner buddies, Pedro, Turk, Crow, and I took a deep breath and went for it. We inched out on the ledge, one by one, and positioned ourselves to spy in, two of us on each side, on each other's shoulders, occupying all four corners of the window. Turk called it. "All right, boys, on the count of three. One . . . two . . ." and just as he was about to call "three," her eighty-year-old shrunken head, made haglike by the decades, was suddenly pressed up against the glass with a flashlight under it. Her face, illuminated against the unlit room, hovered there—suspended—like the unholiest of holograms. Her famous eyes didn't disappoint, either. They were enormous and buggy. "YOU BOYS GET OUTTA HERE OR I'M CALLING THE COPS!" the screen icon squawked, her voice uniquely still hers, and powerful enough to convey murderous rage. She rapped on the window repeatedly, yelling, "GET OUTTA HERE, GODDAMMIT! GET OUTTA HERE!!!"

We were all startled off the wall at the same time, plummeting spazzily, and on the way down emitted a collective "WHOA!" We landed on top of one another and ran a quarter mile down the beach at full tilt before collapsing in front of a burned-out sailboat, laughing our asses off.

"Wow, you have to tell Glen that story," Amy said. "Well, bring him to the gig tonight and I will," I said, as a way of inviting her. "You're in a band?" she asked, her eyes lighting up. "Yeah, we're called Knockout Drops. We're on tonight at nine-thirty at The Wetlands.

You should come and check it out. I'm actually going to get a drink right now. You wanna come?" I asked, really needing a drink. "Sure," she said. I bought a navy blue polka-dot shirt and wore it out of the store. It would do for the gig.

We went into this place called the Holiday Cocktail Lounge, a no-frills gin mill right on St. Marks. I loved it right away but Amy definitely didn't gel with the crap-hole surroundings I'd brought her to. "This place is killer!" I said, loading up the jukebox with the Stones' *Beggars Banquet* album. "Really? You think so?" she said, less than convinced. "Oh yeah, my kinda place," I told her. There were five people in there besides us: two old men sitting separately, both contemplative in the glass; two fat Irish brothers on the other side of the bar, connected at the forehead and slurring to each other in some sort of Gaelic twins language; and the old drunk seated directly to my right who was showing few signs of life at all. Call me old-fashioned but I thought it was the perfect place for love to blossom, a spot where after a few drinks she could pan around the room and I'd seem like a really good idea. I thought it to be strategic genius until the guy next to me literally fell off his barstool, passing out over my feet. "What do I do?" I asked the bartender. "Leave him there. He'll be up in a little while," he said, washing out a glass.

Amy said, "Can we at least move away from him?" "You heard him. He'll be up in a little while. If I move my feet he's gonna bonk his head," I said, thinking it showed off my sensitive side but really just not wanting to move (we had a perfect spot at the corner of the bar). She wanted to leave for the same reasons that I wanted to stay and I lost her off the line. As she was making a hasty exit, I said, "Are you at least gonna make it to the gig tonight?" She said, "I don't know. If he doesn't wake up from his nap in time, are you?" and she stormed out. The bartender said, "Wow! Girlfriend?" "Yeah, we had some good moments. I'm gonna miss her," I said, slamming down the rest of my beer and adjusting my feet to give the passed-out guy a better pillow. "You don't know what you got till it's gone," he said. "Exactly, could you hit me again?" I said, showing him my pint was empty. We both laughed, knowing Amy's incessant chirping wasn't right for the sanctity of the room anyway.

The barman's name was Francis, an old hippie who'd been worn down by the years, no longer believing in flower power but lacking the energy to change his hairstyle (gray ponytail). He'd been tending bar for twenty-five years, had seen his share of shit, was in a less-than-good mood but not cranky, and had a funny way of looking at life. In other words: the perfect bartender.

Sleeping Beauty eventually came to, picking his head up to a streamline of drunk drool that followed him from my sneakers back to his vertical position. I ended up drinking with him. His name was George. He had on this filthy, light blue windbreaker that I assumed he lived in, his hair a fantastic comb-over, going from ear to ear on just a few strands. His face looked as if it had been scorched under a sunlamp from all the broken blood vessels and his teeth were a smoker's Easter egg yellow.

He told me he'd worked for the gas company for twenty years but had recently been laid off. "Wow, that sucks. How long have you been outta work, then?" I asked him. "Oh, about three years now," he said. Time has no relevance when your sun rises and sets in the bar. I knew this and just said, "Oh, sorry to hear to that. Any chance of getting it back?" "What? Uh, not sure . . . haven't been keeping up with it. Do you think if I tried I could snap this cap all the way out the door and onto the street?" he asked me, holding up a beer cap between his thumb and middle finger. "I don't know, dude. That's pretty far," I said. "I'll betcha a buck I can," he said, teeing one up. "You're on!" I said. We spent the next couple of hours doing only that, him snapping 'em, then me snapping 'em, him winning some, and me winning some. After a while more people came in and we had the whole bar involved. Everyone in there was betting and cheering whenever the cap flying-saucered its way through the open door. Passersby kept hearing the commotion inside, curiously stopping in, and before we knew it the joint was jumpin'—an otherwise dead and depressed room resuscitated to gleeful good feeling by two drunks, a bottle cap, and an idea. That's why I love bars. The tide can turn on a dime with something like that.

I split from the Holiday around seven P.M., hugging George and all my new friends on the way out, saying to him, "Dude, come to The Wetlands. I'll put you on the list." "I dunno, Chris, maybe. I rarely leave here," he said. "Understood, my man, but I'll throw you on just in case you get a wild hair," I told him. I'd had a beautiful first day in there and resigned myself to go back whenever in that neighborhood. It would be one of my "day spots," I thought. There is a big distinction between a night spot and a day spot. Night spots have girls in them and mainstream people. Day spots are specifically designed for the damned drinker to imbibe in the loving peace and understanding of fellow damned drinkers—retirees are also welcome. In just a short time I'd forged a profound relationship with that decrepit old dive, much more meaningful than anything I could have hoped for with Amy.

I swung by the apartment for the three Ss (a shit, shower, and shave) before soundcheck—aside from a fat line of coke, the three Ss are the next best rejuvenator after a long day's drinking. My sisters were having a preshow party, so there were about fifteen people over when I walked in. Donna was taking a shower. She poked her head out and said, "I bought you frozen chicken pot pies. They take like three minutes in the microwave. Heat one up." "OK, I'm just gonna grab a beer and say hello to everyone first," I said. "OK," she said, taking a big sip from a glass of red wine that she'd positioned on the bathroom sink within grabbing distance. Ah, the shower libation . . . that's a good one.

My sisters always brought a crowd to my gigs—actually they always brought a crowd everywhere. They are wildly social beings, both with hollow legs. They'd been living in the city for a couple of years by then and had the entire West Village wired. They knew everyone in every bar, having all the barkeeps in their hip pockets. I couldn't have had it easier—I felt like royalty when I said, "I'm Donna and Eileen's little brother." I'd have a cold pint in my hand before I even got the sentence out, always attached to those sweet words the man behind the tap uses when he's buying you a drink, "That's with me."

They had every good bartender's schedule committed to memory. I remember, after a week of living with them, saying, "Whattya say we hit the Corner Bistro for a few?" Eileen looked at me like I'd just suggested we go water-skiing in winter. "The Bistro . . . on a Tuesday? No. We only go there when Dermott or Tommy is working. Tonight we go to the Ear Inn 'cause Brendan is there. You're gonna love him." And love him I did. He later opened up a place on East Eleventh called Brendan's that became one of our favorite places ever. Donna got married there.

I decided to forego the shower, instead partying with the living room crew. When I got to The Wetlands, I realized I had a problem. About a month prior I'd been thrown out by the scruff of my neck for doing blow in the bathroom. I'd completely forgotten about it until I saw the humongous bouncer with the big leather overcoat, long hair, and goatee who'd ejected me, standing by the front door. How the hell was I gonna navigate this? He'd kicked open the bathroom door, rag-dolled me, and dragged me through the entire place like I was going to the stocks. When he tossed me out the door, he said, "Don't ever try to come back. You're barred from The Wetlands for life!" I never told the band about it because those guys weren't coke users and they were already worried about what a destructive drunk I was. I didn't want them thinking I was a pathetic cokehead too, which at the time I really wasn't yet. In a boozed-up existence your life becomes a constant troubleshoot. This was just one more little hurdle I had to get over.

I snuck in through the entrance reserved for equipment load-in, stowing myself away in the kitchen. Tom came in. "What are you doing in here? The sound guy's ready for us." I half came clean. "Look, man, I was thrown outta here by that bouncer a month ago and he told me never to come back. I gotta duck him till set time." "He's outside. Just stand back by the kit with the mic so we can get sounds up with a tune, then ditch it till show time," Tom said, not even a little surprised by the crisis. He just laughed and pulled his amp onstage. He'd come to expect this sort of thing from me. Once, after gigging at Top of the Town, we were eating at the diner in Huntington and the manager came over to our table and said to me, "Let's go, you know you're not allowed in here anymore." Tom just continued eating his burger as the guy escorted me out. "Meetcha by the car," he said, his mouth half full.

I didn't wanna blow this. At the time The Wetlands was an important place to play in New York and it wasn't easy to wrangle a slot. Oasis did their first two U.S. shows there around that time. You had to have a big draw to even be considered for a gig, especially headlining on a Saturday night as we were. It was also the reputed hangout of a lot of A and R people, which at that point were like yeti to us because we'd heard about them but had never actually seen one.

We'd been packing 'em in at places like the Bitter End and the Lion's Den but wanted to be off that lower rung of small clubs. I knew it was vital to us to make a splash there, but to tell you the truth I didn't think the place was that cool. It was considered a cradle to the hippie jam band movement, a kind of music that I vehemently abhor. I like songs. I don't wanna listen to guys jacking off on their instruments for fifteen minutes at a time. Ironically this flavorless, never-ending crap stemmed from these bands all being fans of the Grateful Dead, whom I loved—but the Dead had tunes! It's something that often happens in music. An awesome, ground-breaking group spawns awful imitators who miss the point completely (see Led Zeppelin and hair metal bands).

The room itself I liked, though. It was half dive bar–half rock club, which set it apart. The staff was really warm and friendly too. Our following loved The Wetlands. It was a great place to socialize before the set and after, because it had an enormous bar and standing area in back. All in all, it was a good hang, the pros outweighing the cons.

I remained outta sight till it was time to go on and we hit the stage running, opening with "Burning Bush Chronicles." The hall was full to capacity and all the mainstays in our crowd were there. From the stage I spotted the Humes: Sharon, Vickie, and Tara, three gorgeous sisters from Florida. They were these effervescent party chicks who managed Frédéric Fekkai's hair salon, a chichi place in the Bergdorf-Goodman building on Fifth Avenue that fashionistas and rich socialites patronized. Hillary Clinton got her hair done there when she was First Lady.

The Humes were huge Drops fans, attending every show, and always bringing a gaggle of hotties from their high-end hair world. Another fringe benefit of their fandom was getting free haircuts. I'd go into Frédéric's all cross-eyed and disheveled, and obnoxiously flirt with the pampered older women. My first time at the salon there was a lady next to me reading *Redbook* and I said to her, "Excuse me, does this place do colonics? I haven't shat in like two weeks." She never did give me an answer. Wealthy people can be so rude.

We were three-quarters of the way through our set at The Wetlands and killing beautifully when, from the corner of my eye, I saw my bouncer friend standing side stage. We were right in the middle of a song and when it finished, not knowing what else to do, I addressed him from the mic. "What's up, man?" I said. "Not much, you guys sound rockin'," he said smiling, like he was about to have my dick in a sling. "What's your name?" I asked. He said, "Ronnie." "I don't know how many of you saw this, but Ronnie and I won a dance contest in here a few weeks ago. Oh yeah, we glided all around the room, dipping, and turning. It almost looked like fuckin' pairs ice-skating," I said, speaking in code about it. "We're not gonna do any more dancing, though. Right, Chris?" he said, still smiling. I said, "No, we're not, Ronnie. I'm done dancing." "Good," he said. And that was that.

Ronnie became a good friend of mine after that. We love fielding the how-did-you-guys-meet? question. We tell it tag-team style. It's great 'cause then people get both points of view. Then we argue over the finer points and it always ends with me saying, "But you didn't have to use such brutal force," and him saying, "I still wish I'da kicked your ass outside when I had the chance." Ronnie's one of those gentle giants—everyone loves them.

We finished the night with the song "Dharma," a tongue-in-cheek performance tune of ours with punk sensibilities. It was sung from the point of view of a serial killer on death row, unskillfully pleading his case for a stay of execution. There'd been several of these cases in the news at the time. I got to the last verse:

I got a bone to pick with you, your honor,
about my life down here on death row
a flick of the switch and I know I'm a goner
But there's one thing I think you should know

My daddy done beat me
My momma done left me
And my older sister she molest me
I'm so screwed up
Well, I get an evil chill

Yes, I get an evil chill
All I wanna do is kill, kill, kill
But somehow that ain't enough

Chorus
There's no new direction to Dharma
no resurrection today
no new confessions, your honor,
to wash my transgressions away.

I sang that last line and noticed something weird out in the audience as we were heading into the instrumental outro. The Wetlands had that glow-in-the-dark lighting that made any bright-colored clothing appear blindingly luminescent. I was spazzing out with a drum stick, mock-stabbing the stage while the music swelled, and I looked out and saw a luminous flash of sky blue, yellow teeth, and squinty eyes. It was George! He'd made it and was dancing in the middle of a bunch of hot chicks, raising his arms in the air like he'd just won the lottery. He had a couple of his cronies from The Holiday with him pogoing up and down as well. I said from the stage, "Hey, George, show the crowd what you can do." With that, he pulled a bottle cap from his pocket, we provided him a drum roll, and he snapped it across the room to big applause. I put the mic up to him and asked him like a sports announcer, "So how'd that one feel?" "I got all of it. I just wanna say that this has been one of the greatest nights of my life," he said emotionally. Hearing him say that definitely made it one of mine.

The show was a slam dunk and we were invited back the following month for another headlining slot. We did a ton of gigs at The Wetlands in the nineties. It closed in 2001 and though we'd graduated to different places by then and hadn't played it in years, I was sad to see it go. It was a unique experience in there. I had a lot of vicious times in the bowels of that club. Everyone that lived in New York in the nineties has a Wetlands story. If you know someone that was there, just ask and you're sure to get an earful back.

After the show we directed everyone to the Kettle of Fish on West Third for our customary afterparty. We always went to the Kettle after our downtown shows because Nancy, a good friend of Donna's and Eileen's, bartended there.

Nancy was like family to the Campions, as well as fans of the Knockout Drops and Bogmen. She was whip smart and gave off a warm but tough vibe, like she could've been matriarch to a Hell's Angels chapter. She had long black hair parted in the middle, kind brown eyes, and a beautiful, yet radiantly imperfect, smile. I always saw her as a heavier-set Janis Joplin. She had a vicious-freak-barfly following that sat in front of her every night. She ruled them with an iron fist and caring sense of humor. Everyone loved Nancy. She used to sit back there, pouring beers, with a big pin on that said GIULIANI IS A JERK. The Kettle served big pitchers of beer, and every time I walked in after a gig, she'd say, "Chris, the usual?" and hand me an empty mug, knowing I had no money and would be pilfering out of the pitchers. People caught on and it became a running joke.

Entering the Kettle after a gig later that summer, my friend Rico walked in behind me, saw Nancy and I do our thing, and nicknamed me "Skidder." "What the hell is a skidder?" I asked him. "It's you. One who skids on someone else's back, often going unnoticed. You're a skidder, Chris," he informed. "That's not me at all. I'm a hundred percent overt in my actions," I said. He laughed and said, "Oh, I know. You're living brilliantly. We should all be so lucky as to have your lifestyle." My sister Eileen happened to be standing there and chimed in. "I know, he has the highest standard of living matched against the lowest income in Manhattan. The other night his broker buddy, Danny Shea, had him sitting courtside at the Knicks game, two seats over from Spike Lee. He borrowed money from me for a subway token to get up there." Rico laughed hard. I said, "Lemme ask you a question, Rico. Would you be standing in the middle of all these beautiful girls—who I've just introduced you to—without me?" "No, probably not," he said. "Then buy me a drink, motherfucker," I said. "Not a problem. Go grab those girls and let's do some shots, Skidder!" he said, heading for the bar.

That nickname stuck. I actually kind of liked it. Just don't ever call me slacker by mistake. There are some similarities between skidders and slackers but the differences are bigger. Slackers were unlovely beings that lie around all day, stoned, ambitionless, expecting other my Don Juan capabilities. Still, if you go out every night and do as I did, your numbers will go up.

We (the band, my sisters, the Humes, and about twenty others) took off from the Kettle and went around the corner to the Red Lion, on Bleecker Street, where Willibee and his guitar player, Bill Ryan, were working as busboys. We walked in and the band that was supposed to be on hadn't showed up, so Bill and Bill went on for them, announcing to the crowd, "Hi, we're the busboys. Could you please give your empty glasses to your waitress? We've been called outta the bullpen to entertain you." They rocked the place upside down with their song "Suddenly" and played the Van Morrison classic "Sweet Thing" with my sisters, both great singers in their own right, providing the harmonies on the side mics. Every gal in the joint was swooning. My brother has an awesome voice. Then Phil, Tom, and I joined them for a spirited version of Elvis Costello's "Peace, Love, and Understanding," which I took lead vocals on. The place went nuts. My first night as a New York resident couldn't have been going better.

Peter Cavanaugh, a fun-lovin' Irishman (from Ireland), whose uncle Alan Whelan owned the bar, sat and drank with us afterward. Peter was a good-looking, blond-haired guy my age, who was quick with a joke and had a comedy troupe called "The Fourth Floor," a bunch of maniacal alcoholics who went on stage and did crazy shit. They were like the show *Jackass* meets *Monty Python*.

"You guys oughta stay and watch Mike Tait. He's mad," Peter said. Around three A.M., this guy came onstage, handsome, slender, with long dark brown hair. At first, he appeared to be just another folkie playing on Bleecker Street. He started playing and I took notice right away that he was a proficient guitarist, really unique, and a great singer. Unfortunately for him I was the only one in the place watching it, the hour being late, and the inane drunken bar chatter at a fevered pitch—shit-faced dudes throwing their last Hail Mary passes at the chickies before the dreaded last call.

He finished the song and I guess he didn't feel he'd gotten enough recognition from the crowd and said, "Well, thank you very little." He futzed around with his tuning for a few minutes and then some belligerent douche bag yelled up to him, "Hey, why don't you play something?" Mike didn't acknowledge him and continued fiddling with his gear. The guy didn't like being ignored and pounded on the table, this time yelling louder, "PLAY SOMETHING!" Without batting an eye, Mike, with a starry-eyed-crooner expression on his face, tenderly started strumming and singing to him, *"Something in the way you move, attracts me like no other lover . . ."*

He performed the whole song zeroing in on just the heckler, never changing his loving demeanor. Everyone died laughing through the whole thing. The loudmouth was visibly embarrassed and walked out muttering to himself, "Fuckin' asshole." I turned to Peter and said, "You gotta introduce me to this guy. We have to get a gig together in here." Peter clinked my glass, "You guys would be perfect together. Done."

Everybody went home. Mike, Peter, and I stayed and drank in the bar till well after closing, the first of countless nights we'd do that, and then we went across the street to the Triumph Diner. Mike said, "Oh, cool, Club Triumph, that means we can get some green milk shakes." I found out green milk shakes were just Heinekens in paper cups. We ordered some omelettes and drank up some green milk shakes. Mike was Canadian to the bone. He was a beer-swillin', hockey-lovin', wise ass Canuck, as loveable as they come. Peter set Mike and me up with a slot on Monday nights at ten P.M. that we held for the next five years (we still play together), also gigging on other nights depending on the monthly calendar. Through the Red Lion I got to know lots of folks in the New York Irish bar community, awesome people, who understand the importance of blarney in this world—my stock in trade.

We said our tipping-over long good-byes out on Bleecker Street and went our separate ways. The morning light was on its way and I wanted to beat it home. I walked past the Kettle and it had long since been buttoned up. It seemed like a lifetime ago that I'd been there . . . It seemed like two lifetimes since the Holiday Cocktail Lounge. I lumbered forward, stewed to the bejesus, but had a feeling of total satisfaction propelling me forward. It'd been a great night. I still had the bounce in my step from earlier in the afternoon, but it was being weighed down by the fifty beers I'd had since then.

I rounded the corner in front of the newsstand on Sixth Avenue and this crackhead black guy, the size of a nose tackle, came flying outta nowhere and grabbed me by the throat. "GIMME ALL YOUR

MONEY!" he screamed, in the most threatening way. I was so stunned I just said nothing. "I SAID GIMME ALL YOUR MONEY OR I'M GONNA FUCKIN' KILL YOU," he yelled, this time slobbering all over me as he said it. He appeared to be frothing at the mouth. Being really fucked up and just going on instinct, I said to him, "Well, where's your weapon?" He said, "WHAT?" I said, "You have to have a weapon if you're gonna mug me or else what am I gonna tell my friends? I can't hand you money just to keep from getting an ass kicking. That happens like three times a year, anyway. I can't puss out like that," I slurred.

He tilted his head with the most perplexed look on his face. You'd have thought he was doing a calculus problem in his mind. He was more fat than muscular and I pictured punching him in the stomach to the cartoon sound of a trampoline and not being able to get my hand back out. He still had me by the shirt and I said, "You look like you could use a beer. Here's three bucks. It's the last of my dough. Go get a forty. I'm going home." He snatched the money from my hand without looking back at me and crossed the street in a hurry. I watched him walk into the bodega, having one of those did-that-really-just-happen? moments.

Then it got even stranger. He came out of the store, drinking out of his freshly bought forty-ouncer, and started walking up Sixth Avenue parallel to me on the other side of the street. We kept catching the lights at the same time and having to stop, each time looking across at each other, where to myself I'd say, "Shit, that's the guy who mugged me." We did that for ten blocks, every corner the same deal—stopping and looking at each other. It was the weirdest thing ever. When we got to Tenth Street, out of reflex, I waved bye to him. He waved back, sort of smiling, and rounded the corner. It almost seemed like walking together on opposite sides of the street—like that had somehow made us friends. I fell through the door of the apartment, poured myself a glass of Concha y Toro red wine out of the refrigerator, slammed it, and went to bed—excuse me, couch. I went to couch.

The next night I was in the Corner Bistro with Willibee and my sisters drinking with Dermott the bartender, a lovely Irish fellow with a deep appreciation and knowledge of music. He loaded up the jukebox with Tom Waits, which made me ecstatic—there's no one better to listen to on a Sunday night than Tom Waits. He is the maestro for the melancholy. I held court at the bar telling the story of the previous night's mugging with the all-too-perfect "Tom Traubert's Blues" underscoring me. *"I'm an innocent victim of a blinded alley"* swelled up behind me as I unfurled it. When I finished, Dermott said, "You do realize that this is a good thing, right, Christopher?" "Good? How so? Good that I didn't get killed, I guess," I said, taking a big sip of my beer, still a bit panicked about it all. He said, "No, your cherry's been popped, son. It's a time for celebration. You're a real New Yorker now. You were christened by a crackhead!" Then he handed me a fresh beer with the ever-sweet words, "That's with me."

. . .

Life started to get interesting for the Drops. We picked up a Thursday residency at a brand-new bar that had just opened up in the East Village called Nevada Smiths. This helped our crowd grow exponentially because it was right near NYU and they ran drink specials to entice the kids, so filling it every week was a piece of cake. The owner was a sweet Irish guy named Terry, who was a big fan of ours. "I'll take the bar, you take the door, gentlemen," he said. We charged a five-dollar cover and played three sets a night.

It was the best thing that ever happened to us. I'm a big believer in residencies. The frequency of the dates tightened the band considerably and it also forced us to constantly interject new stuff into the act. We ended up writing a lot of songs as a result and debuting new ones each week. By the end of the summer we had a whole set of new material.

We went into a cheap eight-track studio on Long Island and recorded them. Two days later we emerged with our finest effort up until then, a cassette with eight songs we called *Burning Bush Chronicles.* Here's the track listing:

Mrs. Goodbar
Kopycat
Burning Bush Chronicles
The Dropout Song
Daisy Carnival

Deathbed and Breakfast
Dharma
Give Up the Ghost

We sold 'em for five bucks at the gigs, sometimes giving them away if people didn't have money but said they really liked the band (or if they were just hot chicks). Before we knew it, we had bigger crowds showing up and now they all knew the songs! It was a great feeling. After a couple of months, to our surprise, we'd sold almost a thousand of those little tapes.

While the band loaded out each week I was the clown who'd go around collecting people's addresses for the mailing list. I wasn't a big fan of doing it, but it was better than carrying shit. I felt like I was running for state comptroller (whatever the fuck that is). These weren't e-mails, mind you, but snail-mail addresses. I'd hand the clipboard to someone and lose track of it while they were passing it around the bar. At the end of the night we'd get it back and we could visibly see the signatures got more monstrous the later it got. Tom was our decoder. He had an amazing gift for deciphering drunk handwriting. We'd also get the usual jokey fake names, like Mike Hunt, Ismell Uranus, or my personal favorite, everybody's All-American, Stanley Fuckinger—the reason I like that one is because the person didn't even try to use the device of the first name working with the last to say something dirty. Unless there really is a Stanley Fuckinger out there, in which case, Stanley, I apologize.

We started practicing at a rehearsal space in the East Village four times a week. It was just a little hole-in-the-wall place that had a couple of shoebox rooms with rinky-dink P.A.s in them, but it was cheap and the guys who ran it were cool. One night, after drinking eight tall boys, I opened the door to the bathroom and there—passed out on the toilet, with his jeans around his ankles and a bindle of blow in his hand—was the guy who'd just set up the sound for us in the room. He was sweating like a farmer and bore an uncanny resemblance to John Belushi—and I don't mean he resembled him—he was a dead ringer.

I snatched the bindle out of his hand and he woke right up. "Hey, what the fuck do you think you're doin'?" he snarled. "You're not people to take care of them. I had no such sense of entitlement. I always tried to bring something to the table in the form of excitement. I'd go to the outer limits for my host—I was a jackass in the box, if you will. I had goals and I worked for my drinks in my own odd way and didn't think myself a deadbeat—and I didn't give a shit whether you thought I was or not, so long as you kept buying. It was the same philosophy as with Eddie the bartender at the Shamrock only now I was applying it all over New York City. I also brought packs of thirsty people with money everywhere I went, so no bartender in their right mind would ever charge me and cut off that gravy train. I quickly learned that that's how the game was played. I drank like a Viking every night without so much as a farthing in my pocket and never gave it a second thought.

The Kettle was a quintessential watering hole. There was a long bar to your left as you walked in and booths in back by the dartboard. Beat heroes like Kerouac, Neal Cassady, and William Burroughs supposedly hung out there a lot in the early sixties (there's a famous picture of Kerouac standing in front of the bar sign). Its regulars were long-time residents and colorful characters from the heart of Greenwich Village and NYU students, who came for the cheap pitchers but were seen and not heard. They were usually studious types who would disappear into booths (there was nothing close to a collegiate air in this place). It wasn't out of the ordinary to turn around and almost collide with a guy riding a unicycle (that happened to me once) or see a guy drinking at the bar wearing a one-man-band outfit, with the bass drum strapped to his torso along with cymbals and some sort of multiple horn apparatus (saw a few different guys like that). It was weirdo heaven. We hung out there a lot. I fuckin' loved it.

That night after the gig we partied in there late and I got totally wasted, hanging all over the Hume girls and their friends, falling victim to the poor game plan of hitting on all of them and ending up with none of them. I never got wise to that and did it again and again. I wasn't a real smoothie in these situations, preferring to get good and drunk with my friends first and then going for it. Hookups for me happened more by way of a last call: "Okay, we're both still here. Wanna go fool around?" Leading to sloppy wet kisses and rolling around in the backs of cabs hailed at five A.M. That was the extent of supposed to pass out on this stuff. It's supposed to keep you awake. Here, lemme show you," I said, and dug one out, packing my beak. "You better be careful. That shit's what sent me to the bowl to begin with. It's horrible. I copped it outside on the street. I think it's been cut with alotta laxative," he said. "I'll take my chances," I told him, doing another two hits in a row. "My name is Chris," I said, extending my hand for a shake. "Yeah, I know. I caught you guys at Nevada's the other night. It was fuckin' awesome! I absolutely loved it," he said, unraveling some toilet paper, still in a half squat. "You're sure that's not just the laxative talkin'?" I said, laughing. "No . . . no . . . you were great. I'd shake your hand but I'm wiping my ass with it," he said, and he was.

"My wife, Leslie, is friends with some girls that love you guys and go every week. She took me. I've been wantin' to say something to you for the last few days but was always leaving as you guys came in. Do you need someone to roadie for ya? I'd love to do it. I wanna latch onto something good that's goin' somewhere. I think you guys could be it," he said, pulling up his pants, not the least bit self-conscious. "I'll talk it over with the boys but I don't see why not. I've already been privy to how you handle a crisis and I like what I see," I said. "But you're gonna have to find me some better blow." "Aw, don't you worry about that. I got it covered. This happened because I ran outta the good shit. I have a great connection," he said.

"I still haven't gotten your name. It says EMPLOYEES MUST WASH HANDS so I'm assuming you did," I said, again reaching out my hand. "Nah, wash your hands in that sink and they'll come out even dirtier. Shake my hand anyway, candyass," he said, and gripped mine hard before I could pull it away. "The name's Ponzo." "Ponzo like from *On the Road*?" I asked. "That's the one," he said. "Your parents hippies?" I said. "Nah, Wasps from New England. I'm a huge disappointment. It's awesome. My real name is Wendell but my eighth-grade English teacher nicknamed me Ponzo and it stuck, thank Gawd. I hated Wendell," he said, in his wicked Boston accent. "Why did he give you that name, you think?" I asked. "I dunno. I was always high in his class and he thought I looked like a fat Mexican, I guess." "Oh, yeah," I said, sizing him up. "Feels great to remember. Thanks for askin'." We both laughed. "So you're a rebel then, is that it?" I asked him. "Nah, just a fat slawb alcohawlic and drug addict who loves rock 'n' roll," he said humbly. I found that kind of touching. "Well, I think that concludes our interview, Mr. . . . Ponzo was it? You got the job!" I told him. "Hawt damn! Wait'll I tell Leslie. She loves you guys!"

From that moment on Ponzo became our omnipresent roadie and my personal guy Friday, sidekick, bodyguard when I drunkenly mouthed off to the wrong guy, and trusted friend. He was a prince of a guy. He had a gruff exterior but a soft chewy center. He was perfect for the Drops, able to roll with the punches and find the humor in the many disasters we found ourselves in playing outta town. He was extremely loyal too. "A man isn't shit in this world without honor" is what he'd always say. Short him in a drug deal and he'd be so far up your ass he'd punch your teeth out from the inside of your mouth, but by the same token if a dealer gave him too much change, he'd say, "You gave me an extra twenty by mistake, chief," and hand the money back. That's just the sort of guy he was. Every band should be so lucky as to have a Ponzo.

Our juggernaut continued to roll. On a Monday afternoon as I was decomposing on the couch, colossally hungover from a gig I'd done with Mike Tait, the phone rang. I answered it with a gravelly voice. "Hello?" "Hi, is this Chris Campion?" this low-register voice asked. I didn't have my bearings yet about the night before. Some time had gone missing that my memory couldn't recover and I didn't wanna answer too quickly just in case something fucked up had happened. This is the kind of vigilance one can only learn from a lifetime of phone calls that started with "Is this Chris? Yeah, this is Sergeant Whoeverthefuck from such and such precinct. . . ." I'd never done anything that bad but had learned to at least buy enough time to find out what it was about before blindly giving myself up. I said, "Uh, he stepped out. Can I take a message?" "Yeah, tell him Joe Blaney called. I'm a producer. I'm interested in his band, The Knockout Drops." "Oh, ummm, I'm sure he's gonna wanna call you. What's your number?" I asked, wanting to talk to him now but realizing that he might think me a mental case if I tried to explain what'd happened.

I took down his number, then asked him, "Would he know you? Have you guys met?" trying to ascertain his interest from an outside vantage point but also wondering if I'd met him. "No, my cousin gave me his tape, *Burning Bush Chronicles*, and I think it's rockin'. Great tunes . . . I just wanna talk to him about it," he said. "Have you produced anyone I'd know? Ya know, so I can tell him who you are," I asked. "Sure. Let's see, I've worked with The Clash, Soul Asylum, Keith Richards, Prince, and a lot of other people. Not always producing, sometimes engineering, sometimes mixing, but I'm interested in producing him. . . . Just have him gimme a call. I gotta run. Thanks, man. Oh, and you are?" he asked, just before hanging up. I choked for a second and said, "Ummm, his brother Billy." Billy and I had similar voices anyway. In later years we would do each other's phoners (those are phone-in radio interviews) when one of us was too drunk.

I waited until the following day to call him back. Joe was a really cool dude with an awesome résumé. He'd gotten his big break when, in the middle of engineering The Clash's *Combat Rock* album, they fired their producer, handing him the reins to finish the record with them. He'd then gone on to engineer both of Keith Richards's solo records with the Expensive Winos as well as coproducing Soul Asylum's *And the Horse They Rode In On* with Steve Jordan. He'd also worked with artists like Tom Waits, Mike Scott and The Waterboys, and a whole lot of other people I admired.

He took me for a burger at Joe Jr.'s Coffee Shop on Sixth Avenue. I was shitting in my pants. I couldn't believe that this guy wanted to work with us. For the first half hour of the meeting I peppered him with questions about The Clash. Tom and I had been Clash fanatics for years (we saw them open for The Who at Shea in '82, an amazing night). There was a statement made by the music press back in the eighties calling them, "The only band that mattered"; and I couldn't agree more. Then I moved on to Soul Asylum and finally I got to Keith Richards and just exploded with queries about him. "What was he like? Did he talk about the Stones? Did Mick ever stop by?"

The meeting from my end had deteriorated into the old Wayne's World "We're Not Worthy" sketch when finally Joe said, "You know, Chris, I didn't bring you here to talk about everyone else's music. I'm here to talk about you and yours. You're a great lyricist and the band smokes." I said, "Sorry, Joe. I'm a fan first, ya know?" "Me too. We all are . . . at least the real ones in this business are, I find. I think we can make a killer record together. Whattya say?" he asked, taking a bite out of his burger. "I say let's leave the blood on the tracks," making a Dylan pun. We bumped burgers as a way of cheers-ing. Then I said, "Hey, did you ever meet or work with Dylan?" He just laughed a little and ate some fries, shaking his head.

We signed a production agreement with Joe soon thereafter and began recording what would become our first CD, *Nowadays*. He'd pay for all the studio fees and produce us, taking a percentage of any record deal we got as a result, along with royalties and other back-end payments. When we were done, he would take our album to his friends at the labels. We'd also be contractually obligated to keep him as a producer. "I know some people that are gonna love this," he said, sending me into a kid-on-Christmas-morning state of mind for the remainder of that week. I could hardly contain my excitement every time I walked into the studio to work with him.

Joe was a giant, topping out at about six feet, six inches. He had shaggy salt-and-pepper hair and a calm disposition. We got on great with him. He was a stickler for a good take and would make us go again and again till we got one. He brought a mobile unit and recorded us at a show at New York's most hallowed of rock halls, CBGB. After that he changed tacks with us. "I wanna capture the energy you guys have live so from now on we're gonna try to get our takes as a band and not do a lot of overdubbing. The recording from CBs is phenomenal. I think the studio is sterilizing you guys," he said. "Did you get any of my commentary on tape?" I asked, laughing. "Yeah, and I wanna speak to you about that. I want you to stop doing it. People don't go to a music show to hear comedy. You wanna be a comedian, then go be a comedian but I think when you're standing in front of the band you should just sing. Let the music do the talkin', ya know?"

He was the one with all the experience and was paying the bills so I didn't argue with him but I secretly thought it was a crock. What he didn't understand was that maybe music crowds on the whole were like that, but my audience wasn't. They loved it when I fucked around. I relished looking audiences in the eye and talking to them directly and didn't wanna be one of those timid little shoe-gazing pussies who was mute behind a microphone. What was wrong with having a few laughs in between songs? That's what I'd been doing up to that point and people had always liked it. I just didn't understand this compartmentalized entertainment world where you were either a singer or a comedian. Why couldn't I just be me, whatever the hell that was?

That was the first brush I had with the idea of compromising who I was to fit a certain mold, something that the music business is infamous for doing to people. With Joe it wasn't heavy-handed, it was merely a suggestion based on his own personal taste. I said, "All right, dude. I'll try." "Chris, I know you're a funny guy. I see people laughing. I just don't want anything detracting from the music is all. I want them to take you guys seriously. The tunes are amazing and that's what the band should be about," he said passionately. Joe worshipped at the temple of music and loved the band so it was easy to see where he was coming from. After talking it through I didn't resent his suggestion—but this would be a theme presented later on down the line by other music-biz people and the angle they played with it positively enraged me. Those soulless cunts love to package people. My blood boils just thinking about it.

As a result of our growing popularity we attracted management to our door as well. Michael Solomon and Rishon Blumberg, coowners of Brick Wall Management, had also been given *Burning Bush Chronicles* (which we were now referring to as "the little tape that could") by a gal who regularly attended our shows. They really dug it and came to our next performance at The Wetlands, signing us up on the spot. "We're goin' all the way, boys!" Rishon said, as we all clinked glasses at the bar after the show. We didn't know shit from shoe polish at the time but there was something about them that was impressive—and they partied with us, buying us lots of drinks. The way to this band's heart was through its liver, anyone could see that. I considered that smart business.

But Brick Wall offered more than just that. Michael and Rishon were real players. They were two guys in their late twenties who'd learned the record business from the inside out. Michael had worked at Sony and Rishon had run the office for Ron Delsner Productions before they partnered up to form Brick Wall.

They'd been best friends since childhood and were also very well connected. Michael had been engaged to Barbara Carr's daughter, Kristin Ann Carr, who'd died tragically of cancer a few years earlier.

At the time of signing us he still had a faraway look in his eye about it, which broke my heart. Barbara is Bruce Springsteen's manager and looked upon Michael as a son. Brick Wall and Barbara had started the cancer charity The Kristin Ann Carr Fund. We ended up playing a few of their events. They were always star studded and a lotta fun to do, though we never did get to play with the Boss, which would've been a dream come true.

Michael and Rishon went on to good success, managing John Mayer, as well as a host of other well-earning acts. We were the first real band they tried to break. They fit in well with us and our expanding family, both guys having excellent senses of humor, but make no mistake—they were all about the bottom line at the end of the day. When you take on real management, everything changes. We were no longer just a D.I.Y. band. They came in with a plan and we got started right away. Rish began booking us regional shows.

We were now playing four times a week out of town, up and down the East Coast, mostly shit holes, in front of very few people, and for next-to-no money, but we were happy to be out playing a lot. We did that while they shopped us a deal. We had our team and morale was good. It had only been a year since I'd left Huntington and already things were happening. I sensed a record deal coming—the same way my dog Clyde used to jump up, wagging his tail joyfully seconds before Dad's car even hit the driveway. He just knew. I felt like that.

I'd just done some vocal takes for our *Nowadays* record with Joe at his studio on Sullivan Street and was walking home up Sixth at around three in the afternoon when I was overcome with gratitude about the way things were going and decided to stop in at Saint Joe's Church to give a little thanks. I was still in the habit of lobbing prayers up to what I thought might be God—occasionally feeling like an existential buffoon hurling petitions into the unknowing air—but something about being in a Catholic church restored me to a state of grace.

I dabbed my fingers in the holy water, crossing myself with it, and kneeled down in the pew, gazing upon the life-size crucifix up on the altar. I thanked God for my good fortune and asked him to restore my faith. As always, I waited to be dumb-struck back to believing and when it didn't happen, I got up to go to happy hour.

On my way out, I bumped into an old priest with a full head of white hair and a ruddy face. "I saw you there praying. Is there any special reason that brought you here today that I might help you with?" he asked quietly. "No, not really," I said. "I've just had a run of good luck and wanted to show my appreciation. Most of the time when I pray it's 'Get me outta this' or 'Please, God, I can't afford to get a dee-wee right now so don't let this cop pull me over.' Ya know, stuff like that. I thought I'd surprise him with a change of pace today," I said loudly, overloading him by saying a mouthful. "Well, you're not really gonna surprise him with anything. He already knows all," he said. "I know . . . sees you when you're sleeping, knows when you're awake. I gotcha," I said. "No, I think that's Santa Claus you're referring to there," he said, chuckling. "Well, Father, to be honest I'm not sure they're not one and the same sometimes. If you know what I mean." "If you feel like that, then what brings you here?" he asked. "I'm hedging my bets, Father . . . hedging my bets . . . trying to keep my balloon from hitting the ground but still hoping . . . always hoping and never wanna give up hope. I'm Chris, by the way."

"How do you feel when you pray, Chris?" he asked. "Ummm, disconnected mostly . . . like there's a light out. Then I'll get an occasional flicker . . . a warm feeling, just enough nourishment to keep me trying. I'm not a quitter, Father." "No, you're not. You just keep doing what you're doing and you'll be fine," he said, smiling. "Maybe say a few prayers for me, wouldja? Ya know, we get the old tag team goin' and God might come back faster?" I said. "He hasn't left you but I will do that. Where you off to now?" he asked. "It's almost four o'clock, I'm goin' to get a pint. Wanna come?" I asked. "No, I don't drink," he said steadfastly. "Don't drink? What's your last name?" I asked, sensing he was Irish. "Kelly," he said. "KELLY? Oh, you're a disgrace," I joked, backpedaling down the street. "Bye, Chris." "BYE, FATHER KELLY," I hollered back, walking two more steps to enter McBell's Bar and Grill. Three hours later he walked by the window I was drinking in and we waved bye again.

Chapter Eight

Relationships and Rodeo Clowns

Now begins my sex, drugs, and rock 'n' roll period. Only for "sex," substitute "small intervals of romantic cohabitation" 'cause I'm really not the hit-and-run type—more like the hit-and-stay type . . . the hey-we-had-a-pretty-good-time-last-night-right?-You-mind-if-I-live-here-for-a-while type. So it was small intervals of romantic cohabitation, drugs, and rock 'n' roll.

The cohabitation part would usually last about as long as it took for my charm to slip into alcoholic dementia . . . or they found out I did drugs. Either way I'd always get thrown out.

One would think, given my chosen lifestyle, that I'd naturally seek out a female running mate who would be tolerant of my ways and even costar in my drunken drugged-up vaudeville act, like some coked-up party chick, right? *Wrong.* The last thing I wanted was to have to deal with somebody who had problems like my own so I always chose "good girls" who, in turn, might make me good. Sound logic, or so I thought.

I was the living embodiment of that old joke "Whattya call a musician who's just been dumped by his girlfriend?" HOMELESS. If someone were to draw a *New Yorker* cartoon to sum up the dynamic of these romances, it would be me in a giant baby stroller, tattered and torn in thrift-store rock 'n' roll duds, bedhead and bloodshot eyes, sucking on a Heineken through a nipple, while some sad-eyed, beleaguered young woman behind me pushed it.

These relationships always had the same story arc. They'd start out in some dive, usually after a gig, in a whirlwind of boozed–up laughs and bar smooches. We'd go back to her place that night arm–in–arm, completely smitten (always had to be a road game 'cause I never had a place of my own to take them). One night would turn into two nights, then three, four, and by the fifth night, without either of us even noticing, I'd be living there. There was no such thing as a "moving day" for this skidder. I'd just retrieve clothes, as needed, from the dirty duffel at my sisters' place, making no formal announcements to them about anything.

Martha was one in the procession of which I speak. We hooked up at my gig at The Wetlands, did one of those drunken kissy-face cab rides back to her apartment, and, as per usual, just kept keeping company over at her place every night after that. About a month rolled by in a blink and one night her friend Becky, who lived in the apartment next door and was with Martha the night we met, stopped by with some beers. Becky was a brazen man-hater, with brown hair, brown eyes, two chins, and two eyebrows slanted down toward her nose, giving away her abundantly suspicious nature. She looked at me with total disdain and said in the casually accusatory manner used regularly by passive-aggressive chicks who resent your stealing their best friend away, "You live here now? When did you move in?" Martha and I looked at each other dumbfounded. Neither of us knew, exactly. "Hmmm . . . I guess you could say that you just came and stayed, eh, Chris?" she said, shooting to wound with her double entendre. I had no comeback so I just laughed like a good sport to suck some of the poison out of it. "Ha ha ha . . . yeah, I guess you could say that." I laughed alone.

The good girls would always be enamored of my crazy life and vicious freak friends at first, it being an exciting change to their ordinary workaday existences. Then they'd realize they were actually living with a roaring alcoholic, insomniac, night crawler. My days were numbered going in, and I always lived in fear of the day the jig would be up.

So I was always sneaking around. None of these women was happy about living with a real drunk but some tried valiantly to make it work. Their thresholds of tolerance varied, but one thing every one of them had in common was that they abhorred drugs.

The use of drugs would sometimes be spelled out as a deal breaker so I would always try to camouflage myself as a straight-up drunk who smoked a little weed. In truth, I was a total gack fiend and didn't say no to anything mood altering, really, except for heroin. I'd dick around with that a little too, eventually, but booze and blow was the peanut-butter-and-jelly combo I preferred.

There's no worse feeling in the world than being found out. After a while I'd just come to expect it, feel bad about it when it happened, and then roll with it, always claiming the Popeye I-yams-what-I-yams defense to soothe my guilt. Awful moments all, but the most colossal of these bust-ups was with Martha.

Martha was a Type-A chick if ever there was one. Fastidious and organized, she had her shit together in ways I never even thought possible. She was in her mid-twenties and had a demanding job as a clothing designer at a big international outlet. She got up early, worked exhausting twelve-hour days, came home, ate, and went to bed, a concept so foreign to me I was actually a little in awe of her as I watched her do it . . . from her couch, of course.

She was a drop-dead gorgeous gal, with big blue doe eyes and long flaxen ringlets that fell softly over her ample bosoms. Anyway, she was pretty fuckin' hot. She also had a devilish machine-gun cackle that could get a whole room laughing hysterically with her and was alotta fun when she'd had a few beers. But make no mistake, she was a sergeant at arms once she got you behind closed doors. I was definitely the shit-faced Gomer Pyle to her irritated Sergeant Carter, and if she came home and found a mess in the sink or so much as a sock on the floor, it was my ass.

My brother Bill nicknamed her "the Stablizer" because she kept me in a couple of nights a week and stabilized my life to where it was livable or I would've just been drunk all the time. As much as I complained about her iron fist, I secretly loved that about her too. For chrissakes, I needed stabilizing and her TV was loaded with cable.

After a few months of stepping over me on her way to work (I'd sometimes roll off the bed in my sleep, hammered), she started getting suspicious of my late nights and began asking questions like, "I don't get it. The gig ended at eleven. Why did you get home at six in the morning again?" That's when I'd give her all the engines, Bill

Clinton–style, and say something like, "They had us play a double set, and then I had to run the gear back to the rehearsal space and then I had to talk to Ponzo 'cause he's going through a real rough time right now with Leslie, and then . . . well, then we were starving, and so we stopped at the diner on Washington, but that diner was closed so we had to go to the one on Waverly, and they were packed with all these cops and firemen and cabbies that were getting off their shifts, and they only had one waitress working so it took forever for us to get our food, and then it took even longer to get the check and then . . ."

At that point she would have that I-can't-process-all-this-shit-so-I'll-just-take-your-word-for-it-so-you'll-stop-talking look on her face and say, "Whatever, okay, but you weren't even tired when you got in. Are you doing drugs, Chris?" Then I'd give her my incredulous shocked-at-the-mere-inquiry face and say, "Babe, I had coffee at the diner," and do the embarrassed half-laugh shrug as I looked at the floor.

She'd feel bad for having offended me, hug me, tousle my hair, and say, "All right, well, no more coffee so late then, and maybe if Ponzo got home at a decent hour—hint hint—he wouldn't have these problems with Leslie." I'd exhale and say, "You're right, honey, we'll try not to be such vampires," and I'd hug her, the night-before's eight ball leaking outta my nose onto her shoulder.

Our relationship (or situation-ship as the case may have been) was kind of like *Hogan's Heroes* meets Stockholm syndrome. I was in love with my captor but my life with her consisted of one caper after another, trying to keep her from finding out who I really was.

Martha traveled a lot for her job. She'd go on these long junkets to the Far East, places like Singapore and Hong Kong, to oversee her line being put into production and would sometimes be gone for weeks at a time. During these periods I would have the apartment to myself to do whatever I pleased, enough rope for a savage hanging.

One time she left for one of these trips and within days I had turned her home into the usual late-night opium den of snaggle-toothed reprobates, drug dealers, and anyone else who still wanted to party after the bar had closed. There was no velvet rope in front of this door. If you were still drinking (and especially holding), you were in!

About ten days before she left, I had been hitting the sauce pretty hard and she had given me the ultimatum (or the "old tomato" as we referred to it in the band 'cause it happened so many times), "Clean up your act or get out." I responded by going on the wagon for a few days, just to clear a path and send her on her trip without worry, but I knew I'd be rejoining myself on the dark side as soon as the door swung shut.

Whenever I would go on the wagon our lives would become positively blissful. I'd be really thoughtful sometimes and go get her favorite dinner at Tartine, this French restaurant that she liked, and have it ready on the table when she got home. Or I'd surprise her at work with flowers and rev up the song and dance in front of her work chums (that would really put my stock through the roof). I loved doing these things, loved seeing her happy, loved being a good guy. I just couldn't sustain it, is all.

Anyway, because I had been dry a few days before she left, this time I was really shot out of a cannon and had been partying 'round the clock heroically for weeks, all the while having brief phone conversations with her early in the day to tell her I was still sober and "fighting the good fight." She would tell me she was proud of me and say with such innocence, "See? You don't have to drink to have fun, Chris."

My heart would always sink after she said that. Especially when I'd look over and see what looked like a snapshot of the massacre at Jonestown in her living room: people passed out, red keg cups clutched in their dying hands, the stench of a thousand beer-and-blow farts wafting into the bedroom, practically peeling the paint off the walls. I'd look down and notice the razor scratches from us chopping lines on her favorite CD—to the naked eye it would look like somebody really hated Alanis Morrisette and went to town on her face. That part I liked (I can't stand Alanis Morrisette). The rest just made me feel like the asshole that I knew I was. Then I'd sign off with, "I miss you, honey, hurry home." Part of me really meant that. I might be dead otherwise.

The night before she was due home from this particular trip was gonna be a big one. I had announced to everybody that I had to go back on dry land when she got home or I was gonna be homeless. So I would go out in a buzzed-to-the-beyond blaze of glory.

I couldn't have everybody back to her apartment after the bar because I had to clean the place up and make it all look spit spot, so she wouldn't be suspicious of anything. But I didn't wanna get it too clean either—that would be a dead giveaway that I'd been up to something. The point is I had to designate some time before I went to bed to get the place looking good. *I can do that drunk,* I thought, so long as I still had some gack left to stay awake.

I had a gig with Mike Tait at the Red Lion and had announced to everyone that it was gonna be my last night on the sauce (I was always making that proclamation, BTW) so I wanted to do something that would bring down the house and really put a cherry on top of this particular bender.

There were a couple of really bad movies about strippers out at the time: *Showgirls* with Elizabeth Berkley (the girl from *Saved by the Bell* all grown up in a ridiculous role) and *Striptease* starring Demi Moore. There happened to be a pole to the left of the stage at the Red Lion and as a comic stunt I'd drop my pants, wedgie myself with my tightie-whities to give that thong effect, jump on it, and flop around like a clumsy stripper as Mike and I would sing that Divinyls song "I Touch Myself," making all the Demi sexy-but-tough faces at the crowd. Everyone would get really loud and start stamping their feet and catcalling. I'd be dead stewed, knocking drinks over and shit, but the bit always killed.

On the big night, as I was leaving the house, I decided to slip on one of Martha's hot pink thongs, in lieu of my usual underwear, to surprise everybody. "Wait'll they get a load of this," I snickered.

Mike and I always front loaded a lot of drinks before we went on at the Lion and the results varied. Sometimes we got too drunk and played sloppily, other nights we'd get it done right onstage and be okay, and then there were the gigs we were too shit-faced to play at all. For this one we were just right, energetic but wobbly. We hit the stage with a good glow.

The set was going really well. The joint was jammed with the usual mix of our barfly friends and a host of German tourists who were right on board with our drunken chicanery. We'd just finished playing a rousing rendition of the Violent Femmes's "American Music," and Mike and I both knew that the gig had crescendoed to that point when it was time for "Demi."

He went into the chords and I stood up on my barstool, dropped my pants, and leaped over to the pole, wiping out a table full of drinks. The crowd went wild! Then I started doing my best Buffalo Bill from *Silence of the Lambs*, tucking my door knocker between my legs and gyrating.

"Would you fuck me . . . I'd fuck me . . . would you fuck me?" I croaked, getting right in this old German guy's grill, my thong ass thrust in his friend's face. Then I took our metal tip jug from onstage and said to him in the Buffalo Billy voice, "It puts the lotion in the basket." He was frozen with fear. Again I prodded, "It puts the lotion in the basket," thrusting the tip jug in his chest. He didn't know what to do, so I just stared him down and waited for him as the music rose with intensity, the whole crowd riveted. He wasn't sure what to say, so he started muttering sheepishly, "Is zis some kinds of joke?" As he was trying to get that out, I let it fly just like in the movie, "PUT THE FUCKIN' LOTION IN THE BASKET," startling him off his chair.

Everyone exploded laughing as I leapt back onto the pole and finished the song and dance. That underwear thing was a home run! I knew it would be. Drunks love shit like that.

It was about one-thirty A.M. when the gig ended and I got sucked into partying with Klaus (the guy I'd knocked off his chair) and his friends for a little while, but I had to cut it short 'cause I had the ti- tanic task of getting the apartment clean before Martha's arrival the next day.

She was touching down at Kennedy around noon and with traf- fic would probably be home between one and two, leaving plenty of time for me to clean up what I could that night, sleep off my hammer, and get up for another once-over of the place in the morning.

I searched the Lion for Tino (Bleeker Street's resident coke dealer) to score some blow for my cleaning detail but couldn't find him, and decided to abort that mission and leave. I backdoored everyone with- out any good-byes (a tactic used by drunks the world over). I knew that if even one person said, "C'mon, have another drink," that I would, and I was anxious to get back to being that "good guy" and wash off the top layer of degeneracy.

As I started my zag home down Bleecker and up Sixth Ave., I no- ticed how trashed I was. When you're among other nightly bombers in the forgiving atmosphere of the bar, you sometimes don't notice your state but with each step I detected more gravitational difficulty. I was fucked up, but this was just run of the mill. It would soon get worse.

As I was making my way up Sixth to West Fourth, I started noticing all these trailers, a big battalion of lights, cranes, and all that shit you see when people are filming in New York—a fairly common thing but this looked bigger than most. I was curious, but it wasn't enough to make me stop. I had cleaning to do.

As I was backpedaling onto Jones Street still checking it out, I turned and bumped into this big fat black guy, sixtyish, with a smile like a month-old jack-o'-lantern. "Oh sorry, man, I was looking back at all that gear they have over there," I said apologetically, realizing this guy was skunked out of his fuckin' mind.

"That's OK, I saw what you was doin'. I was doin' the same thing. They shootin' a Whoopi Goldberg movie over there. I been watchin' it for about three hours now. Get this, in this movie she's supposed to be the coach of the Knicks! Can you imagine that nasty, rug-munchin' ho coachin' the Knicks? Whose writin' that shit?"

I realized pretty quickly that he was completely insane, but he was really hilarious and that goes a long way with me so I decided to engage him. "You mean to tell me you have it on fact that Whoopi Goldberg is a lesbian?" I asked him, knowing there would be something good coming back. "I dunno, I heard maybe. She got so much money she could probably go get herself fucked in the gorilla cages at the Bronx Zoo if she wants. Probably not a bad idea neither, for once she'd wake up and be the good-lookin' one," he said as he exploded into a louder-than-bombs laugh that gave way to a gravelly and consumptive cough that sounded like a storefront window shattering. I couldn't get enough of that laugh. He said, "C'mon, let's go have a look, they filmin' somethin' right now."

He'd more than earned his stripes with me and I thought, *Well, it's right in my 'hood so a few minutes with him won't matter.* Besides, he was a vicious freak and I've learned never to say no to them when potential adventure is concerned. They are natural sherpas in the world of human amusement.

"C'mon, Gary, I got us a perfect spot to watch from on that stoop.

We just enough outta the way where nobody gonna push us out, but can see all the action perfect," he said, pointing. "Gary?" I said kinda dumbfounded, not knowing why he called me that. Then I realized he'd gotten the name off of the red Budweiser jacket I had on, given to me by a driver for Budweiser who'd come to a gig of ours upstate.

"That's your name, ain't it?" he asked with a tone of incredulity. He didn't know from fashion trends of the mid-nineties when a lot of people were wearing working-guy shirts with other people's names on them. That's not the reason I opted for it. I just thought it was a cool-lookin' red with Budweiser on it; but when I tried to explain the trend to him and how it wasn't really my name, he interrupted me midsentence. "We ain't got time for this, Gary. Whoopi gonna be comin' out her trailer in just a few minutes. I overheard one of them coffee peons talkin'. We got to get to the spot. You got some money for some beverages?" "Yeah, yeah, what do you want?" I asked obligingly. "Colt Forty-five . . . good lookin' out . . . you my nigga, Gary," he yelled down the block as I entered the bodega on Sixth. *I'll just let him call me Gary*, I thought. *It's probably best he doesn't have my real name anyway.*

Then I popped back out and called to him, "I didn't catch your name." "Xavier Sonsire the third," he growled with great importance, "but you can call me Sonny or Son, just don't call me homeless cuz I can turn this shit around anytime, Gary, specially if I meet a nice lady," he said with the pride of a true veteran of the streets erupting into his bronchial laugh. Jesus, we weren't even that different. The only thing that separated him from me was Martha's keys.

So we sat on these church stairs watching them do take after take of Whoopi strolling with someone, chatting, and drinking a coffee. I kept making deli runs and getting Sonny his forty of Colt and grabbing myself a couple of Bud tall boys.

"What's your story, Gary, that you can take time outta your busy schedule to sit out here and get an old black man drunk?" he asked with a bit of suspicion. "You ain't a fag, is you?" "Me? No, I'm just an alcoholic who likes to feel better than the people he's drinkin' with," I said with a smile curling up but trying to keep a straight face. "You were the only guy I could find."

He looked puzzled by the statement at first, staring out into space;

then he looked over at me and we both busted into uncontrollable laughing fits. Just when we thought we were over it, one of us would think of it again and it would all start over. When you're a drunk, there's no greater feeling than meeting another drunk. They just know.

Sonny was laughing so hard that his cough morphed into a heavy wheeze so I offered him my asthma inhaler. I'd had asthma as a kid and didn't really have it anymore but carried that thing around anyway cuz I would puff on it occasionally for adrenaline before I went onstage. He waved me off at first. "Nah . . . well, what is that shit?" he asked curiously. I said, "It's just an inhalant to help clear your lungs. Here, I'll show you how to use it." I cocked my head back and sucked up the mist, demonstrating, and then he did. "Damn, I think that did something," he said, handing it back to me. "It's all right," I said, "keep it."

"So what's your deal, Sonny?" I asked him, hoping for a long answer 'cause I was good and stewed at this point and no longer felt like talking. "Well, Gary, I'm originally from Mississippi, born to a sharecropper, left home when I was eleven, and started ridin' the rails in pursuit of the American fuckin' dream," he volleyed back with a bit of sarcasm. I gave him a look that cried bullshit and we hung in that moment staring at each other, all stretched out on the stairs leaning back on our elbows. Then he cracked. "What do you want, a story? *Moby-Dick* or some shit? I'm a fuckup just like you, Gary. Look at you in them ripped-up motherfuckin' plaid pants. Looks like you just crawled out of a goddamn Goodwill box or some shit. You know you out here too, Gary, though I suspect you got somewheres to go after this but I'd be willing to bet it ain't your place."

"You'd win that bet," I told him. "See?" he chided. "Stay in your lane, Gary, and I'll stay in mine." I'd forgotten that though we were kin, drunks can be very private people. We house a lot of shame, guilt, and regret, which doesn't really fall under the heading of small talk. Some alkies relish the opportunity to give their life stories; neither one of us was that type.

I made another beer run and now we were *really* well oiled when Sonny started having major continuity problems with the director and decided to address the issue head-on with the camera crew. "Have you motherfuckers lost all sense? Whoopi just had a cup of coffee in her hand, walkin' and talkin', right? Now you shootin' her down the block but where's the coffee? What'd it just magically disappear or vaporize or some shit? People don't drink hot motherfuckin' coffee in one gulp. They sip it. You don't think people watchin' are gonna notice that shit and say, 'WHERE THE FUCK IS THAT COFFEE SHE WAS DRINKIN'?' " he screamed at them, abruptly running right out into the middle of everything they were doing. "I've had it with you people. Y'all have been making mistakes like this all night and Miss Goldberg deserves better." "I thought you didn't like Whoopi," I said, tugging on his sleeve. "She all right, deserves better than these hacks," he said, point-blanking the camera guys. Just when I thought I knew Sonny he trotted out a whole new side . . . Sonny the perfectionist! I looked at him again and could see that something had snapped in him.

With that, two gigantic, stone-faced Teamsters appeared quickly to escort us off the block. One of 'em looked like a young Luca Brasi from *The Godfather*. "Don't you fuckin' put your hands on me or we gonna have real problems then," Sonny warned them. "You know Sugar Ray Robinson? I'll make you wish you was fightin' him." The one that looked like Luca Brasi laughed and said, "Oh yeah, bring him on, he's dead." "Pound for pound, greatest fighter ever, and dead or not, just like me, he can still whup yo ass," Sonny retorted, looking back over his shoulder at them, seeing how big they were, and losing a little steam. "You can put your hands all over me," I slurred. "I kinda like it." Sonny snapped, "You would, Gary. I knew you was a fuckin' faggot."

The sun was rearing its shiny ugly head, reminding me of the doom that would befall me if I didn't get the apartment cleaned up. I said a quick good-bye to Sonny, gave him my last crumpled-up ten, and said, "Go with God, Eggzzzzzzavier the turd! May your travels lead you home . . . or somewhere good . . . or wherever the hell it's gonna be easiest for you." He responded anxiously, "Thanks, Gary. You all right. Gonna break the day down by the river," and off he went without looking back. I kept waving to him from the stairs of Martha's building even after he disappeared from sight around the corner.

I felt a little sad watching him walk off like that, me having a nice place to sleep and all. I hadn't noticed that he had a little limp to him but he still strutted proudly. I stayed frozen atop the stoop with the keys in my hand, lost in an altruistic daydream, the kind you only get when you're drunk. I thought, maybe Martha and I will befriend Sonny and have him over for dinner once in a while. Martha might even be able to get him a job in the clothing warehouse or at one of the retail stores or something. He was such a smart guy too, maybe we could get him into a city college. I'd heard about programs like that where the city would pay. I envisioned Martha and me, beaming with pride, applauding in an auditorium full of people while Sonny accepted his diploma, pumping his fist in the air and calling out to me in the crowd, "You believed in me when I couldn't believe in myself, Gary." He'd know my real name by then but'd still call me Gary out of affection. *Yeah, we'll clean him up and get him back on his feet,* I thought—this rehabilitation being masterminded by the guy standing on the stairs of his girlfriend's building at six in the morning with his face falling off, never having finished college himself, so hammered he can't get the key in the door, his own name not ever having appeared on a lease anywhere.

Wasn't Martha lucky to have me? I thought. *All those great things I wanted to do for Sonny?* You have to have a really big heart to wanna do those things and I did, goddammit. "I genuinely care about people and that's what makes me different," I said to myself, one hand on the key in the door, the other on my cock, pissing over the railing onto the metal garbage-can lids below, causing a thunderous *rat-a-tat-tat* in front of the neighbors' downstairs apartment. *What the fuck was that noise?* I recall thinking as I finally got the key turned in the door and went in the building.

That was the essence of my life's philosophy right there. I always thought I was being judged on my intentions, not my actions. Sure, I did stupid and selfish things, and yes, I drank and drugged too much, but my heart, my heart's always in the right place and isn't that all that matters? I'm inherently good, I just do bad things—and only to myself and in the name of a good time—never hurting or endangering anyone else.

Anyway, it was time to clean up Martha's apartment after repeatedly destroying it for two weeks with reckless parties and jeopardizing her lease with all of the neighbors' complaints. Listen, I know what you're thinking, but those people were lame-os. They got all bent because of some late-night noise and something about someone taking a shit in the hallway. Don't blame me. I can't be everywhere all the time. You see what I just did there? That was my everyday mind-set. *Nothing* was ever my fault. Either I had bad luck or people were being uptight.

I entered the apartment and, as my first order of business, tried to stuff a big empty pizza box into a tiny wastepaper basket. I'd crumple it up and stamp it in with my foot and it would miraculously reanimate inside the can and force its way back out in seconds as if it had never been folded up. I'd squish it again with great force and place it back in and watch it regain life, unfold itself, and pop out again.

After losing my battle with that box I surveyed the rest of the insurmountable mess around the room from a drunken tilt, leaned up against the wall, and let my body slide down it into a sitting position, and that's where I'd break the day, passed out.

The next memory I have I'm out in the hall in nothing but a powder-pink thong at about eight-thirty in the morning with the door slamming behind me, locking me out. There are people out there on their way to work and shit; horribly bad timing for another sleepwalking episode.

My dad's comment, "Go upstairs to our bedroom and maybe you'll piece it together," flashed through my head as I stared down at the bramble bush of pubes poking out from behind my powder-pink gunnysack. "Shit . . . shit . . . SHITTTTTT," I screamed frantically, jiggling the doorknob. I understood the part about the somnambulant stroll into the corridor, but how the hell did I get outta my clothes? What am I, fuckin' Houdini in my sleep? Then it occurred to me that none of that mattered now. How was I gonna get back in the apartment with no one seeing me? That was the question.

I remembered that the super, this Russian guy named Ivan, lived in 12C and Martha's apartment was 13C. He didn't like me 'cause he always saw me coming in late at night, bouncing off the walls, and I suspected that he had a bit of a thing for Martha. He'd always make excuses to come into the place when I wasn't there and a couple of times I came home to find him telling her something about how the heat worked. She'd flash me a look like, "What's he doing here, I already know this." When he'd leave, he'd always say to her, "Rrre-member, I'm rrright downsteerrrs from you eef you have prawblem." Then he'd give me the ol' skunk eye and leave.

My plan was to sneak down the stairs, throw myself on Ivan's mercy, have him open the door for me with his super keys, and get right to cleaning so Martha would think I was still "fighting the good fight."

I got in front of his door and started pounding on it. "Ivan, open up, dude . . . it's me, Chris . . . Martha's Chris from 13C. C'mon, dude, I know you're in there! I can hear the cartoons . . . what's that, *The Bugs Bunny/Roadrunner Hour?* I watch that too! C'mon, beep beep, I'm out here. Ivan, open up!"

I heard some fidgeting around and the TV volume got lowered, but he still wasn't coming to the door. I looked down at the thong and my dirty bare feet, and there was a window that acted like a mirror to the left of me. I could see my hair looked like Medusa's and my eyes were all bloodshot, so I started getting apologetic. "Dude . . . um . . . I know this looks bad but I can explain it. I . . . uh . . . well, I have . . . I guess a bad sleepwalking problem . . . um . . . uh . . . which is further compounded by . . . I dunno . . . I guess what some might call a drinking problem. I . . . which . . . um . . . doesn't really explain the thong but . . . uh . . ."

Suddenly the door flies open, stopping short at the chain lock. I lean my head on the door jamb, my legs crossed in what I perceive to be too feminine a stance so I uncross them quickly, stand up straight, and say, "Thank you, thank you, oh my God, THANK YOU! I re-ally owe you one, buddy." Then I see just a nose poke out and with it comes this lispy, thin, and very afraid voice: "I'd love to help you but I'm not the super. My name is Ralph and this is 12C. Ivan lives in 11C." "Oh, sorry, man, go back to your cartoons," I said, backing away from the door.

I barreled down the stairs, stopping on the landing to peer around the railing. No one was there so I started pounding on Ivan's door. Nothing. *Shit, he must be in the basement,* I thought.

The only way to the basement was via the elevator. I didn't really feel like getting in there during rush hour, but Ivan was my only shot so I had to brave it.

I pressed the button and hid to the side so if there were people already in there I could see them when the doors opened, ditch it, and grab the next one.

The doors opened and there was no one inside so I gingerly got in and started sweatin' it. I watched intensely as the light for each floor flashed, willing that light to keep moving and talking to myself out loud like a deranged craps player. "Ten, okay, we got past ten, now gimme nine . . . all right . . . we're past nine, baby, now let's cruise through eight . . . *yes* . . . just seven more floors to go, lucky number seven . . . c'mon seven . . . yeah . . . through seven . . . I think I'm gonna make it. . . . People this low will probably opt for the stairs. . . . I'm gonna make it! Here we go with six . . . six . . . six? SIXXXXXXX!"

I was staring at the light stuck on six, trying to wave it past with both my arms, jumping up and down à la Carlton Fisk in the '75 World Series but it was no use. The doors opened and this guy and his wife, both in their mid-thirties and in power suits, got on.

I find in these situations the less said, the better, so after the initial shock of seeing me cowering in the corner of the elevator with my hands cupped over my bright pink nuts, they made no attempt at conversation and I felt no need to provide any from my end. I saw the woman's shoulders going up and down a little as she stared at the floor. She was having a good giggle over it. The guy looked horrified.

My little experiment with telekinesis got even worse 'cause the fuckin' thing stopped on two more floors and let even more people on. By the time we got to the bottom the elevator was pretty well full but I didn't care anymore by then. Once one person saw me it got easier with each one after. Don't ask me why.

They all got out on the ground floor and I rode down to the basement where I was unsuccessful in my attempt to find Ivan. Though I did have the exciting revelation that my penis glowed in the dark— rather my underwear did. I mean her underwear.

Back into the elevator I went, dutifully, like an astronaut inviting whatever peril remained. Of course, it stopped on the ground floor where little Jimmy and his Jamaican nanny got on.

Jimmy was about four. Standing there defiantly in nothing but a pair of panties with my hair poofing out like Sideshow Bob's from *The Simpsons*, I think I looked like a cartoon character to him 'cause he couldn't take his eyes off me. "Look away, Jeeemy, dis mon has got troubles but dey not ours," the nanny ordered him, staring straight ahead at the elevator doors. "Yeah, you said it, sister," I grumbled.

I got out on thirteen and resigned myself to curling up in front of Martha's door like a lost cat and being busted when she got home in a few hours. After all, I was a fake and it might feel good to just tell the truth, take my lumps, and live with whatever sentence she handed down. If she threw me out, then at least I wouldn't have to feel guilty about ruining her life anymore.

My collective hangover from the past two weeks was starting to kick in and combined with the anxiety brought on by my hallway thong fright was creating the perfect storm. So I puked out a window down into the alleyway and sprawled across Martha's welcome mat. There wasn't enough room for my whole body to stretch out so my legs ran halfway up the wall, forcing the thong to explore even deeper routes up my ass. I went to sleep looking like some sort of self-fellating pervert-contortionist.

About ten minutes later I awoke to Becky coming out of her place. Her door slammed and my legs flopped down. She turned around to put her keys in her purse and almost tripped over me. "AAAAAAAHHHHHH!!!!! What the hell are you doing out here? You scared the ever livin' shit outta me!" "I got locked out. I was sleepwalking and must've opened the door. Do you have Martha's keys?" I begged, knowing she might say no even if she did have them. "No . . . you look like you were gang-raped by a bunch of sailors at Julius's," she shrieked, referring to the vicious gay bar in our neighborhood. "Well, can you get out your Amex and card the door then? C'mon, I've seen you do it," I humbly and desperately requested.

I'd watched her perform this little diddy once on her own door when she was locked out, sliding an Amex card up between the door jamb and the door to trick the lock.

"Why should I, Chris? It would be better for her to come home and find you like this, as you really are—drunk, lying, scheming. All the things I tell her you are and what does she do when I bring all this to her attention? She immediately defends you. Oh, you don't know him. He's really sweet. He's just really loud around people but there's a more tender side. . . . BULLSHIT, this is the real you, right now. Out in the hall with only pink dental floss covering your balls, which by the way I'm too afraid to even ask you about, groveling, helpless, still smashed, and asking for a favor. That's the person I'd one day love for her to meet. You're a real catch, buddy," she said, shaking her head. But the satisfaction of having told me off seemed to soften her.

"So you'll do it then," I asked, sensing she would. "You're un-believable." She shrugged, begrudgingly opening the door (with the dexterity of a professional thief I might add). "I really should let her find you like this but if Ivan finds you first she could get kicked out of the building for this little caper. That's what they do when people let their pets roam free in the building, and believe me, you look worse than a rabid collie."

I could see she was proud of herself for reeling off that last line. I just stood there and took it like a man, picking the undies out of my ass. We became friends in that moment. I can't explain it. She had just verbally lacerated me and her tone was nothing short of bitchy, but all of a sudden I liked her and not just because she was bailing me out. She was a really smart and funny chick and I could tell she liked me too, as strange as that may sound.

Becky held open the door for me to enter, and when I passed under her arm, I turned around. "She really said I was tender?" She shook her head again. "Unbelievable." "Listen, you and I can keep this just between us, right? I mean there's no sense in getting Martha all jammed up after such a long and arduous trip," I asked, appealing to her friendship with Martha but really just trying to save my own ass—bullshit that she could see right through. She let go of the door and as it swung shut on me all I saw was the back of her head and all I heard was, "Yeah, right."

So it was a disaster narrowly averted (if you discount the emotional turmoil and the public humiliation) but now it was on to the business at hand.

The place looked like a giant drug-and-alcohol-addled hamster lived there, the floor covered in the usual garbage of pizza boxes, sandwich wrappers, makeshift tinfoil pipes, and dented soda cans (for smoking weed), empty plastic cocaine bags, condom wrappers, which actually disgusted me cuz there'd been some toothless cretins in that living room and I had been unaware of any sex, articles of clothing that people had left behind including bras, jackets, a marching band's majorette hat—where that came from I'll never know—your basic smorgasbord wreckage of blackout partying. Given one more day, I might've had a rummage sale. If Martha were to see this, there was no doubt in my mind that she'd have a grand mal seizure on the spot and spend the rest of her life catatonic, occasionally muttering the words, "Fuckin' Chris."

The smell was a combination of B.O., the stale odor of empty booze bottles, and old cigarette smoke. It was kind of like the Jacksonville Jaguars locker room at halftime meets the Blarney Stone bar in Times Square. I had my work cut out for me.

I yanked off the thong, threw on some boxers, got dressed, and went to the store for supplies. It was T minus two hours till her arrival. I got garbage bags, cleaning stuff, flowers, everything.

I was a cleaning cyclone, manic and thorough. I sprayed disinfectant everywhere and after a while had the place smelling like a hospital. I didn't want it to look too clean so I left some clothes lying around and newspapers on the couch. If it were too spotless, she'd get suspicious and pick me off of first base by looking closely at my face for guilt—and finding it. I panned around the room one last time and exhaled. I'd scaled the garbage version of Everest and lived to tell. I couldn't have been more ready.

She buzzed and I went down and grabbed her bags. She was in a foul mood. "I think I wanna quit my job," she said. "Really? What happened?" I answered, playing the role of the conscientious boyfriend, ever so grateful for a topic that would get the focus on something other than me. Martha had a real snout for smells. I hadn't pulled this off yet and was still nervous.

"They don't fucking appreciate me and what I do for them and I'm fucking sick of it," she snapped, looking way overtired. "How was the flight?" I asked carefully. "It was all right, same shit, I'm exhausted. I just wanna go get some lunch, come back here, and go to bed." "Well, then let's do that," I said agreeably.

"Oh my God, you cleaned," she said, her face relaxing. "I gave it a once-over, yeah, but I've been on top of it," I shot back, as I fake fiddled with the stereo equalizer, The Clash's "Police & Thieves" playing softly through it.

"What's this?" she asked, her tone abruptly shifting. I was afraid to look up. I knew there had to be something unexplainable on the other end of that question. I braced myself, turned off the stereo, and answered back without looking, "What?"

Our eyes met, she pointed in the direction of the exercise bicycle, and there dangling from its handlebars was a big, ugly, shimmering, purple bra. I racked my brain (no pun, I promise) for a sound explanation, not just a temporary deflection but a lie that would hold water in the future. I thought long and hard and finally came up with "What's that?" the tried-and-true question-with-a-question time buyer.

"It's a bra, dumbass, can't you see that?" I was feeling the flame big time. "Well, from here it just looks like the bike grew some purple tits." A cold wind vibrated the window as we stood across the room staring at each other, sweat gathering behind my ears. Then a miracle happened.

"I haven't seen this since freshman year of college! Where the hell did you find it?" She laughed, holding it up. "It fell out when I was pulling something outta the closet the other day and I thought I'd surprise you with it," I said, sticking the landing. "You're hilarious, come here and kiss me," she requested. I did, long and hard and for ten full minutes.

We lay in bed naked and engaged in some light pillow talk." What about you? Have you been a good boy? You look tired," she probed but I could tell she wasn't really looking for anything. "I played last night and couldn't sleep when I got home," I said. "Awwwwww, you missed me? Can't sleep in the bed without me?" she teased. "That's it." I smiled back. "Liar," she said, placing her hand on my forehead and thrusting me back down onto the pillow. "Let's go get some tacos." "Cool," I muttered queasily, already throwing them up in my head.

On the way out she grabbed an empty cocaine wrapper from atop the TV set and threw it away. "How many of those little packies that extra buttons come in do we have laying around here? I'm always finding them everywhere." "I don't know, hon, I never noticed," I said, tying my sneaker and thanking the universe for lying for me, love when that happens.

We started strolling down Jones Street on the way to this Mexican joint on Sixth Avenue. "So, you still haven't had a drink or anything?" she asked, her eyes squinting a little, looking for a confession but wanting to believe. "Nope, nothing," I said proudly. "Not a thing, not even a beer?" Her eyes widened in disbelief. "Just cigarettes and coffee, Ma. I'm towin' the line this time," I replied, serving up a jokie Southern drawl to keep things light. " 'Cause when you kissed me at first I thought you smelled a little like booze," she said. Curse that goddamn sniffer of hers! "No, what you're smelling is the Listerine . . . it's got booze in it to disinfect. Gots to have a clean mouth fer my baby," I said back in the Southern voice.

"Okay, well I'm proud of you, babe. I know how hard it must be with those lunatic friends of yours always wanting you to drink. They love for you to be their drunken-clown ringleader so they can feel better about their own going-nowhere lives. But nobody sees what I see when you come home, when you're either throwing up in the sink or having a loud debate with the drapes. You're sick, ya know," she said in a loving but authoritative tone.

"I know, but I'm on the upswing now and starting to feel good. I'm actually starting to meet some new people too, ya know, ones that don't really party. I've been meeting them over at the Strand Bookstore. We have coffee, discussions about books, everything," I said with the calm of a consummate actor.

This was easily the fattest lie that had ever passed my lips. If you turned me upside down by my feet and shook all the friends outta my pockets, you wouldn't find one that didn't have a morose drinking problem and I wasn't really interested in finding any that didn't.

"Really? That's awesome," she said with delighted surprise. "You know this is like you're being born again, Chris; a whole new you is gonna emerge from this and I, for one, can't wait to meet that person." Her face was so full of hope and conviction that even I started believing that it was true. I thought to myself, as I looked at how happy she was with the fake new me, *She already believes it and she's making some good points . . . maybe I'll give this sobriety thing a shot for real. It'll be great. I'll get in shape. I'll eat right. Maybe I'll even quit smok-*

ing too, 'cause that'll only help my voice. Yeah, I think I'm gonna do it. In fact, I am gonna do it!

Just as the triumphant *Rocky* montage music was being cued in my head to go with my ambitious new beginning, I looked past my lovely girlfriend's smiling face and over her shoulder I saw an off-kilter, piss-drunk, old black man playing frogger across Sixth Avenue traffic, cabs whizzing past him, drivers leaning on their horns almost hitting him. His eyes were buggin' out of his head as he was waving his hands spastically to get my attention. "HEY, GAREEEEEEEEE . . . GAREEEEEE . . . YOU SOBER YET!?"

"Who the hell is that? Is he yelling to you? Do you know him?" Martha was back to her interrogative tone, expecting the worst. "Is my name Gary? You know those homeless people . . . they're all crazy," I said, hustling her down the block at double clicks, subtly glancing back over my shoulder to see where Sonny was. I couldn't locate him so I just kept hurrying us along and kept my eyes forward. As we were rounding the corner to safety, I heard him scream out, "ATTA BOY, GARY! I KNEW YOU HAD A GIRL SOMEWHERES . . . GOOD FOR YOU . . . GOOD FOR YOU."

So life resumed as it had been in the days before she left for her trip, with me on the wagon. Becky didn't even narc me out for the hallway incident. I think the ridiculousness of it somehow earned her respect, or as she said, she didn't wanna hurt Martha. Either way I was in the clear. The only difference was, this time I didn't really stay booze free.

I wanted to, but wanting to and actually doing it are vastly different things. I went underground, sneaking drinks and trying to pull up on the throttle before reaching a point of drunkenness. During this short period I stayed out of trouble, never getting fucked up enough to get caught but I do think Martha let me slide a few times knowing I was trying. She never said anything, but the house rules were still emphatically NO DRINKING.

About a month later Martha and I were having dinner at Tartine (on her, of course) and she said, "I'd love a glass of wine right now but I don't want you staring at me like I'm denying you water in the desert." "Do I do that?" I asked. "Oh yeah, you do it full on with the puppy-dog eyes and everything. You don't know that you do that?" "No," I said, really not knowing. "Well, then, why don't we just get some?" I suggested carefully. "Look, I've proven I can quit and it'll be romantic . . . we can pretend we're in Paris," said the serpent to the little birdie. "All right," she said with excited trepidation, "but I'm counting your glasses." "No problem," said the serpent back to the little birdie . . . and to himself.

. . .

The wedding of Martha's sister, Hadley, had been looming for months. Martha was the maid of honor and with that came the frazzled nerves that befall every woman thrust into that role. There were lots of hour-long phone calls with her sister, discussing every last detail—enough to asphyxiate even Martha Stewart, let alone my Martha. She'd get off the phone, look at me, and just exhale, "Uuuuugggghhhh, this wedding," and go in the other room.

She mentioned on several occasions that I was to be on my best behavior because I'd be meeting her family for the first time, giving me a clear indication that her knees were knockin' about that. Once I'd overheard her on the phone with her folks, saying, "He's a musician." Then she stopped talking abruptly and just listened. I knew what that meant.

Her dad was a retired general who now worked as a consultant to a company that manufactured weapons and sold them back to the military. He was just to the right of Barry Goldwater. Her mom was a nice conservative housewife who threw ladies' luncheons and used time-honored and intimate phrases with her loved ones like "That's nice, dear." She looked a lot like Betty Ford, which completely freaked me out, for obvious reasons.

Martha's family hailed from Bethesda, Maryland, but the wedding was in the groom's hometown of Charleston, South Carolina. He was from a prominent conservative family. He might've *been* the groom but I was the one being groomed, it seemed. Martha packed my bag for the weekend with khakis and all this other preppy shit I wouldn't in a million years wear. I looked like the shaggy-haired, unkempt guy with bags under his eyes on the Dockers ads that you just know has an eight ball of blow in the pocket his hand is in and doesn't really wear Dockers. Martha was doing everything she could so I'd pass muster with these people, God bless her.

On the flight down I ordered a beer and Martha shot me a warning look and then just appeared pensive. She turned to me and blurted, "I don't think you should be yourself down here." I said, "Whattya mean?" "Well, I really don't think their gonna *get* your sense of humor is all," she said, not even caring if it offended me, which it did. "You don't think I know how to act around rich people?" I responded defensively. "I've been around richer people than this, I'm from Huntington. We have captains of industry in my town that could buy, sell, and piss on these people," I exclaimed, loud and proud, not just of my town but also my turn of phrase "buy, sell, and piss."

"I'm not saying you don't know how to act around rich people. I'm saying you don't know how to act around people people," she said wryly. "You're loud and fucked up and most of the time oblivious to what's going on around you." "Then why do I have so many friends?" I asked, thinking I'd stymied her. "Cuz they're freaks, they're just as fucked up, and they think that shit you do is funny," she said, ramming her point home. Then there was silence.

A minute later I said, "Well, maybe I think anyone who doesn't think I'm funny . . . that they're fucked up . . . ya know . . . that they're the ones with the problem and that I'm just being me . . . me and free . . . What would you say to that?" "I'd say eat your Salisbury steak, you idiot," she said, laughing at my dramatic speech and eating one of the wayward french fries that had slid off my plate onto my tray. My feelings were hurt. "Well, maybe I won't talk at all." She said, "Yeah, let's try that," and laughed again.

Little did she know that I *was* gonna try that.

We got there in time for the rehearsal dinner. I wore the goddamn beige khakis and white button-down shirt she laid out on the bed, which might as well have been fuckin' Garanimals 'cause it felt like my first day of kindergarten. I smiled and said nothing.

We got to the dinner, which was an expectedly staid affair in some hoity-toity country club, and still I smiled and said nothing. I just acted shy and well mannered and gave her everything she wanted out of spite, thinking that at some point she'd realize what I was doing and tell me that I'd won, that she was wrong, and please go back to being my charmingly loud and quirky self. Instead she fuckin' *loved* IT! She said her parents thought I was "a nice young man" and to keep it up, I was doing great.

Lots of people might be put off by something like this but not me. They might say, "Well if she doesn't love me for me then I'm outta here," but I'm such a people pleaser, and she was so beyond thrilled, that I just decided to go with it. It was nice seeing her that happy. I could play the part of shy and unassuming for a weekend, why not?

The wedding the next day was sheer and unspeakable torture. Just stuffed shirts as far as the eye could see, not a live wire in the place. Usually you can find that one other guy who's there against his will to commiserate with but not here. The guys were all married off or engaged and loving it. To them this was the event of the season.

The best man gave his toast and I remember him saying, "When Tom [the groom] plays golf with us, nobody on the course refers to him as Tom anymore. Out there everybody calls him Paul Bunyon 'cause he's always in the woods," and the entire reception exploded laughing. Who the hell were these people? Who was the band gonna be, Pat Boone's? I panned around and for a moment I thought maybe the plane had crashed and that I was actually in hell, damned for all eternity in a room full of these folks, terminally cemented in the role of smiling mute. The worst part was that I knew, on some level, that I deserved it.

After four excruciating hours of this (power drinking the whole time), the wedding finally ended. We said our good-byes to the happy new couple and went to a bar called Warbly's with a bunch of people from the wedding for a nightcap.

So I was standing in Warbly's with the same fuckin' people, still bored outta my tits, when I heard a big commotion over in the corner. I looked down the bar and I saw about twelve rodeo clowns, whooping it up in the back of the bar in their rodeo attire: the noses, the riding chaps, the funny hats, the whole deal. Now, I'd had a long day and I *wanted in* . . . rodeo clowns, the Super Bowl of vicious freaks!

I kept looking over there and then I ever so slowly, ever so slyly, slid my glass down the bar, periodically looking back at Martha, who was deep into a conversation with one of the merps from the wedding. So I kept sliding . . . sliding . . . turning around again . . . sliding . . . *and I was in!*

I laughed along with their stories, on the outskirts of their circle, just playing it cool. They were all talking about a show they'd just done for the Founder's Day parade in the town square, when the head rodeo clown, Clem, noticed me. "Where you from, boy? I saw you lookin' over here a bunch a times from them people you was with. . . . You looked fuckin' miserable." Well, I told him I was from New York and that·was all I had to say. Clem went wild. "Goddamn, New York . . . line 'em up . . . we got us a miserable bastard from New York here we gotta cheer up . . . You like tequeelar? Yeah, I know you like tequeelar . . . line 'em up," he screamed and pounded on the bar.

Clem was truly something to behold. He was reminiscent of Slim Pickens in a younger day, slightly bow-legged, barrel-chested with a pot belly, a weathered face, and a golf ball–size cud of chewing tobacco in his mouth. If you called central casting looking for an amped-up rodeo clown, you couldn't do better.

His sidekicks were more than complementary. There was Ty or "Ty Quan Do" as Clem called him. He was a string bean of a man, with one of those faces you see in documentaries about the Dust Bowl during the Great Depression. Clem said, "We call him Ty Quan Do 'cause he's prone to gittin' in fights when he's drunk and he tries to pull that Karate Kid shit on 'em, waxin' on and waxin' off and then his opponent just mops the floor with him every time."

His other wing was flanked by Li'l Lou, who was about jockey size with what looked like black shoe polish in his hair and an old-timey curly-cue mustache. I'd put him at about fifty. I said to Clem, "What does Li'l Lou do for you guys, help train the horses?" He glanced over at him. "Oh him . . . we just fling him." "Fling?" "Yeah, I'll show you," and with that Clem picked him up and whipped him fifteen feet across the room, where he took out a table full of empty Bud bottles like bowling pins before skidding off and face-planting into the wall. Seeing this, Clem yelled out to the whole bar, "Steee-rike."

I ran over to the corner to help Li'l Lou up. He let me at first, and then saw his buddies watching and gave me the classic I-don't-need-anyone's-help arm yank back. Then Clem grabbed him and said, "Come here, you. What do you want a shot of, you daredevil motherfucker? Come on, New York, you too. What do you want a shot of?" I was gonna say Jameson's but before I could get it out, Clem shouted, "Cuervo it is then," pulling both me and Li'l Lou into headlocks on each side of him. I said to Clem, "Well, now I know you fling him but how is this used in the rodeo?" "Who him? He ain't in the rodeo, he's just a drinkin' buddy."

So I was partying with these rodeo clowns and feeling like God had smiled on me for being a good boy at the wedding and then my luck got even better. I saw Clem go to his nose with some exaggerated sniffles, then excuse himself to the bathroom. That could only mean one thing.

I gave it a second and then trailed him into the bathroom. All I saw was his rodeo clown hat protruding from the top of the stall and all I heard was keys jingling and this "snifffffff . . . um . . . oh . . . sniffffffffff . . . yeah . . . That is it!"

> *Me:* "Clem?"
> *Clem:* "That you, New York?"
> *Me:* "The kid can't fly on only one wing, Clem, you know that."
> *Clem:* "Huh HAAAAW . . . Truer words never spoke. . . . I'm gonna set you up, New York."

The stall door flew open and out came Clem with a powdered doughnut of cocaine residue all over his red rodeo clown nose. I said, "Why don't you just take the nose off?" "It's a pain in the ass keep taking it on and off and on and off . . . Lemme set you up with a bump," said Clem with a boyish excitement.

He pulled out his huge ring of keys—there must've been five hundred keys on there—and produced a key six inches long, two inches wide. "This one's fer openin' up the big trailer." He then plunged it into the biggest pouch of blow I've ever seen in my entire life, pulled it out, and there was enough gack on this key to choke every elephant they had down there at that parade.

We were out in the middle of the bathroom floor and my head was on a swivel, looking in all directions. I was a little nervous because the door to the men's room was ajar and you could kinda see the line for the ladies' room on the other side of the hall. Clem said, "Don't worry, New York . . . ain't nobody coming in here."

So Clem had pulled the blow out of the bag onto this gigantic key, holding it in front of his massive Texas longhorn belt buckle, unable to move his hand at all because there was too much piled on the key, and he said he didn't want to spill any. So to get it I had to get on one knee . . .

So now I was about to take this hit of blow that could very well kill me. I had Clem baiting me, "C'mon . . . come on, boy . . . you can do it . . . ," feeding me blow and talking to me like I'm some kind of dolphin he's training. I could almost picture him commanding me, "Swim to the key!" I couldn't seem to find the right angle to begin this ominous and herculean snort so I kept having these false starts with it, creating a bobbinglike motion. Clem tried to help me by wrapping his left hand around the back of my head and shoving the key in closer under my nose and saying, "C'mon, it'll sting at first but then you got to just keep goin' till you get to the end. I'm here to help ya." Starting to get the picture yet?

Suddenly I heard something behind me and felt a presence. I turned around and there, framed in the doorway with her arms folded and her mouth agape, was Martha, who must've inched her way up the ladies' room line, heard me in there, and decided to investigate. She'd never even seen drugs, so she wasn't quite sure what she was lookin' at. What she was seeing was me down on one knee, in a dirty bathroom, in South Carolina, with a rodeo clown standing over me with his hand draped around the back of my head, urging me, "C'mon . . . you're gonna be happy you did this now . . . go and git it . . . no pain, no gain."

So I had a decision to make. I looked up at her, turned around and looked back at Clem, motioning for me to hurry up and do it, looked back at her, then back at Clem again, jammed my left index finger into the side of my left nostril, buried my right nostril in the key, exhaled, snorted up the line, *Sniffffffffffffffff,* wheeled around to her, my face looking like a freshly floured cutlet, and said, "I CAN EXPLAIN . . ."

All the blood drained from Martha's face. I know that's an expression people use but I actually watched it happen to her. She let out some sort of sound too. It wasn't a shriek or a cry either. It was more like a yelp—of disbelief and horror.

She immediately started running out of the bar, weaving through the crowd like an Olympic-level slalomer. I, on the other hand, didn't have the same luck. I tried to go after her, yelling, "Babe, just wait a second," but Clem grabbed me by the back of my collar. "Have some dignity, boy, and at least wipe the coke off yer face before ya go and grovel." He handed me his handkerchief, which was so repugnant it defied description. 'No thanks, man, I'll use my shirt," I told him. "Suit yerself but you better git after her, she's gittin' away," he said, pointing.

She was about halfway through the packed bar when I saw her look back at me. She stopped for a second and it looked like she was gonna let me catch up, but then Ty snuck up under me, put his head through my legs, and raised me up on his shoulders. I looked down at him and hollered, "What the fuck are you doing, dude?" "CHICKEN FIGHTS! C'mon, New York, Clems got Li'l Lou. We can take 'em!" He spun me around toward her one more time and she was standing there with members of her family and the wedding party. They looked puzzled. She looked disgusted. I saw her shake her head and start to leave with her older sister and the husband, as well as the rest of the wedding party, following her lead, their heads cocked backward on their shoulders, unleashing fiery eyes of condemnation that landed squarely on me. I motioned for her to wait for me outside and sprang my hands out, giving her the it's-outta-my-control gesture as Ty was dragging me into the seventh circle of rodeo clown hell, all of them chanting, "Fight, fight, fight" stomping their feet, clapping their hands in unison.

After I took down Li'l Lou (which wasn't easy, by the way), I threw people out of the way in dramatic fashion, clamoring to get outside. It didn't take long to realize that she was gone and I was fucked. I had no idea where I was, where I was staying, or who to call. This was around 1996 so I didn't have a cell phone or anything like that. I went into my pockets and pulled out nothing but dog ears—no money. Martha always carried the dough 'cause she's the one who earned it. I never contested that. It occurred to me right then and there that she was gone, wasn't coming back at all, and that I was gonna have to find my way back to New York somehow.

I took a long desperate pull off of my cigarette, flicked it, and turned around to go back into the bar. Clem and company had shifted to the front corner where they'd been watching me. He flashed me his prize-winning tobacco-stained rodeo choppers (three gold teeth in the front row), grinned, and said, "Don't worry, New York, you're with us now." I thought in that moment that I was either gonna die or under Clem's tutelage actually *become* a rodeo clown. I was past the point of caring anymore. Either one sounded good.

Then the whole gang (about fourteen of us) piled in the rodeo clown vehicle, which was essentially a big horse trailer that had something like TULSA ROUGH RIDERS on the side, with a picture of a demented-looking cowboy riding a bucking bronco and swinging a big lasso. "That's supposed to be my likeness," Clem pointed out proudly as I climbed in. "Nice picture," I told him.

Clem said I could stay at their rodeo clown shantytown, which was set up a few miles outside of Charleston. "You're gonna love it, New York. Get a night of true carny livin' under your belt before you go back to your fancy dishwashers and Cuisinarts," he said, chuckling. "Do I look like I've ever used a fuckin' Cuisinart?" I asked harshly, my words now getting a bit slurry. "No, you look like you been through one, though." He pointed out the missing buttons on my shirt and laughed louder. I must've lost them during the chicken fight.

The ride to rodeo clown headquarters was pretty terrifying. I was in the front with Clem and there were gas cans everywhere, everyone with lit cigarettes (including me). Clem was accelerating around the turns so that everyone would roll to one side and then back. "Watch what I do to these clowns," he said devilishly as he sped up. "Look at Li'l Lou flyin' around back there with all them big meaty slobs. He's a survivin' son of a bitch, ain't he?" "He sure is," I said, looking back, watching him run a comb through his black-shoe-polish hair, clowns falling all over him.

We got to the clown village and the rest of the circus was camping there too. Here's where it gets really murky for me. Clem was fumbling through the glove compartment, looking for something and then he looked up with a shit-eating grin and said, "I got a nice surprise for you, New York," and handed me a Baggie of magic mushrooms. "Shrooms?" I asked. "Oh yeah, I think these'll heighten your experience considerably. The bearded lady gave 'em to me. Chew a coupla these caps, you'll be trapeezin' from stars," he said, gobbling a handful and chasing them with the Pabst Blue Ribbon can that he'd smuggled out of the bar and had in his top pocket.

I took a handful, grabbed his beer, and did the same thing. "It's on now, New York! You're a musician, right? Let's go find you a geetar and jam around the campfire. You might even get laid out here if you still know who you are in ten minutes." He was scaring me a little. I'd taken a lot of those shrooms.

The rest of the night was like something out of HBO's *Carnivàle*. I don't even know what was real or imagined. I couldn't swing a dead cat without hitting the biggest freak I'd ever seen in my life, until I turned around and saw an even bigger one. It was pure heaven or hell, depending on which way the shrooms were blowin' me.

As I was on the turn and the caps were kicking in, I got real frightened, which had happened to me before so I didn't panic too much. Sometimes an avalanche of fear comes on you in the very beginning, so I knew I just had to get through that part of it.

I met the bearded lady and she was really hot, aside from the unruly Grizzly Adams beard hanging from her chin (which was real). She let me hold her hand and tug on it while I rode out "the scaries," as she called them. She was about twenty-five years old and had this sexy Playboy Playmate figure. But she was like a modern-day Minotaur, only half centerfold, half ZZ Top guitar player. It was the weirdest thing. I was staring off into space when her breast rubbed up against my shoulder and a raging hard-on came galloping into my pants, only to be quickly chased away when I looked up and found myself staring dead into the face of the fuckin' Unabomber. "I think I need to walk around a little," I told her. "All right, darlin', just remember to summon the drug, don't let it summon you." The bearded lady was wise.

She went by Beardslee but she said, "You can just call me Lee." She said she was Lebanese and that all the women in her family could grow beards and showed me a picture of her fully bearded, eighty-year-old grandmother. It was a ghastly photo. She was a frail and stern-looking old woman with lips like two thin strips of tree bark, staring angrily at the camera like an anorexic Robert E. Lee in drag. She said, "The irony is that she married my grandfather, who went his whole life never able to grow a full beard. Went to his grave never having done it. He was Swedish . . . totally bald face." "That is ironic," I said, not knowing if it was.

I was starting to see traces and trails everywhere, so I told Lee, "I think I have to lay down." "Okay, cutie pie, you all right?" she asked, genuinely concerned. I answered, "Oh yeah, they're just kickin' in hard is all. I think I took too many to start. Can you go grab me a beer? I think I'm gonna need to drink these things down a little." "I think that's a good idea. I say that with all the drugs I do. When in doubt, drink 'em out," and she walked off to find me a beer, laughing; except she didn't take her laugh with her. It kept coming to a crescendo and then dying out to where you could only hear it faintly and then it would come ROARING BACK AND BE LOUDER THAN HELL, then soft again like a summer drizzle.

"It's official," I said out loud. "I'm starting to freak the fuck out," not intending for anyone to hear me. Seemingly right on cue, Clem snuck up behind me with two beers and gave me one. "Well, what the hell did you expect, New York? That wasn't Mama's Toll House cookies you crammed into yer gullet back there. That was drugs, boy! Albeit natural ones, though I've heard they sometimes spray 'em with PCP and pesticides and all sorts a shit to get ya off but that's just some batches, I guess. Who cares, it's done now. You gotta stop pussin' out over here and come join the party. We got a fire goin' and we found you a geetar. We got folks of all shapes and sizes over here, good and loaded, and just waitin' for you to rock their shit, New York style! Li'l Lou's girlfriend just got here. She's three hundred and forty pounds! He's eighty on a good day. We have to send a search party in every time he goes and fucks her! Now come on, Elvis, your adoring crowd awaits!"

He couldn't have been more right about that. They did adore me and I hadn't even done anything yet. There was a raging fire coming out of one of those big garbage canisters and all these vicious freaks were gathered 'round it, playing tambourines and kazoos. There were midgets and clowns and midget clowns who were also fire eaters. One of the wee ones standing next to the fire offered me a roasted marshmallow so I said, "Sure." He lit the damn thing on fire and then stuffed the whole three-and-a-half-foot flaming stick down his throat. I didn't see it come out, so I said, "Where the fuck is it?" He just looked at me nastily and said, "Whattya want me to pull it out from behind your ear like your old uncle? I fuckin' ate it." I couldn't get my shroomed-up head around that one. The stick was bigger than the guy. As I was unraveling the physics on that, they all started chanting, "Sing, sing, SING, SING!"

I don't know that many cover songs on guitar to begin with (I'm primarily a singer) and they weren't gonna know a Knockout Drops tune so I was blankin' on what to play for them. Then I dug real deep and found this old Marshall Tucker song that I knew the changes and words to from years ago when my older brothers used to play it over and over. I started strumming and nobody really knew what I was gonna do yet but I could tell people were starting to pick up on the melody. Then I started caterwauling Grand Ole' Opry style, "Gonna take a freight train down to the station, Lord, don't care where it goes. . . . Can'tcha see, can'tcha see what that a woman, lawd, she been doin' ta me . . ."

They went completely bananas for it and all started singing in unison at the top of their lungs, rodeo clowns and assorted freaks, twenty strong, swaying back and forth in time, linked shoulder to shoulder in a circle singing for joy under an enormous and shining hunter's moon, me pied pipering them to the happiest pasture known to mankind . . . THE DRUNKEN GROUP SING-ALONG!!

Well, I'd picked a pretty good song, and as it turns out, I didn't really need any others 'cause that one did just fine for the next three hours. It went over many bumps and around many bends, almost dying out several times but then someone would get a second wind and jump in singing a spirited chorus and everyone would be back at full power again for another round.

I remember looking out at all of them, singing and dancing and banging on anything that would make a sound, and just loving them. These were people who, like me, had gotten to that intersection where if you want reality and nine-to-five living, you just had to veer to the right and they all had made hard lefts! Some were aided in their decisions by physical oddities or broken homes (I talked with lots of them), but by and large they were just running on freak power and when the time in life came to make that choice they had a yearning to be among their own. They were a close-knit group, a family, fully functional, they had each other's backs, and I could see they loved each other profoundly.

The sun was singeing the horizon and squeaking through the trunks of the trees at us when the pagan dance finally reached its end, everyone's batteries going dead at the same time. I don't recall consciously going to sleep but when I woke up, the guitar was still strapped around my neck, my back leaned up against the tire of the trailer.

No one was around. I guess they'd all crawled off to the corners of the camp where their beds were. There was a high-pitched buzz in my head reminiscent of the old Huntington firehouse siren and a taste in my mouth that, if harnessed, could be used by the military to mass-kill anything in this world.

I got my good-morning vomiting session out of the way first, hunched over the very trash can we'd used as the hub of our celebration the night before, the odor of the charred insides and fermenting garbage reactivating my puke mechanism over and over, and as I was rummaging in my blazer pockets for a tissue I found an invitation to a post-wedding brunch. It had a map on it, giving directions to the house Martha's parents were renting, the place where I was supposed to be staying. If I could get to this thing, I'd be able to get back to New York without hitchhiking, which was my only other plan. SAVED!

I ran around frantically trying to find Clem, opening doors to all of the trailers. I finally found him in the very last camper, sleeping upright in a chair with a Bud tall boy in his hand. I jostled him. "Clem . . . Clem . . . CLEM!" "Huh? You can't park there," he snapped, his eyes opening but no recognition coming my way. He must've just resumed whatever conversation he was having when he conked or was still talking in his dream or something. "Dude, it's me . . . New York?" I said, still shaking him. "Oh, morning, partner, you get a good sleep?" he asked, rubbing his eyes with the heels of his hands.

"I found this map to the house in my pocket. Do you know where this is? Can you take me there? This is my only shot," I said, out of breath and desperate. He took a look at it and then went silent for a second, pondering something. "What?" "I got some news for you, New York, that you may or may not like. If I'm right about this, and I think I am, this place is not two blocks from the bar we was in last night." "Shit, really?" "Yeah, if you had found this last night, you easily coulda walked," he said, handing it back to me.

"You are a U.S. of A, grade A, numero uno FUCKUP, New York, the kind you don't see just every day," he said, hyperventilating from laughter. "We'll git you there. It's on our way and we gotta git movin' now anyway. We got another show to do today for the good people of Charleston. Help me git everybody in motion, wouldja?" he asked, tossing his head back and sucking down the rest of that tall boy.

I ran out of his trailer to rally everyone but most of them were up already and loading gear into the trucks. Those carnies had incredible resilience. Nobody complained about hangovers. They were all packed up and ready for action in no time flat.

I jumped in the front with Clem and we led the convoy of freaks down the highway. There were about six trailers in the fleet. "I wanna know what yer gonna say to this nice young lady to wriggle outta all this. . . . I think we should practice it now," he said, giggling. "I don't think there's much to say, Clem. I'm just hoping she lets me on the plane—she's got my ticket."

"Well, is she Christian? And I don't mean one of them go-to-church-on-Christmas-and-Easter types, I mean really Christian—cuz if she is she's got no choice but to forgive ya," he pointed out like a trial lawyer. "I don't know for sure, I think she's Episcopalian," I muttered. "Oh, yer fucked." He laughed. "Them people just throw money at Jesus and think they're covered. You gotta find a nice Baptist girl like we have here in the South. They understand men like us, who are good by nature but fucked up when it comes to all else—that we're good men with failings. You gotta go and git one of those gals, New York. You ain't gonna cut it with anyone that's got expectations. Jewish chicks are fun—great in the sack cuz Jesus ain't watchin' em but don't ever cross 'em. If you do, you can expect a tidal wave of pain that they'll take right outta yer hide and they ain't big on forgiveness." "Thanks, Clem, I'll keep all that in mind," I said, and threw up out the window. "That's it, New York, git last night outta yer system. We want you lookin' innocent goin' in," he said, patting my shoulder.

We turned onto the street and started looking for the address. Clem had some country station on and he pegged it up to its loudest when "Why Don't We Get Drunk and Screw" came on. "This is one that ya always gotta turn up," he yelled above the music. We came up on a huge front yard that had tables with white and yellow umbrellas and a bunch of people seated, eating. This had to be it. The pit in my stomach turned into a fuckin' cinder block.

"Here's number one thirty-one on the left, New York. It's show-time," and with that Clem sped up and pulled into the driveway, clipping the mailbox, which was one of those real cute ones that looked like a little barn. I heard it hit the pavement as he sounded the horn, which was, of course, "Dixie," the same one as on *The Dukes of Hazzard.*

There were about a hundred and fifty people on that lawn and every head turned my way as I stepped out of the truck, the other vehicles in the convoy idling loudly in front of the yard, rodeo clowns out every window waving to me. I turned around and Clem saluted me. "Bye, New York, 'twas both an honor and a privilege," and he threw it in reverse, laughing hysterically. *What's with the hyena cackle?* I thought.

I made my way across the yard, my hair all messed up, eyes like two piss holes in the snow, everybody staring at me, no one saying anything, but I could hear the courtroom waller behind me with every step. It didn't surprise me 'cause I was wearing the same suit as the night before, and I'm sure Martha had been dirting me to a few of her confidantes. A couple of people were there who had been at the bar the night before and seen me partying with the rodeo clowns, but even so, the looks I was catching seemed a bit weird.

I found Martha sitting at a table with her mom and dad and a few other old aristocrat couples I'd met briefly at the wedding. "Good morning, everyone," I said as chipper and oblivious to the situation as I could possibly pretend to be. I buried my head in a slice of canta-loupe. Martha didn't even look at me and nobody said a word, which was beyond nerve-racking, but I just kept my head down and con-tinued eating.

Martha's father, the general, calmly got up, walked halfway around the table, and ripped off a booklet of light blue, extra-large, ribbed Trojan prophylactics that had been taped in a fan across the back of my blazer. "These yours?" he leaned down and asked, his head about to pop off with rage. "Ummmm . . . no . . . I don't wear them," was the answer that came back.

He killed me six hundred times in his head as he glared at the side of my face for a full minute. I didn't flinch. I just kept my nose in that cantaloupe rind, pretending to eat even though I'd already finished it. Looking up was out of the question, so I just stayed with that same slice of cantaloupe through the whole breakfast. Thanks, Clem.

Not a word was uttered for the rest of the trip but Martha did let me on the plane. We touched down at JFK and got into a cab that made it back to the city in what seemed like no time at all. I took our bags up to the apartment, but when we got to the door she took hers from my hand, opened the door with her keys, and without looking back, slammed it in my face.

Three days later she brought the rest of my stuff down to a gig I was doing at the Red Lion with Mike. She didn't exactly need a fuckin' U-Haul either. It was a plastic Gap bag whose contents were: a Rubik's cube, a couple of pairs of Hanes underwear with the elastic blown out of them, and a Cheap Trick tape, *Live at Buddakhan*. . . . And I don't even think that tape was mine . . .

Three days after that my brother and I placed an ad in the *Village Voice* personals that read, "Blown-out alcoholic lounge singer seeks stabilizer, must have cable, no pets."

Chapter Nine

Maverick Records Doesn't Like Beer Bellies

After being bounced from Martha's, with nowhere else to go, I found myself living back at my sisters'—or should I say, they found me living back with them. I'd gotten used to a cushy life in a big, luxurious bed over at Martha's and had to hit the bottle hard to make the transition back to the couch. The blessing for them was that I was out playing dates most nights so I was rarely there. I'd skulk in around five or six A.M., wasted, sleep while they were at work, and then be up and out to meet Ponzo and the van at the Bagel Buffet on Sixth Avenue before they got home. We'd grab a quick bite, drive up to his coke dealer's place in Midtown, score, then shoot out of town to our next scheduled appearance. The other Drops drove their own vehicles while Ponzo and I transported the equipment, freeing us up to do blow the whole way there.

We both had DWIs and prior drug busts with probationary stipulations so we never drank in the van (even something as little as an open container could get us both thrown in the clink). This didn't stop us from doing blow because that was much easier to hide. Getting gilled on gack without the precious reward of a drink on top, though, really sucked. Alcohol was my great love. Cocaine was just something I did to keep my altitude up—without the necessary gravity that the sauce provided, a coke high just made me uncomfortably pent up and hyper. It had me doing index-fingered drum solos on the dash with Ponzo yelling, "That's it. No more for you for at least three exits." I'd get to the venues like I'd been shot out of a cannon, drinking insatiably till we went on.

Ponzo's dealer was a lively fellow called the Walrus. In addition to being a bionic Hoover of cocaine, he was also a tightly wound gambling addict. I would describe his natural state as pre-massive coronary. We'd walk into his apartment to a wall of TVs, with different sports contests on each one, and he'd be going down the line screaming at all of them. "Fuckin' fab five, my ass! What have they ever won? NOTHIN'! And do they ever cover the spread? NEVER . . . the cockfuckinsuckers," he said, referring to the Michigan basketball team. "And look at these asshole Knicks on this TV. Never bet with your heart, boys. You'll TAKE IT UP THE ASS EVERY TIME if you do that," he told us often.

He was somewhere between three to four hundred pounds, more jowly than the McDonaldland Grimace, and he always had a red pasta stain on his pit-stained, white T-shirt (which rode up his belly above his sweatpants despite being the largest possible human size). He sweated profusely and usually had a towel slung around his neck as if he'd just exerted himself on a StairMaster, but there was no such apparatus anywhere to be found at the Walrus's—only sandwich wrappers, full ashtrays, Coke cans, and empty Dewar's bottles. He made Ponzo look like a toy fat guy when they'd sit next to each other on the couch, chopping lines. The Walrus always did a few scooters with us out of his own stash before giving us our count, which, itself, was always generous.

On our way upstate to a gig one night, we paid him our usual visit. "Where you boys off to tonight?" he asked, dumping some blow onto the glass table in front of the couch. "We're playing Valentine's in Albany," Ponzo answered, hypnotized by the fresh pile in front of him—as if he were seeing it in all its splendor for the very first time. "That oughta be good. There's a college near there, right?" he asked. "Yeah, there is. We played it a few months ago and it was good," I said. "When are you guys playing around here next? I've been playing the *Nowadays* CD for people here and everybody wants to come," he said. "We're having a record release party at Coney Island High in a couple of weeks," I told him. "Count me in," he said.

The Walrus came to all of our gigs. He was big into the music but also did a lot of business there. "Who says you can't mix business with pleasure?" he said to me, winking, one night outside our dressing room at Tramps as some nervous guy in a suit was handing him cash for an eight ball.

We hit the road up to Albany listening to the newly pressed *Nowadays* CD that had taken forever to finish with Joe Blaney. Joe was a highly sought-after producer-engineer in the business and kept having to leave us in the middle of recording to go out of town and work with other people. As a result, it ended up taking us a year to complete the record. "It sounds too compressed to me on certain songs," Ponzo said, critiquing it. "Yeah, I agree. Something was lost in translation but I think it's pretty good," I said. "I don't think it's gonna matter anyway. Whatever label you guys sign with is gonna have you rerecord all this shit anyway, probably. Speaking of which, Rishon called me. We have a meeting tomorrow afternoon up at Brick Wall. He said he has good news. Don't fuckin' disappear on me tonight. If I don't get you there, it's my ass," he said, doing a hit out of the bindle and handing it over to me to do one.

"What good news?" I asked. "He didn't say. It's best for us not to think about it. We've been down this road before. Let's just do the gig tonight and we'll find out tomorrow." I agreed with Ponzo. It was best not to speculate. We had the Pixies album *Doolittle* cranking, and my gaze drifted out the window into a protracted daydream of carefree success and penthouses in the sky while the trees, road signs, taillights, and painted lanes melded into one blurred kaleidoscope of colors.

When we pulled up to Valentine's the band were all out front waiting for us to help load in. A snapshot of how we all looked for the gig is indicative of this period on the whole: I was wearing red-white-and-blue seersucker bell-bottoms, a T-shirt, and the red "Gary" Budweiser jacket. My hair was longish brown with thick peroxide-blond chunks in it (courtesy of the Humes). Phil had just dyed his hair platinum blond, making him look like some kind of ginzo Billy Idol. He was wearing a sparkly banana-colored shirt, black pants, and Chuck Taylors. Tom remained the same with long dark hair, Lennonesque glasses, and a cool vintage blazer à la Peter Buck from R.E.M. And our new drummer, Caveman, was a strapping guy with broad shoulders and a boxer's physique, who wore sleeveless shirts to accentuate his muscles (despite my pleas for him not to). He easily could've been mistaken for Fabio with his long, flowing, shoulder-length brownish red hair that chicks went crazy for. Sometimes we'd overhear them at the gigs asking him, "What kind of conditioner do you use?" Caveman was a warm and friendly sort and would actually engage these women seriously. "The trick is not to wash it every day," he'd say, and then chat them up innocently about it, not even flirting. Women adored him.

We got out of the van with the English Beat's "Ranking Full Stop" blaring from the speakers. *"Said are you ready? Are you ready to stop? Said are you ready? Are you ready to stop?"* Dave Wakeling and Rankin' Roger wailed. We all started spontaneously dancing to the revved-up ska song in front of the club, linking arms, twirling around, and hopping up and down. We continued to half dance as Ponzo dug out the equipment, handing everyone something to trot in. "Did you guys hit a lot of traffic getting out of the city?" Phil asked Ponzo. "A little bit but we cruised once we were on the highway. You ready to rip this place in half, blondie?" Ponzo asked Phil, getting him in a headlock. "Yeah," he said. "I wanna see more enthusiasm than that. Say 'yes, Uncle Ponz!'" Ponzo said. "YES, UNCLE PONZ!" he answered. "Atta boy!" he said, releasing him.

Valentine's was a cool place and became a favorite stop of ours on our swings north. SUNY Albany and Siena College were right there. It was a popular place for students to drink, giving us a built-in crowd, but our first few times there we had to work the room beforehand to get the kids to come watch us. There was a downstairs bar where the students hung out, and upstairs was the performance room, which was pretty big. We'd party downstairs, make friends with the Albany kids by buying them beers with our drink tickets, and then persuade them to come up and listen to us.

We established a beachhead in the middle of the bar and began luring in a crowd, Ponzo standing up on a barstool making the announcement to anyone within hearing distance. "Who wants shawts? The band is buyin'!"

A crowd of five cuties came right over to us, one so gorgeous I was speechless. She looked like a young Catherine Zeta-Jones. She said to me, "Are you guys playing upstairs tonight?" "In about an hour, yeah. You coming?" I asked, praying the answer would be yes. "That all depends. What do you guys sound like?" she asked. "I don't know. We got our own thing goin' on but do you like The Replacements, old R.E.M., stuff like that?" I asked. "I love R.E.M. but haven't heard of The Replacements." "Well, why don't you have a seat next to me right here and I'll debrief you." "Whoa! You're gonna debrief me already? I don't even know you yet," she said jokingly. "Well then, whattya say we start a little slower and work our way up to the debriefing part?" I teased. "OK, you're on," she said, smiling coyly and taking the barstool next to mine.

We talked for a while and she turned out to be a charming girl. I drank ferociously, trying to level off the blow in my system. I handed her a beer and noticed something peculiar when she went to grab it. She had webbed fingers. At first I wasn't gonna say anything but then she noticed that I noticed and there was no turning back. "Pardon me asking but what is that?" I inquired cautiously. "I have webbed fingers on this hand. It's okay. Comes in handy in the water," she said, laughing freely about it. I was feeling a buzz at this point and figured her comment had opened up the floodgates for a few flirty jokes and said, "Yeah, you must be a strong swimmer." She said, "You know I am . . . I am a good swimmer." Being the moron that I am, I completely misread the situation, not even considering that it might be a topic she'd want to move away from, and just kept shooting out playful comments.

She was getting more and more uncomfortable and finally when I said, "Does your mother have a dorsal fin?" she put an end to it. "You know, Chris, we've had our fun with this but it's not really something I wanna harp on all night. I like you but you seem obsessed with this. Don't say another thing about it and we'll be just fine. OK?" she said, a little annoyed. I felt horrible. "OK, sorry . . . um . . . uh," I fumbled, not yet knowing her name, though she'd told me a few times. "Lily . . . my name is Lily, you jerk," she said, laughing, and slapped me on the knee.

I recovered from my whimsical yet insensitive jibes about her finlike hand and we started to hit it off again. She was so fuckin' hot it wasn't funny. It was beyond belief. It was almost time to go on and

I invited her into our dressing room for a private drink before the show.

I gave Ponzo a look and he cleared everyone outta there. She trailed me into our designated room, a glorified closet with a musty old couch, holding my hand. I pulled a beer from the cooler. She was drinking whiskey sours by then, so I didn't need to get her one. When I turned around, she was on me. We started making out furiously. I popped the mother of all boingees. She started to unbuckle my belt while we were still locked in a passionate, ongoing tongue duel. Then she hit a snag and disengaged from the kiss to open my pants. I looked down, saw her webbed hand having trouble getting the belt open, and felt a joke coming on. I tried to hold it back, knowing what was at stake, but when a punch line pops into my head a mechanism takes over that is as involuntary as a heartbeak. It's a severe disorder—my own strain of Tourette's—and way worse than her aquatic appendage. I strummed the side of her face with my forefingers affectionately, and blurted in my best Jackie Gleason voice, "Nnnn . . . go for it, Flipper."

In one motion she wheeled around, threw the whiskey sour in my face, blinding me, and ran out, yelling, "I warned you, DICKHEAD!" Ponzo walked in at that precise moment and on her way past him she said it again. "Your friend is a dickhead. Did you now that?" "Yeah, I knew, but we all have our ways of finding out. Sorry about yours, sister . . . whatever it was," he said, rolling with it. She shrugged and left in a huff. He looked over at me. "Holy fuck, she's wicked pissed! What in the hell went wrong here?" "Fishing accident . . . I'll tell you on the way home. It's way too painful right now," I said, feeling like an idiot. "Well, shake it off. You're on!" he said, slapping me on the fanny, like a high school football coach. "C'mon! Show 'em who you are out there! And get the broad out your head!" he hollered at me, stealing that last line from his favorite movie, *Bull Durham,* as I made my way through people to the stage.

The next day we assembled at the Brick Wall office on the Upper West Side at four P.M. We were all excited to hear this so-called good news. Seated with Michael and Rishon at the conference table was Mike Taylor. Taylor was a fan of ours who, a few years back, had approached us about managing the Knockout Drops. He was at the

William Morris Agency at the time and in the process of leaving, so nothing had ever come of it. However, he'd stayed a fan and had become a friend of ours since then, still turning up at a lot of shows. He would always say to me, "When I get the right label job, I'm signing you guys." He'd been working for Maverick Records as a junior A and R person (which is really just a scout) for about a year, without the power to sign anything, but in recent months his boss had been fired and he got her job as head of the New York office.

Taylor was a way cool cat and unlike anyone else we'd met in the music business up till then. He was a fervent fan of all the same left-of-the-dial music we were, especially the alt-country stuff like Uncle Tupelo, The Jayhawks, Steve Earle, and myriad others. He had dark features and wavy black hair. Chicks dug him. He also didn't have that asshole ego that normally came part and parcel with these music-industry weasels. We (the Drops) would go to the Bistro with him and tip 'em all night, talking music, and if opportunity knocked maybe chat up some gals. He was a solid guy and we all liked him a lot.

"Taylor! What are you doin' here, dude? You here to audition for first clarinet? The spot's open if you want it," I said, kidding around. "I must warn you though, there's a contortionist kid showing up here in a few minutes who we heard can blow himself and play it at the same time, so your competition will be stiff," I said, finishing off the joke. "No, Chris, I'm here to rescue you from anonymity and sign you to a record deal," he said, stopping me dead in my tracks. "That's good too, but we're still gonna have to hear you play a little bit," I said, keeping my cool but doing somersaults on the inside over what he'd just said.

"I played some of *Nowadays* and *Burning Bush* for the people on the coast and they've given me the go-ahead to sign you guys to a development deal. What that means is that we get you into the studio right away, you record the songs I tell you to, and then I take it back to them for the yea or nay. I have every confidence based on the reaction we've already gotten that they're gonna love it. We, in the New York office, want you guys on Maverick," he said. What was misleading about that was, "We in the New York office," meant Taylor and like two other people. The real Maverick offices were in LA and they were the ones who needed convincing.

Phil asked, "Mike, why do we have to jump through all these hoops? You're the head of New York A and R, can't you just sign us?" A good question, to which he replied, "Unfortunately, no. Look, I hate this too, but Guy controls all the signings at the label right now. Everything's gotta go through him."

The person Taylor was referring to was Guy Oseary, Maverick's golden boy, who'd signed the likes of Alanis Morrisette and a band called Candlebox. They'd both gone multiplatinum with their debut albums so he wielded a lot of influence at the label during this time (he went on to become CEO). I considered both of those records repugnant and commercial drivel, so I said, "Mikey, no disrespect intended but your label isn't exactly known for having the same kind of cool taste that you do. How are you gonna push this thing through?" He said calmly, "That's the reason I'm bringing you guys in. I wanna slowly try to change some of that and make it a cool label, at least on my end, but that's really none of your concern." Michael Solomon jumped in. "Guys, let us three worry about the business and you just knock out a great recording with Joe."

The situation Mike Taylor was in over at Maverick was a precarious one. The label was founded and co-owned by Madonna and her manager at the time, Freddy DeMann. Freddy was a big supporter of Taylor's but the label was making a lot of money off of all the garbage Guy Oseary had signed. Mike hadn't signed anything on his own yet. He needed to get on the board. In a preproduction session for the recording with Joe Blaney, I said to him again, "Are you sure you know what you're doing here? We don't really fit with anything you have on this label." "Chris, it doesn't matter. I hear your songs as radio songs. They are under four minutes, have great guitar hooks, lyrics, and memorable melodies. It doesn't matter how they're framed, they're still pop songs. You wouldn't consider Nirvana a commercial band but their songs are catchy as hell and sound great on the radio, yes? I'm not comparing you to Nirvana but it's the same principle. We can do this." He made a good point. I loved Nirvana (though we sounded nothing like them). In my opinion not liking them is like not liking the Beatles. It's just undeniable genius.

We recorded for Maverick for the next two months with Joe Blaney producing and Mike Taylor overseeing the sessions. I kept it together pretty well, drinking moderately while we worked, then going out for beers with the band, Joe, Taylor, and Ponzo after we wrapped. We'd have a few slow ones together and then Ponzo and I would split, saying we were going home, and go out hard.

Taylor's favorite song of ours was a quirky number called "Mrs. Goodbar," about a last gasper's willy-nilly search for love. We tracked that one first. Here's an excerpt:

Second verse
Stare out at the moon, play connect the dots with the stars
seeing that in every constellation there's a star with its own tint
and maybe you don't know just who the hell you are?
Realizing, every implication's in the swirl of your fingerprint

Chorus
Well, I got so sick of American pie today
all washed up and I'm goin' on holiday
I spend my time in a downtown hideaway
Hey, Mrs. Goodbar . . .
Oh, come my way . . . Mrs. Goodbar

One Saturday afternoon as I was laying down a vocal for Joe, Taylor stopped in and said, "Get plenty of rest this weekend. Guy and Freddie are in town and you're doing a special showcase for them at Mercury Lounge Monday, at seven P.M." "Monday, as in the day after tomorrow?" I asked, taking my headphones off in the booth. "Yeah, Michael and Rishon will fill you in. Don't worry about a thing. It's all gonna be great but right now I gotta run."

We had two days to get word out and pack Mercury Lounge for this showcase (no small task considering these were the dark days before everyone had e-mail). We hit the phones hard, enlisting all of our most ardent supporters to get the word out. The band and I stopped by all of our watering holes on Saturday and Sunday, leaving behind quickie makeshift flyers. We walked in Monday to a full club.

Everyone who came knew why we were there, giving the show a specific air of excitement—a pervading feeling that all of our hard work was about to pay off. And I don't mean just for the band—I'm talking about for our fans and friends too. After all, we'd built this thing together.

We got onstage and went into "Mrs. Goodbar" without any of my usual introductory chatter. We were on our game from the very first snare hit. We ended the song to huge applause, the crowd obviously manufacturing more enthusiasm than usual, like they were auditioning too. I was in a great mood and opened the night by saying, "Welcome to the Westminster Dog Show," a sarcastic remark in reference to the fact that it was a "showcase"—a fuckin' cringe-worthy music-business term that I refused to use. I grabbed Phil and started pulling him around by his collar. "Meet our prize poodle, Phil. This is Phil's third trip to the Dog Show and he has placed each and every time, so if you have a problem with his performance tonight it most likely is his handler's fault. So blame me, not him. This dog is proven." He said over his mic, "Thanks, Chris. That was the B-twelve shot of self-esteem I needed up here." Tom launched into the chords of the Stooges tune "I Wanna Be Your Dog," and we all joined in spontaneously. I sang, *"Now I wanna be your dawg . . . now I wanna be your dawg . . .* c'mon everybody sing!" and everyone in the audience hopped in for the impromptu sing-along.

We were having a good time with the folks in front of us, like always, and trying not to let this showcase thing affect our performance too much, but it was hard to be up there and not feel like we were being judged. I never did spot where Freddy and Guy Oseary were in the crowd but didn't really try all that hard either. We plowed through the rest of the set relatively unfettered, stopping to talk a few times. I quipped a little while introducing the songs, saying things like, "Here's one about our ongoing struggles with puberty," but by and large kept it moving along. The show was a total smash! We did two encores, ending with the mercurial epic "In the Returning Hours," a hypnotic Doors meets the Byrds' "Eight Miles High" opus of ours. Here's a little of that one:

> *Last verse*
> *A conflagration once inside a blink*
> *It was there I saw the confidence of your wink*
> *I laugh and think, "Maybe it's all just a joke"*
> *And it echoes . . .*

Chorus
In the returning hours
We're all in the returning hours . . .

Freddy and Guy were late for a business dinner and split right after "In the Returning Hours." Mike Taylor had to go and meet them and just popped his head into the dressing room downstairs for a minute after the show. Everybody was cracking beers, celebrating, giving it more of a locker room atmosphere. It hearkened back to that feeling I hadn't known since my high school football days—the one of a hard-fought victory. I wanted to hang on to it forever. "Hey, Taylor, what did they think?" I yelled across the room. He smiled and flashed two thumbs-up. "Great show, guys. I gotta go meet them now. We'll talk about it all tomorrow. Awesome job!"

We took everyone who was at Mercury over to the Red Lion for a hootenanny. Mike Tait and I were due on for our usual ten o'clock Monday night slot but because of the circumstances converted it into a big jam with him and all the Drops, my brother Bill, and the boys from The Bogmen, my sisters, and everyone else from our little scene doing songs together and separately. It was one of the most joyful good times of my life. We were so moved by the love and support people gave us and on such short notice. We still talk about it from time to time. Our New York City audience has always kept us moving forward, no matter what.

At the end of the night I hooked up with a luscious brunette named Vanessa and I'd go on to have many late-night adventures with her. She was a supremely vicious minx, smart, sexy, beautiful, crazy, and troublesome—more fun than you could shake a stick at.

She took me back to her place in the East Village. We had to do some *Raiders-of-the-Lost-Ark* shit to get to her entrance—running through a rat-infested garbage area, leaping over a lake-size puddle, and climbing up a sliding iron ladder that almost maimed me stepping off of it (it snapped shut like a bear trap). I thought for a second that she may be luring me back there to kill me, which made the whole thing that much more thrilling. When we got into her apartment, she said, "I don't have any blow left, but have you ever done Special K?" I said, "No, I keep hearing about it, though. You got any?" "Yeah, but let's fuck first. This stuff can take down a charging rhino." I'd never had sex before where drugs were dangled in front of me as the dessert incentive. I found it an inspiringly fresh concept. Who was this chick? She was a mad genius. I was a little scared of her—but a good scared.

We ripped off each other's clothes in the kitchen, creating a tornado from there to the bedroom—spinning around, bumping into walls, and knocking down pictures, articles of clothing flying out of the twister. We got to the bed and the lovin' was like a runaway train. It was like the feeling I'd get when I played tennis with someone better and would surprise myself by being able to hit the ball at that level. She was unbridled energy. I was drunk keeper-upper. I survived the initial shock and awe and then we had a fantastic romp.

When it was over, she dumped the K out on her nightstand and whipped out a dollar bill. She said, "Go ahead, you've earned it." I snorted a couple of fatties off the table and it hit me pretty fast. The world was suddenly in slow motion—then came to a subtle halt, leaving me to live by freeze-frame. I said, "Holy shit, what is this stuff? I don't know if I like it." "Well, it's called Ketamine. It's a horse tranquilizer," she said, like *that* was no big deal. She hooved a couple of lines herself and had no problems at all. She could've run a marathon. I, on the other hand, was having major difficulties. "I'm going to the fridge to get a couple of beers. I have to drink my way back to better health," I told her.

There was a long and narrow, winding corridor I had to walk down to get to the kitchen. Naked, I hopped down from her loft bed. My legs went spaghetti upon impact of the dismount, sending me crashing to the floor, knocking over a lamp. I got up but only made it as far as the bedroom door. I was pinging off the walls so badly I decided to crawl the rest of the way. The last memory I have is being on all fours, determined to get to the refrigerator and her standing in the nude behind me, cackling like a hyena. In between laughs she was cheering me on like I was some Special Olympics kid. "YOU CAN DO IT, CHRIS! I BELIEVE IN YOU! VISUALIZE IT . . . VISUALIZE IT!"

I woke up with two empty Bud cans next to my pillow so I know I got there.

· · ·

We finished the recording with Joe, and given the time constraints, it really came out great. Joe had captured the liveliness of the band on tape (back then it was still tape) and we were all confident. Taylor sent the tapes out to Maverick LA, and about a week later I got a call from him at home. "I just got off the phone with Freddy. He thinks 'Wrong Side of Love' is a hit!" he said excitedly. "Whoa! I guess that means that he wants us?" I asked. "I'll put it to you this way, he asked me to see if I could get all of the publishing from your songs too. If he's trying to get the better of you in the deal, then you know he wants it," he said. "Well, God bless him for trying to rip us off!" I told him. "We're not outta the woods yet. They're flying you guys to LA to play for the people out there but it's lookin' really good," he said. "When?" I asked. "The day after tomorrow. We got a meeting up at Brick Wall in an hour but I wanna hook up with you first. I got something I need to talk to you about," he said, sounding serious.

We met in front of Brick Wall's building for a conversation before heading upstairs. "Listen . . . um . . . I don't quite know how to say this but I want you to augment your performance a little when you play for these people," he said sheepishly. I took a second to process what he'd just hit me with. "What are you talking about, 'augment'? You mean change how I am up there?" I asked, not liking where it was headed. "Dude, I love what you do. I wouldn't be doing all this if I didn't but . . . It's just these people . . . they're looking for a certain thing and unfortunately in order to get the deal we have to try and give it to them," he said, not looking me in the eye.

"Mike, tell me what's going on. I thought you said Freddy loved it," I stated. "He does but Guy doesn't. Remember how you had everyone in there laughin' the night of Mercury Lounge?" he said. "Yeah, so?" I said, wondering what that had to do with anything. "Well . . . he didn't like that. He wants a brooding rock star, somebody enigmatic and mysterious," he told me, hating himself for saying it. "That's the most ridiculous fuckin' thing I've ever heard. I just saw Guided by Voices and Robert Pollard didn't do that and I consider him the best frontman in front of the best band in the world right now. He was telling stories right and left, going on and on, and then firing into a tune. Everyone loved it. Tom Waits likes to do that too. You wouldn't tell Tom Waits not to talk in between songs. It's part of what he does, just like me," I said, thinking I was making a good argument. "You just made my point for me, Chris. You just named two acts that don't sell records. I love GBV and Tom Waits but the people that work at this label don't even know who they are, probably. I was listening to a Pavement record in my office one day out there and not one of them knew who it was." "Good God . . . I can understand maybe not knowing GBV but if they don't know who Tom Waits is they shouldn't even be allowed to work in music," I said. "It should be a law."

We were at a stalemate. "What do you want me to do?" I asked. "Just stand there and deliver the songs intensely," he instructed. "You mean not even do my normal moving around? What am I, fuckin' Elvis on *The Ed Sullivan Show*?" I said, getting pissed. "Don't move at all, just sing, and definitely don't talk in between. Look, you only have to do this once and then we can do whatever we want. We just have to secure the deal first. I hate it as much as you do. These people wouldn't know the real thing if it walked up and bit 'em in the ass. They're only interested in sales. You are the real thing but you're also gonna have sales, something we can't prove unless we get the deal. Please, go with me on this. It's the only way," he said, now looking me straight in the eye. "All right, dude, but I'm gonna need an epic number of drinks afterward that you're paying for. I'd imagine it's gonna take most of the night to wash the whorish taste outta my mouth. You best have that expense account handy," I said unhappily. "I was gonna do that anyway," he said.

We all assembled up at Michael and Rishon's to organize the logistics of the trip. Michael said, "All right, Taylor is flying ahead of us. I'm going with you guys. This thing is gonna go like boom, boom, boom. We get off the plane, check into the hotel, and head straight to the big showcase studio at SIR, where you guys will warm up a bit and then they're gonna file in and you'll play, just like it's a real show. Our flight is at seven A.M. Now, Chris, I know you're not used to being up around then but we can't miss this flight," he said sternly. Phil quipped, "Hey, have a little respect. He's used to being up . . . just not WAKING UP." Everyone laughed. "Well, that's why he's gonna stay over with you and Holly tomorrow night. Got it?" "Got it," Phil said.

Whenever we had early wake-ups I'd stay with Phil and his wife, Holly. She and Phil met at a Drops gig, dated for a year, and got married. Tom and I did an acoustic duo version of the Beatles's, "Things We Said Today" as their wedding song. She was an artsy gal, really pretty, and full of spirit. She loved the band. Sometimes she came with us on our short tours. She was adaptable in any situation and made for a good liaison with the ladies for Caveman and me. Tom was married by then too, but he and his wife, Karen, still lived in Huntington. Tom and Phil were both faithful lads and didn't partake in any funny business with chicks on the road even when Holly wasn't with us. I liked that about them.

Maverick had only accounted for the band and Michael Solomon to go on the trip, which left Ponzo out. It sucked having to leave him behind but he took it with grace and aplomb, saying, "Bring back the brass ring, boys." Maverick didn't skimp in any other way, though, getting us a stretch limo to the airport and putting us up in four-star accommodations once we got there.

Staring out the window of the limo on the way to JFK, I thought of Lenny and the gang at the Tuscaroo, if they could only see us now. Then my thoughts turned to Mac Smith and Nud and my family and everyone else who had told me to go after this dream. I thought of all the people who slogged out to the Merc a few weeks before and knew they were all rooting for us. I wanted to bring back that brass ring—I wanted it fuckin' bad. I craved the validation a deal would give me.

Anyone in an unsigned band knows that moment of deflation that occurs when you're talking to someone new about the group, and then they make that dreaded inquiry, "So are you guys on a label or . . . ?" When you tell them, "Not yet but we got a few things cooking," there is an indescribable expression of disbelief and pity in the look they shoot back that's like, "Oh, heard this one before. This poor bastard actually thinks he's gonna make it. Well, I'm not gonna be the one to burst his bubble." And then they'll say something along the lines of "Great. That . . . um . . . sounds exciting," but you know they don't mean it. A record deal would get rid of all that. I wanted to stand tall in the world for a change. The deal was the Holy Grail to me—the key to artistic independence on my terms and a freedom from skidderdom.

The flight got off OK and I sat with my eyes riveted to the seat belt sign, willing it to shut off because I had to take a screamin' leak. I was told by Rishon to hydrate heavily because the pressurized air on the plane dehydrates you and it's hard to sing well with dried-out pipes. I'd been guzzling water since I woke up to combat this. When the light went off, I darted to the bathroom, beating everyone in there. Once inside I discovered a little packie of blow in my pocket that Ponzo had hit me off with the night before, saying, "A little something for the long flight." I pulled it out to do a couple of bumps.

I tried to open the Baggie but the damn thing was stuck. I had bitten my fingernails down to the nubs and didn't have them to get in between the zip lock on top. I struggled with it every which way for several minutes, even putting my foot up on the sink for the leverage to pull it apart but it wouldn't budge. A lot of time had elapsed and a long line formed outside the door. The man next in line started rapping on it. "Everything all right in there?" he asked. "Yeah, just a minute, sir," I said, desperately trying to pry it open. "C'mon, we got alotta people waiting out here," he said, this time forcefully. "OKAAAAY," I enunciated, in a nicely mannered tone.

Finally I resorted to the last thing any cokehead wants to do. I bit into the Baggie—you never wanna bite the Baggie because it can't be refastened and if it can't be refastened it can't be contained so you have to do it all in one shot. I jerked my head back and ripped it open with my right incisor, causing powder to go everywhere. There was still a lot in there so I jammed it into my right nostril and honked all of it at once. I looked in the mirror and it was all over my nose, chin, shirt, pants, and sink console. I cleaned it up quickly, flushed the mangled plastic, and walked out. The guy who was next stared daggers at me as I pushed past him. "Sorry, mister," I said, avoiding eye contact.

The line that had sprung up for the bathroom as a result of my drug-related horseplay went all the way to the back of the cabin and I was the notorious asshole who'd caused it. It became abundantly clear to me how unhappy I'd made everyone as I waded my way through them, saying, "Pardon me. Excuse me. Could I just get past? Thanks. Pardon me. Excuse me," all of them shooting me dirty looks on my way by. I got about halfway back to my seat when I realized that in my hectic obsession to get the packie open I'd forgotten to pee. I paused for a second, then continued to slide through, and instead of going to my seat just got onto the end of the line. The old lady in front of me turned around and said, "Jesus, you must have a bladder problem. If I were you, I'd get that looked at." I said, "I think I'm just a nervous flyer." "And, here, you got a little shmutz on your face. Lemme get it," as she licked her thumb, wiping some overlooked blow powder from my cheek.

We dropped our stuff in the hotel and had an hour to freshen up. I used the time to pound a couple of beers from the minibar and get myself even. I snuck in a fifteen-minute disco nap too, which was much needed. I hadn't really slept the night before but not for the reasons you might think. I'd gone relatively easy, just having a few slow ones with Phil and Ponzo at the bar around the corner from Phil's apartment, but as it turns out that was the problem. I couldn't sleep without a certain amount of alcohol. Booze deprivation and nerves over the trip had delivered me an untimely night of insomnia. I gave up even trying to sleep at around three in the morning and just lay silently on Phil and Holly's pullout till sunup, when I drifted off just in time for the harsh smackdown of an obnoxious alarm clock they'd placed next to the bed. My initial instinct when it went off was to fake an illness, a reflex left over from my working days.

We strode through the hotel lobby with our shades on and guitars over our shoulders, everyone looking at us. We filed through the revolving door and jumped into the limo out front—all of us enjoying our rock star moment. As I was opening the door to the car, a pretty blonde on her way into the hotel asked, "Who are you guys?" I looked at the rest of the band and took the liberty. "We're Knockout Drops." She shrugged and said, "Oh, I haven't heard of you." With that, the air farted out of that fantasy balloon resoundingly, making us laugh hysterically for three blocks. It had been a nice sequence before she inadvertently bitch-slapped us, we all agreed.

We gazed out the window on the way there, looking at palm trees and making nervous conversation. It was a surreal landscape to us. Phil started singing the *Beverly Hillbillies* theme and pointing out the window at different stuff, imitating the opening of the show. We all joined in with him for the line "And up from the ground came a bubbling crude . . . oil, that is!"

Then there was some contemplative preshow silence and I said to everyone, "Don't be freaked out if I'm not talking or moving around much up there. Taylor told me to play it straight. He says these people just wanna hear the tunes, so let's not fuck around tuning and shit in between, okay? Let's just keep the music going." "Can you do that?" Tom asked, visibly concerned. "I'm gonna have to. He says that's what they want. I'm just forewarning you guys 'cause I don't want you to think there's something wrong or that I'm nervous or something," I said. "Like Bobby Brady when he saw the little red light on the camera and couldn't do the TV commercial?" Phil said. "I think that was Peter," Tom said, correcting him. "Actually, wasn't that Oscar Madison on *The Odd Couple*?" I said. "No, dudes, that was Greg when he played Johnny Bravo," Caveman anted up. "You know I feel like Johnny Bravo today. I hope these assholes think I fit the suit," I said, frustrated about how I was being coerced to perform. "You're already calling them assholes? Oh, I feel good now," Tom said, with Phil laughing loudly. "Let's all just settle down and go in there and tear 'em a new asshole," I said, feeling like that was a satisfactory pep talk. "We're gonna tear the assholes a new asshole?" Tom said. "Yes . . . yes we are," I said, lighting a cigarette and ignoring his joke. I had my game face on.

We got into SIR and they put us in this huge performance room with a big stage and sound system. It was specifically designed for label showcases (still have a problem with that word). My voice felt kind of tight so I went in another room and loosened it up with a few vocal exercises. After a few minutes, Michael Solomon came in and said, "All right, Chris, they're here. Just go up there and sing your songs. Don't worry about it. It's the songs they wanna hear anyway."

I walked onstage and could see it was a painfully stagnant environment. From what I could gather from everyone's clothing and hairstyles most of these people were end products of LA's cheesy cock rock-metal scene. They weren't our usual audience but we were a rough-edged, guitar-driven, indie-rock band, who hit hard and had been able to convert our fair share of metal heads over the years so they didn't worry me too much. Among them were a few stiff-looking suits, bean counters I surmised. They weren't exactly our demographic either, but we couldn't do anything about that. The few women I saw out there were on the corporate side as well. Guy Oseary was in Europe so he wasn't gonna be there but Freddy DeMann was and there was a rumor that Madonna might show up. She was very pregnant at the time and Taylor told us it was a long shot but that it could happen.

The room was as cold as could be and I don't mean temperature—I mean people standing there with their arms folded, watching the clock. The bailiff at my DWI hearing showed more interest in the proceedings.

I could see everyone there was uncomfortable and I knew we were. I was dying to break the ice by saying something but followed orders and we went right into "Mrs. Goodbar." We ended the tune to polite applause. I said, "Thanks." Sizing up the audience we did some off roading and shifted gears, playing some harder stuff. It was pandering that didn't sit well with me, but I was the one who suggested it, hoping to get a rise out of these corpses. We did a Zeppesque number called "Best of Enemies," from *Nowadays* and then "The Dropout Song," always a fire starter back home and still nothing, just the same robotic response as before. We were playing great. We were tight, dynamic, and energetic. What the fuck more could we do? I started getting the premonition that Guy had already squashed us (which was later confirmed), and that these folks were just there as a formality. For them it was a work thing—for us a lame-duck show, counting for nil.

The thought of them flying us all the way out there for this exercise in futility really got my Irish up. Then a mushroom cloud detonated in my head. I stepped up to center mic and addressed a woman in a power suit standing right in front of me. "Hey, uh, I don't see Madonna anywhere . . . she comin'?" She was pretty startled that I'd spoken to her, turning to some of her work friends and giggling. "No, I don't think so," she said. "Oh, that's too bad 'cause . . . uh . . . ya know . . . alotta people back in New York think I look a little like Sean Penn. I thought that might help our chances here tonight," I said, aware that I was now violating my pact with Taylor. Then she said innocently, "You know you do a little. She'd probably think so too." "Really? You think if I got her liquored up I could bang her?" I asked bluntly. A pocket of people stage right laughed out loud but quickly muzzled themselves.

Shock waves of silence radiated out over the room. I turned around and looked at the band and I could see that they knew the pin was out of the grenade. My special blend of Tourrette's, demonstrated back at Valentine's, had now poked its head out of the rabbit hole and was here to stay. When at the point of no return there are two all-important words that have always come into clear focus for me when I needed them to—I cherish these words with all my heart. I took a deep breath, opened my eyes wildly, and said to the band, "FUCK IT."

I announced the next song. "Here's one we wrote down at the methadone clinic. Don't be alarmed. We're not heroin addicts. We were just there trying to pick up chicks. Yeah . . . they have such low self-esteem down there that if you tell 'em you own a TV set, you're practically in." Taylor and Solomon stood there, dumbfounded. They were transfixed, like people on the side of a New York street watching a building fire. I locked eyes with Taylor for a brief second before I started singing the tune, and he just looked up at me with his hand holding his chin and smiled a pained smile.

I started hyperactively hopping around too—like Iggy Pop on crack. I jumped up on the bass drum and tumbled down onto the stage, springing up in front of the mic when it was time to sing. Just before the last song I heard someone crinkling a burrito wrapper in the back of the room and maniacally chuckling at one of my inappropriate remarks. It was my older brother Hollywood Bob. He'd been living in Laguna Beach for years and had come down to surprise me. He still maintains it was my finest hour.

We ended the set with an inspired and angry version of "In the Returning Hours," our least commercial song. I had an out-of-body experience while we played it. I glanced over at Phil and Tom and they were murdering their instruments—throttling their guitars with explosive passion. They had followed me down without even questioning it. I loved them dearly in that moment. I rounded out the evening by saying, "Listen, I just wanna thank everyone for coming out and to show our appreciation we'd like to invite y'all back to our hotel where it's HOOKERS AND BLOW ALL NIGHT FOR EVERYONE . . . ON YOU! Thank you very much! Good night!" I left the stage to thunderous applause . . . in my head. My brother Bob was the only one who was really clapping.

After a few minutes we had to come out for an obligatory meet and greet. Solomon came back, pretty even-keeled considering what he'd just witnessed, and said, "Come on, they wanna say hello to you guys." Caveman said, "Are you sure that's necessary? Couldn't you just thank them for us?" "No, get up. It'll only take a few minutes. There are actually some people who liked it, but as you might've guessed, I found out they're originally from New York," he said, looking at me with a little smirk on his face. That expression wasn't there to give me any approval for what I'd done but Michael was always able to see the humor in things and he knew in his heart that asking me to perform without talking was like poking a beehive. He and Taylor both admitted that to me later.

I shook hands with Freddy and said my begrudging hello. He ended up being a terrific guy. We stood in front of the stage and chatted for a few minutes. He said, "Wow, you have alotta energy up there. Where do you get it from?" "I dunno . . . the good people over at Anheuser-Busch?" I said, my apathy a startin' to flow. I could see that he'd gotten a kick out of my performance but was in no hurry to be in business with me. It turned out he was transitioning himself out of there anyway. He sold his share of Maverick about a year later for a reported twenty million dollars. Smart guy. I liked him and would've enjoyed working for him under different circumstances. Mike Taylor also bailed from Maverick not long after this and went on to a very successful career in A and R with Sony. He continued to champion the Knockout Drops's cause, bringing us to other labels, and remaining our biggest fan. He is as true blue as they come. Guy Oseary's Midas touch in the world of schlock entertainment endures. He has his finger in many worthwhile pies, including being the newly ordained sports agent of one Alex Rodriguez—the perennial MVP-winning third baseman for the New York Yankees. As a diehard Mets fan, this only steeps my resentment of him further.

We all went out to dinner after the fiasco at SIR, taking Hollywood Bob and the Maverick folks who liked us. The feeling of failure hadn't quite set in yet. Also, Taylor had a meeting about us up at the office the next day so our jugular hadn't officially been cut yet, but we all knew it was coming. As he was biting into his cheeseburger, Caveman naïvely said, "Maybe it'll hit 'em differently in a few hours and they'll end up loving us. You never know." "Either that or they'll decide to have Chris arrested," Phil said, cracking up the underling Maverick people. "I think we know now that we don't fit in out here with all this shit. Speaking of which, Taylor, is there a bar around here you can take us to that's not all lit up like a fuckin' tanning salon?" I asked, wanting to drink at my frustration in a real bar. "Yeah, there is a place called the Snake Pit on Melrose. You guys will like it there. We'll hit it after dinner," he said. "Perfect," I said, sucking down a Dos Equis, wishing I were far, far away but knowing that I'd be there soon.

Hollywood Bob split after the restaurant, opting out of the Snake Pit excursion to go home to his wife. I hugged him good-bye and said, "Thanks for coming, bro. It meant a lot." He said, "I'm proud of you. If it's any consolation I can't wait to tell the story." I said, "Well, it's not right now but I'm sure it will be someday."

We walked into the Snake Pit determined to drink our sorrows away but a funny thing happened. We got in there and nobody wanted to (nobody but me, that is). We were celebratory people by nature and had always gotten drunk together under the auspices of impending success, not commiseration over failure. It turns out no one was comfortable with it and everyone bailed. Phil said, "I'm just gonna go back to the room and whack that minibar within an inch of its life and go to bed. I'm gettin' somethin' outta this, goddammit."

I called my friends P. J. and Beth to come to the bar. They were a hilarious screenwriting duo I knew from New York who now lived in Venice Beach. They came down and we threw a few back. They had sold a pilot to Fox and were going through a similar ordeal at the time so they made for good company. I drank with cataclysmic intent but couldn't get drunk. My dejectedness weighed me down to the point where I couldn't find any liftoff. I made a futile attempt at finding some blow in the bar but struck out. Then the bartender rang the bell. "Last call!" I said to him, "Last call? It's one-thirty in the morning; what the fuck do people do around here?" He looked at me and started reciting the standard, "Hey, you don't have to go home but you can't . . . ." I interrupted him quickly, "Please . . . please . . . I've had a rough night. Just do me a favor and don't finish that sentence. I hate that fuckin' cliché." "OK I won't but that doesn't change anything. It's still last call," he said unmercifully.

I was sharing a room with Phil and when I got back he'd made good on his promise of ravaging the minibar. The room was semi-trashed. He told me the next day that he was taking expensive bottles of Rémy Martin and bathing in them (evidenced by the empty bottles on the table that I know he couldn't have drunk). He also had invited a bunch of people from the hotel bar up for a little party, running up a seventeen-hundred-dollar bill. They were gone by the time I got there. I saw him passed out in his boxers between the two queen-size beds, snoring, and said out loud, "Good for him." I sat on the bed staring at the TV with a bottle of Jack Daniel's next to me, periodically taking painkilling pulls out of it. The television was on but I wasn't watching it. I was just waiting for the numbness to arrive and it finally did. I passed out fully clothed, sitting up against the headboard, my hand still on the bottle.

We had an early-afternoon flight out of LAX. Phil and I both woke up still semi-drunk. We didn't talk at all. We weren't capable of conversation anyway. We just mechanically collected our things and met everyone in the lobby. We waited outside for our ride to the airport, which was a Town Car. "What, no limo?" Caveman said facetiously.

Taylor met us at the airport (though he was on a different flight) just to give us a rundown of his morning meeting that he said was, "Brief . . . very brief." He said that Freddy wasn't there and that it was just the execs who'd been at the showcase. "Not that I really wanna hear this but what'd they say?" I asked him, sipping on a coffee, my foot resting atop my overnight bag. "They just told me, in so many words, that you guys weren't what Maverick was looking for and to thank you for coming all the way out here," he said with a grimace. "Awwww, isn't that sweet? Anything else?" I asked. He said, "Actually, yeah, they also said that some of you guys had beer bellies making you not really Maverick material." As you can see they were all about the music over at that shop.

Phil and I were seated next to each other on the plane and immediately went the hair-of-the-dog route, ordering two beers at a time, then switching to scotch. It didn't take long to fully reactivate our buzzes. We started getting really loud and the stewardess kept having to come over and shush us. This was a quiet midday flight with a lot of businessmen on it and a cluster of eight Hasidic rabbis traveling together in the section in front of us. It turns out ours was a connecting flight to Tel Aviv.

We were the only ones raging. About an hour and a half into the flight a nice Southern belle flight attendant who was serving us said, "Y'all have had enough. I think it's time for a nappy nap." Michael Solomon turned around and said, "C'mon, guys, there are other people on this flight. Just ease off a little, please?" I felt bad. Michael had worked hard to get this deal too. I could see the disappointment on his face. I said, "OK, dude. Sorry." Tom and Caveman were in the row in front of us and started smuggling us back mini-bottles of booze. We kept drinking on the sly, but tried to tone it down.

Phil's drunkeness was no longer containable. He just wasn't aware of how loud he was. I whispered, "You gotta quiet down or they're gonna bust us." "What?" he said. I repeated, "You gotta quiet down or they're gonna find out we're still drinking." "WHAT? YOU'RE GONNA WIND UP STINKING? WELL, YOU SMELL FINE RIGHT NOW. WHY WORRY ABOUT IT?" he said at a party volume. He was fuckin' gone. I wasn't too far behind.

Caveman's seat was right in front of mine and I noticed he was reading, barefoot, with his moccasins under his seat. I looked at Phil, gave him the, *Shhhh* sign, and slipped the meatloaf from his lunch tray off his plate and into Caveman's shoe. He started to belly laugh and I put my hand over his mouth until he stopped vibrating. We continued to drink, forgetting all about it, and then about twenty minutes later Caveman got up to use the bathroom and we heard "WHAT THE FUCK?" We peered out into the aisle and he was scooping shards of meatloaf out of his shoe and flicking them onto the floor in front of two shocked older businessmen.

Phil couldn't handle that picture. He blew. His crazy cackles were so loud they dominated the entire cabin all the way to the front of the plane. We know that because our nice Southern stewardess came back and said, "Y'all are gonna have to quiet down or there's gonna be some serious trouble. Even the pilot can hear y'all up there. He's the one that sent me back." Solomon intervened and asked the stewardess, "Listen, there's a movie about to start, yes? Can you get them some headphones? Maybe that'll help." She turned to us and said, "You know your manager is a nice guy. Y'all should listen to him." She walked away and Phil said, "WAY TO GO, MIKEY! THE MILE HIGH CLUB AWAITS! YOU SHOULD SEE IF YOU CAN GET SOMETHIN' COOKIN' WITH HER IN THE GALLEY. IF SO, BRING US BACK A COUPLE A JELLO-S, WOULDJA? I DIDN'T GET TO EAT MY MEATLOAF." I looked over at Tom, who had tears in his eyes from laughing. He was just far enough away to enjoy all of this without being implicated.

She came back with the headphones and we started watching the movie, which was terrible. It was *Up Close and Personal,* with Robert Redford and Michelle Pfeiffer. Phil was subdued for about five minutes and then erupted "THIS MOVIE SUCKSSSSSSSS!" and whipped his headphones across the cabin. They whistled through the air like a Chinese star, hitting one of the rabbis and knocking his hat off. Phil said, "OH NO!" and ducked down in his seat. A few seconds later the rabbi appeared in front of us, hopping mad. He looked and sounded just like Jackie Mason, only with side curls. "I believe these are yours," he said to Phil, who kept his head down like a naughty nursery schooler. He glanced up out of one eye. "Um . . . sorry, Father . . . they just got away from me." The rabbi said, "I'm not your father but if I was I'd have a mind to put you over my knee and give you a good spanking." "Why reward me?" Phil said, falling back into an uncontrollable giggle. "Put these back on and watch this stinker of a movie. Maybe you'll even fall asleep. That, it's good for I'm sure," he said, walking back to his seat. Even he agreed that the movie really sucked.

Phil never bothered to put on the phones and the party continued until they got wise to our system of sneaking the drinks. Then our Southern belle delivered the grim news. "I tried to warn y'all, but you wouldn't listen. You're being detained on the flight when we land. When everyone else gets off, y'all just stay put. The marshal wants to talk to you. It's in violation of federal law to interfere with the flight of an airplane." That silenced us pretty good. For the last hour in the air we sat pensively, wondering if we were going to jail when we landed. Michael turned to us. "I don't wanna hear one peep out of you two when the marshal is here. I'll do all the talking. I'll smooth it out, don't worry, but not a peep."

Everyone filed off the plane when we landed, grabbing their stuff out of the overheads and going on their merry way. We sat there with big *Ls* on our foreheads waiting for the marshal to arrive. After about twenty minutes when it became obvious that no one was coming to get us, Michael said, "Maybe they were just trying to scare us. Let's go."

We walked through the terminal at JFK to baggage claim. Something was a little off. We couldn't put our fingers on it but there was definitely something weird in the air. We climbed into our limo, and on the way to the highway our Russian driver informed us, "The plane go down . . . into the sea . . . just before you land. I put on news station for you." That plane was flight 800. It had taken off from JFK and crashed only minutes before we touched down, killing everyone on board. The fragments lay floating somewhere in the Atlantic Ocean, off the south shore of Long Island. These were familiar waters. We listened to 1010 WINS the whole ride back, no one saying a word.

We got back to the city and everyone scattered quickly. I think we'd all had enough of one another at that point and were exhausted. I didn't even go home to my sisters'. I didn't wanna face them and have to see the disappointment register on their faces. I just wanted to drink by myself in a bar. I thought about roping in Ponzo but blew that off for the same reasons. He was so devoted. He was gonna be crushed. Only a few days before, we'd all thought we had this thing in the bag.

I elected to go to the Stoned Crow, a pub in the neighborhood with a pool table in back. Ponzo and I used to bring people there to shoot some stick once in a while. It was a good place. The bartender's name was Terry, a really friendly Irish American guy from Woodside. Being the same age, we used to have alotta laughs talking about the Woodside of our youth and all the characters. We knew some of the same people. Betsy, the owner, was a big fan of ours. She always put up our flyers and played our CD on the overhead. She'd been a Village resident since the mid-sixties, knew everyone, and had sort of a Mae West vibe to her. She was great and the Crow was a nice mellow hang.

I had no money, of course, but Terry gave me drinks on the arm. "You always bring me a good crowd, Chris. Don't worry about it," he said, pouring me a Guinness and a whiskey back. It was a slow Wednesday night in the dead of summer so it was just him and me in the bar. We talked about the plane crash for a while and then the conversation turned to Maverick. "Beer bellies . . . BEER BELLIES . . . CAN YOU BELIEVE THAT SHIT?" I said, getting more unhinged by the second.

Terry liked good music too. He was big into The Pogues. He'd crank them up in the bar and sometimes we'd sing "Summer in Siam," with our arms around each other's necks, trying to get everyone to sing it. He played yes-man to my drunken rant for a while that night. "Yeah, well, what did you expect from a label owned by Madonna?" he said. "Hey, I got no problem with Madonna. She's a lot cooler than the shit on her label . . . and definitely cooler than the assholes that work there," I said, chugging my beer and sipping my whiskey.

About an hour went by and I was still whining, getting really slurry, going into a venomous diatribe about Maverick and the music business. "You know everything has to go into these tidy little packages or they can't deal with it. They need to be able to define you . . . to call you something they can fuckin' understand. But what do they really understand? NOTHING! You know my A and R guy was trying to get me to do some self-absorbed, disassociated, tortured artist, bullshit thing just to get the deal? He wanted me to FUCKIN' PLAYACT! I can't say as I blame him. Everything cool that he brings in there they reject so he tried to put one past them with this. I went fuckin' crazy about a third of the way through the set and threw a match on the whole thing. . . . Tortured artist, my ass," I said, burying the rest of my whiskey and slamming my glass down on the bar.

"You look plenty tortured to me," he said, getting really tired of hearing my misery. He turned up the TV to watch the coverage of the crash, and I said, "I'll tell you another thing, Terry. If those motherfuckers think they're gonna—" He interjected loudly and decisively, "No, you won't tell me another thing, Chris, because I've heard everything already and I don't wanna hear any more. A lot of people lost their lives today. Hmmm? You could be one of them, or worse yet, a family member who said good-bye to a sister or a brother or son or mother never to see them again. Those are real problems. So you didn't get the record contract, big fuckin' deal. You'll get the next one. There are more important things going on in the world than you and your crappy, fuckin' record deal. Now watch with me and have a little respect . . . a little reverence for those people that don't have it so good right now."

I shrunk to the size of a thumbnail. I'd been having the kind of self-centered tantrum that would make even the most spoiled of debutantes embarrassed. Terry was a beautiful guy with a big heart. He had it so right. His speech cajoled me into really feeling the magnitude of what had happened.

I didn't say anything for a few minutes and just watched with him as they showed footage of the clean takeoff and the wreckage in the water. They were also displaying individual photos of the trusting folks who had innocently boarded that airplane, as I had just done earlier that day. I folded my hands, closed my eyes, and started praying for them. I asked God to go to all those families and comfort them, ending it with my usual disclaimer of "Ya know, if you're up there." "What are you doing now?" Terry asked. "Praying for them and their families," I said. "Good man. That's the Chris Campion I know," he said, refilling my glass with Jameson's.

Then I apologized to him. "It's okay, man. Let's forget about it. It's over. You get it now," he said. "No, really, man. I want you to know how sorry I am," I said. "And I do. So let's just move on," he reiterated. Then I went from myopic, mopey, the-world-owes-me-a-favor guy to serial-apologizing guy. "No, really, Terry, I can't apologize enough," I said for about the seventh time. "Actually you can . . . and have. . . . You've apologized enough. In fact, if you apologize again, I'm throwin' you out. Jesus Christ, I never thought I'd hear myself say this but what happened with Maverick again?" Through the very thick haze of my Jameson's high I could see the irritated expression coming off his face. I paused for a moment and said, "Okay, so there's this guy Guy Oseary over there. And he's the one that makes it all go for them. And word is that he hates us, right? You following me?" Lesson learned—lesson lost.

Booze is funny that way. It'll have you believing you're the only person in the world with problems, when it's not telling you you're the only person in the world, period.

Chapter Ten

Always a Bridesmaid

We recovered from the Maverick catastrophe and continued business as usual, playing anywhere and everywhere
within a five-hour driving radius. Sometimes we'd go out
for three- and four-day "hops," as we called them. These mini-tours
were usually a mixed bag of college gigs, dive bars, and opening slots
for bigger acts. Most of the gigs sounded good on paper but we never
knew what awaited us on the other end of the drive. On our way
back up from a gig at UPenn we stopped to play at an outdoor festival on the Jersey Shore. The itinerary showed we were to play a set
from three to four P.M., and be on our way. We got there and saw a
bunch of balloons and different colored flags attached to a makeshift
stage in front of a Rite Aid drugstore. There was a big sign running
across the façade that read, GRAND OPENING. There wasn't anyone in
sight—save for a potbellied dude in a blue smock wearing glasses
and a white name tag, anxiously looking at his watch. He was obviously waiting for us. To streamline our costs we were now traveling
together in one vehicle. We ducked down as Ponzo slowly cruised us
past him. In Knockout Drops lore, this is referred to as the Rite Aid
Festival. Tom came up with that one.

For our first Manhattan dates after the LA trip, we decided to do
two nights in a row at Brownie's in the East Village. Both shows sold
out and were among the best we'd ever done, helping us regain our
sea legs a little bit. We knew how the Russian hockey team must've
felt when they returned home after losing to the Americans. We'd left

town expecting to come back conquerors and instead had to explain the fallout to everyone we saw. We got very tired of the question "What happened with Maverick, dudes? I thought you guys had it." It didn't help that I had gone out drinking every night while we were recording for them and announced to people that it was a done deal. After three beers I had a habit of telling people what I thought they wanted to hear and what I wished was true. The slap back of repeatedly having to explain how the deal fell through was an unrelenting reminder that my reality and reality's reality, however congruent in spots, were seldom the same. I'd compound it with more lying. "Oh, our A and R guy got fired and we lost the deal" is what I'd say for a quick and easy answer to the question. This would garner sympathy and spare me the embarrassment of having to say, "Well, I know I told you we were signed but we really weren't yet."

My ego was being pummeled on another front too. My little brother Billy's group, The Bogmen, had just been signed by Arista Records and were regularly selling out huge venues like Irving Plaza and Roseland. They'd caught a few breaks and sailed right past us. I was seething with envy, of course, but was such a big fan of them and their music that on even my worst day I couldn't hate them for it.

However, when Bill Ryan, their guitarist, gave me the news I didn't take it so graciously. I was at a party and he approached me out on the patio where I was sitting by myself, drunk off my ass on tequila. "Hey, did you hear we got signed to Arista Records?" he asked, anticipating a congratulations. I squinted, Clint Eastwood style, and said in a spiteful voice, "Just call me Jermaine" (as in Jackson). Let's just say it wasn't the easiest thing to be perceived as the flunkie older brother to the toast of the town. My friends might not have been thinking that, but I was. Let's face it, I'd been at it longer and had less to show for it. It gnawed at me like a friendly cancer.

I got particularly morose about it one night. I was at the Kettle of Fish celebrating my twenty-eighth birthday when The Bogmen's video for their single "Suddenly" came on MTV's *120 Minutes*. It was pretty exciting to see Willibee and the boys on TV and I was psyched while watching it. Twenty drinks later, my birthday party morphed into a where's-mine? pity party, ruining the whole evening for everyone.

My sister Donna got stuck with me after we left the Kettle and we ended up at our favorite late-night-snacking place, the Bagel Buffet. I was fairly inaudible at this point. Donna went up to grab our food, a bagel with cream cheese for me, a baked potato with melted cheddar and sour cream for her. I watched her order, admiring her new punk hairdo, which was all frizzed out and dyed red with blond streaks through it.

When she got back, some shit-faced, scenester, party chick came up to me. "Billy? Billy Campion? Oh my God, I don't believe it! Do you remember meeting me at Mark Wike's party? Remember? We all went to Bowery Bar after?" Mark Wike was the bass player in The Bogmen. I grumbled, "I'm not Billy, sorry." "Yes, you are. Don't fuck with me," she said. "No, I'm not. I'm his older brother Chris. Nice to meet you," and I stuck out my hand, not really even looking at her. She halfheartedly shook it and said, "Awwww, I was hoping you were Billy. I just love him." "Well, sorry to disappoint but I'll tell him you said hello," I said, taking a monster bite of my bagel. "Do that. My name is Cher. He might not know it but . . . oh, shit, I wish Billy was here. You're nice but you're no Billy," she said, not knowing the volcano she'd just angered, not in me, but in my big sister Donna.

She continued to go on and on and fucking *on* about how much she loved my brother. My sister could see that this was pure torture for me and said, "You know Chris is in a band too?" The girl looked at me and said, "Pshhh, who cares? Billy's who I want. Who's he? No one. Fuck him." Donna got up like a shot, kicking her chair back to the wall. She'd been putting the fixins' on her potato all this time but hadn't started eating it yet. She wanted the girl to leave first. She had it in her hand and said, "What did you just say?" "I said 'Fuck him.' He's just the brother. I want the real thing," she explained. "I'll tell you what's gonna happen here. Right now you're gonna go back to whatever sycophant, star-fucker hole you crawled out of and leave us alone. You can go hang yourself in the velvet rope of your precious Bowery Bar for all I care, but I'm warning you if you say one more word to my brother or me, I'm gonna smash you in the face with this potato. So not ONE MORE WORD, OK?"

The girl could see my sister was serious and didn't say anything for a minute but was wearing the sourest puss imaginable, so it was only a matter of time. They stood nose to nose, everyone in the Bagel Buffet glued to the action. Then Cher, if that was her real name, said, "No one is gonna . . ." "THAT'S IT! YOU NEED A LITTLE DAIRY IN YOUR DIET, BITCH!" and Donna grabbed her by the back of the head and with her other hand smacked her hard with the potato, grinding her face in it and twisting it all around. "YOU SHOULD REALLY EAT MORE. PEOPLE MIGHT LIKE YOU BETTER WHEN THEY DON'T HAVE TO LISTEN TO YOU TALK," Donna told her as she wrestled her down, keeping her face submerged in the sour cream.

She finally let her up for air and the girl was in shock. She stood there stoically, with potato clumps, cheddar bits, and droplets of sour cream hanging off her chin, not knowing what to do. They don't really teach you how to react to a potato attack in annoying-scenester-chick school. "C'mon, Chris. Let's go. We'll be sure and tell Bill we ran into you. In fact, I have a feeling we're gonna tell everyone," she said to the girl, still frozen in the middle of the room, traumatized. "I know I'm gonna," I said. "Happy birthday," Donna said to me, laughing, putting her arm around me and helping me up the block, home. BEST BIRTHDAY, EVER!

. . .

One of the perks of our bridesmaid status in the business was getting to open for people we really admired. Sometimes friendship would blossom out of these gigs, as it did with Soul Asylum, Violent Femmes, and a number of other great bands. As a result we'd get a glimpse of what it was like "in the bigs," but ultimately it was back into the luxury tour bus for them and back into the rusted-out van for us, eating Doritos for dinner and weathering Ponzo's farts, which lingered longer than any snapshots we took away of what real success looked like.

We'd been introduced to the Soul Asylum guys originally through our producer, Joe Blaney. Once, before I really knew them, I saw them sitting with Bruce Springsteen in a booth at the Corner Bistro after one of their gigs at Tramps. It was Dave Pirner, his girlfriend at the time Winona Ryder, Dan Murphy, and the Boss, hanging out sipping some beers. I could've just gone over and reintroduced myself but instead chose to go the drunken comedy route, running up to their table and bellowing in a Broadway-style voice, *"I'M IN WITH THE IN CROWD . . . I GO WHERE THE IN CROWD GOES!"* I held there for a few seconds waiting for a reaction, receiving nothing but blank stares from all of them, and then slowly backed away into the dark. I still stand by that entrance and can't believe it didn't work. That was my one and only brush with the Boss.

I didn't really get to know Pirner and Murph until a few months later when we opened for them at the Stone Pony in Asbury Park, New Jersey. There was a rumor that Bruce was gonna show that night but he didn't. At that time Soul Asylum had already enjoyed platinum-selling success and Rolling Stone covers and all that, but at the end of the day they were just humble, beer-swilling dudes from Minneapolis, who loved hockey and wrote and played great tunes. Dave was a nice guy, gracious, with a good sense of humor, but Dan Murphy, their guitar player, is who I really became pals with. We shared a bartender in Dermott at the Bistro, and had a lot of fun gallivanting around the city together. Murph was a hoot and a half. He nicknamed me Chaz, for reasons I can't even remember, and would introduce me to chicks that way. He also played in Golden Smog with Jeff Tweedy from Wilco and Gary Louris of The Jayhawks. Through him I got to meet and hang with them a few times, which was a thrill because I was a big fan.

One of the best weekends of my life was when we played the Guinness Fleadh Festival on Randall's Island. It was a two-day affair headlined by Van Morrison. On the bill were some great acts: Wilco, Soul Asylum, Shane MacGowan, Richard Thompson, Billy Bragg, Sinead O'Connor, The Bogmen, and dozens more. We played on one of the side stages, but it didn't matter. Randall's Island is massive and the festival was packed, so there were thousands of people to watch us. There were Guinness trucks parked everywhere. It was perfect summer weather. The sun ashinin', the beer aflowin', and you couldn't walk four feet without bumping into an Irish beauty.

We played on Saturday in the middle of the afternoon. I was way hungover from our gig in Montauk the night before. We'd had to wake up early and drive for four hours to get to the show. I was completely bedraggled by set time so Ponzo popped me up with some gack before I took the stage. Doing blow just before singing was a big risk. It could have me singing like a birdie or systematically take down my voice to a whisper in a matter of seconds. It had gone both ways in the past but I was so exhausted that I decided to take my chances.

I was singing great but felt the tug, like it could go any minute, and then, about three songs in, it went. I started getting that cocaine drip down the back of my throat. Then it dried out my sinuses and totally locked up my larynx. The band all looked at me because they thought I was missing cues but it was really that nothing was coming out of my voice box. I had to find a way to buy some time till it came back. I knew that if I pushed it too hard too soon I'd lose it for the whole set. If I gave it a few minutes before singing again, there was a good chance I'd get it back.

I started doing some crowd work, talking to people in the front row, asking them where they were from and how they were doing. Everyone gave short answers, giving me nothing to work with. I was dying. It was one of our biggest crowds ever and I couldn't sing.

I kept talking, with a sizable lump gathering in my throat. How was I gonna get through this if my voice didn't return? All of a sudden this screaming girl came charging up to the front of the stage. "Can I come up there and dance with you?" she asked. I needed to stall, saw that she was crazy, and said without hesitation, "Absolutely. Come on up."

She was a big girl, with enormous breasts, and had on some kind of low-cut green mermaid dress. Her eyes were caked beyond comprehension with blue eye shadow. She looked like Dee Snider with unusually large implants—but they weren't implants.

"What's your name?" I asked, as she climbed up. "Gladys," she said, breathing heavily into the microphone. "Well, Gladys, we're a professional outfit and need to audition you a little bit before we can just let you usurp our stage. Can you dance for us a little bit, maybe show us what you got?" She said, "Sure," but must've misunderstood what I meant by "Show us what ya got," because when I looked over at her again she'd flopped out those spectacularly large gavones of hers and was shaking them around for all to see. The crowd went fuckin' ballistic! I threw her a tambourine and we went right into one of our new songs, "Hellride." By the end of it I had gotten my voice back to

full strength and our audience had miraculously quadrupled. A little
of "Hellride":

> *Hey you lollygaggers?*
> *Walkin' with a swagger*
> *A Frisbee toss and a smile in the sun*
> *Your memory lost when the night was so young*
>
> *Hey you carpetbaggers?*
> *Your days are gettin' sadder*
> *Wave to the chick in the Winnebago*
> *With the school-girl eyes and tie-dyed halo*
>
> ***Chorus***
> *Lesson for my brooding son*
> *What's done is done*
> *Shake it up real good again and glide*
> *On this Hellride . . .*

We took our bows with Gladys and got a five-minute ovation.
Michael and Rishon had me sit at our merch table afterward and for
the next hour I autographed CDs and talked to people. The line at
our table wound all the way out into the field to where you couldn't
see it anymore. It was a fantastic feeling. We sold out of CDs and I
was released to go and enjoy the rest of the day. By that time, word of
the bizarre happenings had spread through the grounds like wildfire.

The festival had given us a trailer stocked with booze and good
food. I invited a bunch of cute gals back to have some drinks with us.
My sisters, the Bog boys, and some friends were hanging back there
already. The Bogmen weren't playing till the following day. We drank
the trailer dry and then went over to catch Soul Asylum play the main
stage.

We were calling it shoe-on-the-other-foot Saturday because, as
we walked through the field to get to the stadium, strangers were
greeting me with, "Great set, man," or flashing their Knockout Drops
CDs to show me they'd bought one. No one seemed to know my
brother at all and that made him happy. I could see that sometimes

his success made him incredibly uncomfortable around me, which, in turn, made me uncomfortable.

We parked it backstage as Dave and Murph were walking through to go on. As he was strolling past with his guitar, Murph said, "What'd you guys do over there, a burlesque show? Everybody's talkin' about it."

Soul Asylum burned it up, playing all their recent hits like "Runaway Train" and "Misery" as well as a few older tracks that we, in the Drops, really loved. I was a little bummed, though. Murph had told me they were gonna do a tune he'd written called "Cartoon," an awesome song off of my favorite Soul Asylum record, *Hang Time,* but they couldn't squeeze it in. During the set Winona Ryder surprised Dave by showing up and waving to him excitedly from the wings. He looked positively shocked to see her standing there. The crowd could see all this and ate it up. Before they went on, there was a girl who had been hanging all over him and I observed that she mysteriously switched her affections to Murph after the set. I don't know what the deal was there.

When those guys got off we partied with them in front of their trailer, also drinking it dry. We tried to get more booze but couldn't find any festival production people to ask, so Murph got the idea to steal everything from Van Morrison's trailer. "I know how to do this," he said. "Van is in the food tent now and will be taking a golf cart to the stage. I've been watching him. He hasn't been in his camper all day. When the cart goes, we go," he said to Ponzo, Phil, and me.

As Murph predicted, Van got in his cart to go to the stage and as we watched the dust from the wheels kick up, we sprang into action. We popped open the door and scurried around, taking everything we could carry, bottles of twelve-year-old scotch, cases of beer, wine, the works. It felt like an episode of *The Monkees* meets *Mission: Impossible.* We got it all safely back to the Soul Asylum camp, imbibing for a bit, and then went over and caught Van's set from backstage. It was the weirdest feeling to be moved so profoundly by him as he sang, "Into the Mystic," knowing I'd just robbed him of his post-show cocktail. I took a big sip out of my whiskey and got over it quickly.

A while after Van's set, as the party was winding down, a big black guy with a headset on approached us. "Somebody stole all the booze outta Van Morrison's trailer. Would you guys know anything about that?" he said, smiling wryly. All glazed over from the eight one hitters in a row he'd just done, Ponzo said, "I think it was Billy Bragg. I know he goes around singing all those songs about social injustices and whatnot but I have it on good authority that the man's a kleptomaniac." "He's not due to play here till tomorrow," headset man replied. "Really? I thought I saw him lurking around over there," Ponzo said, sipping on a twelve-year-old scotch. The perfect end to the perfect day—the one in a thousand we didn't feel like bridesmaids. Thanks to dancing Dee Snider and her galloping tits.

. . .

While we were out playing all these dates, Michael and Rishon were busy shopping us around. We'd inquire about what was happening but they'd always say, "When we have something real to tell you, we'll tell you." Our old buddy, and booker at Brownie's, Mike Stuto (yet another Mike) had just gotten a gig in A and R over at Columbia Records. Stuto was a widely respected music man, who'd put Brownie's on the map as one of top places to play in Manhattan. He had his ear to the ground and was always being asked by A and R guys, "Who's good?" A lot of bands in the mid- to late-nineties got signed on his say-so. Stuto, like Mike Taylor before him, became a huge proponent of the Drops, always mentioning us to A and R people. Just like Mercury Lounge, we considered Brownie's home base.

When he got his own A and R job, the first thing Stuto did was take us out to dinner with our management. He said he wanted to sign us. We thought our ship had come in. One of our own was in power. Then a few weeks went by, then a few more, and a few more after that. Finally I asked Solomon, "What's up with the Stuto deal?" He said, "I don't think he's gonna stay there. He's planning to buy Brownie's and run it himself now." That's what he did and it turned out to be a much more lucrative gig for him. It didn't surprise us. He was indie rock incarnate and none of us could picture him navigating the corporate side of the music business. Our hopes were once again dashed but nobody blamed Stuto. Who in their right mind would wanna work for those assholes? He still owns the bar but it's called HiFi now. He doesn't have bands there anymore, but it's a great hang with the best jukebox in the city. Stuto is a gem.

I started getting really suspicious as to why we weren't getting a deal. We were filling rooms, playing forceful live shows, and people like Stuto and Mike Taylor were in our corner. *What is it?* I thought. I was getting the feeling there was something they weren't telling us. Everybody in the band was getting antsy. Money was tight. Everybody had to hustle other jobs in between to cover their nut and be able to travel and play.

We had a booking at a place in Connecticut we hadn't heard of called Sparky's, and when we got there it turned out to be a sports bar, with no sound system, and hardly a clue that we were even supposed to be appearing there. We played while everyone watched the Yankee game and the only cheers we heard were for the game. After one really loud one I said into the mic, "Thank you . . . thank you very much," as we watched Paul O'Neill round the bases after hitting a home run. We got back to the city and Phil got really drunk, called the Brick Wall office, and left a message firing them. He woke up the next day mortified by what he'd done but they didn't really take it seriously. They did, however, call us up there for a meeting to clear the air.

It started off with Phil apologizing and everyone kind of laughing about it but then we got down to brass tacks. Michael addressed us. "Guys, you have to be patient. We're doing everything we can. We have good stuff going on. We're gonna set a date for two months from now for you to headline Irving Plaza. If we don't have a deal in place by then, that will surely get us one. We're going to have to promo the shit out of this but I think we're ready. Our draw is poised to go to the next level." Everybody was satisfied with that and we all left happy. Irving Plaza held a thousand people so it was gonna be a tall order but, like Michael, I thought we were up to it. I was the last to leave the room and Rishon held me there. "Guys, we need to talk to Chris for a second," he said.

He closed the door and I could see he had a speech prepared. "Listen, you know we love you and we didn't wanna say this with the rest of the guys here but a lot of the resistance we're catching from labels has to do with you. Everyone loves the music but your reputation is starting to precede you, my friend. People we're talking to hear that you're a drunk . . . that you're a cokehead . . . that you're a drunken cokehead," he said and laughed, but maintained his seriousness. "Your behavior out on the coast has made you a legend but unfortunately not in a good way for us. People don't wanna be in business with someone who's gonna shoot himself and everyone else involved in the foot. This is not the sixties. It's the nineties. We know that drug addicts die now . . . and that drunks are undependable. Labels don't wanna invest in that anymore. More often than not it doesn't pay dividends. It's just a pain in the ass with diminishing returns. Unless you're Kurt Cobain, but for every Kurt Cobain there are countless others who just lose labels' money. Ya know, we're your managers but we're also your friends and we don't wanna see anything happen to you. Michael and I want you to try to get sober. For the good of everything but mostly for the good of yourself," he said, exhaling.

I didn't say anything because I thought if I did I would cry, so we all just hung for a minute while I processed what he'd said. They were such beautiful guys I didn't like that I was letting them down. I knew I was fucked up. I said, "All right, I'll give it a shot." "That's our boy," he said, hugging me. "So I'm a legend, eh?" I said, as we broke the embrace. "Yeah, how many people announce to a room full of Madonna's employees and her manager that they're gonna get her drunk and try to nail her? It's a small business. You don't think something like that's gonna get around? Right now you're a legend in the same way Son of Sam is. We don't want people to fear you. We want them to love you."

I got outside and the boys were waiting for me. "What'd they say?" Phil asked. "Well, I'm gonna have to make some changes," I said, piquing their curiosity. "I can't drink anymore," I said, with a big sigh, then finishing the sentence, "in front of Michael and Rishon." "Good idea. It's a lot easier to get fake sober," Ponzo said, sparking a one hitter right out in the middle of the crowded Manhattan street. "Maybe you shouldn't be doing that here," I warned. "What? That's why I bought it. It looks like a cigarette," he said defensively. "Yeah, but people don't dig their cigarettes into wooden dugouts with Michael Jordon tongues hanging out and maniacal looks on their faces before they smoke," I told him. "How do you know what people do? You're not even up during the day," he said. "I will be now. I'm gettin' fake sober."

So I resolved to keep my drinking a secret from Michael and Rishon. Whenever they were at gigs I'd put vodka in a pint glass with ice to make it look like ice water or I'd have the bartender fill my O'Doul's bottle with Budweiser. It worked for a while and then after about a month Rishon proposed a toast at a preshow dinner we were having out in the Hamptons. "To Chris, who's fightin' the good fight and has one month sober," and he picked up my glass by mistake, which was filled to the brim with straight vodka. He swallowed it, winced, and glared at me. I gestured with the old open-faced palms and said, "I was only gonna have one." The sobriety topic was put on the shelf after that.

Prior to my vodka mishap the Brick Wall boys had announced to us that our Irving Plaza date was set for October and that we had a few more gigs coming up playing support for bigger bands. The first one was warming up for a band called Dada at the Theater of the Living Arts (TLA) in Philadelphia. They'd had a minor hit with a song called "Dizz Knee Land," a few years before and were pretty good. But the one we were really jazzed about was opening up for the Violent Femmes. This was to occur somewhere out in the swamps of Jersey.

We were all big Femmes fans. I remember painting my garage the summer that I was eighteen while listening to that first Femmes record on cassette and just rewinding it over and over again. My next-door neighbor confessed to me years later that it drove her crazy. Every morning she'd wake up to the words, "Why can't I get just one kiss?" from the song "Add It Up," three times in a row. I was so taken with Gordon Gano's lyrics. They were poetic, funny, and packed a serious wallop. His lionhearted voice set something off in me too. He was free in his rawness and would come unhinged within the frenzy of the tunes, letting emotion govern his inflection rather than being careful to stay on the note. To me it seemed real and not like it was cut in a recording studio. Later I'd have a similar reaction when I first heard Frank Black of the Pixies.

Before the Dada show Phil gave us all a scare when his appendix burst. Holly got him to the hospital in time but it easily could've gone the other way. We all visited him and were really grateful nothing worse had happened. They released him after a few days and he hadn't had a cigarette in there so he decided to make that his spring-board to quit smoking. "When am I ever gonna have a four-day head start like this?" he told us.

We loaded in to TLA and Phil was on edge. He'd been about two weeks without a cigarette and was the walking cliché of a person who'd just quit smoking—one ornery motherfucker. He'd had the habit since he was fourteen. He was getting through his days with different combinations of nicotine gum, patches, and good old-fashioned cold-turkey teeth grinding. On this night he was particularly out of his mind so we just assumed he was roughing it. He paced the floor in the dressing room nervously as Caveman was drumming on the wall with his sticks. "Could you please get him to stop that?" he asked me, his face constricting. "Dude, you gotta loosen up. What's wrong other than the obvious cigarette thing?" I asked. "I've never done a gig without one," he said. The drumming suddenly stopped and Caveman turned to him. "Without one what? Appendix?"

Earlier on, while we were bringing the gear in, we'd met an unusual man who called himself "Dr. Ludwig. We asked him what affiliation he had with the club and he told us he was their "rock doctor." He said, "A lot of these groups today come in here with chemically dependent musicians so the proprietors like to have me on premises just in case. Plus, I love the music." Dr. Ludwig was seventy-four years old, with white hair and a ponytail, and he carried a big black medical bag. He was tall but slightly hunched over with an old-man jaw and when he spoke he had a blinky tick. He was like a craggier version of Timothy Leary.

He told us that he'd toured with all of these bands in the sixties and seventies, including Big Brother and the Holding Company. "Janis and I got along famously. We used to toast each other, her with her Southern Comfort, me with my Demerol," he said. He was a first-team vicious freak so we invited him to hang with us all night. He said, "I'll be up to see you guys later. Gotta make my rounds right now," and he picked up his bag and walked off somewhere. As soon as he was through the door we were already calling him Dr. Lude.

About a half hour from stage time I was smoking a cigarette in the dressing room when Phil came bursting through the door and said, "Fuck it, gimme one." He hastily snarfed a Parliament out of my pack that was sitting on the table. Before any of us could say anything, he took two mondo drags, his eyes rolled back in his head, and . . . *boom*, down he went, fainting. We freaked out and Caveman ran out of the room for help. As he got into the hall Dr. Lude pushed him out of the way, ran in opening his medical bag, and said, "OK, everyone, just clear away from him . . . I SAID CLEAR AWAY! What did he take?" I said, "Nothing. He just started smoking a cigarette and fainted." Dr. Lude looked up at us from one knee, where he was tending to Phil, and said, "You expect me to believe that? I've been working in this business for over thirty-five years. NOW WHAT DID HE TAKE, DAMN IT? I know a junkie when I see one. He's a junkie. Look at him. IT'S TIME YOU ALL GREW UP. HE'S A JUNKIE. YOUR BANDMATE'S A JUNKIE!"

Then I saw a crumpled-up patch on the floor a few feet away that Phil must've ripped off just before going for the cigarette. I picked it up and showed him. "Here, I think he had one of these on. See?" Phil was sitting up and conscious at this point, groggy but visibly okay. Dr. Lude grabbed the patch out of my hand, examined it up in the light for a second, looked back at us, and said, "Pussies," as he walked out of the room, disappointed.

We went on and had a good set but didn't see Dr. Lude again. While we were loading out at the end of the night, I started telling the stage manager at TLA the story. I said, "Make sure and thank Dr. Ludwig for us." He yawned and said, "Dr. Who?" "Ludwig. The old doctor I was tellin' you about that works here," I said. The guy just shook his head. "I'm here every day, dude. There's no one here by that name or who fits that description. Why would we have a doctor on call?"

All the way home that night we argued over whether or not Dr. Lude was a ghost. While gunning us up the highway, Ponzo said, "Whether he is or he isn't he's doin' a damn good job of lookin' dead already. I was more interested in what he had in that bag. Phil, you couldn't have stayed down one more minute for us to get a peek?" Phil was in the way back, snoring loudly. I said, "He's asleep." "Poor little guy . . . he really tuckered himself out today doin' all that faintin' and rawkin'," he said, slamming his foot on the accelerator.

Next we had our big gig with the Violent Femmes. It wasn't that far a drive, only an hour and a half or so down the Jersey Turnpike. To rev up for the show we cranked their albums, *Hallowed Ground,* and, of course, their classic self-titled debut the whole way down.

The place we were playing was pretty strange. It was carved into the woods, right off the turnpike, and you had to go down a narrow driveway/road to reach it. After a few minutes we came to a clearing that was a sports complex with tennis courts, swimming pool, and game fields. It almost looked like a high school but it wasn't. Once you got past that stuff, at the end of the drive was the club.

We saw their big tour bus parked out front so we knew we were in the right place. There were loads of people tailgating in the parking lot: skinheads, skate punks, college kids, normal folks in their thirties, and young teenagers (it was an all-age show). We found out the place was a summer camp during the day. I said, "Wow, the Femmes can definitely lay claim to the fact that their music appeals to everyone. I've never seen such a mixed crowd." Ponzo chimed in, "Yeah, well, let's see how many of these people actually know the music first. It doesn't look like there's much to do out here."

The club itself was pretty standard. It was big, holding about two thousand, with ample stage, lights, and sound system. There was a bar that covered the entire back wall of the room, which was up a level. You needed a bracelet to get a drink up there and we saw kids getting them smuggled through the railing by their older friends or friends with fake IDs.

When you're the opening band for a group like the Femmes, who have such a rabid and devoted following, it's not out of the ordinary to come across a few in the audience who are not interested in seeing the opening act. Then there are the impatient ones who just hate you because in their eyes every minute you're onstage is valuable time they could be watching the band they really came to see. We went on and after the first song we heard a few boos among the applause so we knew what we were up against. We'd had hecklers in the past but had never been outright booed, so it was a weird feeling at first but none of us took it personally. We were all veteran show goers and had been bridesmaids before so we understood. However, we did make the decision to segue most of the tunes so as not to give them the chance to boo us, a trick we'd picked up from the Bogmen when they opened for Kiss on their reunion tour. They were mercilessly booed through their entire set by the Kiss faithful but plowed right through, never stopping to acknowledge it.

It started as just a little unrest in the crowd, nothing really to worry about, and we still had the support of a lot of the room but then, stage right, there was a pocket of naysayers that were getting pretty aggressive. "GET OFF ALREADY! YOU FUCKIN' SUCK! BRING OUT THE FEMMES . . . YOUUUUU SUCKKKKKKKKK!" I tried to have a little fun while Tom tuned up and said, "Ok, now we're gonna do something off of Bette Midler's first album that I think you're all really gonna like," and as I was saying that a beer bottle went wizzing by my right ear and into Caveman's bass drum.

Phil whispered in my ear, "Holy shit, I think we need chicken wire." Right then another bottle skid past our feet with a demonic voice attached to it that shouted, "WHY DON'T YOU GET OFF SO YOU TWO HOMOS CAN BLOW EACH OTHER BACKSTAGE?" It was most unsettling to say the least.

The stage was elevated five feet off the ground and the lights were up high so I couldn't pinpoint who was saying it. Then another bottle hit the front of the stage, bouncing back and breaking, and the same guy threatened in an even more gravelly and ominous tone, "THE NEXT ONE'S GONNA BE AT YOUR HEAD IF YOU DON'T GET OFF!"

We had only one song left, thank God, and we made short work of it, fearing for our lives. There were a lot of people clapping, trying to give us some support against the horrid wave of boos, and to them I said, "Thanks very much. We appreciate it. Good night." The voice started in as soon as I finished. "THANKS FOR NOTHIN', YOU FUCKIN' . . . ," and before he could finish his insult the houselights came up and we saw in the corner that the man behind the terrifying voice was a pimply faced, thirteen-year-old kid, about ninety-one pounds soaking wet. He was wearing a *Star Trek, The Next Generation* T-shirt. He'd been yelling at us just to make his friends laugh.

I marched over to him. He knew he was busted and started to cower. I picked up a plastic cup filled with soda off the ledge next to him. "This yours?" He didn't say anything as his little buddies snickered. I dumped it over his head and said to him and the rest, "You guys want a free CD? Follow me." They said, "Yeah!" I gave them all one and chatted with them for a few minutes. They were typical little suburban ballbusters, just as I had been. I got a kick out of them. It ain't easy when karma bites you in the ass but it's important to acknowledge it, accept it, and do your penance with a smile, I think. My little heckler friend said to me as I was walking away, "Thanks for the CD, Chris. It'll make a great coaster for my mom's herbal tea. . . . VIOLENT FEMMES FOREVER . . . YEAH!" and with that gave me the finger. That kid had a freakishly low voice.

We didn't get to meet Gordon or any of the rest of the band. We were in separate dressing rooms, on opposite sides of the club. We did drink with their road manager, sidestage. He had a bottle of Jim Beam up on one of the speaker cabinets that he graciously shared with us.

They hit the stage and sounded phenomenal, playing all their classic anti-hits. We ended up skedaddling a few songs before they finished and going back to the city so as not to clusterfuck their load out. We also wanted to get to the Walrus's and score 'cause we'd run out of blow and he could be tough to track down after midnight.

I ran into Gordon Gano a month later in the city. It turned out he lived in the West Village and frequented the Blind Tiger Ale House. The Tiger was a new place owned by good friends of ours, Brian and Dave. It was a dank bucket o' blood that specialized in microbrews and imported beers. The night they opened Brian asked if I would play there on Sunday nights. He said, "If this works like I think it will, I'll give you an open tab." I assembled an all-star pub band with members of the Drops, The Bogmen, Mike Tait, and other musician pals of mine. We packed it every week with a thirsty crowd of our friends and people from the neighborhood, and because of our Sunday performances, the Tiger became a regular hangout for everyone in our scene—and I was awarded the dubious honor of that free tab. It was on one of these Sundays that I spotted Gordon drinking in the corner, wearing the kind of hat that jazz cats were known for.

We had just closed the show with the Demi Moore striptease thing (the Tiger had an even better pole than the Lion) when I approached him. "Nice lid . . . didn't Slip Mahoney wear one of those?" I said, goofing around. "Nice set . . . does Demi Moore know you're down here every Sunday doing her act?" he said, sipping a Hefeweizen, one of the really good imported German beers they had on tap. "No, but I'm sure she'd be flattered. What'd ya think?" I asked. "I think you're completely insane. I thought you were gonna break your neck when you were hanging upside down on that pole. It shows alotta commitment to wedgie yourself beforehand the way you did, though. I'll give you that," he said. "Yeah, well come down next week. We're gonna attempt a scene from *G.I. Jane*. I'm trying to wrangle the old helicopter from *Miss Saigon*," I told him. He laughed sarcastically and said, "Oh, in that case, count me in." We ended up shooting the shit after that, having a lively conversation.

If you are a fan of Violent Femmes songs, Gordon is a lot like you'd expect him to be. He's bohemian but not in a pretentious way, superintelligent, acerbic, well-read—and a funny, funny guy. He had long hair and piercing blue eyes behind his glasses and was reserved in his demeanor—unlike his vocal style. He was also a huge New York Mets fan, so we bonded over that big time. After talking awhile he sized me up and said, "How do I know you?" "My band opened for you a month ago at that weird place in Jersey," I explained to him. "Oh yeah, that summer camp resort place. Yeah, that place was weird. What are you guys called again?" he asked. "Knockout Drops," I answered. "That's right, Knockout Drops." He loved the story about the kid who'd scared us at the show.

We became great friends after that and have sat in on each other's sets many times over the years. Brian had a strict policy that only cool music was to be played on the overhead in the bar. It was his contention that the kind of music you played dictated what type of crowd you got, and I agree. He would jokingly say to his bartenders, "If I ever walk in here and Matchbox Twenty is playing, you're fired." But he didn't have to say that to them. The staff was all cool guys and gals with great taste anyway, especially our bartender friend Dan. Gordon and I would while away the hours in there drinking beers as Dan would unfurl Television's classic *Marquee Moon* album or something off the beaten path like Serge Gainsbourg. He was one of those guys that had to get everything right as it came out so he'd serve up the latest from Guided by Voices, Yo La Tengo, Radiohead, The Flaming Lips, Pavement, Buffalo Tom, and everyone else making inspired music in the mid-nineties. He was like our human iPod, his extra features being that he got you drunk and could answer any question you had about the band he was playing you. It made for a great hang.

One night I met Gordon down there and I could see when I walked in he'd already been there awhile. He had five cocktail napkins lined up vertically with stanza after stanza of an epic poem he'd been writing scribbled on them. I picked one of 'em up and looked at it. "What's this about Davy Crockett and the Alamo? Who are you writing this for, the History Channel?" "Gimme that. You're taking it outta context. It's gonna all make sense once I'm finished," he said and laughed. "Sorry to break your concentration, Professor," I said, sliding the napkin back to him.

Our good friend Dom was bartending and Brian was managing. Dom was a talented filmmaker and Gordon was providing the score for an indie movie he was filming at the time. Brian had an endless fountain of nickel knowledge when it came to all things cinema, so naturally the conversation turned to movies. Brian had hatched a discussion about an Ingmar Bergman movie, and feeling left out, I instantly derailed it by saying, "Do you guys think the guy who wrote the screenplay to the movie *Mannequin* is a necrophiliac? I mean, the theme couldn't be more apparent. Do the math."

The serenity of our one A.M. summit was being disrupted by a bunch of people sitting at a table behind us. Every few minutes they'd erupt, pounding the table and obnoxiously screaming. They were playing some kind of drinking game. I said to Dom, "What gives behind us?" "Those are Carlo's friends, up visiting him from Mexico. They came in banged up already. I may have to cut them off and I really don't want to," he said, taking a swig of his beer. That was the other thing I liked about the Tiger. All the bartenders got drunk with you. Carlo was a composer who owned a recording studio across the street and hung out in there a lot. He was an amiable Mexican guy who did film scores and music for commercials. I looked around but didn't see him. "Where's Carlo then?" I asked. Dom answered, "Oh, he bombed out hours ago."

At the Tiger there were two bathrooms. The men's room, which was down this treacherous set of uneven stairs, and the ladies' room that was just off the bar. It was understood that the regulars didn't have to hassle with the stairs and could just use the ladies' bathroom in the later hours. I was just about to take a leak when one of the Mexican dudes asked me, "How do I go to the bathroom?" I said, "I dunno, cowboy. However your parents taught ya, I guess." He didn't get it so I said, "It's just down the stairs, my friend. I'll show ya." I pointed him toward the stairs as I walked behind him, past his table of friends. The two of us veered apart, me going to the upstairs bathroom and him going downstairs. I closed the door and heard, "AAAAAAAAAAAAH!" followed by the sound of successive thumps. I rushed out to see if he was okay. I probably should've used better judgment and had him use the upstairs room but how was I to know? Everybody who braved those stairs after midnight was hammered.

By the time I got out of the bathroom, a lynch mob had formed. Eight Mexicans surrounded me. They had their mangled friend in tow, who was legless and barely aware of what had happened. "You knowingly sent him down those stairs while you walked easily into the upstairs bathroom. He could've been killed!" one yelled, in damn good English. I later found out he was a Mexican soap opera actor. "Hey, fellas, I'm not his keeper. One of you should've escorted him if you thought he was gonna take a digger," I said in my defense. They were getting ready to light me up when Brian, who was a consummate diffuser, stepped in and pulled me out of there. "I think you should go. These guys are primed to kill you," he said, walking me out.

The next day I got a call from Gordon. He said, "It got worse after you left. I was found guilty by association. They circled around me at the bar and started asking all these questions about you. What's your name? Where do you live? How do I know you? Do you come in a lot? Then they forcibly read my poem and found that stuff in there about the Alamo. They were about to get my neck size when Brian and Dom threw them all out." I said, "Holy shit, you're kidding?" He replied, "No, I'm not. Personally, I don't understand why they were so angry. Didn't we *lose* the Alamo?" I said, "Dude, you shoulda called me. I woulda come back." "Do you mean after they left or before?" he asked. "Yeah . . ."

. . .

In the fall of 1997, we began recording our first full-length CD, *Killed by the Lights*. We stopped playing so many dates to focus on making the album and promoting our upcoming Irving Plaza concert. We'd composed a number of songs in the wake of the Maverick fiasco and were determined to make an undeniable record—one that would convince any label or anyone. We had no deal so the recording was financed by our number one fan, the Yapper. He was tired of seeing us get "the short shrift," as he called it, and insisted we have the best of everything.

The Yapper was a Wall Street guy who had big bucks and was infinitely generous. He also loved to party and lived for music. His belief in us, and me especially, was a huge shot in the arm at a time when we really needed it. His red, sunburned face and blond hair gave him the look of a wild-eyed Norseman but it was his prodigious gift of gab that defined him—hence the nickname (given to him by his business cohorts). The man could sell snow tires in the desert. He was such a pill of positivity that during a night out drinking with him he could make me believe I'd beat Carl Lewis in a sixty-yard dash if only I'd put my mind to it. He gave me no choice but to believe him. He said, "If Brick Wall can't broker you a record deal, then I will."

Our contract with Joe was only bound to the *Nowadays* CD so we decided to hook up with a new producer, Jim Sabella. Jim had just had success with a group called Marcy Playground who'd recorded their hit song, "Sex and Candy," with him. A lot of other good stuff had emerged from his studio in recent years as well, so we were excited to work with him. He turned out to be an awesome producer, really understanding what we were all about and how to get it recorded.

Some darker themes had emerged in this collection of songs that were rather telling. The title track, "Killed by the Lights," conjured a bleak landscape. The character in the song is composing a letter to an old girlfriend essentially telling her that he's thrown in the towel on his life. That didn't necessarily mean suicide but it didn't not mean it either. Then there was the point of view of the girlfriend represented in the closing song, "Head Full o' Worry."

Killed by the Lights

There'll come a time tonight
You'll find out you were right
I cut short my flight
And was killed by the lights . . .

Head Full o' Worry

There you go
Where I don't know
But you're in such a hurry
Here I stand
Up on dry land
I got a head full o' worry

Feel-good songs of the summer, eh? Don't get me wrong. There were a lot of happy tunes on KBTL too, but looking back there's no denying that some black clouds had rolled in. Later on, a student DJ interviewing me for his college station would ask, "Are you a manic depressive?" I would answer, "No, I'm an exuberant melancholic."

We worked our asses off on KBTL through the autumn, pulling twelve-hour days in the studio. I used discretion around Jimmy but went out and raged after the sessions, often hooking up with Vanessa and cutting a swath through New York's underbelly.

When our big show at Irving Plaza came around we packed it to a near sellout, an unheard-of feat for an unsigned band. We were also getting a lot of nice press including an article in the *LA Times* calling us one of the best unsigned acts in the country. Michael and Rishon told us that there were a lot of labels at Irving and when they'd gotten it all sorted out they'd let us know. "The way you guys commanded that big stage I can't see anything other than a fat deal coming our way," Michael told us. We kept our eyes solely on the recording and decided to let them worry about getting us signed, though it was never far from anyone's mind.

The end of that year brought with it an unexpected change of address for me. My sister Donna had gotten engaged and her fiancé, Tommy O, was gonna be moving into the apartment so I had to find somewhere else to live. My good friends Elmo and Marino agreed to let me couch surf. "Just until I can find my own place," I told them. Elmo said, "Yeah, well, let us know what her name is when you do. We'd love to meet her."

Elmo and Marino were mainstays at all the Drops shows. Elmo was a gifted artist and cartoonist and had designed our *Nowadays* CD cover along with a lot of posters for us. Marino was a business guy. They were heavy drinkers themselves, but were nervous about me living with them because both of their girlfriends were around a lot. They told me to keep whatever craziness I was involved in, especially drugs, out of the house. They lived on Thirtieth Street between Madison and Fifth Avenue in a big railroad-style loft. I hated being out of the Village but you know what they say about beggars? Well, it's the same for skidders.

The actual move was simple: I threw my duffel bag on the floor next to the couch, just as I had done at Donna and Eileen's five years earlier. I slid it with my foot across the floor like I was playing shuffleboard, locating it perfectly adjacent to the armrest. Elmo said, "I can see you've done this before. Is that all your stuff?" "You know me, I'm a nomad . . . gotta travel light, my friend," I said. "I thought you were a skidder," he replied. "Skidders are urban nomads," I said, cracking a beer that I'd forgotten I had stashed in my pocket.

That night we went out for drinks to discuss the house rules. We walked into a chichi bar around the corner, a stupid fuckin' place none of us wanted to be in, and I could see Marino was a little nervous. I tried to reassure him by saying, "Listen, I'm recording right now and behaving myself. My hours are such that you're not even gonna see me. I'll be Mr. Invisible. You'll see." He said, "I don't wanna bust balls. You know me, Campy. I'm easy. It's just that we have the girls sleep over a lot and I don't want them walking out into something weird. I'll tell you right now they don't want you there." "They don't want *me* there," I said, putting my arm around him, "but they're not gonna have any problems with Mr. Invisible."

It was a Monday night so I left them to go downtown and do my gig with Mike Tait. Mike and I engaged the crowd with our usual duo thing. In fact, we called ourselves, "Fonduo," because we used to set up a fondue pot between our stools as we sang. We got the idea one night after the set when I was telling him about the Campion family fondue dinners of the seventies. The crowd would come up and eat it with us while we played. It was a hilarious novelty for the act and Mike made a mean cheese fondue. Everybody loved it but we had to discontinue it after the flame under the pot set fire to the drapes during one of our shows. We kept the name, though.

After our set we hooked up with these two gorgeous and wholesome sisters from the Midwest. They were on vacation so we volunteered to show them around the Village. We barhopped on Bleecker for a while and then, after we were all a bit tipsy, Mike skipped with his gal back to his apartment nearby. I stayed out with the other sister and proceeded to get so whacked that I blacked out.

The next day I woke up with the girl next to me, both of us naked, sprawled out on Elmo and Marino's wraparound couch, blanketless. Through a dense fog I saw my new roommates and their girlfriends all assembled in their business suits peering down at us. I kept my head buried in the girl's long luxurious mane of curly brown hair so they wouldn't know I was awake. She was lightly snoring. On their way out I heard Marino's girlfriend ask him in a whisper, "Oh my God, who's that girl he's with?" He answered, "I guess that's Mrs. Invisible."

We finished recording the *Killed by the Lights* album. The record was far and away our crowning achievement. Jim Sabella (with a lot of help from our brilliant live soundman and studio engineer Phil Palazzolo) had delivered on his promise to get us recorded the right way. We were thrilled. The Brick Wall boys were happy too because now they had our success at Irving Plaza, the good press we'd gotten, and a killer record to work with in their pursuit of the right deal. They gave us the usual, we'll-let-you-know speech after we listened to the demo of the mixes together.

The Yapper had the CD mastered by the legendary Howie Weinberg up at Masterdisk. He'd done Nirvana's *Nevermind* and a host of other iconic records. Howie told us, "This record is a layup. Congratulations, boys." Hearing that kind of praise from a guy like Howie, who normally just couldn't be bothered, sent me into orbit. *This time we can't miss,* I thought. The CDs were pressed and we celebrated with a sold-out show at the Bowery Ballroom. Howie even came down and partied with us. We met with a big A and R guy from Universal in our dressing room after the show, who told us we were all but in! Still sweaty from the lights, we all clinked glasses to our unstoppable future. Our Universal guy said, "Fellas, I just have to go to London for a few weeks and when I get back we'll sign the papers and make it official."

A month and a half passed and we read in one of the trades that

Universal had just fired four hundred employees. His name was on top of that list. The phone didn't ring at all after that. I was starting to believe that we were the bad-luck schleprocks of rock 'n' roll.

A few more months passed and the air slowly seeped out of our balloon. We had little skirmishes with hope—pieces of possible good news that would turn out to be nothing. Everybody who's ever battled this business knows what I'm talking about. Somebody would tell me, "Oh, so and so from Bumfuck Records loves you." It's an immediate adrenaline shot. Your lungs fill up with helium. Hope would spring eternal in these moments, but in the light of day the deal just wouldn't materialize. I fell for it every time. After a little while I'd run into that person again. I wouldn't wanna ask, in my heart already knowing the answer, but curiosity and desperation would get the best of me and I'd say, "Hey, whatever happened to so and so? I thought he loved us." Only to find out that he'd left or been fired from Bumfuck Records—or that it hadn't been true in the first place. It was just some asshole talking in a bar.

Reality had forced its way through my back door and wasn't even allowing me the sanctity of my daydreams anymore. They had been my buffer in life. If things weren't to my liking I would always dial up one of my favorite ones—but not anymore. I fell into a despondency that even the Yapper couldn't pull me from. I just couldn't picture us winning anymore. When hope dies, it can be a long and drawn-out wake. I started spending all my time drunk, abysmally staring into the open casket of my dead dream.

Chapter Eleven

"I Call Him Dribbly"

With no proper distribution for *Killed by the Lights* and hardly any dates to play, I commenced with a daily diet of disappointment, booze, and blow—all day, every day. And I mean crack an eye, run for a pint. That lamp shade I'd strapped on back when I was fourteen had started to feel like a crash helmet that had been compromised by one too many knocks. I walked around sensing it would surely shatter with the next unexpected blow to the head. In other words, I was losing my fuckin' mind.

Still living at Elmo and Marino's, I'd wake up every afternoon for a fun bit of aerobic dry heaving (the aerobic part being the mad scurry to the bathroom). I'd hug the bowl for dear life until the jackpot of scorching hot bile came bubbling up through me, followed by the relieving sting of a cold sweat. Once that activity had reached its violent conclusion I'd wipe the perspiration from my brow and be off to the Blind Tiger to begin my short day's journey into a long-ass night. It felt like the perfect time to fall in love.

Her name was Grace. She walked into the Blind Tiger one Sunday as we were playing and I knew right away she was the one for me. I can't explain how or why but as I was singing a fuzzy feeling washed over me. I then did probably the corniest thing I've ever done in my life and told the boys to play U2's "All I Want Is You" and crooned it to her. The band and I had a weekly ritual of doing a shot at the bar together when the show was over, and according to them I floated right by in a trance without even noticing that they were holding out a shot for me. They watched as I made a beeline to the front of the bar, taking the stool next to her.

"That was really moving. You have a beautiful voice. I felt like you were singing that to me. Were you?" she said, sipping an ice water. "If I say yes, then where do we go from here? I can't give all that away in the first minute," I said, kidding around and feeling a bit stupid about it. "Well, you were looking right at me the whole time and didn't seem to be looking anywhere else," she pointed out.

"That's really more of an autistic thing. I get fixated on one object while I'm concentrating. It's usually that neon Budweiser sign over there. You just happened to be sitting in front of it," I said, pointing over her shoulder. "Are you autistic?" she asked. "I've had so many cocktails that I'm probably that and a few other things," I said, burping and trying to remain cool. "Oh, nice," she said, howling. Her laugh sent my heart spinning out of control. It was un-self-conscious and loud and not at all what you'd expect from someone who looked like her. I love when girls laugh like that.

She had long and shiny light blond hair and the roundest, bluest eyes imaginable. I sensed a lot of compassion and intelligence in them. She moved through the bar with a calm elegance. I watched as she lithely weaved through the chairs on her way back from the ladies' room, pulling out her barstool and sitting in one motion. She was 5 feet 8 with a perfectly proportioned body and was dressed really cool too. She had on tight-fitting pink-and-blue-plaid bell-bottoms and a white baseball T-shirt with red sleeves that extended to her elbows. She was unbearably sexy, almost to the point that it made me uncomfortable. I wanted to yell out, "YOU DO KNOW HOW HOT YOU ARE, DON'T YOU?" but felt it might hurt my chances. She did know how hot she was but she didn't care about that kinda stuff.

After she sat back down I continued to talk fast, trying to stay afloat with some flirty bullshit that ultimately went nowhere. I was glad it didn't work. It meant I was gonna have to be real with her and part of me really yearned for that. I spent so much of my time plastering a fake smile on and entertaining people that it might be nice to engage in a real conversation, I thought. The only problem was I didn't quite know how to do that.

"Your brother is Billy from The Bogmen, right?" she asked. "Oh good God, here we go. Yes, he is. Why, do you know them?" I asked with zero enthusiasm. "Well, my friend took me to their concert when they played with the Barenaked Ladies at Roseland and we hung out a little with them after the show. I met your brother there. He was a really nice guy and they were fantastic," she said. She was right. I was at that same show and they were great, blowing the cutesy Barenaked Ladies off the stage, but this subject wasn't gonna put any wind in my sails, so I tried to tack the conversation somewhere else.

"So, are you new around here? I haven't seen you before," I said, sipping a beer. "Wow, you really don't wanna talk about your brother do you? Are you guys like Cain and Abel or something?" she asked. "No, in fact, he's one of my best friends, not to mention being my brother whom I love dearly. It's just that everyone around here is always talking about him and the band and all the glamorous stuff they have going on and it makes me feel kinda like . . . I don't know . . . an also-ran," I said, and quickly averted my eyes.

Up to that point I'd never addressed the subject honestly with anyone. I was too ashamed and concerned over how it would be perceived. I'd comment on Billy's success and make a sarcastic joke about how my career was going nowhere, so people kinda knew how I felt but I'd never answered a question about it from the heart the way I'd just done. This girl had something in her that made me wanna tell the truth. It was scary. I wasn't used to dealing in the truth that much. It was much too hard to control. "Well, I thought my song was wonderful," she said, batting her long eyelashes. "It wasn't your song," I said, reverting comfortably back to lies.

"To answer your question from before, yes, I'm new. I'm an actress. I moved here from LA about a month ago. I booked the lead in an indie film that's shooting here in the city." "Congratulations, that's awesome," I said, clinking her glass. "I notice you're drinking ice water. Is that some sort of Scientologist, yoga–influenced, recenter-yourself, LA-lifestyle choice?" Whenever someone wasn't drinking, I was the nosiest fuck. I had to know the reason why. Maybe it was because I couldn't fathom it. "No," she said, giggling, "I have work to do on my character when I get home. I need a clear head for that. We start shooting in Soho on Tuesday." I was even more taken with her after she said that. She was beautiful, an artist, and she had it together. I was in love.

We hung out for another hour just kicking it around and getting to know each other. She told me she was originally from New Jersey. I started singing "Jersey Girl" to her. "Cut it out," she said. "You know not all people from New Jersey love Bruce." "Wait a minute, are you saying you don't like Bruce?" I asked, ready to defend him the way I always did with my hipper-than-thou friends. "No, I actually do, his older stuff more, but I'm just saying not all of us do," she said. "Well, that's a Tom Waits song anyway. Bruce just covered it," I pointed out. It turned out we liked a lot of the same music. She was only twenty-four so she didn't know some of the groups I referenced. "I really like Cracker," she said. "Yeah, Kerosene Hat is great but I'm a bigger fan of David Lowery's first band, Camper Van Beethoven," I told her. She'd never heard of them but that was probably less of an age thing and more to do with the fact that they'd never gotten on the radio. "They're such a cool band. Get the *Key Lime Pie* record. You'll love it." We got on the subject of the Beatles and she said, "You wanna hear a good one? My old roommate in LA hated the Beatles." "What? You have to be subhuman to hate them . . . or just a contrarian ass-hole. Which was she?" I asked. "A little of both," she said.

Grace and I were hitting it off magnificently but the hammer was coming down on me fast from all the beers and shots I'd backlogged. Then I hit a wall and said, "I gotta apologize for being so wasted. I got here at like six o'clock to set up." She said, "Wow, you guys have to set up that early?" "No," I said. "Why don't you rest your head here for a few minutes and I'll order you some water," she said, putting my head down on her shoulder. She turned to get Dan the bartender's attention as I addressed God in my head. "Shit, God, I'll never doubt you again. This is your best work since the fishes and the loaves."

I napped on her as she talked to Dan about the Cake record he was playing. "I saw Cake just before I left LA. They were great," I heard her tell him as I drifted in and out. She kept talking to him while stroking my hair like I was some kind of snoozing pet. I was in shambles but the evening couldn't have gone better.

Grace became my girlfriend after that. I didn't do my usual sleep-over-three-nights-in-a-row-and-presto-chango-I'm-living-there thing this time. She was busy with the movie and I didn't want to horrify her with my nightly savagery, so my strategy instead was to avoid her a lot. I ended up seeing her two or three nights a week. I'd make sure not to be shit-housed when I went up to her apartment to call on her. She liked to meet up there because she was usually knackered from that day's filming. We'd have herbal tea and talk a while.

She was an avid reader and had a fervent interest in fine art. She'd talk about how she loved to paint but confessed to not being that good at it, which made her all the more adorable. I'd show her that I was no slouch at the art of conversation by naming every defensive starter on the Super Bowl XXI Giants. She could've cared less but she was so cute when she was feigning interest. It was like an old-fashioned courtship in some ways. After batting it back and forth in her sitting room we'd then adjourn for a splendiferous roll in the hay. The way her bedroom was decorated I felt like I was violating Holly Hobbie in her gazebo. We'd shake the room, always knocking her Indian dream catcher from the wall. It would fall on my ass and she'd throw it aside, saying, "I have to find a different place to hang this."

She'd have an early call in the morning so I'd split around midnight telling her, "You should get your beauty rest." I'd give her a thorough good-night kiss and then zip to the Blind Tiger with an impatient thirst. Thankfully it was conveniently located only fifty paces from her door—my two favorite things in the world in wonderfully close proximity—yippee!

I'd skip out the front door of her building, doing a singing Jim Morrison imitation. *"She lives on Love Street . . . lingers long on Love Street."* I'd keep warbling it into the crisp night air all the way up the block and the timing would always be such that the moment I got to that line in the second verse, "There's this store where the creatures meet," I could see my gang lighting it up through the Blind Tiger Alehouse window. My heart would be pounding when I'd been without a drink for a few hours. I'd pull the door open and, borrowing a line from naughty boy Max in the iconic children's book *Where the Wild Things Are*, I'd cry out, "LET THE WILD RUMPUS START!" And all the creatures would join in.

. . .

I fell deeply for Grace and she for me but even that love, as powerful as it was, didn't prove to be enough of a flotation device for what came next.

From the deep recesses of my drunken psyche emerged a new character, a self-loathing monster my friends dubbed Bizarro. Bizzaro was my belligerent blacked-out alter ego who was filled with rage and darkness—my perfect opposite. He'd come out at the tail end of the night, usually after a lot of whiskey or vodka, inhabiting me and terrorizing everyone else. It was a Dr. Jekyll and Mr. Hyde scenario. One day I got a phone call from Brian at the Tiger and he said, "Dude, are you all right? You were saying some fucked-up shit in here last night. You scared everyone. I just wanna know if you're all right." "What kinda shit?" I asked.

He went on to tell me that after a number of Jameson's I'd gotten a little schitzy. He said, "I was telling you about that crazy woman with the clownish lipstick and the accordion that came in and you cracked up out of control. At that point you seemed like your regular self. Then your laugh died down and you took a long sip of your drink, still giggling a little." I said, "Yeah, so?" "Yeah, so that's when you teared up and told me you were gonna kill yourself." "WHAT?" I asked, in disbelief. "Yeah, you said you were just gonna kill yourself and that you'd made up your mind and not to try and talk you out of it. Then you started partying again like you hadn't even said anything. It was pretty fucked up," he said, concerned. "Listen, man, I'm not gonna kill myself. I've never had that thought, consciously, in my entire life," I told him. "Well, you could've fooled me. In fact, you did," he said, sounding a little pissed at me now. "Sorry, man," I apologized, "it won't happen again."

But it did happen again. And again and again and *again* with always the same sequence of uproarious cackles one second and tearful suicidal diatribes the next. I'd always be mortified upon hearing that I'd uttered those things. What the fuck was wrong with me? It was obviously alcohol fueled but I wasn't gonna blame booze for my problems. Quitting drinking was out of the question. I'd done it before in spurts when I was with Martha and remembered it as being a hellish way to live.

My suicidal rants were not just relegated to Brian at the Tiger but started happening everywhere and with everyone. Ponzo was hearing it, my sisters, my roommates, the Drops, even Grace had witnessed it a few times. My early strategy of keeping her safeguarded from my drinking had become too problematic. If I was only gonna see her when I was sober then I'd never see her, so I started just showing up as is, which was always boxed outta my mind. The cat was now fully out of the bag.

She said, "Sometimes when you come over here late at night, I hear you out in the living room saying weird stuff." I said, "Really? I'm probably just singing." "No, I peeked out once and you were engaged in a heated conversation. At first I thought someone might be with you but I looked and you were the only one there. You looked like someone from acting class doing a monologue into the air," she said, visibly upset. I blew it off and said, "It was probably the Gettysburg Address. I memorized it in fourth grade. I do it when I'm lonely or bored . . . or sometimes drunk." She said, "Oh yeah? Recite a little of it now, then." "I can't. I can only remember it when I'm drunk," I told her. "I think your version is a little angrier than Abraham Lincoln's," she said, walking out of the room.

A few weeks after that conversation when she was again watching me give her walls a talking, she decided to grab the Dictaphone that I used to record song ideas, and get me on tape. Much to my horror, she played it for me the next day. It sounded like Satan dictating his grievances about the world in low and hateful tones or, better still, like Frederich Nietzsche drunkenly trying to pick a bar fight.

I was expounding on anything and everything under the sun. I ended my sunny soliloquy with some uplifting theories on theology and the joy of being alive. "And what of God, you ask? What a fuckin' joke that is. I can't believe I ever fell for that one. It's all one big fuckin' ruse created by humankind so that we all fall in line like good little chickens. God is a chew toy to keep us all from FREAKIN' THE FUCK OUT! I'm sick of God. Is the same God that created me the one that created Stalin and Hitler . . . or Timothy McVeigh? Are we talking about the same God who brought us GUY OSEARY . . . who, in turn, gave us Candlebox . . . And now we all have to listen to fuckin' CANDLEBOX on the radio!" I slurred mightily. "I'm just gonna fuckin' kill myself. What's the fuckin' point anyway? I'm tryin' to find it but there isn't one. Fuck me . . . FUCK YOU, GOD, if you're listening and you exist . . . and FUCK THIS!" the voice on the tape roared, sounding five octaves lower than my normal tenor.

She clicked it off and I sat there dumbstruck and petrified by what I'd just heard. I was mortified by what I'd put her through. I was also frightened for myself. For the first time in my life, I questioned my sanity. I said to her, "I think that thing needs batteries." "No, sweetie, that's what you sound like. You need help," she said, her big blue eyes welling up. "I am so sorry. You know I love you and don't really mean any of that shit, right? I mean, you know that that's just the booze talking, yes? Yes?" I pleaded, needing reassurance desperately, but she didn't give any. She just stared. When she played me that tape I think the response she was looking to get back was, "Oh my God, you're right. I have to get some help," not "I think that thing needs batteries."

I'd love to be able to report that the Dictaphone incident stopped me dead in my tracks and I got sober. Any normal, self-respecting human being would have. Instead, as always, I went the other way by trying to drink my way out of it. For that I have no salable explanation other than that, as a raging alcoholic, drinking was my answer to everything. But that much you already knew. Bizarro's appearances got closer and closer together and so did my blacked-out pledges of suicide. If you say something enough times, drunk or not, people are gonna start to believe you.

So this storm of self-pity continued to swell and one day while my roommates were at work, and by roommates I mean my friends, Elmo and Marino, who were still graciously letting me crash on their couch, I woke up early and started to drink . . . and drink . . . and drink. It wasn't a simple matter of having woken up on the wrong side of the couch, either. It went deeper than that and I knew it. Something awful had washed ashore in my heart. It was D-day—the day I realized I didn't like myself anymore. I didn't like my station in life either. I didn't like that I'd accomplished, in my estimation, nothing. It took me a while to get to these epiphanies because I had begun the day guzzling angrily *at* the world, but when the blame game rang hollow I turned the barrel back where it belonged, on myself. I was the one who'd made these choices. I was the one who wasn't man

enough to live on his own and had become a skidder. I WAS THE
ONE WHO WAS A WASTE OF FUCKIN' SPACE!

I paced. I cried. I swore a blue streak. I drank more—swallowing
vodka furiously, hoping it would change my mood, but it didn't work.
I began drunk-dialing friends at their offices, in the middle of their
workdays, and trying to make them laugh, but I guess getting a call
from an emotionally overwrought and unstable friend at work didn't
make for that fertile a chuckle patch. I remember even the Yapper
telling me, "Go to bed, Campy. I haven't got time for this today." I
desperately wanted something about all this to strike me as hilarious
and rescue me but nothing did. I was all out of jokes. Nothing was
funny to me anymore. That got me really worried.

I then did the most melodramatic thing one can do in the middle
of an ego meltdown/panic attack/boozed-up nervous breakdown/
existential crisis and went in for a little mirror appraisal. Standing
there looking pathetic in my boxers with my dick turtle-ing out, in
crusty black socks and a ripped up T-shirt, holding a big bottle of
vodka, I stared into a full-length mirror and saw a scowl the size of the
Great Divide peering back at me. I wanted to spit at it but thought I'd
seen that in a movie somewhere and chose instead just to give myself
the finger. I wanted the moment to be real and not just an imitation
of something I'd seen. I *really* hated myself. That lamp shade/crash
helmet had finally cracked in two and fallen off, as I'd feared it would.
The light of the world was proving too great without it. This was the
real thing. I *hated* myself—for what I had become—and what I hadn't
become—but mostly for what I was, which was a big fat *nothing*. I
wanted to die.

With all of this swirling in my head, I opened my second bottle
of Smirnoff, called Elmo, and made the dramatic proclamation that it
was to be my last day on earth. I explained how things weren't really
working out for me here and that maybe it would be best if I just cut
it short now before my loser life got any more embarrassing.

I must've been pretty convincing 'cause this really scared the shit
out of him. I'd always just mumbled this stuff before. This time I was
going into some kind of detailed manifesto, even longer than the one
Grace had gotten on tape. I hung up the phone and before I could
say "Sylvia Plath," he and Marino were at the door with the boys

from Bellevue. It felt like I literally put the receiver down and there they were. "C'mon, Campy, they're just here to take you to detox, dude. You need it, you know you need it," Elmo pleaded. I said to myself, *Holy shit, these guys look like fuckin' white coats. What the hell have I done? I thought Elmo'd just feel sorry for me and maybe bring home a pizza.* Seeing all the emergency medical personnel gathering in the living room scared me straight (not really) and I supplanted suicidal me with what's-all-this-commotion-about? me. Fear of incarceration will do that.

I sat on the ottoman and bummed a cigarette from one of the butterfly catchers to buy time, but there was nothing to think about. They were there to take me and something told me they were gonna do just that. The straitjacket kinda gave it away. Not knowing what else to do, I began flirting with a female cop who'd just arrived at the scene with her sergeant. "Hi, these guys were kind enough to grant me a smoke to mull this thing over," I said, catching her up on events. She was Latino with a very pretty face. "Well, I don't know how much mulling you should be doing. You have to come with us right now," she said, chuckling, with ten EMTs standing there next to her. "Answer me honestly, under different circumstances do you think we'd have a shot? When I'm not suicidal, people say I can really be a lot of fun. I might need a new living situation, though. I hope you don't find this too personal a question, but do you have cable?" I asked. Everybody in the room laughed but the sergeant, a big dude with huge, hairy forearms and foreboding eyes.

He looked thoroughly annoyed and I could see he was about to give the order for all of them to bum-rush me. "All right," I said, "maybe you guys are right. I'll go to detox. Just let me freshen up a little." "Oh, you're going to detox, pal, but you'll be doing your freshening-up down there. Let's go! I've had enough of the comedy show," the sergeant said, giving the signal for them to seize me. A bunch of them grabbed hold of me and ushered me out of the building and into an ambulance. It was a relatively smooth exercise, with me giving no struggle, and we sped off to the detox. What they didn't tell me was that *detox* was just a cuddly word for "psych ward."

I walked into Bellevue peacefully from the parking lot, two attendants at each arm, giving me a perverse feeling of importance, but as soon as the antiseptic smell of the hospital hit my nose and I got a good look at some of the snarling, wild-eyed inpatients, I started bucking hard. I went headfirst through the swinging double doors and, with slapstick timing, broke away just as the doors were swinging back, flattening me cartoon style. They picked me up off the floor and had me completely off the ground so I started bronco-kicking like you do when you're a little kid and some bigger kids are about to throw you in the water.

I was fighting like an animal being brought into captivity, more out of reflex and terror than being pissed off at them. It was as if all the claustrophobia I'd felt in the world for the last thirty years was being unleashed, giving me herculean strength, and since I was going against four of them with no way to win, I could fully detonate and it wouldn't look that weird. I mean nobody blamed King Kong for taking a few swipes at the helicopters, right? It was surreal in that sense, kind of like I was robotically playing out a scene in a movie.

They wrestled me onto a gurney, strapped me down, and jammed a Thorazine needle into my left arm. I'd given a good account of myself and just before the lights went out I remember popping my head off the pillow and apologizing to the four orderlies. I said, "You guys would make a good front four for the Giants," and the one on my left, a black guy with a kind face, laughed and came back at me with "Yeah, well, you'd make a helluva rubberman in the circus, Chris." Rubberman, eh? So much for Hercules.

I'd love to have you believe I'm some sort of Steve McQueen but I'm not. I'm just as chickenshit as everyone else. I'm just a kid from Huntington, Long Island, who grew up playing wiffleball in the backyard. What was I doing on this flight deck of damned souls? This place was for true crackpots with irreversible damage. I sure as hell wasn't one of them, was I? Who was the maestro of this madness? Was it my heroic intake of cocktails and drugs? I sure as shit hoped not, 'cause in my opinion those were the only things that *kept* me sane. I knew a lot of people with the same consumption levels and I didn't see them being thrown into any booby hatches. Where was all this existential gloom coming from? I'd always been a happy person by nature. In fact my mom had told me that my very first word was *happy.* I really didn't want to off myself and yet I kept threatening to do so, so maybe I really was going crazy?

I had decided to treat these suicide threats like a passing phase. In my mind it was the same as when, for a few weeks back in '93, I kept getting up drunk and pissing in my sister Donna's sock drawer. I'd stopped doing that after a couple of weeks, hadn't I?

When Grace had gotten me on tape I briefly questioned my sanity, but quickly dismissed it thinking I'd just had another bad night out—a clunker. NOW I was really questioning it. *Then again, if I were truly going crazy would I know? Probably not,* I thought. One thing was clear. None of the hows and whys fuckin' mattered anymore 'cause I was on the Isle of Misfit Toys and it was about survival, nothing else. These off-kilter action figures I was in with would poke my eye out with a pencil in my sleep if I wasn't careful (no choo-choos with square wheels here, just homicidal tendencies).

Strapped and shackled, I entered oblivion by way of a Thorazine dream. They're just like real dreams, but on Thorazine what would normally be a tweeting little birdie becomes a squawking pterodactyl. If you happen to be holding a baby, it'll try to eat your head—that sort of thing. Your dreamscape is radioactive. And that's just when you're asleep. The perks keep on coming once you're awake. It's a wonderful recreational drug.

Do you know why Thorazine is so great? You get to be higher than you've ever been in your entire life and have the added educational advantage of knowing what it must be like to be a fucking mongoloid. If you thought you had sympathy for severely retarded people before, just try a few hours on Thorazine. You'll never laugh at another Farrelly Brothers movie again, because guess what? You've been there. And it ain't easy.

· · ·

There are a lot of places in this world that will fall short of your expectations. They get a big build-up and you're left disappointed. Bellevue is not one of these places. Bellevue is everything you think it will be. If anything, it eclipses your imagination. It is a never-ending Fellini movie.

I woke up in this boiling cauldron of the criminally insane and immediately wanted out. I was still zooming on the Thorazine but in my brain I was lucid and I marched right over to the desk with an intended speech of "Hey I think you made a little mistake here . . . I'm not like these people . . . I can't remember exactly what happened but I think I may have said some things I didn't mean . . . Is there any way to rectify the situation?" I made my approach looking fairly legless, stared at the nurse for a second to compose my thoughts, decided on an opening sentence, and then let it go. "Geh," I said, pointing my finger at her with conviction, my eyes crossed. She said, "What?" I stood there and wobbled for a second, regained my composure, concentrated hard this time, really wanting to get my point across, and with my face about to fall off I let it fly again, "Geh." That's the only sound I could muster.

Following my dramatic attempt at speech, they shuffled me back to bed and I slept for, I don't even know how many hours. I woke up again and now I was hell-bent on getting out of this cuckoo inferno by showing the head nurse that I was normal. As I was walking briskly and purposefully toward the desk, a guy appeared out of nowhere dribbling an imaginary basketball. He started throwing his shoulder into me like he was driving to the hoop. No shit. You had to see what he looked like too. He was five foot nothin', bald, standard-issue crazy eyes, and bushy eyebrows. He looked like a deranged Martin Scorsese. I call him Dribbly but not just for his basketball prowess. He drooled like a motherfucker too.

I couldn't get past Dribbly 'cause he kept dribbling into me, so to get by him I started faking to the left and going right and vice versa, but he was too quick. He kept beating me to the spot. This went on for a minute or two and finally out of frustration, I yelled, "Dude, stop it. I GOTTA GET PAST!" And I screamed it pretty loud. The nurse looked up and what did she see? At a glance it was him dribbling feverishly like a point guard and me huffing and puffing and moving side to side with him. *Great,* I thought. *Now it looks like I'm guarding him!*

I threw him out of the way, went right over to her, and said, "Listen, I don't remember all that happened here last night but you guys made a mistake," and as I was talking, Dribbly returned more determined than ever, and now he was up on my leg, backing his ass into me, doing these Shaq Big Man moves, all the while still dribbling.

I was trying to persuade this lady to let me go and this lunatic was knocking into me like we were underneath the basket in the NBA finals. I had to be able to speak with her without all of this if she was ever gonna release me so I thought I'd try something. I started guarding him as if he had a real ball and when he turned, I reached in and slapped at where the ball was supposed to be. The first swipe I took nothing happened. I must've missed. The second time I did it, I got *all ball* and he scurried down the corridor, diving under a gurney after it. I turned around and she said, "Havin' fun?"

The nurse had the kind of hard shell that is common in New York. She was tough but funny with a foggy, tobacco-ravaged voice and an Italian face. She was about thirty-five-ish. I said, "Look, I think we both know I don't belong here." She said, " HA! Believe it or not, there was a time when I actually heard that from him," referring to Dribbly in her thick New York accent. I said, "Yeah but I think you know this is different." She said, "Hey, I don't know nothin'. The first thing ya learn on this job is not to judge a book by its cover, and by the way, your cover ain't looking so good. There was a rich Wall Street guy in here last week who kept tellin' everybody he was Greg Louganis. Then he tried to do a half gainer off his bed and broke his arm," she said, laughing and shuffling some manila folders. "He gave me his autograph, see." On her desk was a drawing done in red, blue, and yellow crayon of a man in a Speedo at the end of a diving board and below there was a note that read "Dear Marcy, Don't be afraid of the high dive in life or in the pool. Love, Greg Louganis." "What's that in the backround, a screaming meteorite?" I asked. She snapped, "That's the sun, moron. Yeah, you don't belong here at all."

She then told me in no uncertain terms that I'd be staying the rest of that day and night and to go back to my room. I turned around and right up on me was Dribbly again, only now he was pissed. He glared at me for a minute, his eyes lit with hostility, and said, "Thanks a lot, asshole. NOW I LOST IT!" I had nothing better to do so I put my arm around him and said, "C'mon, dude, I'll help you look for it."

I walked the ward with Dribbly for a while and then had the rest of that day to think about my life, and let me tell you, it was a hell of a place to do that. They gave me some Valium at bedtime but it didn't do a thing to offset the hypermanic activity in my brain. There was a chain of you're-a-piece-of-shit choruses echoing through my head that wouldn't turn off until I settled in and just listened to the sounds of Bellevue at night. Then I got scared.

The guy next to me had a library of sound effects going in his sleep. It was an orchestrated ensemble of snoring, groaning, the occasional night scream, and some sort of whistling. It almost felt like listening to a drum kit with the snoring and groaning providing the kick and snare and the screams and whistles acting as cymbals. There was some psycho-soprano humming coming from the room next door with just the right amount of hallway echo to make it completely chilling. There's nothing more frightening than crazy people humming because it seems like they're doing it to stave off their own terror.

There were new people being brought in and raging like I had done, however many hours before. It seemed like decades had gone by since then. All these noises together comprised some kind of twisted symphony. I prayed to Jesus and wept. I was too exhausted and upset to get into the whole God debate. I just did it out of instinct. Every once in a while I let out my own involuntary scream of agony and didn't feel the least bit self-conscious about it. *When in Rome*, I thought. Then I'd see Dribbly dart past my door, occasionally stopping to dribble around in a circle. It's gonna sound weird but I took a great amount of comfort in that.

Alone that night I sat at the windowsill, head in hands, gazing out at the city lights, and realized that I didn't know the first thing about how to live in this world. Then I let my imagination fly me over the horizon onto windblown landscapes. I'd be happier there . . .

Chapter Twelve

Freeze Dried and Born Again (in the Bar)

arly the following morning, I was released from Bellevue into my
parents' custody—a great feeling at thirty-two. I can still see my
dad's expression. It was not unlike the one I remember getting
after a tough Little League loss. You know the one that says, "You
gave it your all, pal. Whattya say we go to 7-Eleven and get you a
Slurpee?" The body language was the same here but his face read
more helpless and said, "This one's outta my hands, kid."

On the way home to Huntington in the car, he confessed to me
and my mom that the last time he'd been to Bellevue was in the early
fifties to visit his dad who was dying of cirrhosis of the liver due to severe alcoholism. He died long before I was born and was rarely talked
about. I'd never even seen a picture of him. He'd only told us Gramps
had won a Purple Heart for his heroics in World War II. He'd been
one of the last men off his destroyer, which had struck an underwater
mine and blown up off the coast of North Africa. In the process he'd
caught a lot of shrapnel in the face, leaving him slightly disfigured and
prone to nervous blinking for the rest of his life. In the years after the
war he systematically destroyed his liver from a barstool. "It only took
him about six years. He wasn't even fifty years old," Dad said. This
revelatory piece of family history was, of course, lost on me. I was too
busy crying, blowing my nose, and letting my eyes wander out the
window onto the majestic L.I.E.

We drove through Queens, passing several auto garages, Laundromats, and supermarkets, all with seemingly happy folks going in and out of them. I cursed my racing mind as I observed them, craving blissful simplicity. "Jesus, I am a fuckin' nut bag," I muttered under my breath. My mom turned around and said, "What?" "Nothing, just talking to myself. Don't be alarmed. It's just leftover behavior from the looney bin. If you don't talk to yourself in there the other kids make fun of you."

"Not all the crazy people are inside, ya know. We had a real doozy with us out in the waiting room," Mom said, handing me a tissue. "Really? Who?" I asked, wanting desperately to hear a story and not be in my head anymore. "I was sitting there chatting with this charming little Ethiopian lady. She was very slight of frame and soft-spoken with these delicate features, probably about sixty years old or so. She had this very dark black skin with a brilliant smile—really beautiful. She asked me in her timid way how many kids I had and I told her six. She said that was nice. I said, well, we're Irish and the Irish are known for having alotta kids. Well, to that she didn't say anything and then I let a moment pass and asked her if she had any kids. She nonchalantly told me that she'd birthed twenty-seven children by Haile Selassie," she said, hysterically laughing. Dad jumped in saying, "She couldn't have been more than four foot ten and maybe ninety-five pounds. I told Mom I was having trouble picturing her having even one, never mind the size litter she described. We got the feeling that she might've been stretching the truth a little. Whattya think? My guess is that she wandered in from triage." "God bless her. She was precious," Mom added, still giggling a little.

I know this may all sound rather glib considering where we'd just come from but my folks were well versed in the way of the booze malady by then. They'd been through multiple car wrecks, alcohol-related arrests, and other assorted dramas due to my and my siblings' hell-raising, not to mention my dad's, so nothing surprised them anymore—not even Bellevue. My mom had this to say: "God has a plan for you. You have to ask him what that is. I know what it's not. It's not you getting high all the time and feeling sorry for yourself. You have something that we used to refer to in the old neighborhood as the 'Irish crazies.' You can't drink. You're too sensitive. I've been telling you that since you were a teenager. I've always known it about you. If you continue this way you'll see that place again . . . or worse. You need to turn your life and your will over to God and seek some help. Can you do that?" "I don't know," I said, being honest.

My dad jumped in. "You don't know? What don't you know? You threatened to kill yourself yesterday. Scared the hell out of everyone, especially your mother. We just picked you up from Bellevue. Where's the tricky part of the question?" "I don't know where I'm at with all of that right now," I said, clamming up quickly. "With all what? Getting yourself sober? God? What?" he said, becoming frustrated. "All of it . . . I guess God, mostly . . . I don't know whether I believe anymore," I said, really not wanting to open that can of worms with my very Catholic parents. "Oh Jeez, I'm gonna let your mother take this one. This is over my head. Pat, would you take it, please?" he said, pushing down on the brakes, slowing with the traffic.

I thought Mom would freak out hearing me say I didn't believe, but she didn't. "If you're angry with God, then tell him that. If you don't believe in him anymore then tell him that. All I'm asking is that you don't stop talking to him and whether you believe or not you still need help with your drinking." I responded, "I don't need any help with it. I'm at it most every day, all by myself. Ask anyone." "You know what she means, wiseass. We won't be picking you up from Bellevue again. That's for damn sure. Next time you're on your own," Dad said. "What's wrong with Bellevue? You got to meet Haile Selassie's wife, didn't you?" I said. "I know . . . twenty-seven children, can you believe it? She must've been squeezing 'em out every nine weeks," Mom said, riffing with me.

"Don't encourage him, Pat. We have to stay mad at him for at least the rest of this ride. This only confirms to me that he gets that smart mouth of his from you," Dad said. "Yeah, well, everything else about this episode he got from you, Bob. Whattya think of that?" Mom answered. "Maybe so . . . There's no questioning that he gets his singing talent from me. Here, I'll prove it. *'KAW-LIGA WAS A WOODEN INDIAN STANDING BY THE DOOR . . . KAW LIGAAAAAAAA,'*" he sang in a spazzy falsetto. "Bob, see if you can find a diner on the way home," Mom said, wincing. "What's a matter? You don't like Hank Williams? How 'bout this one then?

'I'M GONNA BUILD ME A DOGHOUSE NINETY-FIVE MILES LONG . . .' "

I dried out with the folks for a week and fell right into a pattern of sleeplessness, doing nothing but shaking, sweating, and rolling over a lot. When I did drop off, I found myself smack-dab in the middle of some dark dream. Booze was the central theme in all of them. There was one in which I was running in the New York City Marathon and people were lined up along the barricades, handing me Dixie riddle cups full of vodka with the butterfly catchers hot on my heels. I woke up and had the sad realization that only a few days before that had kind of been the case.

There was another one that was most unsettling. It was almost as much a vision as a dream. In it I'd woken up and at the end of my bed was an older blue-collar guy sitting there in one of those Irish knit caps. He was sipping on a whiskey in a rocks glass and smoking a Lucky Strike. He was melancholy in both appearance and manner. I asked him who he was and he said nothing. I asked him again and he smiled gently, leaned in to whisper something to me, affectionately touched me under the chin, and morphed into the most demonic gargoyle that hell had ever spit onto the earth.

When I broke out of this harrowing mare, I gasped so hard I'm surprised I didn't suck the lamp from the nightstand and into my mouth. Years later I saw a picture of my grandfather and he bore an uncanny resemblance to the guy in the dream. I'm ordinarily not all trippy-dippy like this but it still haunts me. I'm sure the story Dad told in the car is what brought that one on but it didn't take an expert in Freudian dream analysis to understand what it meant. It was time to get off the sauce. There was no doubt in my mind.

I called Sir Bobs Alot and told him the whole story about going to Bellevue. I didn't give it any kind of inflection to make it humorous but true to form he laughed his ass off anyway and said, "You know you did that whole I-wanna-kill-myself thing with me a few times at 'Nova?" "Really," I said, surprised. "On a couple of occasions, sure. I just told you to shut the fuck up and go to bed and you did," he said. "How come you never told me?" I asked. "People say shit when they're all fucked up. Besides, I did tell you. You blew it off, remember?" he asked. "No . . . no, not really. This whole thing's got me pretty spooked. I'm thinking about hangin' it up for good. Do you think I should? I mean, do you think I have a drinking problem?" I asked him in earnest. He replied swiftly, "Nah. You don't have a drinking problem—you have a roommate problem."

I had to go back into the city to play my gigs. Mom dropped me at the train station, and as we pulled up, she said, "You know, I asked your father the other night if back when he was having his troubles with the drink did he ever ask God for his help and he gave me an interesting answer. He said no. I asked him why not and he said because he knew if he asked that God would help him. You see, he's stubborn just like you. He didn't wanna give it up, either. But he did eventually ask for God's help and look at what happened. We have a really happy life today and he doesn't miss it at all. He's the same life-of-the-party guy I married—even more so. Sometimes we go to these things and he's the one that doesn't wanna leave . . . just something for you to think about. You're gonna miss your train, go! I love you."

I got back into Manhattan and had to go straight to the Red Lion for the Fonduo gig. The usual collection of rabble was seated in front of us, none of them privy to the Bellevue incident, therefore, all of them egging me on to fall off the wagon. I felt like a diabetic in a confection factory. I was clocking every beverage that went by on the waitress's tray—noticing for the first time the decorative nuances in all the drinks.

At one point I was looking behind the bar at all the sparkly bottles as Mike was starting a song and leaning off mic, he said, "What are you doing?" I spoke through a deep trance. "I never realized how much effort liquor companies put into the design of their bottles. They're beautiful. Have you ever had Cutty Sark?" Mike looked at me concerned. "Oh, man, Campy, you gotta get a grip on yourself. If I were you, I'd split the second our set is over or you're goin' down for sure. In fact, I'll walk you out." He'd heard what had happened, and although he was one of my best drinking buddies, he understood the seriousness of me trying to stop.

I had nowhere to live now. Elmo and Marino had to boot me out. The pressure from their girlfriends to get me outta there after the whole mess at the apartment with the police and EMTs was too much. I wouldn't have tried to stay anyway. I'd put them through enough. They were the sweetest guys in the world and didn't deserve this kind of mental anguish, nor did Grace, or the band, or my family, or anyone. My veins coursed with guilt. I made sure to pick up my duffel bag when they were out so as to avoid any awkward good-byes. I was no stranger to this kind of exit. I composed a very long note thanking them for their generosity and patience, signing off with an apology that to an outsider probably looked like it was scribed by one of the Hell's Angels. "Sorry about drinking all your booze and scaring your women. Love, Mr. Invisible."

Grace took me in upon the condition that I "stay sober and seek help from a support group." So that's what I did. I knew a guitar player at the Red Lion who was clean and he gave me the address and time of a place right in the neighborhood (I can't mention it by name). I said, "I'm not natural to these sort of things. Does it help you?" He said, "I know you're not, Chris. You're more natural to throwing up on yourself and ruining your life. I've known you for three years and you don't even know my name. Dude, we've played gigs together. Do you realize in all that time I've never once seen you sober?" "Well, whattya want? We only see each other at night," I said defensively. "Just go down there and give it a try—nothin' to be afraid of." What's-his-name could see right through my veneer. I *was* afraid.

I was also bullheaded and diametrically opposed to group therapy or self-help of any kind. I thought it was all born out of rampant emotionalism and self-obsession. I'd spit on these concepts many times from a barstool and now I was gonna have to subscribe to them? Self-examination wasn't my strong suit, either, and I sure as hell wasn't comfortable unfurling my problems in front of a bunch of strangers. It seemed unlikely that this place would help someone like me but I didn't have a choice. It was either that or the street. I couldn't put Grace through any more drunken psychodramas. The truth of it was that underneath my blanket of bullshit and excuses lay a very frightened individual who didn't wanna find out what he'd be like sober—it was a terrifying notion.

It was Sunday night and I kissed Gracie good-bye like I was walking the plank. She said, "Jesus, you look like you're about to jump out of a helicopter into the middle of a hostile Vietnam jungle or something. It's no big deal. Just go and keep an open mind. You'll be fine." And with that, she pushed me out the door.

I walked up and down the block several times before having the guts to go in. It was cold, rainy, and windy. I saw people surreptitiously strolling up, closing their umbrellas, and entering quietly. Every time the door swung open I heard the rumble of applause. I said to myself, "What's with the clapping? Is someone fuckin' juggling in there?" Curiosity finally got the best of me, so I summoned my nerve and went in.

I creaked open the door and a line of old men in foldout chairs against the wall all looked up at me at the same time from sipping their coffees. To me, they all looked like Vincent Price. I muttered to myself, "Oh God, am I fucked." I chose to stand there like a statue even though there were plenty of seats available, a dead giveaway to everyone in there that I was the FNG (fuckin' new guy).

There was a kid on the podium, about twenty-two years old, who was telling his drinking story. He was going along talking about how his boozing was out of control and then he got all choked up and said, "Finally one night me and my friends threw this kegger at our apartment and I got all fucked on Jägermeister. I blacked out and woke up with this girl in my bed. She was just in her bra and panties . . . and . . . and . . . ," he pushed through the sobs," and . . . I DIDN'T EVEN KNOW HER NAME!" Someone got up and handed him a Kleenex. I stood there, totally confused. Where was the bad part of the story? Where was the part that was supposed to make me wanna stop drinking? As far as I could see, he'd thrown a kickass party with his best buds, gotten smashed, and hooked up with a hot chick. Isn't that why you throw a party like that in the first place? I mean, for fuck's sake, mission accomplished, dude. Drinking didn't rob him of anything. In my mind he owed booze—HE OWED BOOZE BIG! None of that ever would've happened to him sober. Talk about your lack of gratitude!

Suffice it to say, I didn't have an easy transition into my new support group but I continued to go, faithfully, and on a daily basis, simply because those were the conditions of my treaty with Grace.

Her career was starting to gain momentum. She'd wrapped the movie, then straightaway booked two national commercials, and landed a recurring role on the soap *One Life To Live*. Her role was that of a female police officer—a flatfoot, which made for some kinky fun in the bedroom. I used to have her whip out her baton and club me like a baby seal, then patch me up, and screw my brains out. I'm just fuckin' around. We never did anything like that. She wouldn't even let me wear the hat. She always whined, "Take it off, you're stretching it." We did have a lot of fun clowning around about it, though. She didn't look anything like a cop.

Gracie was kicking ass and taking names while I was . . . lemme see . . . what the hell was I doing? Oh yeah, I was doing nothing. I had to get my shit together. I didn't wanna end up being one of those loser boyfriends that you see clapping at the Emmys or the Oscars—the obvious bum appendage in a rented tuxedo. It was quickly amounting to that since I'd been living with, excuse me, *off . . . living off Grace*. Let's call it what it was because I was paying no rent. I needed to get my ass in gear.

In the haze of my last bender, which had culminated with Bellevue, we'd split from Brick Wall Management after three years of working together. They'd scheduled a show at a rock club in Huntington called New York Avenue, but I got drunk and blatantly disregarded it. After my no-show they called and fired me. I was so hungover on the phone with them that the details escape me now but I remember it being pretty heartbreaking. Michael and Rishon took turns talking but both said basically the same thing, the key line being, "We just can't do this with you anymore." I didn't fight them in the least. I knew they couldn't. As a manager, when your artist can't show up for things it's pretty cut and dried that it's time to call it quits.

That relationship ending was entirely on me and I knew it. I closed out the call saying, "OK, guys, you've done a great job. Good luck with everything." I ran into Rishon a couple of years later in a bar downtown and he said at the time of my disintegration they had been in the final stages of securing us a deal. That one still stings. He's not one to bullshit so I believe him. Caveman flew the coop, finding a real job, cutting his hair, and getting married. Ponzo remained loyal, saying, "It's a long way to the top if you wanna rock 'n' roll. I have wicked belief that someday we'll all be sippin' champagne in the winner's circle. We'll get some sparkling cider for you if you're still doin' the sober thing." I wasn't seeing much of ol' Ponz because we weren't playing out much and he, in turn, had to get his shifts back at the rehearsal place. I missed him but knew it was probably for the best—just seeing his face made me wanna party.

I was a kept man over at Grace's, feeling useless and miserable. She'd come home every night from the soap opera gig, all excited and happy. She was flourishing. I was dying on the vine but putting up a brave face in an effort not to sandbag her enthusiasm. I'd have dinner waiting for her and listen to her stories from the set. "The people are so nice and everybody gets along. I know this sounds corny but we're like one big happy family up there. It's amazing," she'd say, messily shoveling in her food—all wound up like a little kid. I loved her so much and was really proud of her but was suffering from that manly desire to be a breadwinner—imagine that, me wanting to be a bread-winner? This girl *was* special.

I decided I needed to get back on the horse and set up a meeting with Tom and Phil. I told them I'd been sober for a few weeks and they could see by the way I looked that I was. I said, "Let's find a new drummer and start over." They agreed and we found a hard hittin', wiry, Italian guy named Rich Pagano—thusly preserving our McKnockout Wops status.

Rich was a much-sought-after drummer who was also a producer and owned his own studio. A session drummer who was frequently hired to play with legends like Patti Smith and Robbie Robertson from The Band, Rich was a consummate musician, a pisser to have around, and an all-around pro. When we asked him to join, he told us he was a fan of ours already. "I've seen you guys a couple of times. You have great songs! I think you should write some new ones and we'll record them at my studio—I'll produce. Screw the past. Let's go get ourselves a record deal!" We were all down with that plan. I was psyched just to have some purpose back in my life.

We started rehearsing up at Rich's, wrote some new songs that we were all really jazzed about, and played a sold-out Brownie's show to introduce the new songs and new incarnation of the band. Rich was finishing up producing Ian Hunter from Mott the Hoople in his studio so we had to wait a few weeks to get in and record. I went up there to check Ian out one day and ended up having a cigarette with him. He was about sixty years old, so I said, "Glad to see you're still sounding so good and, more important, sounding so good *and* smoking. It gives me hope." He looked at me cockeyed, ironically asking, "Why? Are cigarettes supposed to be bad for your voice? Oh, don't believe it, mate." He was a fantastic guy and an awesome singer.

Our goal was to record a four-song EP/CD, shop it around to whomever we could, and sell it at gigs. Rich worked high up in the business and said he had some people waiting on it. He also told me, "Stay off the drink. I've already talked this project up some and have gotten a couple of questions back as to whether you're really sober. You are, right?" "Oh yeah. Clean as a whistle. Watch this," I said, and guzzled out of my big Poland Spring bottle. "Good, let's keep it that way. We need you." It felt great to hear him say that, but was I truly sober? Did pot count? I found out down at my support group that it did.

I'd been scoring a little weed at the Tiger and getting stoned before going down to the place where the group met. My nose was getting all out of joint because in these meetings they encouraged you to find a "Higher Power" to help ease the struggle. I thought, *So I'm just supposed to snap my fingers and locate God all of a sudden?* Hadn't I been trying to do that for years? I was fairly certain it wasn't an overnight kinda thing. I didn't know where I fell on the belief continuum but I did know one thing: I wasn't interested in hearing what other people in the group had to say about it. That was for damn sure.

I was sitting in there one afternoon, in pain listening to this dude get all flowery and evangelical from the floor. He said, "I just want to thank my Higher Power for finding me a parking spot today." A bomb of sarcasm went off in my head as soon as I heard that. *Oh, I get it now! I know who God is. God is this guy's personal fuckin' assistant. How could I have missed that? God is who gets him his parking spots on West Fourth Street. It all makes sense now.* It was right around then I began getting high before going.

One day I went in there with an insatiable case of the munchies. I had two Suzie Q's from the deli that I noisily unwrapped and ate in the room, making stoner groans of delight with each bite. "Mmmm, oh man, mmmm." I could see everyone staring at me, annoyed, but I didn't care. I was starving. I was seated right in front of the guy who was telling his story. He kept pausing and looking at me like, "What are you doing?" but I was oblivious, focused only on the task at hand. After I'd finished the second Suzy Q, I got up in the middle of his talk, went across to the deli, grabbed another one, sat back down, and did it all again—fumbling and making a crackling racket with the plastic, then loudly chomping on the Devil Dog's bigger, more delicious cousin.

After the meeting adjourned and I was standing outside talking to this chick, a senior member of the group, Patrick (not his real name), came over to me. He was a nice old Irish American guy with graying temples, blue eyes, and a big red honker. He looked like someone I'd probably tip 'em with, so I'd become friendly with him. As a way of cheerleading you to sobriety the group required new people to give their day count off booze before they started the proceedings. Earlier I had chimed up that I had thirty days sober and everybody made with the obligatory clapping. Patrick asked me somewhat suspiciously, "How many days is it for you today, Chris?" "Cruising along at thirty, dude," I said with pride. "Really? Yeah, I thought I heard you say that," he said, still with a modicum of disbelief in his voice. "You know it's not just booze. It's drugs too. You still have thirty days?" he asked again.

I wasn't gonna give him the satisfaction of busting me in front of this pretty girl and the four other people standing there on the sidewalk, so I said casually, "Yeah, thirty days. I feel great." He reached into the girl's purse and pulled out her compact mirror. He opened it, held it up for me to see my reflection, and there was Suzy Q cream all over my face, including a big goober of it at the end of my nose. My eyes were burgundy and nearly shut with a playful twinkle in them. He kept the mirror in front of my face for a minute and for the third time asked, "How many days you got, Chris?" I collapsed it shut and said, "Upon further review I hasten to say, no days, Pat." I started my day count over the next day, only bringing in a coffee this time—which I opened outside.

I felt like an open sore in the world without a drink. Everything seemed to irritate me. Colorful panhandlers and freak street performers that I would normally stop and chat up now seemed like a nuisance. I'd whisk past them not even acknowledging their existence. I was turning into such a dick I couldn't stand it. But that was only half of the time. The other half I was so foggy I didn't know what the fuck was up. I preferred the fog but wasn't really comfortable with either.

The good news was that the recording up at Rich's was going really well. This little project had a very alt country sound to it. I was in a listening phase that had me constantly throwing in Johnny Cash and Dylan's *Highway 61 Revisited*. It's weird the way you can go through something like that and not know why. Tom and Phil were both heavily into a group called Velvet Crush (in particular their album *Teenage Symphonies to God*) and Uncle Tupelo's *Anodyne*. The confluence of all these albums was birthing our EP, as often happens. For years I'd always just thought that the lyrics I'd written for the first track were sort of a pastiche of Cash and Dylan. Musically I think that was true, but lyrically I think what was going on in my life at the time was the biggest influence. The song was called "Freeze Dried (and Born Again)." Here are the first couple of verses:

> *Well, Amy doesn't wanna go to the stirrup man*
> *She found out about a week ago she can't drink them Black*
>   *and Tans . . . anymore*

> *She took home a rifleman, with a toothy smile*
> *He threw her one leg over and she was countin' tiles*
> *It was wild*
> *Now she's with child*
> *and she's freeze dried and born again*
> *Freeze dried and born again*

> *Wally doesn't wanna be in trouble anymore*
> *Wakin' up on the ceiling with them fifty-dollar whores*
> *Says he's fine . . .*

> *He just shoots up his hand and spills it to the group*
> *He's got a very different plan to go out and get looped*
> *Says the wine*
> *Just screws his mind . . . up.*
> *But now he's freeze dried and born again*
> *Freeze dried and born again*

Rich's studio was in what we NYC musicians refer to as "the music building" in Midtown. He'd carved out a cool place for himself up there and had a lot of good projects coming through. The music building was a bustling place with a lot of recording and rehearsal studios as well as storage places for gear, so you had nothing but musicians going in and out of there constantly. Wherever you find music cats there are going to be some strange characters. I went out in the hall for a smoke break during one of our sessions and ran into a really weird guy.

He said his name was Ricky and I got the sense that he was smacked out because he was nodding as we talked (a dead giveaway). He had an orange 'fro (not dyed) and a HANG LOOSE T-shirt on. He looked lost so I asked him, "Do you need help with somethin', bro?" Appearing discombobulated, he asked me, "Do you know Dorla?" I said, "Darla?" "No, Dorla," he corrected me. "Oh, I thought you meant Darla like from *The Little Rascals*. Remember Darla?" I said, hoping that would brighten him. He studied my face for a second and said, "You look like you have great wisdom into things." I said, "Well, you're dead wrong there, kimosabe. I don't know shit from Shinola and that's becoming more apparent every day, but thanks for thinking that." "Do you know where I might find Dorla?" he asked. "Stay here. I'll ask for you," I told him. I went into the control room where Tom, Rich, and Phil were listening to a playback. I said to Rich, "There's a lost guy in the hallway. He seems a bit out of it. He's looking for someone in the building named Dorla. Do you know anyone by the name of Dorla on any of these floors?" All three of them at the same time said, "Darla?"

Rich came out in the hall with me to talk to him. Ricky tried handing us his cassette tape, desperately asking us, "Can you guys learn this tune and I'll sing it? I was gonna do it with Dorla. I came a really long way." Rich asked, "Where are you coming from?" He panned around, his eyes going all over the place, and said, "Oh, everywhere, Santa Fe . . . Paris . . . Yaphank." Yaphank was on Long Island and being from the Island too, Rich glanced at me and mouthed, "Yaphank?" It didn't really fit with the other exotic locales. He steered him back downstairs and said, "Check with the doorman. There's a directory in front, and if she's in here, he'll be able to tell you." He looked at Rich as he was getting in the elevator and then pointing to me said, "Listen to this man. He's got great wisdom." We watched as the doors closed on him and Rich looked over at me and said, "All right, Yoda, get back in the booth. We gotta finish all these vocals tonight."

We ended up not getting everything done and returned the next day to get all of our overdubbing and vocals completed so we could start mixing. We'd been in since the early afternoon and it was our custom to take a dinner break around seven P.M. so we could all eat, unwind a little, and watch *The Simpsons* before hitting it again. As I was doing one of my final takes, we heard a wall-shaking thump out in the hall. I pulled the headphones off my ears. "What the hell was that?" Rich hit the talk-back from behind the glass and said, "Don't worry about it. Someone probably just dropped some equipment out there. It happens all the time." I started doing another take and Rich stopped the tape. "I gotta fix something in here now. Go have a smoke . . . be ready for you in five."

.   .   .

Phil came with me to have a cigarette. We weren't allowed to smoke in the hall. We had to go to the end of the corridor and through a door to have our puffs in the airshaft. Each floor had a little balcony with a metal railing within the airshaft. It was kinda spooky. There was no light out there so you had to leave the door cracked just to see a foot in front of you. You could look up and see the sky through the top but when you looked down it appeared dark and bottomless—like an elevator shaft. We were on the ninth floor of the high rise.

We popped our ciggies into our mouths as I pushed open the door to the airshaft terrace. I turned to Phil, gesturing for him to light me, and his face became snow white with terror. He was hyperventilating and pointing at the metal railing. I thought he was fucking around so it became like an Abbott and Costello routine with me in the Bud Abbott role, feeding him unintentional straight lines. "C'mon, light me. What? Cat got your tongue? What's wrong with you?" He grabbed me and turned my body all the way around and there, slunk over the railing was the lifeless body of a long-haired male stranger. The look of fright he flashed when he'd fallen was still frozen on his face—wild-eyed and mouth agape. He reminded me of that Stretch Armstrong doll I had when I was a kid. Remember those? They were made of petroleum jelly and you could leave them stretched out over chairs and stuff. On his way down he must've ricocheted off the wall and he'd landed back first. His spine had been severed so his torso, with nothing to keep it in place, had stretched to about eight feet long, hanging over the iron banister.

At first glance I thought it might be a life-size mannequin of some sort. The guys that rehearsed across the hall were in a death metal band and I'd seen them going off to gigs with all sorts of horror stage props in tow. I went to poke him to see if he was real and Phil yanked me back by the collar. "WHAT ARE YOU DOING? ARE YOU CRAZY? We need to tell Rich about this and get the cops here." He was freaking out. I was mesmerized.

The detectives showed up and we felt like we were trapped in an episode of *Law & Order*. The trench coats started right in with their gallows humor. The detective running the crime scene was a tall guy with a box head, one eyebrow, and gray hair. He told his partner to check out what was on the landing. The cop pushed open the door and turned back around right away. "Whadja come up with?" he asked him. "He's dead," he said, deadpan. "Good work. Lemme know if anything changes," the head detective said. The death metal band was practicing at the time and the hallway was filled with the sound of their guttural screams, nonstop pounding drums, and earsplitting guitars. He asked me, "What the hell is that awful noise? I said, "The band down the hall is rehearsing." He snapped, "Jesus H. Christ, no wonder he jumped." And it went on like that for another fifteen minutes, one-liner after one-liner. These New York homicide cops are a different breed, boy. Not just on TV. They're so desensitized to the daily gruesomeness of their jobs that nothing fazes them.

They wanted to get my and Phil's stories separately, which sent Phil into a state of total panic. "We found him together. Can't we just do it together? You're a better talker than I am. I might fuck up." I said, "Phil, it's just standard procedure," looking to the box-head cop for reassurance. He said to Phil, "Hey, we don't know nothin' yet. Go back inside the studio. We'll talk to you when we're done with your friend here." "You guys are in a band, right? Don't you have any alcohol in there you can give him?" the second detective said to Rich and Tom, who were standing in the hall. I turned to Box Head and said,

"You're fucking with him, right?" "Him? Yeah. Sorry, but you gotta have some fun on this job or you'll go outta your mind. The nervous ones give us the most laughs. Is he always like that?" he asked. "Only when he quits smoking, which is every other day, or when he stumbles across dead bodies," I replied. "Yeah, quitting smoking is a bitch," he said, lighting a cigarette and offering me one, which I took.

I gave my version of the events, as did Phil, and there weren't any holes in our story so they let us go back to work. I jumped into the vocal booth but soon it started to sink in what we'd all just been through and we sat around and talked about it into the night, foregoing any further recording. There was a bottle of Jack Daniel's in there that was demolished within the hour. I missed booze a lot, especially when I saw the way everyone else was using it to calm down. I was resentful that I had lost my privileges with it. I wanted to be anesthetized so I didn't have to feel all the uncomfortable feelings that seeing the dead guy had dredged up in me. *Such fragile mammals are we,* I thought, slugging out of my Poland Spring bottle in pursuit of the same wanton relief they were receiving from the whiskey—imagining it was vodka and trying to placebo myself into believing it.

Rich buttoned up the studio and we went to this bar in the neighborhood, a seedy part of Eighth Avenue in the Broadway district. The bartender, Mickey, frequented this acoustic gig I did up around there at a cops-and-robbers joint called The Collins Bar. He was in his mid-forties with a classic Irish frying-pan face—as gin blossomed as they come. I told him about what happened and he said in his thick New York accent, "I know, right? Two weeks ago I'm catching the number 7 train to work from where I live in Queens and this lunatic next to me up and jumps in front of the train . . . *Splat!* . . . Dead on the spot." I said, "Holy shit, what'd you do?" "Whattya mean what'd I do? I waited for the next train and came to work," he said, pulling a pint for Phil. Only in New York do you enter a bar fresh off a story like ours and the first person you run into comes back at you with something worse.

I met Rich up in the studio at one P.M. the next day. He told me that the detectives had come back and confirmed that the dead body in the airshaft was Ricky. We hadn't been able to see his face because it was down so far on the other side of the railing. "Can you believe it was that guy we were talking to?" he said. He went on to tell me that they'd found a suicide note in his pocket that contained a poisonous tirade against the music business and him not getting a fair shot. Rich shook his head and said, "This is a tough business but, Jeez, it sure as hell isn't worth that, am I right?" "He was probably so fucked up that he didn't know what he was doin'," I replied, knowing he knew nothing about my own good-bye-cruel-world speech of only a month before—and feeling grateful that he didn't.

Straphanging on the downtown E train after the session, my thoughts turned to Ricky. I think in the chaos of it all I had somehow pushed aside what a sad thing it really was. It started to hit me. Who was this guy? Where was his family? I said a prayer for him and them. With my eyes shut and mouth closed, I asked God to heal and ease his tormented soul, jokingly throwing in, "And mine too." I ended it with "There but for the grace of God go I," and I felt a little flicker—that twinge I'd described to Father Kelly. I just had this feeling that the prayer had landed somewhere. Maybe it was because it had the word *grace* in it and I was on my way home to see my Grace. She was a godsend.

As an homage to Ricky, we chose to call our EP *Falling for Dorla,* never explaining to anyone why.

. . .

It was getting harder for me to go to my alcohol support group. There were some cool people in there but I wanted to drink so badly that any worthwhile stuff that was being said was going in one ear and out the other. Sometimes when people would share about their drinking I'd have visceral reactions. Once a guy was describing a gin and tonic and I could've sworn my saliva started tasting like it—and I didn't even drink gin and tonics. I felt like a phony sitting in there sometimes too, clapping and shit. I wasn't really that on board with it. I was just there to keep everyone off my back.

I was talking to this old-timer in front of the place one afternoon, a really amusing guy named Marty who was a retired Teamster, when I saw Dan from the Tiger walking toward us. The building was well-known in the neighborhood as being a place that helped people get back on their feet from alcohol and drug problems, so I didn't want him to see me hanging out there. After all, I had an image to uphold.

I ducked behind Marty till he passed. After he was gone from sight I popped back out as if nothing had happened.

"What was that?" Marty asked. "What was what?" I said. "Why were you using me like a human shield? You owe that fella money or somethin'?" I said, "No, he's my . . . excuse me, *was my* bartender and I just didn't want him to know anything about this. He'll tell everyone in the bar." "I guess we're really crampin' your style, huh?" he said. "For lack of a better term . . . yeah. I just don't know how I feel about all this yet." "Lemme be the first to tell ya this because I'd rather you heard it from me than someone else. You're a helluva nice guy, Chris, and I enjoy our conversations out here so it pains me to burst your bubble, but based on everything you've told me about yourself it's my expert opinion that you are a garden-variety, shits-his-pants drunk. YOU HAVE NO STYLE TO CRAMP!" We laughed long and hard at that one. I loved Marty. Then he said, "If he was your bartender I think it's safe to assume he already knows about your drinking problem." "Oh, I know he knows. I just don't want him to think that I'm one of those people that's doing something about it," I said. His laughter stopped on a dime and he said, "Did you hear that? That's your disease protecting itself. If you don't get humble and admit what you are, you'll be out drinking with your next broken shoelace." That broken shoelace came in the form of the next guy I heard speak at the group.

I was particularly thirsty on this day. Gracie and I had gotten into a fight because one of her actor boy costars in the film she'd just done was blatantly all over her shit and she, being her naïve self, was completely clueless about it. He called her incessantly, always wanting to get together to talk about "the work," as he called it. I could see he was just trying to get into her pants. He was one of those prefab pussies you see in New York and LA, with not a hair out of place, and trying to be cool in the world but you could just tell from looking at him that he was probably president of his high school drama club and got his ass kicked every day for the first eighteen years of his life. He had one of those Tom Cruise smiles that, whether you knew him or not, made you wanna put his head through a window. After a few cocktails at their wrap party I volunteered to be the one to do that and he nearly choked on the celery stalk he was eating.

His name was Grant. How perfect is that? Good Lord, was he ever punchable. She told me she was meeting him for a drink. I reacted jealously, but more to the fact that she was having a drink than anything to do with Grant. He only added insult to an already injured alcoholic pride. *I'd like to be able to have a social drink with my girl,* I thought. The whole idea of someone else getting to do that had me bubbling like molten lava with resentment.

"He just wants to discuss the work," she said. "What work? The work's done. The movie is over. What work is he talking about?" I said angrily. "Just acting in general . . . different breathing techniques, stuff like that," she replied. "Breathing? Since when is breathing a technique? Last I heard it was an involuntary reflex that starts in the brain. Watch me closely . . . look . . . I'm breathing," I said, huffing in and out. "It practically takes care of itself. In fact, it does. I don't have to do anything. Leave it to actors to take the one thing in this life we all get to rely upon as a given and complicate it." "You know what I'm talking about, wiseass, and don't pretend you don't," she said while brushing her hair. "OK, well, I'll bet you any amount of money that he makes a move," I challenged. "You're wrong and even if he did like me like that he'd never make a move now. You scared the shit out of him the night of that party. Remember? He thinks you're crazy. He told me," she said. "He's right, I am. I'll see you later. Have fun drinking with Grant. I'm also willing to bet he drinks Amstel Light," I said sarcastically, leaving the apartment to go down to the support group.

I was in a foul mood and ready to blow. I'd had just about all I could take of this no-drinking thing. I got into the room a little late and the speaker was a guy who looked like a young Julio Iglesias. He was an ex-professional soccer player/international playboy from Italy, who, in recent years, had mended his ways. He extolled the virtues of sobriety simultaneous to divulging details of his former jet-setting glamour life, a style that really heated me under the collar. The last straw came when he said, "I used to be out till all hours of the night partying with lingerie models till you people in here gave me a bridge back to life." Unable to take any more, I blurted, "Dude, why don't you go relapse right now and I'll follow you?" I meant it as a joke, but you're not supposed to talk out of turn and when no one laughed, I got squirrely and made for the door. Bells and whistles went off in my head. It was game on.

I intended to go to the Corner Bistro where I knew my buddy was working, but I impatiently ducked into the first place with a neon Budweiser sign. It was a joint called The Cubby Hole. In the middle of the afternoon there were only about eight people in the bar. I sat down and without blinking ordered a Jameson's with a beer back. I slammed them in two point two seconds and ordered another round. I had fifty bucks on me and put it all on the bar and told the gal on the stick to keep 'em comin'. She said, "Any particular reason for the sixty-yard dash here?" I didn't want her to think me a problem drinker and lied. "I have my in-laws coming in an hour. I'm trying to front load." She said, "I don't see any wedding ring." I answered, "I was just doing some gardening and took it off." Leave it to me to find the only avid gardening bartender in all of the five boroughs. She talked at me at light speed about her green fucking thumb for the next twenty minutes. I just nodded, drank fast, and "Uh-huh-ed" her.

After a little while I looked up and realized that the Cubby Hole was a lesbian bar. I'd lived in this neighborhood for six years and never noticed. I think I'd even drank in there a few times—late night. There were five bull dykes down the bar talking loudly and drinking. I think it was someone's birthday. They didn't strike me as regular twinighters. Under normal circumstances I probably would've gone over and started partying with them but I was in such a weird way that I just kept to myself.

Some more time went by and I was feeling a good buzz coming on. I hadn't had a drink in a month and a half and felt out of drinking shape. I could feel it going straight to my head. Just to be an asshole, when no one was looking I loaded up the jukebox with the Fleetwood Mac song "Rhiannon." I played it nine times in a row just to see what people's reactions would be. The first time it played some of the gals were singing along and everyone was happy. Then it came on again and I heard someone say, "Oh, an encore I guess." It finished and that annoying guitar intro came on immediately. Now they started getting wise. I didn't make eye contact with anyone, playing it straight, and staring into space as I drank. Then the sixth time it came on they noticed me giggling to myself, and the jig was up. I looked up and a chick the size of a linebacker was in my face.

She had a husky voice and manly sideburns to go with her pompadour and leather shirt vest. "What kind of game are you playing? Do you like to annoy people, is that it?" she said. "I don't know what you're talking about," I replied. "You do too. What the fuck are you doing in here anyway? No one wants you here. Just get the fuck out," she said, grabbing my arm. "C'mon, ladies, we can work this out. 'Tusk' is coming on next. I only played that four times," I said, with four of them now surrounding me. "It's too bad you won't get to hear it 'cause you're leaving now," she said, all of them pushing me off the stool and escorting me out. We got to the door and I surged to get back in but they thwarted my forward progress and pushed me out the door, all of us tumbling out onto the sidewalk. As we were hitting the ground, I yelled out, "I JUST WANNA PROVE THAT I CAN PARTY LIKE A GENTLEMAN WITH YOU LESBIANS!" and I spotted Patrick and Marty as well as a few other members of my support group standing right there.

As fate would have it, the group had just let out and as the gals and I were getting untangled from one another, they stood over me and Patrick asked, "How many days today, Chris?" I made the sign of a goose egg with my hand, removed one of the girls' sneakers from the front of my mouth, and said, "No days, Patrick."

This drinking escapade was merely the starting gun of a cataclysmic backward slide that would once again see me being dragged off to Bellevue. Only this time I wouldn't be sticking around.

Oh, and I was both right and wrong about Grant. He did make his move, going for some titty touch while showing Gracie a breathing exercise, and she shot him down. But he drank white wine spritzers, not Amstel Lights. She told me the whole story a day and a half later when I got home. . . .

Chapter Thirteen

The Sleepkins Diet

settled back into my vampire existence getting up with the sunset. This lifestyle might not sound healthy to a lot of people but I gotta tell ya, *I looked great*—maybe a little sallow around the eyes but svelte. My lifestyle in those days yielded a revolutionary new diet. I'm gonna share it with all of you now. I know a lot of you are out there struggling to lose weight on Atkins and The Zone but I found an easier way. I call mine The Sleepkins Diet.

What's the most important thing to do on Sleepkins? The answer is right there in the title. YOU MUST SLEEP THROUGH THE FIRST TWO MEALS OF THE DAY. I can't stress this enough. You don't wanna wake up and have to ask yourself those nagging questions like, "What can I have for breakfast? What am I allowed to have for lunch? Can I have carbs? Do I have to measure shit? Fuck it. You will never see breakfast or lunch again on Sleepkins, my friend. This much I can assure you.

When you do wake up, the first thing I recommend is to find your way to the nearest APPETITE SUPPRESSANT. In most cases this will be a cigarette. If you have a little blow left over from the previous evening then by all means, pack your beak. After partaking in that you're gonna feel real chatty so the next step is to get on the phone and LINE UP THE NIGHT. You go out every night on Sleepkins—preferably with other people doing Sleepkins 'cause they know what you're going through, right? The second part of this step is to get yourself to the bar before your wife or significant other (if you have one) comes home. You don't wanna hear those keys of horror opening the door before you can get out. That'll mean an evening in and you can't have that on Sleepkins.

While out, feel free to indulge in a sensible dinner. Handfuls of cheddar Goldfish and bar nuts always make for a nice light meal and they won't slow you up the way a hamburger or a slice of pizza might. The only thing left to do from there is set yourself on autopilot, drink and drug with a carefree and gluttonous abandon, and count on waking up that much lighter (and later) the next day . . . or should I say, night. It's of the utmost importance to stay out as late as possible (or early depending on how you look at it). No going home before five A.M. And you're going to wanna stay out that late anyway if you're going to . . . SLEEP THROUGH THE FIRST TWO MEALS OF THE FOLLOWING DAY.

If you take my advice and do all this, without cheating by staying home and taking care of yourself, you're going to lose weight. And you're going to lose a lot of other things that are just cluttering up your life, as well . . . like YOUR JOB . . . YOUR FAMILY . . . ANY AND ALL PERSONAL RELATIONSHIPS. . . . You know, stuff that's just getting in the way of YOU having your valuable YOU time. Sleepkins isn't just a diet. IT'S A WAY OF LIFE.

Of course, I'm fucking around. Stay in school, kids. But that's how I was living. Food just wasn't a priority. On days when I'd wake up before five P.M. I'd often call the Chinese place on the corner and order up their $4.95 lunch special. I never had any money and would often have to pay the delivery guy with Grace's laundry quarters. Then a few days later she'd go to do a wash and become incensed that they weren't there. After a couple of times, she got fed up and said, "Did you use my quarters again? How am I supposed to do laundry now? I have no clothes for my audition. Thanks a lot. You're a grown man. Am I gonna have to hide them from you?" She started stashing the jar of quarters where she thought I wouldn't be able to find them.

Lots of times I'd be searching the house for them while the same smiley little Chinese guy stood there in the living room holding the hot bag. I'd eventually locate them in the linen closet or under the bed and then count out the quarters into his two cupped hands—him smiling away. One day I was desperate to find them. She really had me stumped. I was running all over, checking in the usual spots, and coming up empty. Smiley was standing there for ten minutes while I did this. Frantic and on all fours, with my head under the couch and my ass sticking straight up in the air, inhaling drifts of dust bunnies, I heard him say, "Missah Chris . . . Missah Chris . . . I find them! She hide in bathtub this time. She put where you no find. She know you don't like to showah." He started laughing and I said, "Hey, I like to shower. It's just that my schedule doesn't allow for it sometimes. Hold out your hands, boss, so I can count these out." Even Smiley knew what a dirtbag I was becoming.

My other free food source was the bodega downstairs. There were a bunch of Dominican guys working in there and for the longest time they only knew me as the souse that would stagger in late at night, knock over a box of Nilla wafers, and then buy a pack of cigarettes with more of Grace's laundry quarters. But one night that all changed.

I'd been drinking all day and night in the Tiger with this Hispanic guy, Lupe, I'd just met in the bar. He told me he worked for a landscape architect in the neighborhood so I regaled him with some stories about my old landscaping career and the crew from El Salvador. It turned out he was from El Salvador so I said, "Really? Do you know Hector and Nestor?" He laughed and said, "No, the country's a little bigger than that, Chris." I said, "Please, call me Cristobal." We had alotta laughs. Lupe was a funny guy and loved to party. He was fat with a big round face and jet-black, longish, rock-star hair—so thick and wavy it looked womanly.

It'd been a lot of years since working with Hector and Nestor so I wanted to see how well I remembered my Spanish and asked if we could practice for a while—just to see if I could hold my own. Before we switched to Spanish he asked me, "Did those guys ever teach you any curse words?"

At about four in the morning I popped into the deli and blurted out the line that would change my life from that day forward. I stumbled up to the register and the guys in there were getting ready for my usual routine of pulling out the quarters, having them drop on the floor and roll away from me, and then fumbling with them on the counter. Instead I stared them down, thrust my index finger in the air, and declared, *"¡YO QUIERO CULEAR TORTUGAS!"* Lupe never explained to me what it meant, saying, "Just say it. People will love it." He couldn't have been more right about that. These guys doubled over, holding on to each other to keep from falling down, they were laughing so hard. It was obvious to me that it was the last thing they expected to hear. It means, "I wanna fuck turtles in the ass."

They ended up hooking me up with a free sandwich and we sat down and drank beers into the night. If something works once you gotta go back to it, right? It became a nightly thing. It was like watching the tower fall in *F Troop*. Every night, somewhere between four and six A.M., I'd march into the bodega, my catch phrase in tow (taking the place of actual currency), and I'd yell out, *"¡YO QUIERO CULEAR TORTUGAS!"* And the same thing would happen. They'd laugh hard, make me a sandwich, and we'd sit down for beers.

The owner of the bodega, Oscar Granados, a dapper but slightly less handsome Desi Arnaz, took a real shine to me and nicknamed me Tortuga. I'd walk in and he'd say, "How are ju doing today, Tortuga? Did ju get into trobble today, Tortuga? Sit down . . . sit down." Then he'd holler over to the counter guys, "Get Tortuga a sandwich." I'd then light him and the rest of them up with stories till dawn, drinking Coronas and munching on whatever they put out (which was always delicious). I'd tell them some real whoppers too. My life was going pretty well according to these stories. I was doing stuff like opening for the Stones and plowing my way through the supermodel community. I got a sense that they knew it was all bullshit and let me spew it anyway. Guys that date supermodels can usually afford a three-dollar grilled cheese. Most of the time I was telling them about my booze-related mishaps and resultant problems with Grace. It was my life as a bum that they got a real kick out of. Especially when I began turning up in my pajamas.

I was skating on thin ice with Grace. I'd broken our agreement by drinking, so every day became an exercise in trying not to get thrown out. My strategy was to see as little of her as possible and because she was so busy with her various acting jobs it was doable. I'd leave messages on the machine before she got in and say that I wouldn't be coming home because we were recording late into the night and that

I was just gonna crash at Phil's or Ponzo's. Meanwhile I was out getting fucked up and didn't want to have to pass muster with her when I got home. Sometimes she'd listen to the machine, hear bar noise in the backround, and come right down to the Tiger and bust me in front of everyone—dragging me out by the ear.

Some days she'd get home around six P.M., before I could pry myself out of bed (adhering strictly to Sleepkins), and she'd say, "Don't even think of going anywhere tonight." Grace was an early-to-bed-early-to-rise person, and a heavy sleeper at that. One night I tiptoed out of bed around one A.M., in hopes of making it down to the bar, but she busted me while I was putting my clothes on. I got wise and the next time I just opened the window and went down the fire escape in my pajamas. They were these cool, silk, evergreen-and-black-plaid pj's she'd gotten me for Christmas that I'd wear with a Gomez Adams robe.

I pushed open the door to the Tiger and received an unexpected hero's welcome. Everybody died laughing at my apparel and I hadn't even done it to be funny. I bellied up and ordered a drink from Brian. He shook his head, cracking up. Pulling me a pint of Guinness, he said, "Jesus Christ, you've really lost it this time. You're gonna drink in here like that?" "Dude, it's either this or I'm gonna be staring at a test pattern on the TV while Grace sleeps. Besides, don't look a gift horse in the mouth—look around, people are digging this. I'm like a lovable mascot in here," I said, as everyone hollered at me from the back. "Actually you're just some dick in here drinkin' in his pajamas," he said. "Hey, you know what desperate times call for, don'tcha?" I asked. "Desperate measures?" he answered. "No, vodka. She's gonna smell this beer on me when I slither back in. Vodka has no smell, right?" I asked. "I think it's a little late for you to be covering your tracks, pal, but here's an Absolut and soda," he said. "I might even get up and do a few tunes like this tonight. This could be my new thing," I said, making my way to the back.

At about seven A.M. I crept back up the fire escape and into bed like a seasoned cat burglar. Still sleeping peacefully, Grace rolled over, threw her arm across my chest, and kissed the side of my neck. She hadn't even noticed. I'd done it! It was one of the most thrilling moments of my life—of course that statement alone made my life pretty pathetic. Still, it wasn't an easy task. Her apartment was way up on the seventh floor.

Like everything else in my life, this second-story act became habitual. I even had a foolproof alibi if she busted me coming back in the window, which was that I was out on the fire escape having a smoke—something I did on occasion anyway. One night I was hanging out talking to Gordon Gano in the back of the Blind Tiger, sipping a whiskey in my pajamas, as usual, and this music business friend of Michael Solomon's walked in. His name was Jimmy, a nice guy who worked in music publishing, who used to come to a lot of our gigs. He said, "Chris, holy shit! I never see you around anymore, man. How are the rest of the Drops? What're you doin' with yourself these days?" Somehow in that moment I felt exhausted from a lifetime of having to find new and creative ways to make my life sound good to people. It's as if the PR guy in my head got fed up and just quit right there on the spot. I put my chin on my chest, waved my hand up and down my body showing him my pajamas, pointed at my whiskey, and said, "This is it." Brian and Gordon were sitting right there and Brian said, "We'll vouch for him," with Gordon adding, "He's definitely not embellishing this time." I just remember Jimmy backpedaling to his table with a weird look on his face and saying, "Um . . . OK, man, well . . . it was good to see you."

Gordon was right. I wasn't embellishing. I'd thrown in the towel and didn't even know it. I was no longer showing up for band rehearsals. We didn't have management anymore so there was no one booking any gigs and I just subsisted off Grace, drank at the Tiger, and did my two weekly canteen gigs to put a little jangle in my pocket. The gig pay would never make it home with me. It would go to the Walrus, one of my other drug dealers, or I'd carelessly piss it away in another bar—an asinine move considering I drank free at the gig. The next day Gracie would ask, "They pay you a hundred dollars and you eat and drink for free. Where's your money?" I'd usually tell her that I forgot to grab it at the end of the night and she'd say, "Well, don't forget next time. I'm running out of places to hide the laundry quarters."

I was getting really tired of myself and bored with my routine. I walked around with that feeling of just wanting to break out, a mood that always spelled trouble for me. The Drops got hired to play a party on this old rusted-out World War Two lightship called *The Frying Pan*, down at the pier on the Hudson River. The boat never left the dock and was specifically used for this purpose. Gracie had landed another small role in an indie film and couldn't make it because she was shooting. She said, "It's a street scene so the director said we'll be working till the early morning around seven." This freed me up to get as loaded as I wanted. Tom and Phil were tired of policing my actions and just accepted the fact that I was drinking again and partied with me. I didn't give them much choice. Neither one of those guys is the nagging type. Also, we were grateful to have a gig where we could just rock out and, for once, make some money. It'd been months since we'd played live.

The gig was great, a good old-fashioned beer blast that was packed with our fans and friends. We did three sweaty, high-energy sets and blew the fuckin' roof off of that boat. The girl that had hired us paid us fifteen hundred dollars in cash. After we finished I went up on deck and bumped into Ponzo. "Awesome set, governor! You still got it, kid. Did it feel good?" he asked, rubbing my shoulders. "Yeah, it did. These long layoffs sometimes make me forget how much fun it is," I said. I saw him casually take out a tab of acid and go to put it in his mouth. "Whoa! What is that, blotter? Where the hell did you find that, hippie?" I inquired curiously. "Never you mind, chief. This one's all me. Leslie's outta town visiting her mother for a few days so I got nothin' but open water in front of me. I'm going on this voyage alone, though, dude. I don't wanna get you into any more trouble," he said. "What's with all the nautical references, Gilligan? Or should I say, Skipper . . . you fat fuck. You know you're ripping off half of that for me," I said, sleeving him hard. "Why do you gotta be so hurtful. Did I tell ya I only gained seven pounds this month?" "No, but good for you. Now tear me off half," I urged him. He was still on the fence but I could see his thumbs and forefingers were in position to do it. "C'mon, Ponzee, you know you want me along for the ride," I said, egging him on—knowing he'd cave. Then I started singing the first verse of the World Party song "Ship of Fools," *"We're settin' sail to a place on the map from which no one has ever returned."* I kept singing it and dancing around him. Finally he tore the tab in two and placed one half on my tongue, which was already sticking out in eager anticipation (a reflex of my Catholic training). "Don't tell anyone I gave this to you," he said. "I don't wanna be the one responsible for sending you back to the rubber room."

"Whattya say we go and visit the Walrus?" I asked, grinning wide. "Can't. Gotta get the equipment back. I wanna do it now before this shit kicks in. Tom and Phil are gonna help me. You go and I'll meet you there," he said. "Dude, what are you, a rookie? You know the rules of acid? Never leave your tripping buddy. It's a recipe for a bummer," I said, reacquainting him with the acid handbook. "I know but it'll be easier this way. Besides, I don't even think this shit's that strong. I got it off some kids in the park and they were playing some pretty mean Frisbee. They couldn't have been tripping that hard," he said. "That doesn't mean shit. Dock Ellis threw a no-hitter on acid," I said. "Yeah, but he walked eight batters. These kids looked mellow, I'm tellin' ya. Meet you at the Walrus's in an hour," he said, walking down the dock and jingling his keys on his way to get the van. As his pace grew into a slow trot I heard him start to sing, *"We're setting sail . . ."* I never made it to the Walrus's.

Having just taken the acid I felt weird about going back into the party and opted to split right away. I had some time to kill and a fresh four hundred dollars in my pocket from playing the gig—more money than I'd seen in a decade. I figured I'd hit a bar by the docks, have a few pints, and cab it up to the Walrus's in a half an hour or so. On my way down the gangplank I saw a shady character hovering around. Identifying him instantly as a drug dealer I approached him. "Whattya got for me, friend?" I asked. "What do you want? I got a smorgasbord tonight," he said.

This guy was classic in every way—a tall black guy with a stringbean body and a scruffy beard. He was shifty, never looking directly at me as he paced around, poised to go into a dead sprint. He had a toothpick dangling out of the corner of his mouth that he constantly chewed on and every time he spoke he lifted it out, giving his words added dramatic effect. I asked him, "Howzabout a little gack? You got any gack?" He looked at me and smiled. "Why, yes, I do. I got stuff that'll knock you into tomorrow. I got tens . . . twenty-fives . . . what you want?" he asked, moving it along like a pro. "Tens? How much is in that, like two blasts? Never heard of a ten before," I told him. He said, "I don't know what you talkin' 'bout, son. These is the units we go by unless you want a whole bundle."

This was street coke and probably stepped on a hundred times with God knows what, so I said, "Well let's have a little taste and then I'll tell you." "Oh, I can see I'm dealin' with a businessman here. OK, let's dump a little out. You mind this right here for your sample tray, sir?" he asked, dumping it on a rusty, dented garbage-can lid and chopping out two dinky lines, In fact, you couldn't even call them lines. They were more like nubs. "Not at all. This'll do fine. It looks a little yellow, though. What did you cut it with, dried piss?" I said, taking a straw from him. I snorted it up and right away knew something was off. It was harsher than blow and the immediate postnasal drip tasted different. I started choking a bit and through it said, "Ohhhh, fuck, WHAT IS THAT SHIT?" "It's what you wanted," he said, surprised. "What did you think I wanted?" I asked him, now worried. "SMACK . . . you said smack, right?" he answered.

I stood there frozen for a minute with the straw still in my hand. I thought about writers like William Burroughs and the Velvet Underground song "Heroin" that Lou Reed had written. I said to myself, "You owe it to yourself to at least do this once." I turned to him and said, "Yeah, this is fine," and leaned down and snorted the other puny rail. "Where to now?" I asked. "You go your way, I go mine, son. You know how it works," he said. "No, I'm with you tonight, my man. Lead on, I'm buying," I said, committing fully to this misadventure and wherever it was gonna take me. "OK, but I'm headin' back to Harlem," he said. "You got a bar that you call your spot up there?" I asked. "Right on the corner of where I live. My uncle owns it but ain't no white folk ever go in there unless they hos," he said. "We can say I'm a male prostitute then," I said. "C'mon, we're going to your uncle's bar. I got the cab." "Whoa! I can see see nigga's got some bills burnin' a hole in his pocket. I'm with that. Follow me . . . uh? I didn't get your name yet, did I?" he said. "Chris," I answered, shaking his hand. "Why your jacket say 'Gary' then? He some friend of yours that works for Bud?" he inquired, admiring my red Budweiser jacket. "No, it's a long story. I'll tell you later at the bar," I said, feeling the first signs of drug unevenness. "I'm a call you Bud. It fits you better," he said.

I pulled out the little Baggie and did some key hits in the back of the cab. "What are you doin, Bud? Go easy. That ain't cocaine. That's smack. You don't hit it like that every five minutes. Ain't you ever done this before?" he asked me. I said, "No. I wanted gack, which to me means coke but you musta thought I said smack. After we had that miscue I just decided to go with it." I saw a smile curl up in the corner of his mouth. I wouldn't be able to translate what it meant until the next day. He said, "Well, go easy, Bud. It ain't popcorn. You can die from that shit, you know . . . even just sniffin'." "I'm on half a hit of acid too but it hasn't kicked in yet," I told him. "Damn, who you think you are, Jimi fuckin' Hendrix? I ain't gonna babysit you at my uncle's place, Bud. If you fall apart, you on your own." "You know it just occurred to me that I haven't gotten your name either. What is it?" I asked. "What the fuck does it matter? You ain't gonna know yours or mine in a minute. . . . It's Ronald but everyone in the neighborhood calls me Rollo," he said. "Like on *Sanford and Son*, Rollo?" I asked him. "That's it. You like *Sanford and Son*, Bud?" he asked. My eyes lit up. "Redd Foxx is one of my heroes—him and Jackie Gleason." Rollo's eyes opened wide. "Me too!"

That cab ride is the last complete sequence of lucid memories I have from that night. Everything from that point on seems like a murky, David Lynch–directed dream. Rollo and I swapped favorite episodes of *The Honeymooners* and *Sanford and Son*, quoting and imitating Fred Sanford and Ralph Kramden the rest of the way up there. We had each other going good—laughing and slappin' backs and shit. Rollo did a spot-on Ed Norton impersonation. By the time we pulled in front of his uncle's bar, we were best friends. He was a great guy.

Rollo gave me a big introduction as we entered the bar and I was warmly received. The place had a great energy to it. It was your basic blue-collar dive with a pool table in back—nothing any different from what I was used to except for the fact that I was the only white guy. I didn't feel self-conscious, though. Rollo had my back and everyone seemed to like him a lot. I asked for a Guinness and that got big laughs. Rollo's uncle Reggie, a bald old man with glasses, said with a nice smile, "How 'bout a Budweiser, instead, to match your jacket?" That's the last real memory of any conversation I have—that and Rollo taking me into the bathroom, splashing water on my face, and saying, "You can't nod out in here, Bud. My uncle don't like smackheads in his joint." "I'm not a smackhead. This is my first time I swear. Let's go back out there. I'll explain it to him," I said naïvely, pulling out the packie of heroin to do another blast. "No, you won't 'cause we leavin'. Gimme that shit," he said, yanking it out of my now-feeble hands. "I told you it ain't coke. I'll give it back to you when it's time to do another hit. Just try to be cool, Bud. We going to a spot I know around the corner where there's gonna be some ladies. Pull yourself together."

We bounced in and out of a bunch of places after leaving Reggie's. He had no choice but to get me out of there. I was a walking facsimile of soup, hallucinating up a storm, talking a lot, and then not at all. The acid would deliver these episodes of fantasia and I'd try to articulate them but the heroin had reduced me to such rubble that instead I ended up being a guy using a lot of hand gestures and really not saying anything. I'm sure it was a sight to behold. The night morphed into a big ball of colors, crowds, and cigarette smoke after that. Rollo gave me the same big this-is-Bud-everybody intro everywhere we went, which would be accompanied by big laughs. Then I'd buy a round of drinks. The next thing I knew he'd be waking me up and dragging me somewhere else. I was able to identify those laughs the next day as the acknowledgment of me being his pigeon, but at the time I just thought I was a funny guy.

I woke up the next morning on a bench on Avenue C in the East Village. How I made it all the way back down there from Harlem is anyone's guess. I was shivering uncontrollably—quaking, actually. My jacket was soaked with puke, enhancing the chill of the morning frost. I was so wet I felt like I'd been hosed off. I must've been vomiting intermittently for hours.

A cop was standing over me beating me on the leg with his baton. "Wake up! WAKE UP, JUNKIE! THIS ISN'T A HOTEL. GO SLEEP SOMEWHERE ELSE." He was whacking the shit out of me with it but I was still sort of dreaming. Then he gave me a sharp crack on the knee and that got my attention. "OW! WHAT THE FUCK? IT WAS MY FIRST TIME TRYING IT. I SWEAR!" I said reactively, not knowing who he was yet. "MOVE IT ALONG, JUNKIE, UNLESS YOU WANNA GO TO CENTRAL BOOKING." I got up and just started aimlessly walking down the block, looking back once to see him motioning me with his club. "THAT'S IT. KEEP WALKING. THE AIR'LL DO YOU SOME GOOD."

It took about a half a block for everything to sink in. I felt sicker than I'd ever been from any hangover—anytime. I ran over to a garbage pail and started hurling . . . and hurling . . . AND HURLING— good God, was I ever hurling. I could've thrown up a Volkswagon. I reached out my hand and hailed a cab. It was about nine o'clock in the morning. "West Tenth Street and Sixth, please," I told the cabbie. "My friend, you don't look so good. Why don't you get near the window and crack it open?" he suggested. He was a Pakastani guy who spoke good English. "Thanks, man," I said. I began thinking about the entire chain of events and getting really upset. It was like a bad movie. All I could hear echoing through my head was that cop saying, "WAKE UP! WAKE UP, JUNKIE!" I started crying. I thought, *Maybe this is it? Maybe I am a junkie now? This is how it starts, right?* That didn't end up happening. I was no William Burroughs. My heart belonged to alcohol. No drug would ever replace the precious juice. God got it right the first time if you ask me. I rolled the window all the way down and threw up out of it for the rest of the trip. The cab driver said, "That's it, brother. Get it all out. You'll be fine." He was a prince.

I was headed to my sisters' apartment. I couldn't go home to Gracie's in that condition. I'd have to come up with an excuse later as to where I'd been and why I didn't come home. I started trying to compose that lie in my head as we whipped around turns, the wind conveniently holding my hair back, as I blew chunks out the window but I decided that it could wait. What I needed right then was a safe haven to be infirmed in.

We pulled up in front of the building and I groped through my pockets for that wad of bills I'd had but couldn't find them. "Shit, dude, it's all right. I have money somewhere. I have to," I told him, apologizing. "Take your time, bro," he said. I pulled out dog ears in both pants pockets then finally in the top pocket of the barf-covered Bud jacket I found a lone crumpled-up ten spot with a yellow sticky note attached: "Dear Bud, Hope you got home safe. Your friend, Rollo."

After reading the note, I connected the dots as to what all the laughter was about. He, along with everyone else we came in contact with, knew that he was gonna roll me from the get. He could've taken it all but left me ten bucks cab fare—there are many in his profession that wouldn't have. I liked Rollo and wasn't mad at him for what he'd done. I likened it to the old parable about the scorpion and the frog. The scorpion asks the frog for a ride across the pond and the frog says, "I can't give you a ride. You're a scorpion. You'll sting me and I'll die." The scorpion replies, "Hey, I need a ride and I don't swim. I promise in return not to sting you." So the frog tells him to climb on his back and off they go. About halfway across the pond the scorpion stings the frog. As they're both about to drown the frog looks up at him and says, "I don't understand. Why'd you do it? Now we're both gonna die." And the scorpion says, "I'm a scorpion. That's what I do." It would have been against the rules of the game to get pissed at Rollo. To me the most perplexing forensic question of all was, at that time of night, where the hell did he get a yellow sticky? Perhaps we'll never know.

My sister Donna opened the door to find me paler than paper, weeping inconsolably, and sick as a dog. She put me in her bed where I spent the entire day and night violently puking into a pot. She was afraid I'd been gang-raped by a bunch of drug-addict ex-cons till I was finally able to give her the whole story the next day.

My sisters, plenty disturbed by my latest foray into the darkness, told my mom that something had to be done and, unbeknownsts to me, they all began circling the wagons. It was intervention time. We've done so many of these in my family, we refer to them as "surprise parties."

Chapter Fourteen

Escape from Bellevue

lmo came and picked me up in his car to bring me to a dinner party Leslie was throwing over at her and Ponzo's place. He said, "Listen, I have some business over on Hudson and I'm gonna have my car. I'll give you a ride." Something seemed a little off—we weren't dinner-party kinds of people. I said, "All right. I'll meet you outside."

Ponzo and Leslie owned a huge loft. She had a good job and Ponzo let on that his rich family had cut him off but it had been obvious to me for quite a while that this wasn't the case because of his opulent pad and his carefree purchases at the Walrus's. He never complained about money.

I walked in and there they were in my honor—thirty or so of my closest friends and family with expressions of dread on their faces. I'd been duped. My mom and dad, brothers and sisters, Gracie, the band, the boys from Brick Wall, and a bunch of friends, were all there— Mom in tears. It was just the worst. I sat in the middle of the "circle of love" as they went 'round the horn, each one addressing me personally, telling me how my drinking and drugging had affected them. It was fucking gut-wrenching. I didn't realize how much pain and worry I'd inflicted on those around me. When you're a lifelong incorrigible fuckup, it is required of you to sit patiently through a lot of speeches from people. Someone's always pleading with you to "get it together" and "act responsibly," so you spend a good portion of your life staring at the floor and half listening. This was an ambush. I was under siege and being bombarded from all sides so I instinctively hit hyperspace and went up into my head. They were talking to me but I was a human armadillo, unable to hear anything through my protective shell.

My aunt Mary spoke first. She was my mom's best friend growing up in Woodside. She'd always been a favorite of mine—a beautiful woman, inside and out, with dark hair and eyes. Like all of my parents' friends from the old neighborhood, she had an edgy sense of humor. She'd been working as an alcohol counselor for many years. She'd been the one who helped educate my mom on these matters and had also been instrumental in organizing the family's very first intervention back in 1980 for my dad, an event now looked upon with great reverence in the Campion family, like the First Continental Congress. As she was pouring her heart out to me I drifted back to those days. It was surreal to be at my own intervention and thinking about my dad's. Her voice wafted up over my head as I sank into heavy reflection about it.

It was almost as if I'd blocked it out completely—like it had never happened. The house had emptied out a little that year and wasn't the vibrant party headquarters it used to be. Hollywood Bob had moved out, eventually migrating to Orange County, California. Kevin and Donna were in college, leaving Eileen, me, and Billy at home. Eileen was seventeen, I was fourteen, and Bill was nine.

Dad had always been a heavy drinker like everyone in our town, but in the two years that led up to his intervention, something in him had busted and gone haywire. He was turbo-drinking, every day, taking five-hour liquid lunches and then coming home to finish himself off in front of the TV. When I'd try to talk to him he wasn't mean or anything but would just smile a crooked smile, content in his cocoon, and go back to viewing an old rerun of *The Honeymooners*. Gleason reminded him of the characters he knew in his youth back in Woodside. He would drink and get fuzzily nostalgic, making comments as we watched. "When you walked into Driscoll's Bar back in Woodside, half the guys in there were Ralph Kramdens . . . and the other half were Nortons," he'd say and laugh, forgetting he'd already told me that a thousand times. "You see that old icebox? We had one of those" was another of his go-to lines. It was a comfortable time capsule for him, filled with fond memories that were being nurtured by booze. He was as happy as a pig in shit with a drink in his hand in front of that TV.

I just kind of sat there and watched him get his load on. As weird a spectator sport as that was, I soon found out that it was the perfect time to hit him up for money. He couldn't part with the green fast enough when he was lit. "Here, whattya need? Will twenty do it?" he said one night, shuffling bills in his hand. "Thanks, Dad, but I'm just going to the kitchen to get some soda. It's free." "Take some money anyway. You never know," he said, urging me. "Dad, I'm only going to the kitchen," I said. "Oh, I thought you were talking about something else. Take twenty anyway. You may need it for something," he said and smiled. In this state he became a prime target for late-night commercials too, ordering stuff with his credit card and forgetting about it. "Another set of Ginsu knives came in the mail today for you, Bob," Mom deadpanned one evening while setting the table for dinner, casually throwing the brown package in front of him in lieu of his plate.

My whole life we'd always bonded over football but at this point he was turning up to all my games hammered and embarrassing the shit out of me by yelling loudly to me on the field during the games. "C'mon, Chris, don't be flat-footed or it's easier for them to block you. Get those feet movin', c'mon! Shed that block and make the tackle! Remember to hit low!" he hollered from the sideline. This is actually sound football advice he was dispensing. I was playing outside linebacker at the time and that is what you wanna do, but he sounded more like Foster Brooks than Vince Lombardi in his delivery. I'd cringe when I'd look over and see his off-kilter smile and overzealous handclapping, knowing I was gonna be hearing those commands barked at me for the rest of the game.

Mom tried talking to him about his drinking but he was either unreachably bombed or crankily hungover and would blow her off till he could get out the door to go to work. He didn't know what he was up against. Pat Campion is not one to be toyed with or ignored. She has an unshakable faith and inner sturdiness. After a few too many of these morning exchanges Mom had had enough and called my aunt Mary. The two of them conspired to get Dad sober through this new confrontational device called an intervention. Cue the music, "Dum . . . dum . . . DA!"

Mom snuck us into the city once a week to go to the place where Aunt Mary worked called The Freedom Institute. They dealt in helping families, like ours, organize and go through with these interventions. When I first heard the name I thought it sounded like a place high school dropouts went to obtain their equivalency diplomas and get placed in flunky jobs. It turned out to be just a regular office where they educated us about the disease of alcoholism and what to expect when we confronted my dad.

Every time we came back from there I felt like we were betraying him. The lady that ran the program was a spunky gal named Mona. She said to us on the first day, "I love drunks . . . and I am a drunk, sober twenty years now. I never met one I didn't like. Your dad's a drunk, so I love him. They are very charming but also very manipulative people. He's got you all eating out of his hand and that's gotta stop. He's making everyone closest to him sick with the disease of alcoholism. He doesn't know that that's what he's doing but I'm here to tell you, THAT'S WHAT HE'S DOING." "Really, 'cause I feel like we're all stabbing him in the back by being here and he's gonna be furious when he finds all this out. I, for one, don't really wanna be here for that. AND DON'T CALL MY DAD A DRUNK, LADY," I said defiantly.

"Good. We'll start with you. What condition is your dad gonna be in when you guys get home tonight, drunk?" she asked. "Yeah, probably," I said, looking away. "OK we're making progress. Now what about tomorrow night, drunk, you think?" she asked me. "Odds are, yeah," I answered. She then asked more forcefully, "How 'bout three days from now or a week from Tuesday, think he'll be sloshed on those days too?" I glared at her, my eyes welling up with pissed-off tears. She hugged me and whispered in my ear, "What if I told you by doing all this you could have your dad back to his good old self every night of the week. Would you like that?" I just nodded yes, unable to speak. I didn't wanna full on cry in front of this lady. "Good, 'cause that's what we're gonna do but I need you to be brave and to listen to me. Will you do that?" I nodded yes again.

Also on this dream team assembled by my aunt Mary was a

6-foot-4, blond-haired, former Fordham football player priest named Peter Schweizgood. He was a sober alcoholic whose life's work was helping families with this problem. He reminded me of the actor Ken Howard, who played the basketball coach on the show *The White Shadow*. Father Pete was a super-nice guy and a tough dude who my dad had already met through my aunt Mary years before all of this. They liked each other a lot. He was a more down-to-earth kind of priest and hipper to the quandaries of modern-day people.

On a cold winter's night a week before the intervention I heard my parents arguing. It was around eleven o'clock and Dad had come home drunk as usual. When the front door slammed I knew that meant he was headed back out to do some more drinking at a bar. I looked out my window and saw him bobbing and weaving his way to the car. I watched the car bomb down the driveway just barely missing the front pillar at the bottom and swerving up onto the neighbor's lawn before straightening out and continuing down the road. I followed the taillights till they disappeared into the tree cover. I kept my eyes on that driveway for hours, from my windowsill, waiting for the car to come back, and praying the phone wouldn't ring with that fateful call. I played it out in my head. The phone would ring, my mom would scream, and you know the rest.

I stayed there perched like a sentinel, waiting and worrying, like I'd done so many nights before. I'd fallen asleep on that windowsill lots of times, more than I could count, but I never told anyone about it.

On this particular night I was extra-anxious because the intervention was soon and I had that feeling you get when you're watching a cop movie and the good-hearted sergeant says, "Can't wait till my retirement next week," and suddenly with the sound of a gunshot he's found dead in the next scene. We were so close I just thought, *Please, God, help him make it home this one last time.* I waited till about one-thirty A.M. and when he hadn't come home yet, no longer able to take it, I snuck out of the house and went down to have a look at the lighthouse.

We were coming off a blizzard followed by a week-long cold spell that had left the bay entirely frozen over. The last two days had been slightly milder, melting it a bit. Whenever this happened my friends and I had a danger game we liked to play called Berging. You played by jumping from iceberg to iceberg and going out as far as the bergs would let you—the guy that made it the farthest won.

The wind was whipping the snow from the tops of the drifts and shaking it off the trees. Every house on the block was dark except for Richie Blackmore's. His bedroom light was on and I could hear some classical music playing faintly through the cracked window. I saw him walk by and sit at a desk with a cup of tea. *A side of rock-star living people never see,* I thought. Shutters were clanging back and forth on houses and the air had that crisp, cold, suburban charcoal flavor to it. I loved that. The woods were alive as I hit the path to the beach. The trees all tangled up in each other, fighting furiously—the wind in my ears and the sound of the forest rustling, deafening.

I came through the brush and laid eyes on the lighthouse. It was solid stone, impervious to anything Mother Nature could throw at it. Ever since I was a little boy, seeing it always calmed me down. When no one was around, I used to talk to it out loud like it was a real person. It was out about three football fields from shore and before I even realized what I was doing I was berging toward it. At first I just wanted to see how close I could get to it and then something else took over. I didn't have control over my feet anymore. I felt like I was being compelled by a death-defying vision quest.

I feverishly went from block of ice to block of ice, laughing like a madman—jumping, sliding, and falling on my ass. Some parts of the bay were totally frozen, enabling me to run full tilt over those stretches. Then I'd encounter a big hole in the ice and have to berg it to the next frozen-over part. I was on a mission. I stayed focused, with my head down, not even thinking that with one wrong step I could lose my life. If I fell in and the ice shifted, that was it. A couple of times my foot fell through and the water came up to my thigh, giving me a momentary fright, but I quickly pulled it out and kept going. My laughs turned into grunts and snarls, which then gave way to random screaming and cursing. "MOTHERFUCKER . . . I'M GONNA MAKE IT, MOTHERFUCKER!" Who I was yelling at is anyone's guess. God? My dad? The elements? They're all good stabs but the truth is I was just temporarily insane. No one in his right mind would've attempted to go out on that ice at any time of day, let alone one-thirty in the morning—and on a school night. Before I knew it I was almost at the lighthouse. I had a face full of tears and wasn't even able to see the bergs. I stepped recklessly, angrily, and cried—not caring anymore if I fell through.

I made it to the jagged rocks surrounding the lighthouse and stood on the highest one. They'd been put there to fortify it from storm waters. The wind was gusting with a mad gale force. The bay resembled a Russian tundra, blanketed with unblemished snow, frozen and painless. The full moon shone brightly overhead, lighting the scene to its highest grandeur. It felt like a private moment with God. In the presence of that kind of beauty it would've been hard to doubt him but I never doubted back then anyway. Standing there in front of the lighthouse, under that encroaching moon, I offered up my fear to him, like Mom had taught me. It seemed like the right thing to do while I had his ear.

My eyes were drawn left to the lights flickering along the Connecticut shoreline. I remembered my dad taking me out on the deck to look at them when I was a little kid and couldn't sleep. It was like peering down at life on another planet. I wondered if there was another kid over there wandering around with my same troubles.

Then I turned around and admired the lighthouse. I'd never seen it up that close. It was magnificent, more cracked and eroded than anyone could see from shore but nonetheless impressive. My imagination insisted that its decay wasn't due to the pounding it took from the water and weather but rather from years of worry that the boats wouldn't make it into the harbor safely.

I started singing The Who song "Love, Reign O'er Me" to see how far my voice would carry. I sang it with all the lung power I could muster—putting in the Roger Daltrey screams and all. It sounded as if it was going clear across to the smoke stacks in Northport. I imagined it waking people out of their beds over there. *They probably think I'm right outside their window,* I thought and laughed. I loved the feeling of being the only one out there and in a place where no man had ever stood or at least had ever gotten to the way I did. I look at this as my psycho-teenage Neil Armstrong moment.

Staring out over the ice I felt like I'd achieved something. I wanted the world to stop for a second, just for one little moment, so I could catch my breath, and it did. It was as if I'd summoned the Ice Age and frozen everything to a standstill in order to understand it better. I stayed in those thoughts for a few minutes till it occurred to me that I was freezing my dick off and that I'd better get back to shore. I had a big uh-oh revelation as it dawned on me how far that was. In my daredevil trance I hadn't calculated an exit strategy and hadn't a clue left over as to how I'd traversed it in the first place. I had no choice but to start moving. It was either that or I could stand there and freeze to death.

I headed back slowly and carefully, petrified. I stopped a few times and had to wait for bergs to drift close enough to hop to—once waiting for over ten minutes. I actually saw myself as a possible goner while standing there, at the mercy of the ice floating over, but it eventually did and it was relatively clear sailing from there—save for a few leg dips.

I got back to the house and went up the stairs to my little brother Billy's room. He was sleeping peacefully—his arms wrapped around his pillow. That kid could sleep through a nuclear blast. I lay down next to him. I just didn't feel like going back up to my room yet. This was the same room I'd had when I was his age and Hollywood Bob used to sneak in my window. I pictured him coming through, splattering on the floor with his teenage load on, and smiled a little. I was really scared. My dad wasn't home yet. I looked around at Bill's toys and saw a dusty Vertibird in the corner we'd fought over one Christmas. It was under the tree with no tag on it and we both thought it was ours. It ended up being mine but he used it more, so over time it became his. He was such a funny kid—crazy, loud, and wildly passionate. This thing was taking its toll on him too. He'd been much brattier lately, which had never been his nature before. I sniffled through some half tears and then got to a point where I couldn't cry anymore. I was exhausted.

Finally I heard my dad's car rumble up the driveway. I scrambled upstairs to my room before he got his key in the door, which, in his condition, was no small feat. I set the alarm on my clock radio to get me up for school and, as always, left the radio on low. I fell asleep to Steve Winwood singing the opening line of that classic Blind Faith song, "Can't Find My Way Home." He sang, *"Come down off your throne and leave your body alone. Somebody must change."* I remember thinking, *This might be a good song to play to start off the intervention.* I've always had great production instincts.

Intervention day came and we were all as nervous as hell. My stomach was killing me so I snuck into my parents' bathroom and popped one of Dad's Gelusils before we left for the city. He ate those things like candy to relieve the pain of his ulcer.

Bobby, Kevin, and Donna had come home to participate in the proceedings but had to be kept out of sight till the intervention so they stayed with friends the night before. My aunts Claire and Joan—Dad's sisters—were there, as well as my aunt Mary, of course. We were all sitting in this cozy meeting room waiting for my dad to show up. Mona said, "OK, everyone, Bob's gonna be here any minute. Father Peter will be bringing him in momentarily. He hasn't been made aware that you were all gonna be here. We didn't think he'd agree to come otherwise. You can expect him to react to that at first, but just stay calm and let us handle it. How's everybody doing?" Hollywood Bob said, "Will he be bringing him in blindfolded?" Everybody laughed. "No, Bobby, it's not pin-the-tail-on-the-donkey," she said. "Well, then could you at least blindfold me?" Kevin said.

I guess they'd hoodwinked my dad into going under the guise that this was gonna be some kind of marriage counseling thing with him, Mom, and Father Pete. The two of them walked in, Father Pete between my dad and the door, and when Dad got a good look at the family lynch mob sitting there, he quickly added up that he'd been shanghaied. "Oh no . . . no way. What the hell is this, Pete? They teach you about how wrong it is to lie back there in the seminary?" "Bob, just sit down and listen to what everyone's got to say. You've got a lovely family here that loves you very much. Just sit down and listen. That's all you have to do." "All I have to do is leave, which is what I'm doing. I never agreed to this. My children are here, for chrissakes. Was this your doing, Pat? You really think having them here is a good idea? 'Cause I don't. No one consulted me on this and I don't have to be party to it," he said, and made for the door.

Father Pete blocked him. "Now, Bob, alotta people went to alotta trouble here to make this happen . . . and it was all done out of love. You owe it to them to hear them out," he said. "I don't owe anybody anything. I wasn't consulted. Now out of my way, Pete." "No, Bob," Father Pete said. "I'm not gonna tell you again. Get out of my way," Dad said, in a threatening tone. Father Pete didn't budge. "Fine, suit yourself," Dad said, and pushed him aside to get past. Father Peter then grabbed him and the two of them started scuffling. They had each other in headlocks for a minute, moving side to side, bonking into the furniture, and then went tumbling to the ground. They were rolling around at everyone's feet, talking to each other while wrestling it out. Dad said, "Whattya say I kick your ass, Pete, and then maybe after you can take my confession?" To which Father Pete replied, "Or I can kick your ass, Bob, and we can *call* it your confession. I can do this all day with you if you'd like, but one way or another I'm getting you in that chair." I think Father Peter's words hit home because Dad seemed to stop struggling at that point. He said, "All right, enough, Pete. You're scaring everyone." "No, Bob, I think you're gonna find out today that you're the one that's doing that," Father Pete said, re-adjusting his white collar.

Dad sat in the middle chair while we all took turns giving him examples of how his drinking had let us down. He was stoic. He looked everyone in the eye as they were talking but you could see that the rage he felt at being tricked into being there was rendering him impermeable to any of our pleas. I got the feeling he thought the whole thing was just emotional blackmail by Mom. Dad wasn't one for this kind of talk therapy. He was a tough nut to crack. Obviously I am my father's son. It was my turn to talk and I choked, clamming up completely. I couldn't blow him out of the water like that. I had a whole speech planned that Mona had coached me through but I abandoned it or forgot it—I can't remember which.

All I ended up saying was, "Dad . . . you're a great dad . . . but you just gotta stop." And I broke down in a torrent of tears. He said, "It's OK, buddy . . . it's gonna be OK. Would somebody please get him a Kleenex?" A heavy moment passed as I blew my nose, nobody saying a word. Then Billy, who was right next to me, fearlessly blurted, "IS IT MY TURN YET? WELL, FIRST OFF, I DON'T LIKE HOW YOU JUST MADE CHRIS CRY. HE'S CRYING 'CAUSE YOU'RE ALWAYS DRUNK!" Willibee, like my mom, wasn't one to fuck around. He always went right for the throat. He gave it to the old man good. At nine years old he understood what tough love was better than I did. Or he was just more pissed off.

. . .

"ARE YOU HEARING ANY OF THIS?" Willibee said to me, popping the bubble on my flashback. I'd been up in my head for the first half of my own intervention thinking about my dad's. "Yeah, I'm just taking it all in. I don't have any rebuttals. I know that what everyone's been saying is true." "I know you do but do you care? You don't really seem like you're listening," he said, knowing me well. "No, I am. I'm listening. Go ahead," I said. He glanced at me like he didn't quite believe it and continued to say his piece.

At the time of my intervention Willibee had been sober for about a year. Before that we'd been major running buddies, galvanizing the gin mills together with our respective bands (the Drops and Bogmen were inseparable in the downtown bar scene). His reckless boozing and drugging had been derailing Bogmen business so his management lowered the boom on him, spinning him dry through rehab. I felt abandoned by him when he'd gone over to the other side, as selfish and insane as that sounds.

The intervention pressed on with Bill ending his pitch to me by saying exactly that: "Look, you probably feel like I abandoned you out there and in a way I did. I realized I was headed for the same fall as you are now. If you don't get help and sober up we're all afraid you're going to die. I speak for everyone in the room when I say that." The rest all took their turns giving me a different version of the same speech Bill made and then it was my dad's turn to talk.

"Christopher John, I'm not gonna bullshit you. You know as well as I that this is up to you. You can give us all a bunch of mood music about how you're gonna stop but it doesn't mean anything until you actually do. I know that from experience. What I can tell you is that your life will be better than ever you imagined it could be when you do," he said. He started speaking about the support group I'd been attending before falling off the wagon (the same one he'd attended to get sober). "My suggestion is go back into the room and really try to listen this time. I mean, the pearls of wisdom that you'll hear will really help you, even from the women." My mom, aunts, and sisters all gave up a collective groan when he had that slip of the chauvinist tongue. "Even the women? Jesus, Bob, what century do you live in? Did you know we're allowed to vote now?" Mom said. Everybody in the room laughed hard. It was the one moment of comic relief I can remember in the whole thing. "I just meant that sometimes it's hard for guys like us to relate to a broad's story and to keep an open mind 'cause they have good things to say. What's wrong with that?" he said, making it worse. "Who uses the word *broad* anymore besides you?" Mom said. The Yapper was there and he found my dad's comments particularly hilarious and said, "It's OK, Mr. Campion. We understand you." "Thank you, John. If you asked this crew here," he said, pointing to the ladies, "they'd have you believing I was Attila the Hun." Dad is actually a gentleman's gentleman but he is old school.

I heard nothing but crumbling crackers in my head through most of the rest of it. Gracie spoke and I couldn't even look at her. I had such titanic guilt. She said, "Look at me for a second." I kept my eyes down. "LOOK AT ME. I want you to hear this. YOU'RE LOSING ME. Did you hear what I said? YOU'RE LOSING ME. That's all I have to say," she said, sprouting no tears. I could see I'd almost run my tab up there. There was no disputing that.

Lastly it was Ponzo's turn. The gracious host of this gut-wrenchingly emotional event stared me down, jacked to the nines, with his teeth grinding and jaw moving back and forth at the speed of a professional Ping-Pong match. Sweating buckets, with his eyes darting around, twiddling his thumbs and shuffling his feet, he said, "We're . . . um . . . all worried about you, man . . . and . . . uh—" I interrupted him, "Dude, what about you? You're so gacked up your jaw's about to slide out the side of your face like a broken typewriter!" "HEY, WE'RE NOT HERE TO TALK ABOUT ME, MAN," he said, looking over his shoulder at Leslie, who was rolling her eyes. At least I was making him feel comparatively healthy.

I was really appreciative of everyone's taking the time out and participating in the intervention but it didn't take. I knew it hadn't as I hugged everyone good-bye and thanked them from the bottom of my hollowed-out heart for coming. On their way out I latched on to the mantra, "You guys saved my life and I won't soon forget it. I love you." Their tremendous outpouring of love and concern rolled off me like water off a duck's butt. I was covered by a protective sealant of denial. "Sure, I was fucked up. It didn't take a great mathematician to calculate that. But all that stuff about me dying, well, that's just something people say at these things," is what I told myself. I didn't wanna know myself sober. I knew that much. I just wasn't done. I had every reason to be but I wasn't.

I was too afraid to live life the legitimate way. I didn't feel as if I had what it took to do it, but how the hell was I supposed to explain that to everybody without sounding like a mental patient? Another thing I couldn't elaborate on is that destroying myself felt good—it felt *natural*. I wasn't *about* to tell anybody that one. Imagine that being my response at the close of the intervention. I can just picture it. "Listen, I just wanna thank everyone for their support but . . . uh . . . it's not necessary. You see, I like being in abject emotional and physical pain. I like being drunk to the point of cerebral implosion. It's . . . uh . . . the only way I wanna live . . . but . . . um . . . everybody be careful getting home . . . and try not to worry about me. I'm right where I wanna be." Even I don't have balls that big.

When Gracie and I got home I looked in the fridge and said, "We're out of your soy milk. I'll run and get you some," as she was changing in the bedroom. I went and had a couple of beers at the Tiger. Dom put a pint of Guinness in front of me and asked, "So what's new, Campy?" I said, "Ahhh, same old, same old," and sipped the froth off desperately, not even giving it time to settle. "Do you know if that deli next door has soy milk?"

. . .

As a way of placating everyone at the intervention I agreed to go to an outpatient drug and alcohol rehab. I had to report to this place over by Union Square every morning and attend lectures about alcoholism and drug addiction as well as group therapy. I was trying to pull it off for a while, going through the motions, hungover, but they soon got wise and started piss testing me. They busted me a couple of times with alcohol and cocaine in my system and threw my ass out.

My counselor was a really cool black guy with dreadlocks named Carl. He said, "Chris, you know, you're gonna find yourself back out there wishing you could come back and now you've blown your chance." I said, "Carl, I'm thirty-three years old. I think I know how to live my life a little better than you do. I'll be fine but thanks a lot."

About a week later I was stumbling around on the street at seven o'clock in the morning. I'd gone out the night before, blacked out, gotten into a fight, come home beaten and bloodied only to have Gracie toss me out of the house. I'd slept on the front stoop and had woken up with one shoe missing. I saw my reflection in the glass door and I had a fat lip, an oozing shiner, and half my shirt torn off—the other half was spattered with dried blood.

I got up to look for my other shoe and there was Carl. "How ya doin', Chris?" he asked, smirking. I said, "Good . . . good . . . just out getting some morning air . . . early bird and all that. You know the deal, Carl." "Yes, I *do* know the deal, Chris, but the question is *do you*?" I said, "Whattya mean?" "I mean how's it goin' out here for you? Have you had enough yet? How's your drinkin' been since you left us?" he asked, knowing the answer. "It's going all right. . . . Not gonna lie to you . . . been havin' a few beers here and there but otherwise . . . you know . . . good . . . everything's good," and I gave him a thumbs-up, my eye swollen half shut, and blood caked all over my hand. "Okay, then. You keep tellin' yourself that and maybe someday everything will be good, but just in case it isn't, here's my card again," he said and started walking away. I stood there for a moment reading his card and then called down the block to him, "HEY, CARL!" He turned around. "Yeah?" "Uh . . . ," I stammered, wanting in that moment to ask for his help to get sober again but then changing my mind. "If you see a black shoe between here and the corner it's mine," I said. He stayed there for a second and then said, "OK if I see it I'll kick it down to you. Don't lose my card."

What good was that conversation gonna do, really? I'd had a hundred just like it with a hundred different people and it never amounted to anything. I was what I was. Why not just accept it? They were always talking about "acceptance" down at that group I was going to. What about this kind of acceptance? I accepted that I was a piece of shit who wasn't gonna change. It might not be noble but at least it was the truth and the truth is supposed to set you free, yes? I embraced my new worldview and after pondering it for a few minutes went as far as to say out loud, "Fuck it, I feel better now." But I didn't. And my eye was killing me.

I went down to the Hudson River and bummed around for a few

hours until the bars opened up. When I say "bummed around," you can take that literally because there was nothing but bums down there with me (the city has since cleaned it up and made it a nice park). The sun was warm and the familiarity of the salt air, however mixed with sewage, was still nice. I felt right at home sashaying up and down the dirty walkway, lopsided, with one shoe on. I didn't receive any strange reactions from the bunch down there.

I went out on one of the rickety, tar-soaked piers and, leaning over the side, guzzling out of a brown paper bag, was none other than Xavier Sonsire the third—Sonny. He turned from the railing, toward me. "We gotta get outta here. Cops are gonna be by again soon. We not supposed to be out here. They never used to hassle us till them dick-suckin' cowboys started turnin' tricks out here. Now they doin' all kinds of sweeps. . . . goddamn hustlers . . . ruinin' it for every-body," he said before walking off and repeating it to himself several times.

He appeared to be way crazier than the last time I'd seen him. The time spent living outside through the harsh New York City winters had obviously beaten him up a lot too. It'd only been about four years since our night out together but in bum years that's a lifetime. He was gaunt with a nappy gray afro now and way more twitchy and punchy. He didn't recognize me without the Gary jacket on but I don't know if he would have anyway. I only talked to him for a second but mentally he seemed to have crossed over to the point of no return—possibly even wet-brained. I was sad about it.

I lay against a rusted metal fence, bagging rays on my face, and catching splinters in my ass, napping on and off, until it was time to go to the bar. It was early spring but I managed to catch a little burn. Sunburned, shoeless, and now a bit hobbled from a gigantic splinter I'd caught in my toe on the way out, I walked through the city streets with my torn shirt open, looking like Ratso Rizzo on spring break.

I went up to a place called Tavern on Jane, which was right across the street from the Corner Bistro. The Tavern had become another neighborhood home base to the Knockout Drops–Bogmen crowd in recent years. Dermott had left the Bistro and it was starting to crowd up with a yuppie element so when the Tavern opened we bailed for the cooler (and less crowded) environs across the way.

The owners, Michael and Horton, were two charismatic, fun-loving, and generous guys who loved rock 'n' roll, and in the beginning before their place became a success, they used to man their own taps. They'd keep the place open late for us when we'd get back from gigs out of town and we'd hang with them drinking and listening to tunes till the sun came up—most of the time just us and them. Ponzo and Leslie conceived their first child in the bathroom there and when he was born, Michael and Horton put his picture on the wall.

They were big supporters of ours—coming to all of the shows and promoting us to everyone who came into the bar. We, in turn, made that our go-to spot after gigs—filling the joint with our notoriously thirsty crowd. Before long it was like our own clubhouse. Michael and Horton felt like family to us from day one. Sometimes you just know right away with people. They were also good friends with Brian and Dave, owners of the Blind Tiger just down the road, which made my life all the more wonderfully incestuous.

I sat down in front of the bartender, Sandra, a sweetheart of a gal who I loved to talk Giants football with. She, like me, was a devoted lifelong fan. "You look a little banged up there, fella. How's the other guy lookin'?" she asked, chuckling a little bit. "I don't even know who the other guy is yet," I said, feeling pretty sick at this point. "Oh, that's never good. Why don't you try eating something?" she said sympathetically. I said, "Thanks, babe. How 'bout a burger and a bloody?" She said, "Sure, coming right up."

About an hour later, as I was licking my wounds and trying to drink off a full-body hangover, P. J. walked in. He was a close friend who also happened to be the percussionist in The Bogmen. He put his hand on my shoulder gently and said, "I have some news for you. I'm the one who did that to your eye. We were havin' a good time and then out of nowhere you took a swing at me. Sorry, I had to return fire like that but you had this look in your eye like you weren't gonna stop." "Was it the eye of the Tiger?" I asked. "More like the eye of too much Tiger . . . too much BLIND TIGER. Sorry about your eye, dude. I didn't mean for that," he said. "I know you didn't. It's me that owes you the apology. Let's just have some beers and forget it. It's actually starting to look kinda cool anyway. It's been a while since I've had a good shiner," I said.

We partied together for the rest of that afternoon but I couldn't get drunk. I hit a plateau where the pain of my headache prevented any possibilities of worthwhile inebriation. Every drink became like another punch to the face so I did the only thing I could do in a situation like that. I kept taking punches to the face.

This episode worried me, though. I'd never been a fighter before. Over the years I'd gotten in my fair share of scrapes. That's par for the course when you drink a lot and have a big fuckin' mouth, but I'd had only a few instances where blacked-out belligerence had taken me to a point of actually lashing out. It wasn't my nature—my nature was to try to make everyone laugh and have a good time. This was obviously all Bizarro's doing. I'd gone hard on the whiskey all night before striking P. J. so I played chemist for a second and came up with a plan.

I called Brian at the Tiger from the Tavern phone all excited. He answered, "Blind Tiger." I said, "Hey, Brian, it's me, Chris." "Really? 'Cause you sound more like Mike Tyson. Do you have any idea what you did in here last night, asshole?" I said, "I do and I'm sorry. I'm hangin' with P. J now. I have a new plan. Don't serve me any more brown liquors." He said, "I've been trying to enact that plan for years but you always end up begging me for it." "Well, this time don't give it to me. I'm going on an all beer-and-mashed-potatoes diet. I'm gonna try to get as fat as Meatloaf. I need a new angle anyway and I feel like I can bring something fresh to the fraternity of fat male singers," I said. "Get some mash to go and get down here. We'll get started right away. I'll have you looking like Burl Ives before Christmas," he said, laughing. I loved Brian, not just for his forgiving nature but also for his sense of humor. He just had a unique way of looking at things and he loved vicious freaks every bit as much as I did.

I switched to nothing but beer and life got semi-good for a few days. After crashing on Mike Tait's couch for a week or so, I went back to Gracie's to get some stuff and while I was throwing socks and boxers into a plastic bag, she fell into my arms. "I've missed you," she said. "Really? I figured you were happy to be rid of me," I said, surprised. "Not the *fucked up you* but the *you* you," she said, her eyes misting up. "You seem OK. Are you sober again?" she asked. "Kind of," I said. "I only drink beer now. It keeps me out of trouble because I don't really get drunk." She said, "I have a big audition tomorrow for a film. Can you run the lines with me and we'll just stay in tonight and go to bed early?" she asked, her eyes melting me. I couldn't believe she was taking me back. "I'd love nothing better," I told her.

We ran the lines, drank some chamomile tea, and went to bed at midnight. She put her script under her pillow for good luck like she always did, fell asleep on my chest, and after a few minutes of light snoring, rolled over. I tucked my hands behind my head and stared up at the ceiling, so grateful for another chance. I fantasized about marrying Gracie someday and having a family. I imagined myself out on the lawn telling my ten-year-old boy to do a buttonhook and then zipping that pigskin in to him—hitting him right between the numbers. Then Gracie would call us in for lunch and I'd tackle him in the grass on the way in, muddying the two of us up. We'd eat grilled cheeses and I'd gaze across the table at Gracie's radiant face and smile. I watched her sleep and thought, *If I could ever get my shit together I'd love to marry her.* Lucky girl, right? I closed my eyes and tried to sleep.

An hour later I was walking into the Tiger with my pajamas on. "Which one of you skidders is buying me a drink?" An hour after that I had a Jameson's in my hand. The only wrinkle in my strategy of "only drinking beer" is that it didn't get me drunk—which I'd forgotten was the only reason I drank—a pretty big flaw now that I look back.

Darkness once again ensued. It didn't take Grace long this time to catch wind of my descent and one night around dinnertime, as she was getting on me about my "lifestyle," I excused myself to go get a pack of cigarettes and promptly returned three days later—looking like Belushi in his final hours. She asked me where I'd been and I couldn't give her a plausible answer 'cause I didn't have a plausible answer. I'd been drinking and doing blow in different bars, passing out at different friends' apartments, and drinking again since last I'd seen her. It was uneventful but continuous and I was only home because my body had run outta gas. I love when celebrities have to go to detoxes and their flacks say they've checked in due to "exhaustion." That's what I had by the third day, a nasty case of exhaustion. Grace was sick of me but not nearly as sick of me as I was.

She started in on me as I sat on the couch, wallowing in it, as fatigued and self-loathing as one could possibly be without actually hauling off and belting myself. There was quite an ugly pity party going on in my head as she laid into me. She said in a very stern voice as she clomped back and forth, "THIS IS UNACCEPTABLE. YOU'VE GOTTA CHANGE." I contemplated that word for a moment and slurred back miserably, "Change? Oh, I have a plan to change completely. IN FACT, you won't even recognize me when I'm done because I'M JUST GONNA FUCKIN' KILL MYSELF!" Remember that one from the hit parade? This time I said it not in a blackout but in a defeatist and spiteful way and you know something? It doesn't matter.

When you say these words people take it seriously, and well they should. It's not a sentence anyone should be playing around with for any reason. It's like saying BOMB on an airplane. No one wants to know why you said it or what was motivating you when you did. No one has time for that. It's an urgent and incendiary statement that will always end with you hearing the same four words from a higher authority. "COME WITH ME, PLEASE." And if you say it below Forty-second Street on the isle of Manhattan, I'll give you three guesses as to where they're gonna take you.

Clearly out of patience and short on empathy, Grace looked at the pitiful pile of a boyfriend she was harboring and went into the bedroom disgusted. I kicked off my shoes and decomposed in front of the TV for a while. About a half hour later there was a knock at the door. "Who the fuck is that?" I said. I opened the door. "Are you Chris Campion?" a very large emergency medical worker, with an Italian face, asked me. I responded slowly and skeptically, "Yeah?" "Um . . . we got a call saying you were having some trouble and to come over right away," the big walkie-talkie man said, flanked by two more to the right and left of him. "Oh, for chrissakes, ARE YOU FUCKIN' KIDDING ME? I don't wanna kill myself, fellas. That was just something I said in the heat of the argument," I explained. "Sir, it doesn't matter. If we get a call saying that somebody's threatening to do themselves harm we have to respond," he told me nicely, but firmly. Having been through this drill once before I knew there was no talking my way out of it and said, "All right, I'm familiar with the law. I'll come peacefully. We can straighten it out down at the hospital. Just do me a favor and don't put the cuffs on too tight."

Grace was hovering in tears as they slapped the handcuffs on me. She said, "I'm sorry, baby, but it's the only way." I said, "THE ONLY WAY . . . TO HAVE ME COMMITTED? It's a way but I don't know about the only way." "I didn't know what else to do. I called your sister Eileen, and she told me to call," she said, blowing her nose. "DO YOU HAVE ANY IDEA WHERE THEY'RE TAKING ME? THERE'S DANGEROUS FUCKIN' PEOPLE THERE! I WAS HALF ASLEEP JUST NOW. YOU KNOW I WASN'T GONNA DO ANYTHING. I WAS JUST PISSED OFF AT MYSELF," I exclaimed. "Well, how am I supposed to know that? Half the things you say are lies and everything else half-truths. YOU BROUGHT THIS ON YOURSELF!" she yelled. She stymied me with that one. That couldn't have been more true. I said, "Whatever . . . I'll see you when I get out, I guess." "No, you won't. This is it for us," she said, looking at the floor. I directed my next comment to the EMTs, who were letting us have our final words. "How's this for a happy breakup scene, fellas?" "None of my business, boss. My business is to get you to the hospital. Let's go," the big EMT said. They led me down the stairs and out of the building.

When we got outside my Dominican buddies from the deli were out having a smoke. They saw the cuffs on me and came over. Oscar Granados, the owner of the deli, came charging up and said to the big EMT, "Where are ju going with Tortuga, meng? Why are ju taking Tortuga? He's just drunk, leaf him alone." I said, "It's OK, Oscar. They're just doing their job, dude." "No, it's not OK, Tortuga . . . just because he's drunk ju take him? He's drunk all the time, leaf him alone," Oscar pleaded with them.

They put me in the ambulance, and as we're pulling away Oscar started running alongside the truck, pounding on the side." "No . . . don't take him . . . he's just *mucho boracho, meng*. He's drunk! GIVE HIM A SANDWICH . . . HE CALMS RIGHT DOWN!" And off I went for another involuntary visit to the world's most famous mental hospital.

I chatted up the boys in the ambulance and was real charming. I said things like, "You know women, guys . . . they overreact." I struck gold with the big guy, who spoke for all of them and said, "Yeah, we know. We're all married." They all laughed in agreement. This was a pivotal moment. I was trying to do that "guy thing" with them to earn their trust and it seemed to work. I did all this for two reasons: (1) I wanted to lull them into complacency on the off chance that maybe at some point during the transition I could make a break for it, and (2) I did not want the THORAZINE.

I had been a good boy so once they got me behind the electronic doors they saw no need for the handcuffs anymore and big walkie-talkie man said, "Sit here for a few minutes, Chris, and a doctor will be out soon." I knew they weren't letting me go 'cause I had a history. Once they pulled my file I was toast—probably in there for a week or more.

I sat there scouring the ward, looking for any opening at all, a door, an open transom, anything to get me the hell out of there, when all of a sudden from down the hall I heard the most ungodly screams. It sounded like a fuckin' velociraptor. "Aaaaaaaah! Aaaaaaahhh!!! Get me the fuck outta here!" I looked inside the room it was coming from and there was this cantankerous gray-haired old man in there, with a cast on his arm up to his shoulder, cocked out of his mind, bellowing in his thick New York accent, "GET ME THE FUCK OUTTA HERE!" I said, "What happened to you?" "I fell down some stairs and now THESE FUCKS WON'T LET ME ATTA HERE. WHO THE FUCK ARE YOU?"

Just then this snippy orderly poked his head in, looked right at me, and said, "Try to keep him quiet, OK? There's people trying to sleep." I thought, *Wait a minute . . . Did he just ask me to keep him quiet? Hmmmmm. He must've thought I was visiting him. Hmmmmmm. If he thought I was visiting him, then maybe others would too?* While the plan to escape was busy being hatched in my head he really erupted. "WHATTA I GOTTA TO DO GET ATTA HERE? I wheeled around and said, "Shhhhhhhh. I'll tell you what you gotta do but ya gotta play ball." That quieted him some. He said curiously, "Yeah . . . play ball? Who the hell are you? Whatta you work here? GET ME THE FUCK ATTA HERE!" I said, "Shhhhhhhh. No, I don't, but I think I found a way to get us both outta here but you gotta play ball. Now, what's your name?" "Ernie McCormick," he barked. I said in a gentle voice, "All right, Ernie, just let me do all the talking, go along with whatever I say, and I'll get us outta here."

Now Ernie was warming to me but he was one of those guys who even if he was warming to you he'd still insult you. "Yeah, you're gonna get me outta here?" he asked. "Yeah, I am," I promised. He winced a little from the pain of his injury, putting his hand on his shoulder, then shrugged it off, looked me in the eyes, and said, "KNOCK YOURSELF OUT, FUCKFACE." I said, "All right, you stay right here then." "WHERE THE FUCK AM I GONNA GO, GENIUS?" he snapped.

I looked out into the hall to do a little recon and I noticed some different guards on, with doctors exchanging clipboards and shit like that. I said to myself, "Everything must be changing over." So not many people saw them bring me in to begin with and now it was all new people so it was the time to make my move. I saw a lady doctor down the hall, staring at a clipboard and walking toward the room. I waited patiently for her to pass and popped out. "Excuse me, doctor, is there any way I'm going to be able to take my *uncle* home tonight? My aunt wants to know." She said, "Who's your uncle?" I said, "Mr. McCormick right in there," and I pointed in at Ernie. As I was saying this Ernie let out another drunken, "You fucks better lemme go tonight!" She took one look in there at Ernie, saw his angry, drunk, red face and without hesitation said, "Oh no, he's not going anywhere." I reacted with phony disappointment and said, "Oh, well, I'd really better let my aunt know then. Is there a pay phone somewhere I could use?" She answered, "Sure, there's one right down the hall. Let me buzz you out." I recognized these to be THE SWEET WORDS OF FREEDOM.

Ernie heard all this and knew he was being double-crossed so I had to get out before he rolled on me. "Hey . . . HEY! WHERE THE FUCK IS HE GOIN'?" he shouted over to the doctor. She buzzed me out and as I was going through the door I heard her shush him. "Shhhh, he's just going to call your wife. He'll be back." As the door was closing I could hear Ernie freaking out. "My wife? My wife's been dead for fourteen years. YOU FUCKIN' COCKSUCKA!!!" and that's the last thing I heard before I started speed-walking through the halls of Bellevue.

I weaved in and out of people, past gurneys and shit, trying to find an exit sign. I felt like a runaway rat in a labyrinth. I slowed down and sped up according to who I was seeing in front of me. If they seemed official I slowed it down and tried to look inconspicuous. I was careful to make good eye contact and give a facial gesture of hello so as not to arouse any suspicion.

Finally, after a few heart attack minutes of searching, I found a side exit. There was no one down that hall so I started sprinting. I got up a full head of steam and hit the metal cross bar on the door like it was a blocking sled. I was outta Bellevue like a bullet and charged headlong back into the New York night. It was a feeling of exhilaration the likes of which I'd never known and will probably never know again. I had only experienced it vicariously through movies but that wasn't even on the Richter scale compared to this. Going through that door with that kind of force and hearing the loud metallic clink when it crashed open made me realize why they called it "busting out." It was an indescribable feeling of emergence.

I ran down First Avenue, found the nearest pay phone, and called Gracie. After two long rings she picked up. "Hello?" Then I got to say the most empowering words anyone could ever even hope to say in this lifetime, which are, "HA-HA! THEY HAVEN'T BUILT THE MENTAL INSTITUTION THAT CAN HOLD ME!"

Chapter Fifteen

The Triangle Trade of Misery

ollowing my escape, I spent the rest of that year losing things. I lost Grace, my family, the band—everything I held near and dear. No one wanted to deal with me anymore because I was a moth-eaten barfly with a death wish—not exactly a prized dinner guest. I'd gone to all that trouble to escape from Bellevue but what had I escaped to? A far worse incarceration than anything Bellevue could've served up and the fucked-up thing is that I was at the helm of it.

I was homeless but really had no idea that that was the case. Mike Tait came to my rescue. One night after our gig together he said with his disarming Canadian delivery, "Hey, guyser . . . um . . . you do know that you're homeless, right?" Indignant to the accusation, I said, "I am not. I'm just in between living situations right now." He responded, "Well, you can situate yourself on my couch till you're not so 'in between' if you want." I ended up crashing at Mike's sometimes after that but the truth was I slept wherever I landed and that's what became normal. Often it would be on the couch or floor of the person I was partying with or if I'd gotten lucky maybe in the bed of some party chick. The latter wasn't happening as much as it once did. At the end of the night I'd either look too wild-eyed or not house-broken enough to attract any quality takers.

Early one morning I woke up on cold concrete steps and felt something pinching and pulling on my hair. I opened my eyes and saw these two young boys playing with little green army men next to me. They'd factored me in as an intricate centerpiece in their battle scene. I felt like I was in some twisted bum version of *Gulliver's Travels*—surrounded and covered by little plastic figurines. They were making the noises of bomb explosions and machine-gun fire when one of them yelled out, "TAKE COVER! THE BEAST IS WAK-ING UP!" I rolled over onto a pile of sharp ones. "AHHHHHHH! C'mon, get these fuckin' things off me, guys," I said grouchily, as I untangled army men out of my hair and brushed them off my ass and back.

I spotted what appeared to be their nanny talking to some people in front of a café and said, "Hey, I'm not gettin' paid to do your job, ya know. Because of you I'm probably gonna be shittin' plastic bayonets till Wednesday." She was a pretty hot, young, Scandinavian honey but I wasn't flirting. I was still drunk and cranky. "I tried to move you sree times but you wouldn't wake up so I just leaves you there," she said apologetically. Then she realized that I was in no position to be chastising her and said, "Zis is not your living room. You should go home." I needed to say something to make her feel bad as I walked away and said, "For your information I was mugged last night and conked on the head but thanks for the sympathy, lady." She came back with, "File a report wis za police. I think they will find out you are za one they are looking for." "Maybe I'll do that," I said, walking away, knowing I'd lost that exchange badly.

I was starving. I hadn't eaten anything at all the day before that I could remember. I checked my pockets and, much to my surprise, found six glorious crumpled-up ones and decided to hit McDonald's on Sixth Avenue. I was looking pretty beat up. This was day num-ber four in the same clothes with no shower. I noticed I was draw-ing some looks from people as I walked in, which was only adding to my bummy self-image and paranoia. I contemplated leaving and just heading back to Mike's but I was already in there and had to eat something.

I stepped up to the counter and ordered a Big Mac value meal. It was $4.99—perfect for my budget. The man behind the counter was in his thirties and obviously a manager of some sort because on the other registers were kids in their late teens-early twenties. He ap-praised me for a second and then said coldly, "We don't have those." I said, "Whattya mean you don't have those? Of course you have those, it's your bread and butter. Whattya think, I'm stupid?" "No, we don't have those. Now, I suggest you step aside and let someone else order, sir. There's a line," he said snippily.

It was a fairly easy situation to read. He didn't like the way I looked and wanted to get rid of me but I wasn't gonna just stand idly by and take it. I wanted justice. I glanced back at the people behind me and launched into a speech worthy of the highest and finest soapbox. I cleared my voice and enunciated, "Listen, if you don't like the way I look or how I'm dressed or the fact that maybe I'm a little dirty then just say so, but don't stand there and smugly look me in the eye and tell me that you have no Big Macs because that just insults my intelligence." I then ratcheted it up to, "THE BIG MAC IS THE CORNERSTONE OF THIS FINE FRANCHISE. YOU'D BE NOTHING WITHOUT IT. IT HAS BOUGHT EVERY BRICK AND HUNG EVERY GOLDEN ARCH IN EVERY MCDONALD'S ACROSS THIS GREAT LAND. AM I WRONG?" I shouted passionately, posing the question to him and the rest of the crowd. He said, "No, you're not wrong but it's nine-thirty in the morning and right now we're only serving breakfast." I stood silent for a second and replied to him in a timid voice, "Egg McMuffin, then."

I felt a security guard's hand go on my shoulder. He was an older guy about my dad's age. He smelled like he'd done the backstroke in his aftershave that morning, so I said, "Whattya got goin' there, a little Aqua Velva?" He said, "Good guess. I wear that sometimes but today it's Brut." "You switch up your aftershaves? Most guys just stick with one. How long you been doin' that, if you don't mind me askin'?" "I get them as gifts from my kids. It's all the same shit. You gotta go now. You're gonna do that for me, right?" I said, "Oh, yeah, sure. Tell them all sorry. When he said no Big Macs, I thought it was personal. I haven't been myself of late," I said. "Will do," he said. As I was walking out the door he stopped me. "Wait a minute. Hold still," he said, as his hands went into my hair and delicately untangled and plucked out another army man. "Here you go," he said, smiling and giving it to me. "Thanks," I said. "I was lookin' for that."

I still had clothes over at Grace's but didn't dare go there. I'd disrupted her life enough. I'd get drunk and get the itch to call her but would fight it off with everything I had. I told Brian at the Tiger, "Whatever you do don't let me use the phone, even if I'm telling you I'm calling someone else. I'm telling you in advance that I'm lying." "Wow, preemptive truth-telling. You're a pioneer in the field of compulsive lying. What are you doing whiling away your hours in here? You should really be out there helping people," he cracked.

I'd now entered what I like to refer to as my days-unaccounted-for period. During this time I was primarily spending all my waking hours in three bars—the Blind Tiger Ale House, Tavern on Jane, and Fiddlesticks, a newly opened Irish pub on Greenwich Avenue.

The owner of Fiddlesticks was a terrific guy from Ireland named Peter. Johnny, the head bartender, was another colorful Irish character with red hair and a mad twinkle and together we all struck up a great friendship. I'm never more comfortable than when in the company of Irish folks. I just feel understood by them on every level—drunk or sober. Peter gave me a gig on Thursdays that I did with my friends Bill Ryan, Mark Nilsen, and Paulie the G—three consummate musicians and all-star vicious freaks. We called ourselves Ponderosa because we thought the bar reminded us of the set on *Bonanza*. There were all sorts of barrels and wagon wheels and shit like that lying around. We had some killer nights in there when I wasn't wasted and falling apart onstage, which was about half the time.

My average day in the days-unaccounted-for-period would start at the Tiger usually, and then I'd feel myself getting too drunk and rather than wear out my welcome entirely and do something I might have to apologize for later, I'd get up and move it to one of the other two bars. Then once I was at, let's say, Fiddlesticks, I would start to feel the same thing happening, and I'd move it over to the Tavern, trying to stay one step ahead of myself—always figuring new surroundings would yield a new me. It never did.

Fiddlesticks was halfway between the Tiger and the Tavern but a few blocks east, making the route a perfect triangle—which I now call the "triangle trade of misery." What I didn't know was that every time I left one place really drunk they'd phone ahead to the next bar and warn them I was coming. Sometimes I'd get cut off before I could even sit down.

I wasn't in touch with Tom or Phil at all at this point. I'd stopped turning up for rehearsals and returning calls. They'd thrown down the gauntlet and given me "the old tomato" to either get sober or leave the band. Because I had no real place to hang my hat and couldn't afford one of those newfangled cell phones that were becoming annoyingly more ubiquitous every day, I got a voice-mail box that I paid seven dollars a month for. (Remember those?) It was cheap but I still managed to get it turned off on me every so often for not paying the bill.

I was checking it one afternoon from the Tiger's phone and Phil had left me a long message that ended with, "We're not gonna sit back and watch you do it anymore, dude. It's too painful and you're dragging us all down with you. Now what's it gonna be?" I never gave them an answer. I just stopped showing up but I'd occasionally see Ponzo and he'd tell me they were still getting together to jam and write songs. "Bro, you're gonna lose your band if you're not careful. I know a lot of people that would kill to play with Tom and Phil. Swallow your pride and go back," he said. "Pride? You think this is about pride? Try lack thereof . . . Anyway, they said I've got to be sober and you know I can't do that. I wanna go back but I just can't right now," I told him. "Suit yourself but don't say I didn't warn ya," he said. Ponzo wasn't in my life very much either during all this. He and Leslie had just had a baby and he was busy at home being Mr. Mom while she worked.

I figured when it was time to go back I would, but didn't give it much thought otherwise. I was still bitter from all the beatings we'd taken at the hands of the fuckin' music business and drank with fury at it every day. By this time Clive Davis and his crackerjack team of know-nothing flunkies up at Arista Records had systematically ruined The Bogmen. This is a band that was growing exponentially until Arista signed them. One would have expected that to be a good thing but it turned out to be the kiss of death. They spent a lot of money in the wrong places, trying to break them on their first record *Life Begins at 40 Million* and when it didn't go they simply let them die on the vine, spending no money on the second one, CLOSED CAPTION RADIO. Arista said, "We don't hear a single," showed them no commitment on that album whatsoever, and dropped them.

The Bogmen ended up breaking up and all going their separate ways. I was furious with the idiots up at that label. As envious as I was, I really did want to see them make it.

My resentment for all things music related was at an all-time high, so I thought, *Maybe it's time for a break from the Drops.* The bigger truth was, like the situation with Grace, I didn't wanna fuck up Tom's and Phil's lives anymore with my alcoholic shit. I decided it was just best to stay away for a while. Of course I could've conducted myself professionally and told them that, but instead I opted to hide from them.

It may sound like there was a lot of deliberation going on with these decisions but there really wasn't. Once I took the first drink of the day, which was right away, there were no real choices to make anymore. I was getting fucked up and that was that. I watched from a barstool as my life floated downstream, making no effort at all to retrieve it. I quit everyone and everything and just drank—the funniest thing being that there wasn't much to attend to anyhow. I had it set up where I only had to be a couple of different places a week. But when your responsibilities are that few and you miss one it is glaring.

I couldn't even make my gigs with Mike Tait at the Red Lion anymore. I might turn up and I might not. Sometimes I'd call from the Tiger and tell them I had a sore throat. Brian said, "Chris, they're paying you to sit on a stool, get drunk, tell stories, and sing. Where's the hard part? These are all things you'll end up doing in here tonight for free. Why not just go and get paid?" I just couldn't, for the life of me, picture being able to get through a three-hour set anymore without collapsing into myself and said, "No, dude. I just don't have it in me tonight." "I understand. You've had a rough day," he said sarcastically.

My status as America's guest was in some serious jeopardy too. Word was getting out that it might not be such a good idea to have me stay over. My good friends Hank and Joel put me up after a night of partying and I went all Keith Moon on them, smashing up their apartment in a drunken, blacked-out rage. They lived in a big place with a few different roommates who I didn't know at all. I woke up the next day and their living room was in disarray with a big framed picture ripped off the wall, lying on the floor shattered into pieces. It didn't take the help of Scotland Yard to figure out who'd done that and I high-tailed it outta there before anyone woke up. I didn't even stick around to take my lumps and hear the story. I just blew out like a hurricane—the maniacal eye in my own dizzying storm.

One of the lowest moments of this downward turn was when I showed up at my sister Donna's place, at four in the morning, hoping to crash on her couch. She'd given me keys before the family had made me persona non grata and had since asked for them back, a request I conveniently ignored. Unbeknownst to her, I was letting myself in to flop in the basement of her building. I discovered this was possible one night when, desperate for a place to shut my eyes, I headed over to her apartment intending to beg her to let me sleep on the sofa bed. I got there and really didn't wanna have to wake her, her husband, and their newborn baby, Maggie, so I got the bright idea just to pass out in the basement. I got down there and found a musty old box spring, which I pulled off the wall and in one motion fell onto. "A drunkard's dream if I ever did see one," to quote The Band. I made it my fail-safe sleep spot after that. It wasn't the greatest. I'd opened my eyes nose to nose with mice and huge water bugs more than once but at least it wasn't outside.

On the night I speak of here, I was trying to give a soft landing to an exhaustive five-day cocaine-and-booze binge and craved a real bed. I blew off the basement and instead snuck into her apartment, silently slithering onto the couch.

My sly entry was successful but then I must've gotten up and started sleepwalking and TALKING and SCREAMING and WAIL-ING and CURSING, and right as I was about to start breaking shit my sister came out and put me back down on the couch. I remember coming to and hearing her say to the baby, who I'd woken up with my psycho-somnambulance, "Shhhhhhhh, don't cry. You'll wake your uncle Chris and we definitely don't want that." She was shushing her baby not to wake me for fear of what havoc I might wreak. Correct me if I'm wrong, but wasn't it supposed to be the other way around? I tiptoed out of there before they got up too, leaving the keys on the kitchen table. I couldn't face them—I couldn't face anyone.

. . .

Rudderless, homeless, and joyless, I shuffled around the streets of Midtown, killing time before doing my Wednesday gig at The Collins Bar. I played it with the Ponderosa band from Fiddlesticks. At the Collins we called ourselves Night Train. I didn't feel like doing it but desperately needed the fifty-dollar payday and the free drinks.

I was feeling weary and sick. I put a quarter in the pay phone to check messages and got an unexpected voice mail from my good friend Ian McCulloch, the lead singer of Echo and the Bunnymen. I'd first met him in the spring of '97 when my career was still on the upswing and Echo had come to New York to kick off a nationwide tour behind their comeback record *Evergreen*. "Shakes, I'm back in town doin' some work on me new album. They've got me at the Soho Grand. Give a bell when you surface, you fuckin' geezer," he said in his unmistakable Liverpudlian accent. He referred to me as Shakes the Clown, a nickname Phil had given to me, referencing the classic Bobcat Goldthwait movie by the same name. I'd earned that moniker because I shook mightily with a pool cue in my hand and I was somewhat of a clown, I guess. I became reanimated by his message and headed to the Collins with a jolt of enthusiasm. Life was always fun when Ian was in town, no matter how bad I felt.

In 1997, the Bunnymen had a couple of nights in a row scheduled down at Mercury Lounge. The performances were sold out but I used my connections down there to get into the closing night concert and the subsequent afterparty at the Orchard Bar down the street.

Echo and the Bunnymen had been one of my favorite bands since I was a teenager. The show at the Merc was killer. Ian looked exactly the same as the last time I'd seen him in concert way back in February of '88 at Cornell University. I'd gone to that Cornell show with Kim Pearson and I remember being wedged up against the stage in front of Ian's mic stand when, just for a lark, Kim took a swig out of his water cup. Unexpectedly repulsed, she spit it in my face, and winced. "OH MY GOD, THAT'S STRAIGHT VODKA!" I figured if I got a chance to talk to Ian I might tell him that story. Though it was now 1997, his style hadn't changed much. His hair was still dark and mussed and he had on this killer fitted suit and shades. He looked fantastic—a rock star if ever there was one. He forcefully belted out song after song, in between drinking, smoking, and mumbling stuff over the mic that only he could understand—his Liverpool accent mixing with the reverb effect on his voice rendering it unintelligible to the audience.

I blew through the door at the Orchard afterward with my brother Bill, sister Eileen, the Ryan brothers, Billy and Brendan, Phil, Tom, Ponzo, Paulie the G, and a few more guys and gals from our crowd. Eileen, knowing what a huge fan I was, said, "There he is. Go and talk to him." She'd been the one who'd turned me on to the *Ocean Rain* record back in high school. I admitted to being a little nervous to go over there and I was never really one to get star-struck.

I was reluctant to talk to Ian because he had a reputation in the American music press as being difficult and standoffish. I was afraid of being let down. He was, as it turns out, the complete opposite. I walked up to him and said, "Great show, Ian!" and shook his hand. "And who are you?" he asked. "Larry Hagman," I said. "Oh, are you the *I-Dream-of-Jeannie* Hagman or the latter-day J. R.-Ewing Hagman?" he asked jokingly. "I'm the I-NEED-A-LIVER-TRANSPLANT, bloated, alcoholic Hagman," I said, accurately timed with a burp. "That'll do perfectly," he said. "I love that Hagman."

We started talking and I led with the story about Kim and his cup of vodka up at Cornell. He laughed his ass off, saying, "That'll teach her to mess with me cup." "That was an incredible show. It was on a Sunday night. Do you remember it?" I asked him. "Not very much . . . Just that there was some crazy bird there who kept swiping my cup and throwing the whole thing off. I cursed the moron that brought her."

Ian and I hit it off famously, as did our respective party crews. They were vicious—we were vicious—and we recognized the viciousness in one another. It was Shangri-la-VICIOUS! And I was thrilled to be hanging with my hero. He invited us all to an after-afterparty up at the Paramount Hotel where he and the rest of the Bunnymen were staying. "Grab everyone and we'll keep it goin' in me room," he said.

As we were all on Houston Street doing the mad four A.M. scramble for cabs, we saw this bearded and disheveled homeless guy sitting on the sidewalk, in front of Katz's Delicatessen with his pants pulled all the way down to his ankles—dead nude. He was carefully placing slices of bologna over his filthy cock while petting a small mutt next to him who had his snout buried in his crotch eating the pieces off.

Letting out groans of excitation, the bearded pervert would then stuff a slab of bologna in his craw and chew, mouth open, rolling his head back and forth. One of the gals that we had with us took serious issue with this and said, "You stop that right now or I'm calling the police. That's animal cruelty!" He stared at her cross-eyed and in a very gruff voice said, "He gets to eat and I get my balls cleaned. . . . It's win–win. He licks his own balls anyway. Mind your own business, lady."

We were all pretty sickened by what we'd just witnessed. Ian jumped into his limo and putting the window down, quipped, "Bring the guy with the dog and we'll set him up in the lounge."

We raged well into the next morning and then Mac (we'd switched to calling Ian Mac by then 'cause that's what he went by) had to go get snapped for some press photos. They were filming a video for the beautiful single off of *Evergreen*, "Nothing Lasts Forever," the day after that and he told us he was gonna be in town for the rest of the week and back a few more times over the next few months. That summer my brother and I ended up taking him and his boys out whenever they were in town, acting as their guides to the downtown underground and afterhours scene.

I hadn't seen him in over a year when I got his message on my voice mail. He hadn't heard just how far down the dial I'd gone. I desperately wanted to give him "The same old Shakes" and rev it up to a roar. However emotionally unstable and booze logged I felt, I figured just seeing him might be the pill to restore my good-time-Charlie persona and enable me to have fun.

I pounded vodka and breezed through my two sets at The Collins Bar—the anticipation of partying with Mac buoying me to the finish line with relative ease. This was obvious to me considering how I'd felt before I'd gotten the call from him. I'm embarrassed to say that there was a bit of hero worship going on here. We'd become great friends but when you boiled that away I was still the same kid who was up in his room listening to "The Cutter" with the volume pegged. The other thing I felt hanging around him, that I'd never dare tell him, is that he'd made his mark on this world and was a success while I'd fallen way short of that—an ego-bruising fact that made feel diminished in his presence at times.

I scored some blow on my way out from a scruffy guy wearing

an army fatigue jacket who was a regular at the gig and rumored to be in the Westies, the infamously violent Irish Mafia. I saw that he'd been digging the show, and taking pride in the fact that my brand of barroom entertainment soothed something in degenerate criminals, I decided to take advantage of it. "Yo, you think you could float me another half and I'll pay you for a gram next Wednesday? I'm a little light at the moment." He answered, "Sure, you're a funny fuckin' guy . . . good voice too. You remind me a lot of my cousin." I said, "Oh, is he a singer too?" "No, he's dead . . . knife wound punctured his lung." "I'll have the money for you next week, no problem," I reassured him. "Yeah, I know you will," he said. I needed to keep a little cash in my pocket. I didn't wanna be on dead empty whilst partying with my rock star friend.

I did some key hits in the bathroom, said my good-byes, and hopped the C train to Canal Street by myself to go meet "The Macca," as he was affectionately known to his Liverpool cohorts.

On the train my thoughts turned to Grace, who I hadn't seen or spoken to in months. I wondered what she was up to. Did she have a new boyfriend? Probably, I surmised. Gals like her don't stay single for very long. The train screeched and labored around turns as I sank further into my melancholy. I was such a loser. How could I let her go? She was bright, soulful, and selfless, with a great wisdom and insight into deeper things. Sometimes people with high ideals like that can be strident and humorless but she wasn't like that at all. She laughed out loud at everything.

I remembered her watching me in the batting cage at Coney Island, cheering me on from behind the backstop, when the machine went haywire and beaned me in the head. It was set on "superfast pitch." I was on the ground struggling to find my helmet, covered in dirt, as the automated pitcher kept rapid-firing balls at me. I was ducking them and getting pelted by them, trying to get back into the batter's box to take the rest of my swings when I heard these cackles in back of me that were loud enough to ignite Mount Saint Helens. I turned around and she was on the ground, holding her sides, belly laughing. We were both in grass skirts and had green body paint on because we'd been at the Mermaid Parade. I never loved her more than in that moment. She was my one and only. I was sure of that.

We went and rode the Cyclone a bunch of times after that. She wanted to go on it over and over—I dragged her away kicking and screaming like a little kid. We went and rejoined our friends who had a spot staked out on the boardwalk in front of Ruby's Bar. Everybody we knew was there. It was the best fuckin' time.

The after-parade revelers were still in their mermaid costumes and whooping it up all around us as we leaned against the railing and got lost in a long kiss—the breeze blowing our skirts up like a couple of Hawaiian Marilyn Monroes. A mixture of ocean air and barbecue smoke wafted into our noses as we admired the unique backdrop, beach brushing up against the urban decay and the dilapidated amusement park and dirty Ferris wheel—every third light broken on it. There was a Dixieland jazz combo playing on the boardwalk next to us. I did this spontaneous spazzy dance that used to really crack her up. I'd lean forward like I was about to fall and kick up my heels, running in place, while making a demented beaver face. She laughed that infectious laugh and we submerged into another long kiss. I realized as I came out of that fond remembrance that I had traded her in just to be able to drink. *If there was a bigger dumbass than me in the world, I sure as hell haven't met him yet,* I thought, as the train pulled into Canal Street station.

I bought a Bud tall boy from a bodega for the three-block walk to the hotel. I cracked it and sucked on it hard, trying to stuff back down the feelings for Grace that I'd foolishly let bubble to the surface. Instead of continuing to walk, I guzzled it next to a trash can, crushed it on my head, and tossed it out with excessive force, thinking one more time about Gracie. "Gone is gone," I uttered out loud, not caring if anyone caught me talking to myself. I went in and bought another one and started walking with it—cocking my head back, doing stutter steps, and chugging.

I needed to turn this mood around but quick. I wanted to have good shtick for Mac and the boys. I couldn't walk in there some sad sack. I took stock of myself in the street and felt like I was rotting from the inside out. I didn't even wanna go up there now. Who was I fuckin' kidding? I didn't belong there. I didn't belong anywhere. My life had become a perpetual purgatory of guilt and remorse spurred on by a racing mind and a faithless fear that lingered in my system like hepatitis C. Reducing it down to simpler terms, I was a drunken bum and at that precise moment I didn't really feel like being anything else. I wanted to bag it, go to the Tiger, and relax with my fucked-up self or, better yet, just remain alone and drink.

I walked back and forth trying to figure out what to do. I polished off the beer and decided to go through with the night as planned—still in the back of my mind convinced it was gonna restore something in me that had been lost. I watched like a spectator as my feet took me there. I got up to Mac's room and knocked on the door. It swung open. "SHAKES THE CLOWN, AS I LIVE AND BREATHE!"

There was a small crowd of about ten people in the room, partying, some of whom I already knew from past times through. I loved the guys in Ian's crew. They were all aces—real characters with sunny dispositions—each one having an exceptional capacity for drink. Actually I've never met anyone from Liverpool who didn't. With Ian on this trip were his road managers, Hienzy and Peezy, and a few roadies whose names I've forgotten now. Seeing those guys and laughing it up did the trick for a while, but the laughter you enjoy when you're staving off a nervous breakdown has a strange slap-back to it. When it subsides the memory of your life and your troubles twists into you like a knife. It's kind of like when somebody says something funny at a wake. Everyone breaks up and the comic relief feels good momentarily, but when it stops you realize that the reason you're even standing there is because someone you love is dead. Then no one says a thing.

Ian's personal manager, Paul, was hanging in the room too, with the usual bevy of hot chicks that no one seemed to know. Paul was a really sweet guy who I loved talking music with. I asked him, "Where'd you guys find them?" and pointed to the girls. "Oh, we met them in the lounge downstairs and invited them up for a drink. I haven't even gotten their names yet. How've you been, mate? You look a bit knackered," he said. "Well, that's one way of putting it. You English have a lovely way of telling someone they look like shit, you know that?" "Ahhh, Shakes, you know I didn't mean it like that," he said, smiling, and he didn't. "I know, buddy. You actually couldn't be more right. I'm nick nack paddywack give the dog a fuckin' bone KNACKERED," I told him. "Long night last night?" he asked. "Yup, and it's still goin' . . .

but I think it started before last night. Don't make me pinpoint it for you, though. That might start some kind of brain hemorrhage," I said. "Been where you are, mate . . . been where you are. At least you're in the right crowd now. You won't see any judgment out of these vampires, I can tell you that. Speaking of which, I'm not feeling all that well so I'm gonna knock it on the head in a few. Try not to keep him out till dawn, OK? He's got a session tomorrow. I know telling the two of you that is worth nil but it's my job to say it. You do understand?" "Loud and clear, Paulie . . . loud and clear," I said. "All right, Shakes. We'll see you tomorrow then," he said, and quietly cut out.

After Paul left, I hung out holding court with Mac and the crowd in the room. We were entertaining everyone with some stories of our past escapades together and then he wanted me to fly solo on one and said, "Shakes, tell them the one about the time you scored the heroin by accident." "I dunno, man, that one's kind of epic," I said. "Oh, c'mon . . . then do a little of the guy who sold it to you for them," he said. He loved when I imitated Rollo because I wore a retainer plate with fake eye teeth on it that I would drop down, like fangs, and talk jive through. "Okay but let me hit the bathroom first," I said. I was the only one gackin'. Mac and his crew were big boozehounds but they weren't druggies.

I went in there ostensibly to pack my beak and get a second wind but when I looked in the mirror, something else happened. I started bawling uncontrollably. It was the last thing I expected but there it was. I looked so awful it was alarming. I was bloated and blousy and looked like I hadn't slept in years. The mirror shocked me. Once after a four-day run Grace had told me that it looked like I had "a face on top of my face." I saw what she meant by that now. I splashed cold water on my face, dried myself, took a deep breath, and went back into the luxury suite living room like a dutiful Borscht-belt comedian, sucking it up for the second show. I sprang to life and told the heroin story when I got back in there—full on with the teeth and everything. It killed. I had 'em all rolling.

As the night wore on I kept returning to the bathroom, pulling out the blow, crying, throwing cold water on my face, and emerging with a manufactured smile. I was losin' it.

Keeping my word to Paul (somewhat), I encouraged everyone

to leave the room around seven A.M. so Mac could crash out for his afternoon recording session. The gals had hung with us all night but it wasn't a sex, drugs, and rock 'n' roll kind of thing. It'd just been a bunch of people sitting around, getting loaded, and bullshitting— normally my favorite thing in the world but I was anxious to get away from them. I could see Mac was shot too, and I said, "Get some sleep, dude. I'll drop in on you guys at the studio later." He said, "Nice one, Shakes."

Two of the party chicks offered to let me crash in their room. They were these really cool girls from Madrid, both sexy as hell. I almost took them up on it but was so fragile of mind that I politely declined, saying, "Thanks, but I really gotta be gettin' home." "OK, sweetie, maybe we see you out later. You are so funny," the cuter of the two told me, giggling, and giving me one of those Euro kisses on both cheeks. I kept watching them as they walked down the hall holding hands. I'll be sitting in an old age home someday kicking myself for that one but I had no choice. I was short-circuiting and I definitely didn't wanna be having any crying jags in front of them. I needed to be among my own. I went to the Tortuga deli and broke the day there instead. Those guys had seen me cry lots of times.

. . .

I finished off the rest of the blow in the bathroom at the bodega. I was in a walking catatonic state by then. I sat down at a table but the guys didn't sit with me this time, knowing I was too far gone. They just went about their business as I drank a slow beer and let my eyes wander out the window. The morning commute was just begin- ning. People were coming in and getting coffee and newspapers. I was drinking out of a can in a paper bag, vegetating. I'm not even sure how long I did that before Oscar sat down across from me.

"You look pale, Tortuga. When was the last time ju had sleep, my friend?" he asked. "Ummmm . . . not sure. What day is it today?" I asked him. "Eees Thursday," he answered. "Oh, then . . . I dunno," I said, sipping. "Why don't ju go in back and lie down on the couch, huh? Diego will wake you when he goes at noon. Unless ju have an- other place ju'd rather go," he said. "No . . . no . . . I don't. I mean, I could go somewhere but it's a bit of a walk. You're a real pal, Oscar. Thanks," I said, walking in back with him. "Eees nothing . . . what happened with you and the pretty blonde? She throw ju out again?" he asked. "Yeah, but I'm afraid there's no going back this time. She found me out, old-timer," I said, stretching out on the couch. "Old-timer? I'm fifty-two. Who ju calling old-timer? Ju know, Tortuga, we like when ju come in and make us laugh but ju got to stop feeling sorry for jourself. How old are ju?" he asked. "God, don't make me say it. I'm thirty-four . . . I'm thirty-fuckin'-four!" I said, groaning, my hands covering my face. "Ees well past the time for ju to be a man. Ju got to be a man, Tortuga," he emphasized forcefully. "Jour life will pass ju by if ju don't. Are ju listening to me?" "Yes . . . I know . . . a man . . . gonna start right after this nap," I said, passing out. He flicked off the light.

I slept for two hours or so and bolted from the deli upon waking. I had a cloudy recollection of Oscar's speech and, out of instinct, fled the scene right away. He wasn't even there anymore and I still ran out like the building was on fire. He'd never given me one of those talks before, a sure-fire sign that the walls were closing in again. The day had that kind of feel to it right from the very start. In terms of what lay ahead, I consider Oscar's bedtime warning to be STRIKE ONE.

I hadn't really spent that much money from the gig at the Collins so I went to a different deli and got a six of tallies and sat in the empty fountain at Washington Square Park, drinking. It was a nice day. I watched a fire-eating juggler do his act for the crowd. He rode around on a unicycle that had to be ten feet high, tossing up spinning torches, snatching them out of the air, and eating them. It was pretty cool. Watching him made me think back to my time spent with the rodeo clowns. He was an Asian dude with a vaudevillian flare. He jumped off the unicycle and went into the magic portion of his show.

"I'm on a mission and I need help on this mission. Whose gonna help me on this mission?" he carnival-barked to the sizable crowd that was gathering. "You, sir. Will you help me on my mission?" he asked, pointing to me. I was reclined with a beer in my hand. I flashed it and said, "I'm on a mission of my own," and chugged. Some of the NYU kids watching saw this and started chanting, "CHUG . . . CHUG . . . CHUG!" I held up the can and winked at them, egging them on. "C'mon, you're gonna love this trick but I need your assistance," he pleaded. "Only if you're gonna make me disappear . . . but I only want it one way. No worries about bringin' me back," I said, unintentionally killing his momentum. He moved on to something else. I felt bad. Normally I would've helped him out, as a fellow performer, but today I couldn't be bothered.

My self-pity needle was jammed all the way to the right and it had only just struck noon. I was in trouble and I knew it but I also knew that I was in the throes of a compulsion that was too powerful for me to turn off. I would see it to its end as I'd done countless times before. It's weird when you're running amok and you know it. I liken it to going over Niagara Falls in a barrel. Once you're in the barrel the deciding part is over—you're just goin' and that's it. This time was different, though. My indifference to it felt darker. Maybe I was on a mission.

I got good and drunk pounding that six-pack in the sun but I chalked that up to it just being a continuation of the previous night's work without much sleep to separate it. I'd been having a difficult time of late gauging my buzzes. Sometimes I could drink all day and night and just be a little woozy; other times, I'd drink three beers and be embarrassingly wobbly. I had no idea when I was gonna black out either. The episodes used to be far apart. Now it was happening more and more. Doing blow sometimes helped but it wasn't a guarantee—lots of times I blacked out anyway with Bizarro lurking behind every drink, poised to pounce. I was full from the beer so I went and got a pint of Popov vodka at the liquor store to maintain myself, cheaply.

I took it back to the park where I shifted around to different locales, boozing out of a brown paper bag, and killing time.

The park was bustling with activity as it does every nice day. It was early April so there was that spring renaissance vibe in the air—the release of everyone's collective cabin fever was palpable. It'd been a long, cold winter. Frisbeers frisbeed, hackie sackers hacked, buskers busked, and drunks drank. I was the latter and drank till I sank. That's what Dr. Seuss would sound like if he were a suicidal alcoholic, kids.

I flashed back to my first summer in New York City when Donna and I used to come to the park. We'd always be so hurtin' from the night before. She'd get a raspberry frozen fruit bar from the cart, under the mini Arc de Triomphe, as we walked in. She said she needed it to put the fire out. Then we'd sit in the fountain, sunning ourselves and letting the water spray us down. I loved hanging in the fountain. I used to hit it a lot by myself too. It's maybe the best people-watching spot on the planet Earth. I'd go there and just let my mind meander. I'd daydream about my exciting future with the band—my eyes closed and the sun beaming down on me. Sometimes I'd just lie there, languidly, formulating faces in the clouds and working on melodies. Then I'd lightly float away into a pleasant little siesta and wake up feeling awesome—recharged and ready to tear open the night like a brand-new box of Cap'n Crunch.

I was so goddamn lonely it physically hurt. I really missed my family. I hadn't spoken to any of them in I didn't know how long. I loved them deeply. The same went for the band, Gracie, hell, lots of people. I didn't see anyone anymore save for my barfly friends. There was a we're-all-going-down-together level of camaraderie that I got from them but many of them were estranged from their families and had become hardened over the years and impervious to it—especially the old guys. Conversations with them in the late hour would sometimes only compound my loneliness.

I remember trying to explain how much I missed my family and Grace to this old drunk named Whitey at the Blarney Cove one night. He said, "Don't worry, the miss goes away. Either they accept you for the guy you are or they don't. It's not like you're gonna change, right?" I said, "The guy I am? Who's that?" "That's easy, the one that's drinkin' with me at three-thirty A.M. on a Monday night," he said, slurping down a Schlitz. "You're a self-contained organism, eh, Whitey?" I said. "Nah, I walk over to Eighth Avenue and get a blow job every once in a while. I'm not made a stone," he said matter-of-factly. About an hour later, that wise old sage passed out on the bar and crapped his pants.

While I was missing everybody I started thinking about God again. It'd been a little while. I loved and missed him too—even if he wasn't there. I tripped myself by my own wire with that, and in no time flat the black-hole fear of a godless world gripped me by the throat once more. I crinkled the brown paper bag away from the spout and sucked vodka like it was a life-saving blood transfusion. I continued walking aimlessly.

I can take a physical beating pretty well. In fact, I think a good part of me gets off on it, but emotionally I'm a softy. My mom told me that once when I was four I fell down the stairs and rapped my head against the iron radiator at the bottom. The family were all seated at the dinner table and looked over, expecting me to cry, and instead I laughed like hell. I had a big bump and cut on my forehead and never cried even as she administered the iodine. So I guess I've always been tough in that way (if a bit crazy), but I wasn't equipped to be an island. I knew that. When I was a kid my mom used to say, "You're very sensitive, Chris. You should know that about yourself." I used to hate when she told me that. I wanted to be tough, like my dad, but I just wasn't wired that way. The alliance I'd chosen with booze instead of the people I loved was choking my heart into submission, and I knew it, but I soldiered on. I couldn't fathom a life without it. I lived to drink and drank to live—sadly, I knew this too.

Some more fond remembrances of my early days in the city came to me while I strolled but rather than entertain them I stopped myself midstream. This little skip down memory lane, where every recollection was capped with the phrase "That was when life was good" would certainly lead to a cul-de-sac of incomprehensible despair if I didn't nip it in the bud. I'd fallen victim to guilt-ridden sentimentality in this hammered state before and I wasn't gonna let that happen again. I needed to stay in motion—like a shark. "Why don't we go down to the studio and visit Mac?" I suggested to myself. When you start using the pronoun *we* and you're only referring to yourself, that's when you know you're in for some serious shit.

I blew through the doors of the studio on Crosby Street like Shecky Green on crack—jokes flying out of my mouth like bullets from a tommy gun. This wasn't a Bunnymen session. Ian was in there collaborating on a track with the Fun Lovin' Criminals, a rock-rap act that had had a minor hit with the song "Scooby Snacks" a few years earlier. They were doing a version of "Summer Wind," a song made popular by Ol' Blue Eyes and featured in the classic movie *The Pope of Greenwich Village.*

Mac and the band were sitting in the control room discussing ways to layer the track and I kept slurrily interjecting stuff like, "You know what we could do? I could puke into that pail over there and we'll slap a lot of reverb on it and nobody will know what it is. You could run it faintly underneath the entire track. It'll be just like Pink Floyd. I've been told my ralphing is otherworldy." I got the who-the-fuck-is-this-guy? stare from the engineer while the rest of the band, Mac, and Paul just seemed annoyed.

I became such a nuisance that Paul had to get me outta there. He had no choice but to speak to me like I was toddler. "C'mon, Shakes, let's go to the lounge for a beer. There's beer in the fridge. You'd like that, wouldn't you? C'mon, the boys have some things to figure out," he said, grabbing me by the elbow. "But I can help," I said. "We know you can but let them work awhile and then maybe later we'll come back," he said.

He stowed me away downstairs on the couch in front of the TV. "Have a beer and watch some TV. I have to go back up for a minute. You're gonna be okay here, right?" he asked gently. "Dude, I get great ideas. I just have to hear the track some more. I'm tellin' ya, I CAN HELP!" I implored, my eyes half shut. "Maybe later, Shakes, but for now promise you're gonna stay here, all right?" he said. I didn't say anything and just faked watching the TV. He backed out of the room subtly, so I wouldn't follow him back up. I stayed put for about two minutes and then was up like a shot. I swung open the doors and ran up to the mixing desk. I said to the producer-engineer, "I have some great backing vocals. Lemme sing 'em to you. I'm telling ya, you're gonna wanna use 'em."

I was gumming up the works to the point where they had to throw me out of the session. Apparently I got really belligerent and nasty on the way out (Bizarro showed up and took the reins). I have no clue as to what I said or what went down. I'd ask Ian about it a few years later and he soft-soaped it for me, saying, "Better that you never know, Shakes. You were a one-man wrecking ball. Let's just let it go at that."

They ushered me out of the building and I heard them dead-bolt the door once I was on the other side—STRIKE TWO.

I grabbed a roadie beer from the deli, cracked it, and started walking—destination: Blind Tiger. At this point in my life the only thing keeping my self-esteem above sea level was my ability to at least make people laugh in the bar. It was my only currency. Without it, I was nothing.

I got to the Tiger and Brian took one look at me and said, "Dude, I'm not serving you so don't even ask." "What? Whattya mean you're not serving me? We had a deal, remember? Are you reneging on that?" I asked, pissed off and embarrassed in front of my barfly cronies. "We made that deal back when you were sane. Look at you. I'm your friend, I'm not gonna be an accomplice to you murdering yourself. The reason I've let it go on this long is because I know you can just drink somewhere else and I figured you were safer here. But I got a call from your family and they told me not to serve you anymore. They called Tavern too so you won't be getting a drop there either. I can't go back on my word to them," he said sternly.

"So that's how it's gonna be then, huh? Well, can I at least hang out, then?" I asked, having nowhere else to go and feeling lower than the curb. "I think you should go check yourself into the nearest detox. I'll take you right now if you want," he said, softening. "Nah, I'm not much for hospitals. I'll just go on the wagon tomorrow. C'mon, man, lay one of them cool and delicious ice waters on me. I'll be good, I promise," I told him, obviously having another plan in mind. "Whatever, dude. You need help," he said dejectedly, putting a pint of water on the bar for me.

I mixed and mingled, moving as far from Brian as I could get. The bar was packed so I got some of my drunkard friends to shuttle me some shooters that I surreptitiously snarfed in the corner when Brian wasn't looking. He knew what I was up to, though. I migrated back to my usual corner and tried to hold court but it wasn't happening. Nobody was listening. I was so fucked up and pathetically tattered that people just ignored me. I couldn't string two good sentences together but I kept trying—repeating myself, mumble-slurring.

I was desperate to patch things up with Brian. I couldn't stand the thought of him being mad at me. He was such a beautiful guy who'd done so much for me. I summoned all the charm I had left and tried to win him over. I said, "Hey, Bri . . ." He was busy talking to customers and didn't turn around. "Bri!" I said louder, thinking maybe he hadn't heard me. "BRIAN . . . COME HERE, I GOT SOMETHING I WANNA TELL YOU!" I shouted, standing up on my stool. Everybody saw this display and must've sensed that there was some drama coming because suddenly it got really quiet—like they say in war movies, "too quiet." Brian cut the overhead music and stomped over.

"What, Chris? *What?*" he asked, as irritated as a person could be. I saw that everyone was watching and said, "DID I EVER TELL YOU ABOUT THE TIME I PARTIED WITH THESE RODEO CLOWNS?" It was dead silent. With a look of complete disgust he said, "We've all heard the rodeo clowns story a hundred times each. It was funny for the first fifty. I don't think anyone in here could stand to hear it even one more time. You need a new act. Go home, Chris. . . . Excuse me, I mean, go somewhere else. None of us wanna watch this anymore."

I froze up, hovering above the crowd, still standing on the stool. The smile slowly disappeared from my face. Waves of horror shot through me and with them came a sickening revelation. I WASN'T FUNNY ANYMORE. Everyone, including the cretinest of cretins, was looking at me with pity, visibly embarrassed for me. What do you do when the laughter stops? You get the fuck out of there, that's what.

I hastily hopped down from the barstool and pushed through everyone to leave, not saying a word, and on the verge of tears. By the time I got three-quarters of the way through, the music kicked back on loudly and people were chattering as if it hadn't even happened. I took a look around and everyone was having fun again. They didn't need me in this place to have a good time. That was just another thing I told myself to keep the game going. I walked out the door into the night feeling more worthless than ever. Did you just hear the thump of the ball hitting the leather? That was the sound of STRIKE THREE. I was out.

. . .

It was the strangest sensation I've ever known or probably ever will know. The closest thing I can relate it to is the rematerialization scenes on the old *Star Trek*—you know, when Kirk and company would beam back up to the Enterprise and you'd see that special effect of their bodies crystallizing. That's how I felt upon my reentry from a three-day blackout in midstride on Houston Street. I'd woken up from countless blackouts over the past twenty years but never had I been upright and walking when I came to. My innards felt bruised, like Mike Tyson had gone to town on my rib cage, but I hadn't been in a fight. I was so dehydrated that to look at me you would've thought I'd just crawled out of the Mojave Desert. I had a case of morning mouth that was unparalleled in its foulness. It was as if I'd meandered into the mist and magically reappeared three days later.

The last thing I remembered after that humiliating scene at the Tiger was trying my luck at the Tavern and being turned away. My two sisters and brother-in-law happened to be in there and they left, abruptly, as soon as they laid eyes on me. I felt like some boozy pariah. I said to Michael, the owner, "Where the hell are they going? What am I, O. J.?" He said, "Chris, you know we love you, pal, but did you just see how fast your family left here? You gotta go and get yourself some help. Horton and I will be here for you but only after you've straightened yourself out . . . till then there's nothing we can do for you." I turned tail and left without incident. I didn't want another public lynching of my ego. I got another cheap bottle of Popov at the liquor store next to the Tavern and after that, my memory went *poof.* I could've flown to Switzerland, gotten married, and climbed the Matterhorn and it all would've been news to me.

In a state of sheer panic I checked myself for needle marks thinking maybe I'd run into the wrong people and gotten talked into banging some heroin. That would explain all that lost time, but much to my relief, I was clean. I wasn't one to do smack but in the state I was in anything was possible. There were no cuts or bruises or bumps on my head and I hadn't been violated in any way. Everything checked out. The only things that really hurt were my calves and the bottoms of my feet. It felt like I'd been walking for days. When I finally did get my shoes off later on, my feet were all blistered up.

There was a fuzzy filmstrip flying around my head and in it were lots of bars and unfamiliar faces, sitting in an apartment with some people at one point but nothing specific. This was definitely "the mother of all my blackouts," but I'd emerged unscathed—except for my foot fatigue.

Sounding like Ebenezer Scrooge not knowing how long he'd been with the ghosts, I went up to the newsstand dude and asked, "What day is it today?" only I didn't get the same reprieve Ol' Ebenezer did. The Pakastani guy stacking the papers said, "It's Sunday, sir." I guess I was looking a bit worse for wear so he asked, "Are you OK?" I said, "Yeah, I'm just a little jet-lagged and trying to get used to the time change. I flew here all the way from Thursday." He shot me a curious look but I didn't bother stopping to explain.

I was feeling deathly ill and needed to cut through my infirm state with a pint of Guinness. But where the hell could I do that? I was shut out of my usual spots, had no money, and I was afraid to show myself in public to begin with because I had no details as to what I'd been up to for the past fifty or so hours. I didn't wanna walk in somewhere and get bounced or have to face the music about something I knew nothing about. I needed answers. I decided to head over to Mike Tait's. He might be able to piece it together for me. Maybe I'd seen him along the way and he could fill in some of the gaps.

My feet and my respiratory system seemed to be the only things barely left working—everything else was numb or shut down. I felt like a car on its two hundred thousandth mile. I slogged up Sixth Avenue to Mike's and rang his buzzer for five minutes straight but he wasn't home. Then I puked in front of Da Silvano, a fancy eatery near Mike's place.

A bunch of wealthy people sat outside enjoying their brunch till I came bumping along. I held on to the barricade in the corner that separated the sidewalk from the dining area and unloaded buckets of bile accompanied by loud and successive guttural grunts. It was quite a show. I tilted my head to the right in between discharges and there was a rich young woman in her thirties eating with her Diamond Jim hubby, gazing upon me with her napkin over her mouth in disgust—aghast with horror. I said to her, "Stay away from the clams casino. They did this." With that, I descended into my final flurry. When I was done I wiped the yack off my chin, not giving a shit in the least about the brunchkateers, and continued my walk up the street. I felt better but was still toxicity in motion.

I sat on a park bench in front of Joe's Pizza on Carmine Street, rested my feet, and tried to gather a game plan. While I was sitting there a musician friend of mine, Herbie, rolled up on me without me noticing. He kicked the bottom of my feet out from under me, playfully. "AHHHHHHH!!! SHITTTTTT!" I said, grimacing in pain. "What the hell's wrong with you, dude?" he asked. "Oh . . . I've been tryin' to break in these shoes and I got some blisters," I lied. He inspected them closely. They were completely blown out. I'd been wearing them every day for months and they had holes in the soles and both heels were practically in half—on a sharp diagonal. "They don't look new to me, dude," he said. I realized my fib wasn't gonna hold and corrected myself. "I mean this other pair gave me the blisters, that's why I'm back to these."

He was a really good guitarist-songwriter that I'd known a while and was always trying to get me to jam with him. He asked if I wanted to sing on his new record. I said, "I dunno, dude. I'll have to check with The Drops first, and see if it's cool." An uncomfortable expression appeared on his face as he said, "You're not in that band anymore, Chris. I see those guys all the time . . . you're out." I'd been so out of my mind and for so long I didn't even know that. Herbie knew he'd startled me with that news and we said an awkward good-bye.

I was immediately transported back to Tom's basement in Huntington where we used to practice and wrote our first tune on New Year's Day back when we were still in high school. I remembered running all the way home in the snow with that cassette in my hand, pumping my fist in the air, and heading straight up to my room to listen to it. I couldn't believe we'd written a tune of our own. I was brimming with the joy of discovery. How did I go from that to limping up the avenue, simmering with self-hatred, and wondering what had happened to my life? The whole thing felt like one long wrong turn.

I decided to try Fiddlesticks for my relief pint. I didn't know whether or not I'd been there during my blackout but they were pretty forgiving and I was now a little less paranoid because I didn't have a scratch on me and really didn't have that lingering feeling like I'd gotten into trouble. They'd fired me from my gig the month before because I couldn't always show up, and when I did it was reliably disastrous, so we called it a day amicably. I'd been in there many times since, though. Like I said before, Irish folks are my heart.

I trudged past Saint Joe's church and out of habit crossed myself. I prayed, "God, help me find my way back." I didn't even really know what that meant entirely—back to what? Faith? Normalcy? Well, I'd never known normalcy so it couldn't be that. I wasn't even seeking that out, really. Anyway, those were the words I chose.

I lingered for a second, waiting for some kind of magic to kick in but it didn't. I wanted to be transformed, like you see in the movies— a big turnaround moment. When it didn't come, I gimped on up the block and then a voice spoke to me from within the confines of my own mind that I knew, definitively, wasn't that of God. It wasn't mine, either, but it did come out of my mouth. It started in my weary feet, volcanically rose up through my body, and popped out, "YOU ARE FUCKIN' WORTHLESS. WHY DON'T YOU JUST KILL YOURSELF AND GET IT OVER WITH?"

It scared the shit outta me. I picked up the pace. A beer and the distraction of a conversation might be enough to extinguish it but I'd never felt it this strong. I was in so much pain that I just wanted out. It was like an overpowering undertow. I hurried along and again it came, just the same word over and over this time. "Worthless . . . worthless . . . worthless . . . WORTHLESS." By the time I got to the bar it was too late. I had listened to it too much. It had me in its clutches. I was convinced that I WAS WORTHLESS AND WANTED TO DIE.

It didn't help when I saw my reflection in the mirror as I walked in. All the evidence supported my unwanted mantra. My fight got weak. I took the baton from the voice and ran recklessly through the minefield of my alcoholic mind—seeing everything through a distorted prism of bitterness, loneliness, spitefulness, regret, shame, guilt—all of this corroborating the one solution I'd been able to fig- ure: SUICIDE.

I sat down in front of Karen, the bartender, a pretty, raven-haired Canadian gal who used to work on the nights I played there. She sweetly put a pint of Guinness in front of me, knowing I had no way of paying for it. "That's with me, Chris," she said, and went to the other side of the bar. Normally we would chat and share a laugh but she could tell I was in a bad way and just let me be. I sat there blankly staring at the TV. Vanna White turned the letters on the *Wheel of Fortune* as I contemplated colorful suicides. I thought, *Maybe I'll throw myself in the Hudson and just let the river take me.* Then I thought again, *Is that gonna work? I'm a really good swimmer.*

I hatched several other scenarios that all ended the same way. I considered hurling myself from the observation deck of the Empire

State Building but then shot that down with, *I don't know if it's open now and my feet hurt too much to get all the way up there.* Then there was the carbon monoxide idea that was quickly dashed by *Shit, I don't have a car! Howzabout jumping in front of a city bus?* I pitched to the burgeoning suicide committee in my head. They dismissed it, reasoning, *You might endanger other people if you do that.* It turned out that one had to be a pretty good planner for something like suicide and as you know from my trials in the workplace I'm in possession of no such skills.

The bartenders kept feeding me drinks as a gesture to my once-good service while my thoughts stayed on practical ways of killing myself. *All right, maybe traditional suicide isn't the answer. Perhaps, I could comb all the bad neighborhoods in the city and try to break up a violent crime in progress, thusly, dying in the process. This way I could go out with an act of selflessness, and by so doing, undo my legacy of selfishness,* I visualized. This was a suicide to be remembered by. People wouldn't even know it was suicide. I thought I had it that time. I even named it: vigilante-hero suicide. Then I realized, yet again, that this plan would involve a lot of walking. But I liked where I was going with it. I harvested several other grandiose death scenarios and finally punched myself out on them. Who the fuck was I kidding?

The truth was I had neither the balls nor the will to off myself and I knew it. This, however, rectified nothing. I still wanted to die, I just couldn't handle the responsibility of having to kill myself—I wasn't able to do anything for myself, why should this be any different? I slurped down beers and got even more maudlin with the realization that I was too much of a hapless loser to even kill myself. Something had to give.

I snatched some quarters from atop the bar, went upstairs, and called my brother Billy from the pay phone.

He answered and I said, "I want out." "Out of what? Out of life or out of your misery? Because I know of a way out of your misery," he said. "I don't know, dude . . . just out. I wanna die but I don't know how," I mumbled, crying hard. "Oh, you know how. You're already doing it. The same way I was doing it and Dad was doing it and everybody in our fucked-up family tree all the way back to Saint Peter did it. You're already committing suicide. Can't you see that? You're just in the slow lane, that's all. It's much more painful when it's slow," he said. I was crying into the receiver so profusely I couldn't collect a response. He waited a minute for me to say something and could tell by my sobs that it wasn't gonna happen and just said, "Listen, sit tight. I'll be right there." With that, he hung up the phone.

Gathering myself in front of the pay phone, I then felt a wellspring of anger come up that had me shouting a little prayer from the book of the shaking fist. I said, "HEY, GOD, KILL ME OR FIX ME . . . Amen. In the name of the Father, Son, and Holy Spirit." That's a beautiful prayer, isn't it? Feel free to use it. I took a deep breath and ever so briefly felt that twinge that someone was listening. All tolled that twinge accounted for only about three seconds of relief but they were a sublimely precious three seconds. Emotionally wrung out, I went back downstairs and did a swan dive into my pint.

Bill showed up about a half hour later with my good friends Mark Nilsen and Knockout Drops photographer, Chris Cassidy, who we all called Cass. They put me in the car and I was under the impression that Bill was just gonna let me sleep it off on his couch and that we'd talk over what I was gonna do about my life in the morning. I was looking forward to crashing out, knowing, for once, where I was gonna be waking up.

Willibee lived in Williamsburg, Brooklyn, so when we started heading east I paid it no mind. Before I knew it, he was pulling in front of Bellevue. He said, "I worked it out to get you into a rehab but you gotta do three days here first." I said, peering out the window at the ominous bricks, "Here? Why here? Why not St. Vinny's or Cabrini? Anywhere but fuckin' here." He explained that without insurance I could get Medicaid and go to rehab but it all had to go through Bellevue. "I still don't understand. Why here?" I panicked. "This is not like picking a college, asshole. I had to pull some major strings to get you this deal. I suggest you take it."

"Uh-uh. No way. If you guys think I'm goin' in there you got another thing coming. I'll blow outta here right now," I said defiantly. "Oh, I don't think so. That's why I have these guys here, Mr. Houdini. We're walking you in," he said, laughing. "Fuck it. Fine, walk me in. I'll just bust out. I've done it before," I told him. "That won't be happening this time. They know all about you now. What's it gonna be?" he asked. "I ain't going without a fight and you're gonna have to catch me," I said reaching for the door handle, but he'd already locked them all down. Frustrated and afraid, I said, "Do you know what kinds of people are inside there? It's a fuckin' zoo! It's full of free-roaming, chemically unbalanced, homicidal maniacs!" "Yeah, and you're the picture of mental health. You called me an hour ago crying and wanting to off yourself! NOW WHAT'S IT GONNA BE?" Clearly I'd run out of road.

I sat in the car, my eyes fixed on the entrance, just trying to summon the courage to go in. I didn't think about my family or Grace or the band or anyone in my life, past or present. I'd done enough of that already and this wasn't about me cleaning up for them as it had been in all my other halfhearted attempts to get sober. It was about me really looking at myself.

My relationship with booze was an abusive one and I was the classic "abusee," always believing its promise that it would be better the next time. *So you passed out on the sidewalk last night . . . so what? You just had a bad night. Just be more careful tonight and we'll have fun—haven't we had fun before?* it would tell me and I'd buy it every time. It handed me things like DWIs and drug busts, alienated loved ones, severed relationships, sabotaged dreams, public embarrassments, and, overall, a chasm of shame and yet I stayed with it—fearing a life without it—afraid of the unknown.

I had a mile-high pile of glorious yesterdays in which booze was the undisputed superstar. Then there was an equally steep stack of regret and suffering—and now regret and suffering were all I knew. I wasn't making any good new memories with it. Alcohol took from me the three things I loved most in the world: my family, Grace, and rock 'n' roll. Music had always been sacred to me but now, like everything else, it was a joyless chore.

It was a gut-wrenching breakup and I was the jilted lover. How could booze do this to me? The truth was hard to face. I had loved it unconditionally but it didn't love me anymore. If it did, it wouldn't be treating me this way. Look where I was again. Suicidal and checking myself into Bellevue—a place I swore I'd never go back to. How come it kept coming back to this? In my right mind I'd never even think of suicide—*ever*. I wasn't a blackheart. I ruminated hard on that.

It was easy to see that alcohol was the constant in all of this but another thing became abundantly clear to me as I sat mesmerized by the yellow glow of the hospital windows. It wasn't *me* I wanted to kill—it was *Bizarro*. It'd been Bizarro the whole time. He wanted me dead and I wanted him dead and that power struggle was the source of my suicidal rants. We disagreed on everything but shared one common solution—*killing me*. I also realized that I'd never be able to kill Bizarro. He lives in me. The best I could do was arrest him and keep him caged. Drinking was like handing him the keys. I was never able to put that together before. But I still wasn't sure if I could live without alcohol.

It didn't really matter at that point what I wanted or didn't want. Willibee had made it pretty clear that I'd be going in regardless and was growing impatient. Looking back now I find it funny that I was homeless and hopeless but still acting as if I had options. I was presented with two doors. Behind the first was an opportunity to go somewhere to clean up, get sober, and start anew, and the second held the choice to go back out, drink, maybe die, and at the very best, stay miserable. Incredibly I was hovering between the two doors still deciding which one to pick. That's how badly I didn't wanna have to face myself.

My eyes roved around to the sign that read BELLEVUE HOSPITAL and seeing it made me realize that my life was an undeniable breadcrumb trail of bad decisions that had led me to these doors. I'd blown every chance I ever had by taking the easy way out. It was a feeling of irrevocable failure and one I never wanted to revisit. I had to change—first into an ass-less smock. And whatever came after that, I was just gonna have to be okay with.

"It's getting late, dude. I think we oughta get you in there. It's gonna be fine. You'll see. You'll remember this as the greatest night of your life," Willibee said cheerfully. Looking as mucked up and depressed as a person could be, I shot him a look that said, "Dude, are you kidding me?" He saw the expression on my face and readjusted the statement. "But all in due time . . . all in due time." And he gave me a big bear hug. "OK, I'm ready. Let's go before I change my mind again and we all end up rolling around on the sidewalk together," I said, defeated. "YESSSSSSSS," Bill shouted out, with gusto. "THAT'S OUR BOY!!"

I got out of the car and walked into Bellevue, calmly and under no assistance, with Willibee and Co. trailing a few steps behind me. It would be a first in a series of firsts. This time there'd be no gang tackling, no Thorazine, and certainly no masterminding of an escape. I was just exhausted and in my heart I knew I didn't wanna die. I wanted my life back.

Once inside, the nurse came over and said, "I just have to check your vitals, hon, before I can admit you." I said, "Good luck fuckin' finding any." She laughed. Then some of the attendants came over. The one who did all the talking was a really nice tall black guy about ten years older than me. He said with a grin, "Are you Chris Campion? *The* Chris Campion?" For a second, I thought maybe he'd seen me play or something. I started to get some of my pride back and then he said, "We were all working last year the night of your escape. You were the talk of this ward for months. I just need to shake your hand. Can I ask you something? How'd you do it?" I said, "I could tell ya but I want to see what kinda treatment I get around here first, 'cause I haven't decided if I'm staying yet." And I winked. "Oh, you're staying, partner, 'cause you came to us this time, and I can see that you want to get better. Besides, we're all getting fired if you disappear again," he said, chuckling as he walked away. Then as he pushed a gurney out of the way to clear his path he turned around and said, "You know, I heard they hadn't had anyone slip outta here like that since 1963. Good luck, Chris."

Wow, 1963? I guess that made me the Steve McQueen of rock 'n' roll, I thought.

I got a kick out of him but it wasn't long before I realized just where I was again. I heard a mishmash of echoed screams trickling at the end of the corridor and looked down at my new plastic bracelet. C. CAMPION—PSYCH WARD, it read. Then I found myself just standing there in the middle of the hallway under one of those fluorescent lights with an overwhelming amount of fear coursing through me. What the hell was gonna happen to me? I don't know how to live like normal people.

I stood there, motionless, groping for God in the worst way, and unable to keep out the most terrifying notion of all—that He didn't exist. This was the one that had dogged me for sixteen long years, never letting me enjoy a fearless breath. I was as alone as alone could ever be—adrift with no land in sight in any direction. I prayed intensely, "God, if you're ever gonna come back to me, let it be now." I waited. Nothing.

I wept, head down, like a child lost in the supermarket. All I heard was the buzz of the fluorescent light. I closed my eyes and continued to pray. I thought about some of Jesus's last words on the cross. He'd cried out, "Father, why hast thou forsaken me?" I wasn't about to say something like that. He'd had it a lot worse than me, I reckoned. Instead I growled, "C'mon, where the hell are ya?" I kept my eyes shut like that and then a weird thing happened. It's like somebody had clicked on the knob of a loud radio in my head—I actually heard the click. Through the static I heard Janis Joplin singing *"Freedom's just another word for nothin' left to lose"*—that famous line from "Me and Bobby McGee." My eyes opened wide. I heard it again. It came on one more time but this time she continued to sing through to the end of the song. With that a script popped into my head—not a voice, but words. I recited them aloud. "If you put down your gun, your hand will be free to take mine." I didn't know what any of this meant at the time. It wasn't a white light experience but I felt love in it coming from somewhere—where I didn't know . . . or care. For once I didn't question. I just let it in.

Then, out of the corner of my eye, I saw something streak past on the other side of the ward real fast, like a leaping shadow. I thought, *Wait a minute? I know that run. Is that? . . . Dribbly?* I couldn't believe my eyes—it *was* him. He'd obviously worked on his game too and added a jump shot. Before he'd just been a scrappy little playmaker. I went over to him. "Hey, Dribbly, remember me?" He didn't. And he was way too caught up in the heat of the contest to talk.

I started to play with him and what happened next is something that I'll never forget. While I was chasing him around I couldn't stop laughing—I just couldn't stop. It was a different brand of laughter and one that I'd completely forgotten about—the kind I remembered from when I was a kid and I'd have one of my buddies sleep over and something would trigger us into a spontaneous laughing fit after my dad turned the lights out. It was that kind—silly, joyful, and impossible to turn off. I jumped up to block one of his shots and for the first time *ever* I had one of those I'm-right-where-I'm-supposed-to-be moments. I looked over at the night nurse and she flashed me a big smile. My light was back on . . . MY LIGHT WAS BACK ON.

Chapter Sixteen

"Blackout, Baby"

On the afternoon of August 14, 2003, I was in a hell of a hurry. I was leaving for a minitour of New England—four one-off dates in Providence, Boston, Portland, and Cape Cod, with the Knockout Drops. Since it had never really gotten its due, we finally released *Killed by the Lights* on an independent label and were doing pretty well with it. The CD was in stores all across the country.

We were getting airplay on college and indie radio stations and receiving rave reviews from regional and East Coast press. All of this combined enabled us to get out of town and play a bunch of small joints to some decent crowds—not the rock star life I'd once coveted but I was happy. Actually happy is an understatement. I was beside myself ecstatic. I was back in the van with my best friends, making music that I loved, laughing a lot, and entertaining vicious freaks the countryside over. I was having a blast everywhere we played—out there talking to people and getting to know them a little before we moved on. And I was doing all of this sober. Un-fuckin-believable, right?

Three years had passed since Bellevue and my subsequent twenty-eight-day rehab. Early recovery was tough. I'm not gonna lie to you. I didn't know whether to shit or whistle most of the time and I'd never done anything without a drink in my hand. I used to take beers into the shower with me, for chrissakes (if you've never done the shower beer you really should try it—it's heavenly). However uneasy I may have felt in the beginning, it was always nice to get into bed not smashed, and with time the days got easier—just being out of trouble was a great fuckin' feeling.

Singing without that familiar heavy hammer weighing me down turned out to be a real eye-opener too. Once I had six months clean under my belt, the guys could see that I wasn't just crying wolf this time and we reunited—writing a new batch of songs right out of the gate and rehearsing a lot. I'd always subscribed to that tired cliché that an artist had to be tormented and fucked up to produce anything meaningful. I found out that that was some more bullshit I'd bought into. My imagination was more vivid and unhinged than ever, and now that I was clear-headed I had the ability to harness it.

My first show back with the Drops (also the first one I'd ever done truly sober) was at Brownie's. I remember feeling so strange after the fifth song that I just stood there, spellbound, looking out into the crowd—almost in the same way I'd done that time I drank the Thai-stick tea in Boston, but this occasion had me lingering there with a shit-eating grin on my face. Tom came over to me and said, "Everything all right, Captain?" I answered, "Yeah, but I'm in uncharted waters here. This is the point in the set where I used to feel like I was gonna faint."

Sometimes I'd be chatting up the crowd over the microphone, just having some casual yucks, and I'd look down to see a Poland Spring bottle in my hand and say to myself, "Is this really me?" It almost felt like I was playing the part of someone else. It was surreal—but it was a beautiful surreal as opposed to the scary surreal I'd come from.

I felt like a teenager again when we were onstage—hopping around like a madman with puppylike energy. Everything felt new again and I discovered, as corny as this may sound, that my love of rock 'n' roll came from giving, not receiving. I didn't care about big record deals or commercial success anymore. I don't know exactly how or when that change of heart came about but I do know that it was a goddamn blessing. I'd wasted a lot of time in my life worrying about things I didn't have and all of a sudden realized, "Who needs that shit?" I was happy with the audience that was right in front of me—however big or small. I'd had the tiger by the tail all this time and didn't even know it.

On the day we were to take off for the New England tour, I was coming from my alcoholic support group and rushing back to my apartment to throw some things in a bag and split. Our first date was that night in Providence and we had a long drive ahead of us.

Are you surprised to hear, given my donkey pride, that I was willingly attending that support group thing again? After I put the plug in the jug I decided to go back to check it out, and wouldn't you know, nobody looked like Vincent Price anymore. It was a miracle—well, not really. That they all looked like that in the first place was probably my imagination or my thirsty liver's doing—at that point in my drinking any bullshit excuse would do so I could go get my load on feeling like, "Hey, I tried." I had all these prejudices built up against it—seeing it as a thing of weakness. The truth of it was that the group was nothing more than just a bunch of fuckups, like me, who had gotten their shit together and, in turn, were helping newer fuckups get their shit together. And what could be more beautiful than that? I'm not the kind of person that can handle staying sober alone. Also, I like it. There are loads of vicious freaks in there—maybe even more than in the bar.

My attitude about the support group shifted when, after doing my three days in Bellevue, I went to an inpatient drug and alcohol rehabilitation center in upstate New York called Arms Acres. This was not one of those rehab-spas for rich folks. This was a place that had a lot of court-mandated cases—hard-core addict-cons who had taken pleas to go to rehab rather than doing a bid in the state pen. Some of them wanted to get sober, some didn't. It was a nice facility with excellent counselors, but it wasn't an Ivy League crowd I was bunking with in there, that's for sure.

My roommate was a Latino drug dealer from the Bronx. Our first day together Arturo (not his real name) was sizing me up from his bed across the room, giving me what I perceived to be dirty looks. I avoided his eye daggers and stayed busy putting my socks away. He looked as mean as a snake. He was muscle bound, wearing a T-shirt with cutoff sleeves, and had a do-rag wrapped over his head. I was looking like an unmade bed in beige plaid pants and a blue workman's shirt that said NAIL ME HARDWARE on it, with an illustration of a hammer on the pocket.

I wanted to break the ice because the silent hostility was becoming unbearable. Cheerfully I asked him, "So, dude, where ya from?" He ran over to me, ripped off his shirt, and on his back was a constellation of gunshot wounds—black bullet holes in an almost horseshoe pattern. He shouted angrily at me, "YOU SEE THAT? THAT'S WHERE I'M FROM! ANY OTHER QUESTIONS?" I quickly pulled up my pant leg and pointing to my knee said, "See that right there . . . thirteen stitches . . . crashed my bike." He took a moment and in a much calmer voice asked, "Whattya got, a Harley?" I said, "No, a Schwinn . . . that's where I'm from."

We became best buds for the next twenty-eight days. Here was a guy who I had nothing in common with whatsoever, except for the fact that we'd both run our lives into the ground, boozing and drugging. It turned out that was enough. I met a lot of people like Arturo in there and forged great friendships with all of them.

One late night a bunch of us had an impromptu bull session in the lounge, swapping stories and talking over some deep shit. I'd gotten some stuff off my chest that I didn't even know was bothering me and when my head hit the pillow I felt a lot lighter and less afraid of the future. I guess it'd helped just to let some air out of the balloon. I remember thinking, *Maybe there's something to this whole thing of recovering with other people.* It was a profound experience and one I'll forever cherish.

When I got out of "the hab" as we who have been in call it, I took my new attitude to my old support group in the neighborhood and they accepted me back with open arms. My first time returning I saw that old Teamster, Marty, that I used to hang with out front, and he greeted me with a big smile. "Welcome back, Christopher! Have you done enough research out there to know you belong in here with us now?" I said, "And then some, Marty . . . and then some." He said, "Good, as soon as you get your sea legs then you can help someone else out when they come in. That's how it works." Right as he said that, we observed a guy stumbling down the street, drunk. I pointed and said, "You mean like him?" "Exactly, only he looks like he's gonna go a few more laps around the track on just the rims. Remind you of anyone?"

Just as he made that comment the guy turned into the bar on the corner, pulling on the door handle and slipping off it three times before he finally got it open. He frighteningly looked a lot like me—thin with brown scruffy hair and about my same age. That drunken doppelgänger kept me from wanting a drink that day—I'll tell ya that much. He looked like death. "Let's head inside," I said to Marty. "That guy just spooked me a little for some reason." Marty said, "Some reason? You know the reason. There but for the grace of God go you." "Yeah, well, it's too early in the day for me to start talking about God so let's go in," I said. "Someday you're gonna wake up and realize just how much God's been there for you." "I hope you're right, Marty," I said, opening the door for the both of us.

The group encouraged me to find a Higher Power of my own understanding, which was how they referred to God. I couldn't stand that they called it that. To me that phrase smacked of cult language or something—plus Higher Power just had such a horrible ring to it. It didn't matter anyway. I was sawing the same wood I always had with the God thing—praying, then questioning, and ultimately running in place.

Every day when the group adjourned I would go get salami sandwiches with Marty and a few of the other old guys from the group. "Salted meats are a big part of our recovery, Chris," he said to me once, taking a huge bite and chewing through his words. If you think I have stories, you should've heard the Marty crew. They were a tough group of guys, all over sixty and lifelong New Yorkers—a couple of them longshoremen . . . nuff said. They helped me stay sober and had a good time doing it and for that I'm forever grateful to them. Marty died when I had about a year and a half off the sauce. Every time I order a salami on rye with American cheese I think of him. He was aces.

Anyway, where was I? Oh yeah, the day we were leaving for the New England tour. So I was hustling back to my apartment because I had to hop a train uptown and meet the guys on the Upper West Side so we could leave at four-thirty P.M. The post-me-being-fucked-up incarnation of the Knockout Drops was Tom Licameli on guitar, Phil Mastrangelo on bass, me on lead vocals, Paulie Giannini (aka Paulie the G), now providing inventive percussion for us, and our latest addition, Vinny Cimino on the kit. When Vinny came into the band he really gave us a supersonic kick in the ass (a great drummer will do that). We never sounded better. As you can plainly see from everyone's surnames the McKnockout Wops theme was not compromised. This is our same lineup today AND WE'RE COMING TO A DIVE BAR NEAR YOU!

On my way home, I ran past Saint Joe's Church and saw Father Kelly on the front steps. "Will I see you in Mass again this Sunday, Chris?" he hollered. "I dunno, Father, are there gonna be any chicks there?" I said, maintaining a trot. "Yes, but I've warned them all about you," he shot back. "You know you're only doin' me a favor with that, right?" I said, smiling. "Yes, I've heard but what am I to do? I have to tell the truth," he said with a laugh. "Gonna be outta town giggin' this Sunday, Father, but I'll defo see you the next," I said, continuing to jog. He said, "Okay, Chris. Sing for the Lord." I yelled back from up the block, "WILL DO, PADRE."

I threw open the door to the apartment Grace and I shared, a different place from the one near the Tiger and one I actually paid rent on. We'd gotten back together around the same time as the band. I had to court her all over again—only this time I was actually myself and not some trumped-up version of something I was trying to be in her eyes—namely a rock star. It wasn't easy. It took a lot to win back her trust.

I'd written her every day from Arms Acres. These were desperate and epic letters, dripping with guilty apologies that clumsily begged for her mercy and forgiveness, but none of them worked. I didn't get a return letter. Then I tried my hand at some passionate love notes, barraging her with an array of rhapsodic and romantic words intended, first to dazzle, and then melt the ice around her heart. She was supposed to read them, be overcome by the gesture and the beauty of the poetry, and sprint to the nearest phone to call me. I never got a call. Finally I broke down and just wrote her an honest letter about how scared I was to get out and face my life, sober, and that I still loved her but I wouldn't be writing her anymore. That one got a response. It was one line that read, "Don't tell me, show me."

I gave her space after I was released from rehab, not calling her or anything, and when I reached ninety days, clean and sober, she rang me up out of the blue to congratulate me. I was surprised that she was even keeping track of my day count. We went on some awkward dates after that. I was really nervous. I didn't know how to act around her anymore. I didn't know how to act, period. I think the big lesson I was supposed to be getting was that I wasn't supposed to *act* at all but just be my normal self. But I still hadn't found a comfortable place to perch. I'd spent the last twenty years anesthetized most of the time. When in that state you're not as aware of yourself so you're used to always being at ease. Take that away and there's some weirdness to get through before you settle down. I was a fragile bundle of nerves.

One night we were going to the movies and I picked her up at her old place. It was our second time seeing each other in this new courtship—the *Chris and Gracie II*, I guess we'll call it. Our first date had just been a simple walk through the neighborhood. I was talking to her from that front room while she got ready when I plum ran out of conversation. Then, fishing for a kickstart, I picked up a picture that I'd seen ten thousand times and asked her, "Is this your mom and dad in this photo?" She laughed out loud. "You know that it is. What are you doing?" I didn't say anything and set it back down carefully. Then it collapsed and fell off the table. I tried to catch it and dropped it on the floor. "Oh my God . . . Chris Campion, are you being shy? This is a side I've definitely never seen before," she said, genuinely surprised.

I said, "Well, you could probably loosen me up with a kiss." "Nope. That'll have to wait till the end of the date. I want to see how you conduct yourself first, mister. What are taking me to see, anyway?" she asked. "It's a *Porky's* marathon down at the Film Forum. I figured it might get you in the mood," I said. "And we're back with the jokes," she said. "Sorry," I said. "I don't know what else to do. I've never dated before." And I hadn't. I'd always met gals at gigs, gotten bombed, and woken up in relationships. I'd never before felt the pressure of having to win someone over and that's what this felt like, despite all we'd been through. She said, "You're doing fine. I think I like this new Chris Campion. Humility is sexy on you." I said, "Well, I'd gladly go back to being a cocky fuck in a second if I could think of one thing in my life to be remotely cocky about." She grabbed me under my chin and shook it. "You'll be cocky again—don't worry. Till then I'm gonna enjoy this. Do you mind?" I said, "No, I'm half enjoying it myself." She said, "Bullshit, you hate it." "I know but I like seeing you happy," I said, opening the door.

At the end of the evening I kissed her in front of the door to her building and the next night she came to my gig at the Red Lion. Mike Tait and I had recently resurrected Fonduo and slid back into our old time slot. Grace walked in and I reached into my tried-and-true bag of tricks, singing, "All I Want Is You," right to her just as I'd done two years earlier at the Tiger but this time sans the slurring. I framed every word, passionately, communicating to her just how I felt—something I hadn't been able to do in regular conversation. After the gig we went for coffee in the Village at a place called Esperanto. We sat outside and talked all night under a full moon.

It was warm out and MacDougal Street was busting at the seams with vicious freaks. Right as we sat down a guy rode by our table on one of those giant tricycles you see in the circus. Gracie had been looking at a menu and set it down momentarily to ask me what I was gonna get, and as she did that, tricycle man was five inches from our table and hanging ten feet over us. "AAAAAAAAAH!" she screamed. "I didn't know what that was at first." The coffees came and the conversation flowed easily—the only thing wrong was that the subject matter wasn't exactly of my choosing. She had an agenda and did all the talking.

She poured her heart out, telling me just how much I'd hurt her with my drinking. For once, I sat there and listened, not trying to defend myself or spin it in a direction to benefit my cause. She needed to vent and get it all out. She'd never been able to before because I was always trashed. You can't talk sense to people when they're drunk. She didn't take a pound of flesh. She just told me what a harrowing nightmare it'd been for her, watching me sink lower and lower. "I just felt so helpless, ya know?" she said, fighting through tears. I ran inside and got her some tissues.

I wanted to serve up a verbal panacea—an immediate antidote to rid her of all the pain I'd caused her. I searched myself to find the right words and was only able to locate the two that I'd thrown around carelessly for years, using them more to deflect trouble than as a form of sincere apology. I learned the true meaning of them the moment I said to her, "I'm sorry," my heart aching with regret, now sniffling through some tears myself. I owned up to all the awful things I'd put her through and the remorse I felt was excruciating. I wanted to wind back the clock and undo it all. This would normally be the time that I would find a way to wriggle away from her and go get a drink to dull the pain. I dismissed that thought immediately, picturing Marty saying, "One drink is too many, Chris, and a thousand aren't enough."

We hugged from our chairs, not saying anything for a few minutes. I broke the embrace and said, "I'm going in there to buy us a half dozen crullers. Oprah calls this emotional eating and it's supposed to be bad, but I think the situation calls for it." She cracked up as she dabbed her eyes. That stupid little comment broke the spell of tears for both of us. We stayed there for hours under that gigantic and bright unblemished moon, eating crullers, drinking coffee, and falling back in love.

On the afternoon that I was leaving for Providence with the band, Grace was in Florida filming. She'd landed the lead in a low-budget horror movie. We talked on the phone briefly before I started packing. She said, "Babe, I gotta go. I see them bringing out the buckets of chicken blood now. This is so disgusting. I love you. Have a good show tonight." I said, "OK, love you too . . . have fun getting your head cut off."

I put the phone down and threw the rest of my gig shirts into a bag, grabbed my keys to leave, and just as I did that I noticed the fan sputter out. Construction guys had been doing work on the building all week and I figured they'd just shut off the power, temporarily, while they installed a cable or something. I had no time to ask anyone about it and just trusted that they'd turn it back on by the time people got home from work. It was around four o'clock.

I got outside and saw traffic lights out and people acting weird. I bumped into my mailman, Clarence, in the street and asked him, "What's all this about?"

Clarence was a black man in his mid-sixties—a real quiet, gentlemanly type. He reminded me a lot of Morgan Freeman. Every so often I'd run into him as he was putting the mail in the slots and I'd always try to chat him up but could never get more than two words out of him. I'd say, "Whattya say there, Clarence? How are ya?" He'd just look over his shoulder at me, with his glasses down to the tip of his nose, and in his even-keeled way say, "Doin' fine, Chris, just fine."

It was obvious to me that I was encountering a different Clarence when I asked him about what was going on. His expression was that of a caretaker's at a haunted house—like he knew something I didn't. He stared at me for a second, his eyes wide-open, and said, "Blackout, baby." I said, "What?" "You heard me . . . *Blackout, baby*," he repeated, his eyes bulging even more as he said it the second time. I told him, "But I gotta get a train uptown." "No trains," he said, cutting me off. Panicking, I said, "But I gotta gig in Rhode Island tonight." "NO GIG . . . BLACKOUT, BABY," he said unsympathetically. "You never been through a blackout before?" he asked. "No, I remember when I was a kid on Long Island hearing something about it on the news, but no, I guess not," I said. Then he got really amped up and started telling me, in great detail, all the things I could expect to see happen because of the blackout.

"You see these nice folks 'round here? They gonna be changin' when the sun goes down—blackouts do strange things to people. They gonna be LOOTIN', SHOOTIN', SCREAMIN', HOL-LERIN' . . . CARRYIN' ON!" he said, his voice on the brink of shouting. I said, "I dunno, Clarence, that seems a bit . . ." "Oh, so you the expert on blackouts now. Lemme ask you somethin'. How many blackouts you live through? NONE. How many blackouts I been through? MANY. Don't sass me on this, Chris. DO NOT SASS ME!" "I'm not sassing you. I just don't think it's gonna be World War Three is all," I said calmly.

I noticed a big vein pulsing in his forehead that had surfaced while he was issuing his initial warning that I thought was sure to blow after I said that. Frustrated that he wasn't getting his point across he frantically grabbed me by the arm, pulling me over to a line of parked cars. He pointed to one, shouting, "You see this pickup truck parked in front of the building? THAT'S GONNA BE IN MOTHERFUCKIN' FLAMES BY MIDNIGHT! NOW MY ADVICE TO YOU IS TO GO BACK INSIDE, LIGHT A CANDLE, GET UNDERNEATH YOUR BED, AND PRAY FOR FUCKIN' DAYLIGHT. . . . And if I make it, I'll bring your mail tomorrow."

Well, as you know, Clarence's fiery prophecy of a blackout-induced apocalypse never did come to pass and we who were on the isle of Manhattan that night ended up having a wonderful time. It turned out to be a magical evening, really, morphing into one big citywide block party—everybody out on the sidewalks with coolers, raging merrily, and cooking on hibachis.

As the orange glow of sunset faded off the buildings and gave way to nightfall, there was an undeniable wildness in the air, almost like we were all kids on Halloween again—frolicking on the lighter side of anarchy. There were packs of people roaming around with no streetlights to illuminate them so you could only make out a shadowy outline of someone coming toward you and the brightest piece of their clothing.

Everyone was catcalling into the air, free of inhibition, knowing that this was the blackout and there'd be no harsh judgment of silly behavior. It seemed like everyone in the borough simultaneously stood up and proclaimed, "LET'S GET STUPID! Our adult lives will be waiting for us when the lights come back on, but for now let's let out a collective 'WOOOOOO-HOOOOO!' That's what it seemed like to me, anyway.

People were banding together too. Everywhere you went folks were asking if you were hungry and offering food and drink. Restaurants were cooking up all their perishable stuff and giving it away. It was as if the spirit of Woodstock had descended upon the metropolis—a far cry from the hairy night of violence and lawlessness that befell the city the night of the 1977 blackout (Clarence's fear didn't come out of nowhere).

I remember walking down the street, gazing into the twilight between the buildings, and watching the smoke from different barbecues twist up into the sky. I thought, *This is probably what it was like back when the island was first settled and was nothing more than one big grassy shire with everyone outside eating at the same time.*

I also think that 9/11 had a lot to do with it going down the way it did. We'd been through such an unspeakable nightmare only two short years before and had grown closer together as a city as a result. We all hate the reason why but I do think it's true. During that time we learned, firsthand, that we had one another's backs.

The night might not have been the glass-shattering melee Clarence predicted but he had been right about one thing. Our gig was cancelled. There were power outages throughout the Northeast, including Providence. It didn't matter, though. We couldn't get off the island with all the gridlock traffic and chaos anyway.

Instead we took our acoustic guitars and set up in front of Tavern on Jane, leading everyone on the street through an all-night sing-along. We played a bunch of Beatles and Stones tunes—and a lot of other stuff people knew the words to. It was an absolute pisser. It felt like we'd turned the whole neighborhood into Whoville. I was singing, *"You can't always get what you want,"* and when we hit the chorus we heard a hundred voices out there belting it out with us.

Billy Ryan, Willibee, and Brendan Ryan showed up with guitars and accordions along with my sisters and brother Kevin. Everyone lent a helping musical hand—each person taking turns singing and spurring on the crowd around the urban campfire. We did some Knockout Drops and Bogmen songs, as well.

It was peculiar to be sober in the midst of all of this. It was a really hot night, scorching, and almost everyone I ran across was completely annihilated, drunk—giving the city a New Orleans feel. People were cruising around freely with open containers of booze from their houses or the bars. They were smoking weed out in the open with no fear of reprisal—strangers handing each other joints on the sidewalk like an outdoor rock show. In my ten years living in the city I'd never seen anything like it.

At one point I turned around and saw this guy, Headphones Pete, making out with this woman—a total stranger who'd just walked up. Headphones Pete was a beloved character in our scene, a painfully shy guy who always wore gigantic headphones. I suppose we could've come up with a more creative nickname for him. We were leading our street singers through a rendition of The Band's, "The Weight," when Billy Ryan sidled up to me and said, "Hey, checkout Headphones Pete gettin' a little." I said, "I know. It's like Victory-in-Japan Day out here." 'Twas a beautiful thing to see ol' Pete mashing with that girl. Under the usual circumstances he would've been way too bashful for a bold move like that but on this night the playing field was level for everyone. It was anything goes and Headphones Pete hopped right in the pool.

This party would've been like a hundred Christmases to me in my not-too-distant past but a funny thing happened that night. I didn't once itch for a drink. My spirit was too busy soaring. I was having such a good time helping people have a good time that it just didn't occur to me. It wasn't until my walk home at four in the morning that I realized I hadn't jonesed for a drink or a drug all night. Normally, in a situation like that, with people bombed to the bejeesus all around me, I would've entertained the idea at least once. Something had shifted in me.

Everyone was off the streets by the time I made my way back to my apartment, including the cars. There was no rumbling of air conditioners, buzzing of streetlights, beeping of car horns, or any of the other familiar street noises that I heard all the time and lived with but couldn't identify. It was so quiet I could hear my own heartbeat. The combination of silence and darkness had my senses tingling. I tread lightly. It was one of those rare occasions where spooky meets beautiful.

I pushed open the door to my place and I couldn't see a thing except for the pilot light in my stove. It was still burning. There was something about the glow of the lone flame that drew me in so I pulled a chair over, let my eyes get lost in it, and started reflecting on the whole day.

I wore a big smile as I sat there thinking about the guys in the band, my family, good friends, all the strangers in the street singing, and, of course, crazy Clarence—whom I would run into the next day as he was delivering the mail. I gave him an I-told-you-so look and said, "Clarence." He peered back over his shoulder, as was his style, and knowing he'd gotten it way wrong, said, "I know. When I got home my wife surprised me with a picnic basket out on the stoop . . . my daughter came by with the grandkids . . . it was delightful."

I continued watching the flame—allowing myself to become transfixed by it. Then, in that trance I was compelled to write something. I didn't know what it was yet but reached for a pen and paper and there, by the light of the stove, I wrote the lyrics to "Pilot Light," the opening song on what would be the next Knockout Drops album, *Escape from Bellevue*.

Pilot Light

Even though you hide
I think I will keep looking
'Cause if I should stop looking, darkness owns the road

Chorus
And oh I can catch such a fright
If I swallow the unknown
Then I feel that pilot light
And, baby, I'm just thrown . . .

I finished jotting down the words but never let my eyes stray from the flame for very long. Something was happening—something important and I knew it. It was a transformation—an emergence. I wasn't just mesmerized by the flame anymore but was feeling its heat in my heart. I recognized that heat as faith—A FAITH IN SOME-THING BIGGER.

I dropped to my knees and folded my hands, as I'd done thousands of times as a little boy. I tilted my head up and, with confidence, called out, "GOD, THANK YOU . . ."

Acknowledgments

A
hhhh, how to do this? Well, if I start thanking everyone in my life that I owe a sincere thanks to this thing is gonna start sounding like the fuckin' begats in the Old Testament. I was a skidder for alotta years. . . . I OWE EVERYBODY.

I'm gonna try to keep these acknowledgments book-centric for the sake of brevity, but it's important for me to say that I never intended to write a book in the first place. I just didn't fancy myself a writer. I'm a songwriter, of course, but that's a different thing entirely. As a storyteller I've always just talked shit behind a microphone or spun manic yarns in the bar, at house parties, in the street, wherever and to whoever wanted to listen. I'd never even flirted with the idea of actually writing any of this stuff down. It wasn't until I asked my good friend, Horton Foote, Jr., to direct the *Escape from Bellevue* stage show that I discovered I was a writer.

Before I started working with Horton I was an unbridled windbag (still am most of the time), prone to wisecracks and easy exits. It was he who encouraged me to harness my ideas and dig deeper for the story (I wasn't even gonna script the *EFB* show before he talked me into it.) Had I not been the benefactor of his friendship, wisdom, patience, generosity, and expertise, prior to the curtain going up on the first run of *Escape from Bellevue*, the show would not have succeeded and this book would not exist. Thanks, Horton. I love you, bro, and am eternally grateful to you.

There were two separate runs of the show. The first one was at Tom Noonan's Paradise Factory Theatre in the East Village of Manhattan (thanks Tom!) and the success of that graduated us to the bigger, more lush, Village Theatre on Bleecker Street. I wanna thank everyone involved with both of those productions, in particular, Jim Rogers and

Paul Paternoster (and all who fall under the flag of Rogers and Hammered-stein Productions.) Without their extraordinary efforts on my behalf there wouldn't have been a show at The Village Theater. My gratitude knows no bounds, my VF brothers! I also wanna thank Alex Timbers for his directorial brilliance and the keen insights he brought to that Village Theater production of *Escape from Bellevue*. He inspired me to take it to greater heights, and for that I owe him a tremendous debt of gratitude as well.

Jane Dystel and Miriam Goderich, my literary agents, saw *EFB* as a book before I did. I just didn't recognize my story as "book worthy." I'm not an ex-president, some famous Hollywood person, or Papillon. I remember thinking, *who, in their right mind, would find all this interesting for a couple of hundred pages?* When Jane and Miriam called me into their office to sign me as a client they asked me about the show and told me to just start talking about it. I started slinging some hash, doing the usual, when Jane stopped me and said, "You do know that this is not just a show but a book too, right?" I said, "Well, not at the moment, but if you think so then I'm willing to give it a shot." Then they made me write up a fifty-page proposal (a major pain in the arse) and before I could blink they were waiving offers from publishers in front of my nose. It was that fast. Sending alotta love to Jane, Miriam, and all the guys and gals over at D and G Literary Agency.

Profound and heartfelt thanks also go to my distinguished publisher at Gotham Books, William Shinker, and to my original editor, Erin Moore. They really understood what I was trying to accomplish with this book and encouraged me to pull the ripcord on it and do it my own way. Erin's guidance was of vital importance to me, especially in the beginning stages of writing. A gigantic thank you also has to go to my second editor, Jessica Sindler, for taking the tiller from Erin and steering me ashore with a great and steady hand. The transition was seamless, ladies, thank you so much! Thanks to everyone over at Gotham Books. You all rock!

From the lobotomy bottomest of my heart, I wanna thank my band, Knockout Drops, all members past and present, who I lived (and continue to live) this story with. I love you guys. You are my rock 'n' roll brothers to the last gasp. . . .

Special thanks to (in random order):

John DeNatale, Lou Licameli, Kevin Campion, Paul Schmitz, Tom Shea, and Eric Munson for their generosity and commitment to me and the band through the years.

Chris Cassidy for his loyal friendship and faithful service as The

Drops' photographer, videographer, and coconspirator . . . thanks for loaning us your genius, Cass!

Knockout Drops sound engineer and good friend Phil Palazzolo, whose great ideas and sense of sound (and humor) have made us a better band.

Chrisie Penna for her love and the sacrifices she made during the writing of this book (I love you, honey! Kitty pages comin' your way . . .).

Hillary Scheerer, my good friend and neighbor, who believed in *Bellevue* when it was no more than a sapling of an idea (and had to hear about it a lot on our walks home from my Tuesday-night gig at West).

My sister, Eileen Campion (and all at Dera, Roslyn, and Campion), who went above and beyond the call of duty in the name of *Escape from Bellevue* and whose Herculean efforts brought forth many good tidings. I think now's the time for a long overdue apology. I'm sorry about my G.I. Joe's pillaging of your Barbie's beach house back in 1973. Oh . . . and for tying up Ken and making him watch.

Gordon Gano for his invaluable friendship and inspiration to my music and to my life.

Mark Nilsen for his unselfconscious and hilarious portrayal of Mr. Flarf in the show (as only he could do it). You're the best, my good friend. Let us all come together in this still, relatively new, NILSENIUM!!!!!

Bob Donnelly, The Drops beloved "Musik Atty," for being the best rock 'n' roll consigliere a band could ever want.

My good friend Jason Cilo for the great care he took in documenting the *Bellevue* show and all the sound advice along the way (Thanks, Cheelo!).

Kyle Crowley for his comic genius. Long may you ride, Conquistador!!!!

Larry Goodman, my good friend and cofounder of the annual Huntington Christmas Pageant. He was a big influence on me as the lead tenor in our (my and Kyle's) high school acapella trio, "The Pietro Pizzi Singers." Our first album "Leave Pietro Alone!" is now available on Columbia Records and Tapes . . . (not really).

Holly Mastrangelo, matriarch of Knockout Drops!!!

Stacey Lavalle for her love, friendship, and for showing me how to dress.

Hank and Little John, Laura Pedone, D and B-Mac, Nost and Rog, Hollywood Bob, Young and Tender Willibee, KC, Robert Young, and all our friends and fans that made anonymous donations to help us get the show at the Paradise off the ground!

Acknowledgments

Jim and Sarah Rogers for the use of the Rogers' outpost in Amagansett for writing. The battle, for me, was most certainly won on the beach.

The 2007/08 New York Giants for giving me blissful (more like cardiac and fitful) breaks from the manuscript whilst watching their magical run through the NFL playoffs (capped off by their spectacularly glorious Super Bowl victory). So long as I live I won't ever forget it, fellas. . . .

Regis and Amy O'Neil (and the kids) for taking such good care of me in Amagansett while writing.

Scott Padell and everyone at Scott Padell Business Management.

Stu Jenkins and Kevin Sussman for all the great times we had in our video collaborations and for showing me the fun that can be had in writing.

My good buddy Carl for helping us out and graciously posing for the *Escape from Bellevue* album cover. Your professionalism was only overshadowed by the generosity of your time. And if you don't mind me sayin' I think you proved yourself one helluva good ass model.

Robert Ambriano, known to many as "Big Bear" or "The Pleasure King" as well as numerous other party aliases, for his friendship and for always having bail money handy.

Bill Falvey, the singer/songwriter who wrote "Magic Lips" and many other underground Huntington hits. Your songs live on in the hearts of all the men and women that ever crossed the threshold at Mother Magee's, my friend.

Chelsea Lagos for believing I could get sober (even when I didn't) and for all the years of laughter, love, and great friendship.

The Bogmen for all the great times and great music.

Niki Drew for showing me that romance and laughs should always go together.

Fans in the Knockout Drops Hall of Fame who, due to 9/11 or other tragic circumstances, didn't live to see this book get published. I miss you all so much and wish you were still here. I love and salute: Danny Shea, Jeremy "Caz" Carrington, Kristy Irvine Ryan, Big Mike Leonard, Brian Yaussi, Lyric Benson, Billy Oliva, John "Red" Wallace, and Billy Oehmler.

Victoria Derose for her backbreaking efforts on the part of myself and the Drops. We love you, Vic!

Rafer Guzman at *Newsday* for his championing of the Drops and *Escape from Bellevue* (long before anyone else was) and for his great friendship.

Jonathan Clarke at Q104.3, Harlan Friedman at WLIR, and Julianne

Welby at WFUV for believing in the show/band and touting us on the radio.

Robert Pollard (and GBV) for the unparalleled inspiration through the years.

Frederick Exley for *A Fan's Notes*.

James Levin for suggesting the name "Knockout Drops."

Brick Wall Management for everything and then some.

Dave Nugent, Chris Marino, Steve the Limo Driver, and Ponzo for their collective effort in getting me to my first spin dry (sorry it didn't take).

Dennis Clapp for his years of faithful service and belief in Knockout Drops.

Ian McCulloch for his great friendship and the incalculable impact he's had on me musically and lyrically. Thanks also to him and Peasy for listening to me pitch them the *Bellevue* show over dinner in Liverpool (before The Drops' set at the Cavern Club, remember?). That was the night the ball really started rolling in my head. Thanks for the encouragement, my Scouser compadres!

Oliver Platt for his friendship and mentorship through the years. "Captain, oh my, Captain!"

Colin Broderick for his friendship and correspondence during the writing of this book. Thank you, Mr. Orangutang!

Westbeth Entertainment (Arnold Engleman, Kirsten Ames, and Chris Petrelli) for all their hard work in producing *EFB* at The Village Theater.

Vic Thrill and The Saturn Missile and the Vic Thrill Salon for inspiring me to move unflinchingly toward new frontiers and for all that mind-blowing music and spectacle.

Dr. Paul Siu, my rock 'n' roll dentist!

Chris Genoversa for bringing me some enriching reading material during my final stay at Bellevue Hospital.

Tommy O and Donna Osterling Campion for all their love and support (and for keeping me indoors).

The Hume sisters, Gina Angelocci, and Catherine McDermott for all the snazzy haircuts through the years.

Mom for always understanding me, loving me, and laughing with me (especially during the writing of this book). I don't know what I would've done without our daily phone calls, Ma! The example you've set as an artist, especially by the incredible pieces you've created, has been a special source of inspiration to me and taught me to always step out of the way and let the spirit be the guide. I love you, Mom!

Dad for instilling in me the confidence to handle any situation life can serve up even when confidence is unrealistic and unwarranted. I love you, Dad.

Erin Koster, Isabelle Gregory, Scott Sexton, Stephen Davis, Tracey Westmoreland, Kieran Blake, Drunk Mike, Justin, Tom Distler, Marsha Brooks, Luke Rosen, Chris Chaberski, Brett Haines, Harry Rosenblum, Mike Studo, Matt Mahurin, Bob Holman at Bowery Poetry Club, Jerry Downey, Alex Gardega, Bert Moss, and Adam Riviera for their hard work in support of *EFB*. Thanks, guys!

The Archangels of Bellevue are Paul Paternoster, Jim Rogers, Scott Paternoster, Jim McCormack, Ellen Shea Meagher, Cousin Chris Fiore, John McCusker, Steve McAuley, Dave McCarthy, John "Woody" Derham, Gavin Coman, Tim McDevitt, Kevin King, Peter Schellbach, John Nugent, Kevin Doyle, Tony Greer, Eric Schlanger, Chris Scaring, and Taymore Zarghami. Thanks for being there for me when it counted the most, my brothers (and sister)!!!

Lastly but not leastly, I'd like to thank everyone mentioned in this book . . . even Guy Oseary.

If I've overlooked anyone in these acknowledgments please forgive me. I love all y'all and you know who you are. Actually, that's not good enough. Maybe I should start over? Abraham begat Isaac. . . .Isaac begat Jacob. . . . Jacob begat Judah. . . .

—CJC

About the Author

Christopher John Campion is the lead singer of the indie rock band Knockout Drops, and he is the creator, playwright, and star of the hit off-Broadway rock musical, *Escape from Bellevue*. He lives in New York City.